FEDERAL-PROVINCIAL DIPLOMACY

RICHARD SIMEON

# Federal-Provincial Diplomacy

## The making of recent policy in Canada

UNIVERSITY OF TORONTO PRESS

Toronto and Buffalo

Printed in Canada

ISBN 0-8020-1783-5
Microfiche ISBN 0-8020-0151-3
LC 74-163822

## STUDIES IN THE STRUCTURE OF POWER

## DECISION-MAKING IN CANADA

The series 'Studies in the Structure of Power: Decision-Making in Canada' is sponsored by the Social Science Research Council of Canada for the purpose of encouraging and assisting research concerned with the manner and setting in which important decisions are made in fields affecting the general public in Canada. The launching of the series was made possible by a grant from the Canada Council.

Unlike the books in other series supported by the Social Science Research Council, the studies of decision-making are not confined to any one of the disciplines comprising the social sciences. The series explores the ways in which social power is exercised in this country: it will encompass studies done within a number of different conceptual frameworks, utilizing both traditional methods of analysis and those prompted by the social, political, and technological changes following the Second World War.

In establishing the series, the Social Science Research Council has sought to encourage scholars already embarked on relevant studies by providing financial and editorial assistance and similarly to induce others to undertake research in areas of decision-making so far neglected in Canada.

J.M.

STUDIES IN THE STRUCTURE OF POWER:

DECISION-MAKING IN CANADA

EDITOR: JOHN MEISEL

1 In Defence of Canada: From the Great War to the Great Depression. BY JAMES EAYRS

2 The Vertical Mosaic: An Analysis of Social Class and Power in Canada. BY JOHN PORTER

3 In Defence of Canada: Appeasement and Rearmament. BY JAMES EAYRS

4 Canadian Labour in Politics. BY GAD HOROWITZ

5 Federal-Provincial Diplomacy: The Making of Recent Policy in Canada. BY RICHARD SIMEON

# Foreword

*Federal-Provincial Diplomacy* is the most apposite of the studies to be included so far in the series of books on decision-making sponsored by the Social Science Research Council of Canada. It makes a major contribution to our understanding of how Canada's eleven governments, trying to act together, responded to the country's regional and ethnic, political and economic differences, when attempting to formulate policies dealing with pensions, taxation, and constitutional change. At the same time, its fruitful theoretical framework permits generalizations to be made about decision-making in other instances and in other federations than those explored here.

The vast majority of studies of Canadian politics have focused on problems which seem to appear in only one jurisdiction, and they have therefore tended to neglect the degree to which much of Canada's life is influenced by the interplay of forces manifesting themselves at two or more levels of government. Richard Simeon's subject and way of approaching it have compelled him to examine the interstices of at least two layers of our politics. But in addition to studying the interaction between two sets of sub-polities in relation to problems jointly and directly concerning them, Simeon has also shed suggestive light on the interdependence of, and interaction between, the various levels of government even with respect to problems which, on the face of it, appear to concern only one of them. Moreover, by partly casting his analysis in terms of diplomacy and strategy, Simeon has looked at federal-provincial interaction from a seldom-employed and rewarding perspective and has also shown that the virtually universal – and often necessary – distinction in political analysis between intra-state and inter-state interaction may conceal important aspects and may limit our understanding of phenomena. His broader-than-usual definition of his field in this sense has, for instance, provided an additional dimension to our understanding of the much-criticized attitude and style adopted by the federal government vis-à-vis the provinces. Quite apart from the current explanations (some of which are extended and amplified by Simeon's study) of the traditionally haughty posture of Ottawa, the 'diplomatic framework' utilized in the present book implicitly suggests that the Ottawa leaders have acquired many of the psychological traits and general attitudes invariably developed even by the best-intentioned imperialist powers when dealing with their possessions. This enables us better to understand, for instance, why 'For the provinces cooperative federalism implies they should be involved in policy formation at an early stage; for Ottawa it is less a question of joint decisions than a willingness to listen to provincial views after a policy has been developed' (p. 182).

The diplomatic framework not only yields rewarding insights, its use also provides a significant commentary on the changing power relationship between the two senior levels of government. It is most unlikely that in the thirties or forties any author would have characterized the relations between the Canadian governments by terms which suggest as much independence between the participants as is implied by 'diplomacy.' Only the sixties and seventies could have produced the title of the present study.

More important even than looking at federal-provincial negotiations from a viewpoint inviting comparisons with international politics is the general analytical framework as introduced in the first chapter. It lays bare the factors and constraints which affect the relations between the federal and provincial governments and thus permits an understanding of some of the 'givens' of Canadian federalism which cannot be exorcised by changes in personnel or party. It does nevertheless also take into account the more ephemeral or fortuitous occurrences which play a part in the decision-making process of even so formal a kind as that requiring the participation of eleven governments.

*Federal-Provincial Diplomacy* is, however, considerably more than a study of federal-provincial relations. It also illumines the nature of the relationship between politicians and bureaucrats, top party leaders and backbenchers, the two senior levels of government and municipalities, and mass publics and élites in Canada, and it points to an important informal means of bringing about constitutional change. It is, in short, a major contribution to Canadian studies, offering important data and insights not only to students of federalism but to all 'Canadianists.' This being so, it is not irrelevant, at a time when United States influence on Canadian life is so ubiquitously decried, to note the genesis of this book. *Federal-Provincial Diplomacy* is the substantially revised thesis of a Canadian student prepared for a PHD at Yale University. The exacting standards and excellent resources of a first-class graduate school have encouraged a gifted Canadian scholar to tackle an important Canadian problem, to do so within a framework drawing on a number of relevant United States and European studies, and to conduct the extensive fieldwork in Canada, assisted and encouraged, as the author's Preface indicates, by numerous Canadian and American scholars and decision-makers. It is also not unimportant that the author's graduate studies received moral and financial support from both Canadian and American sources. The result is a work which could not have been written by anyone but a Canadian (or at least by someone long steeped in the very essence of Canadian life) and one which, had it been produced completely within a Canadian environment, would have missed the fertile influences and perspectives provided by the site of its creation: an outstandingly good political science department, situated at an international intellectual thoroughfare, in a country operating under a federal system vastly different from that of Canada. The book thus reaches us at an appropriate time not only because of its obviously major contribution to studies of federalism but also for this more tangential reason. There *is* danger to a small country in being influenced by a neighbouring colossus: there are also advantages. Richard Simeon's book shows how fruitful interaction between Canada and the United States can be when it occurs under suitable circumstances, and how insular is the *wholesale* condemnation of American influences on Canadian academic life. It is perhaps not out of place to note, in this context, the positive and sensitive role played by thesis supervisors like Professor Joseph LaPalombara of Yale, in encouraging and guiding Canadian scholars to do graduate work on Canadian subjects in a manner creatively combining the required United States and Canadian resources for the sake of a satisfactory intellectual enterprise.

John Meisel

# Preface

This study examines the workings of a central feature of Canadian policymaking: federal-provincial negotiation. Much of this process takes place outside public view and goes unreported in the press. Therefore a great deal of the data used must come from those most knowledgeable about it: the participants. Without the cooperation of these civil servants and politicians the study could not have been written. Despite great pressures on their time they endured my questioning for periods ranging up to five hours. They were generous with their recollections, their attitudes, and documentation. Many of the respondents have spent a good part of their lives labouring in the federal-provincial arena. They understand its workings far better than I or any outsider ever could. I hope they will not object to the conclusions I have drawn, or feel that I have taken too many liberties with their confidence. They must remain anonymous, but I hope they recognize their contribution on virtually every page.

Several other persons familiar with Canadian federalism provided invaluable assistance. In particular I would like to thank Professor Ronald Burns, director of the Institute of Intergovernmental Relations at Queen's University. His familiarity with federal-provincial negotiations since before the Second World War made his advice and counsel invaluable. He opened many doors and provided me with many of his own ideas. In addition, Professor Donald V. Smiley of the University of Toronto and Professor Edwin R. Black of Queen's University provided helpful advice and were largely responsible for first kindling my interest in the subject. Professor

John Meisel of Queen's provided valuable advice and assistance in revising the work.

The study was first prepared as a dissertation for the degree of Doctor of Philosophy at Yale University. Considerable new material, primarily on the constitutional issue, has been added. My adviser, Professor Joseph LaPalombara of the Yale Department of Political Science, was an indispensable guide from the first formulation of the topic, through the field research, to the actual writing. His advice diverted me from many pitfalls and rescued me from several of those I did fall into. I have also greatly benefited from the comments and suggestions of Professors Charles E. Lindblom, James Fesler, Sydney Tarrow, and Joseph Hamburger, all of Yale University.

Finally, my wife Joan has provided continuous support, from sitting in parliamentary libraries sifting newspapers to critically reading the final draft.

The Canada Council and the Woodrow Wilson Foundation generously contributed the financial assistance which made the original research possible. The book has been published with the help of a grant from the Social Science Research Council of Canada, using funds provided by the Canada Council.

I benefited greatly from the help of all these people, but, as the traditional caveat goes, the responsibility for errors of fact or interpretation are mine alone.

Kingston, November 1970 R.E.B.S.

# Contents

# Chronology

Debates on all three issues covered a long time span and a bewildering array of activities in different arenas. The following is a brief chronological outline of the most important events in each case.

THE PENSION PLAN

1963

8 *April* Liberal government elected, with a minority of seats in Parliament
19 *June* Canada Pension Plan resolution placed on Commons order paper
26–27 *July* Federal-Provincial Conference on pensions and other matters
9 *September* Ministerial conference on pensions; Old Age Security increase separated from federal pension proposal
26–29 *November* Federal-Provincial Conference, devoted to financial and other matters, including pensions

1964

11 *January* Revised federal proposal sent to provinces
14 *March* Bill C-75 introduced in Parliament
31 *March*–2 *April* Federal-Provincial Conference, Quebec City: Quebec pension plan unveiled; impasse on all issues

2–16 *April* Intensive Quebec-Ottawa negotiations
17 *April* Telegram from Prime Minister Pearson to provinces outlining accord
19 *June* Parliament passes address to the Crown for amendment of the British North America Act
9 *November* Bill C-75 withdrawn, new Bill C-136 introduced

1965

3 *April* Royal assent to the Canada Pension Plan
23 *June* Quebec Régime des rentes passes National Assembly

FINANCES

1964

31 *March*–1 *April* Federal-Provincial Conference, Quebec City: Tax Structure Committee established
14 *October* First meeting of the Tax Structure Committee

1965

19 *July* Second meeting of the Tax Structure Committee
*August* Federal and provincial officials meet to compile and collate Tax Structure Committee projections of revenues and expenditures
8 *November* Federal election: Pearson government returned with another minority
*December* Third meeting of the Tax Structure Committee; projections received by the committee

1966

5 *June* Quebec provincial election: Union Nationale government takes office
1–2 *August* Interprovincial Conference of Premiers
14–15 *September* Tax Structure Committee meeting
24–26 *October* Federal-Provincial Conference on financing higher education
26–28 *October* Tax Structure Committee meeting
28 *October* Federal-Provincial Plenary Conference

THE CONSTITUTION

1967

27–30 *November* Confederation of Tomorrow Conference, Toronto

1968

5–7 *February* Constitutional Conference, First Meeting
6 *April* Pierre Trudeau elected Liberal leader
*May–December* Meetings of the continuing committee of officials; propositions submitted by the governments
25 *June* Liberal government elected
26 *September* Quebec Prime Minister Daniel Johnson dies; replaced by former Education Minister Jean-Jacques Bertrand
22 *October* Two per cent Social Development Tax announced in federal budget
5–6 *November* Federal-Provincial Conference of finance ministers

1969

10–12 *February* Constitutional Conference, Second Meeting
11–12 *June* First working session
25 *June* Manitoba provincial election: New Democratic party government replaces Conservatives
7 *July* Federal Official Languages Act passed
8–10 *December* Constitutional Conference, Third Meeting

1970

27 *January* Joint Committee of the Senate and the House of Commons to discuss the constitution is established
29 *April* Quebec provincial election: Liberal government elected
14–15 *September* Second working session
13 *October* Nova Scotia election: Liberal government replaces Conservatives
26 *October* New Brunswick election: Conservative government replaces Liberals

1971

8–9 *February* Third working session: apparent breakthrough on amending formula and other issues
14–18 *June* Constitutional Conference, Victoria: Constitutional Charter proposed
23 *June* Quebec rejects Constitutional Charter

# FEDERAL-PROVINCIAL DIPLOMACY

CHAPTER ONE

# Introduction

What is the relationship between federal and unit governments in federal systems? What factors shape this relationship? What are the consequences of federal structures and institutions for the processes of policy-making? And what part does negotiation among governments play in shaping policy? These are basic questions for understanding the nature of federalism. Yet the answers are elusive. For while federalism is one of the most common ways in which nations have organized their political institutions, the relationship of federal *structures* to the behaviour of decision-makers and ultimately to the kinds of policy which result is largely uncharted territory. This study explores that territory through an analysis of how the federal and provincial governments in Canada have negotiated and debated some major issues in recent Canadian politics.

A central characteristic of modern federal systems is the coexistence of governments which are at the same time *interdependent* and relatively *autonomous*. They are, as M.J.C. Vile writes, 'in a mutually dependent political relationship.'[1] Interdependence implies that, in very many fields, what one government does will have implications for others. Each government's decisions will have spill-over effects to which the others must adjust. Interdependence also means that many of the fields with which modern governments concern themselves – welfare, economic policy, transportation – cut across formal divisions of responsibility.[2] Govern-

1 *The Structure of American Federalism* (London, 1961), p. 199.
2 'As colours are mixed in the marble cake,' writes Morton Grodzins, 'so functions are mixed in the American federal system.' 'The Federal System,' in

ments share functions; demands from citizens do not necessarily respect constitutional lines of authority. The result is that governments must somehow coordinate[3] their policies, not simply to avoid frustrating each others' policies but also jointly to make overall policies for the nation. 'Whereas the guiding principle of eighteenth and nineteenth century federalism was the independence of state and federal authorities, the guiding principle of mid-twentieth century federalism is the need for cooperation between them.'[4] And, as Daniel J. Elazar has suggested, even nineteenth century American federalism involved a great deal of collaboration and cooperation.[5] To say that a central characteristic of modern federalism is 'sharing' leads us to ask through what mechanisms and processes and with what effects does it take place.

The other side of the coin is autonomy. Neither central nor unit governments have hierarchical controls over one another. Except where authority is allocated unambiguously, one cannot dictate to another. Coordination between them cannot take the form of 'authoritative prescription.'[6]

These considerations mean that the governments will inevitably interact with each other. Such interaction could take many forms. The governments might adjust to the decisions of others through what Lindblom calls 'adaptive adjustments,'[7] reacting to the conditions posed by others' actions and acting themselves without trying to directly influence others' policies. A great deal of adjustment within all federal systems undoubtedly takes this form. But another important form of adjustment is one in which the governments try to coordinate their policies, resolve disagreements, and reach mutually desired goals through direct relations with each other. 'Each can influence, bargain with and persuade the other.'[8]

Aaron Wildavsky, ed., *American Federalism in Perspective* (Boston, 1967), p. 257. For a collection of articles epitomizing this point of view, see Daniel J. Elazar *et al.*, eds., *Cooperation and Conflict: Readings in American Federalism* (Itasca, Ill., 1969).

3 'Coordination' is a difficult word to define. Charles Lindblom's definition is useful: 'A set of decisions is coordinated if adjustments have been made in them such that the adverse consequences of any one decision for other decisions are to a degree and in some frequency avoided, reduced, or counterbalanced or overweighed.' *The Intelligence of Democracy: Decision-making through Mutual Adjustment* (New York, 1965), p. 154. This definition is obviously a minimum one, in the sense that it does not require that the resultant coordination be satisfactory or result in 'good' solutions to major problems. We will be more concerned with coordination in a slightly higher sense as well: does it lead to solutions which some or most decision-makers feel is satisfactory in some sense?

4 A.H. Birch, *Federalism, Finance and Social Legislation* (Oxford, 1955), p. 305.

5 'Federal-State Collaboration in the Nineteenth Century United States,' reprinted in Wildavsky, *American Federalism in Perspective*, pp. 190–222.

6 Lindblom, *The Intelligence of Democracy*, pp. 76–7.

7 *Ibid.*, p. 33 and chap. 3.

8 Vile, *The Structure of American Federalism*, p. 199.

These direct and explicit relations are the subject of this book. Even here federal systems can differ greatly. Not only can the relative impact and influence of the governments vary from the comparatively centralized, as in Germany, to the decentralized, as in Canada, but also the particular channels and forms through which the interaction takes place can vary. Thus, in the United States the process is extremely diffuse, taking place inside the Congress, in discussions between federal and state bureaucrats, in the Supreme Court, and so on. In Switzerland and Germany the Council of States and the Bundesrat give some direct representation within the national parliament to the cantons and Länder respectively.[9] And differences in forms and procedures may be expected to have consequences for how policies are raised, debated, and shaped.

In Canada, too, the interaction takes many forms, but one process stands out as a distinctive characteristic of the Canadian federal system and has played a vital role in the development of many national policies. This is a process of direct negotiation between the executives of different governments, which D.V. Smiley has termed 'executive federalism.'[10] My central task is to understand it: what factors help to account for its importance; how does it operate in national policy-making; what are some of its consequences? In seeking to understand it several questions immediately present themselves:

1 What underlying general characteristics of the system foster or facilitate this process?
2 What is the scope and intensity of the disagreement between governments, and what kinds of issues are handled through the process?
3 What kinds of interests do the governments represent?
4 What kinds of institutions and procedures have been developed?
5 What is the relative influence or weight of the different governments in this process?
6 What kinds of activity do they engage in as the process operates?
7 What is the effect of this process, as opposed to other possible forms of interaction, on the kinds of policy which is made and on the values and interests that are taken into account in policy-making?

The negotiations will be examined largely through the eyes of those who participate in them. They include cabinet ministers and senior officials in Canada's federal and ten provincial governments, though five provinces

9 See George Codding, *The Federal Government of Switzerland* (Boston, 1969), pp. 72–3, and Edward Pinney, *Federalism, Bureaucracy and Party Politics in Western Germany* (Chapel Hill, NC, 1963).
10 *Constitutional Adaptation and Canadian Federalism since 1945*, Documents of the Royal Commission on Bilingualism and Biculturalism, 4 (Ottawa, 1970), p. 3.

– Ontario, Quebec, British Columbia, Manitoba, and New Brunswick – were chosen for more intensive analysis. What are the goals, beliefs, perceptions, and attitudes of this governmental élite as its members seek to resolve their differences and shape public policy? They play a vital role in the operation of the federal system.[11] Their behaviour reflects the nature of the system of which they form a part; their actions and attitudes help to determine the future direction the system will take. To understand the operation of the system, therefore, we must focus on the decision-makers themselves.

This analysis of a central element of the operation of Canadian federalism should help to illuminate a number of related questions about federations and other decentralized systems. First, it should shed some light on the crucial link between some of the basic social, cultural, and institutional characteristics of political systems and the processes by which policy is made. One important approach to the study of federalism focuses on its cultural and sociological underpinnings. 'The essence of federalism lies not in the institutional or constitutional structure but in the society itself,' writes William S. Livingston. 'Federal government is a device by which the federal qualities of the society are articulated and protected.'[12] This perspective leads writers to examine such factors as the degree of social and economic integration which produce a balance between desires for separation and unity, and a division of loyalties between central and regional authority.[13] Thus Carl Friedrich defines 'federation' as a process leading to 'a union of groups selves, united by one or more common objectives but retaining their distinctive group being for other purposes.'[14] Karl Deutsch and his associates list nine conditions, including such factors as a certain degree of social communication and expectation of economic gains, as conditions for formation of a federation.[15] This approach is

11 For an example of a study of decision-makers in the United States, see Edward Weidner, 'Decision-making in a Federal System,' in Arthur W. Macmahon, ed., *Federalism Mature and Emergent* (Garden City, NY, 1955), pp. 362–83; William Anderson, *Intergovernmental Relations in Review*, Research Monograph no 10, Intergovernmental Relations in the United States (Minneapolis, 1960). See also other volumes in this series.

12 'A Note on the Nature of Federalism,' reprinted in Wildavsky, *American Federalism in Perspective*, p. 37; see also his *Federalism and Constitutional Change* (Oxford, 1956), esp. chap. 1.

13 See Peter Merkl, 'Federalism and Social Structure,' paper presented to the International Political Science Association, Geneva, 1964.

14 'Federalism National and International in Theory and Practice,' paper presented to the Oxford Round Table Meeting, International Political Science Association, 1963, pp. 3, 8; see also his *Trends of Federalism in Theory and Practice* (New York, 1968), chap. 1.

15 *Political Community and the North Atlantic Area* (Princeton, 1957), p. 58.

particularly useful in examining the origins of federations, and in explaining some of the gross differences between them. But even here, A.H. Birch notes, the goals and strategies of dominant élites must be taken into account.[16] Moreover, overall social differences are too general to provide a satisfactory explanation by themselves of the varying patterns of adjustment found in federal systems.

A second broad approach to federalism is to concentrate on the legal and institutional framework. K.C. Wheare is perhaps the best-known exponent of this approach. He starts from a legal definition of federalism as a 'principle' or a doctrine – 'the method of dividing powers so that the general and regional governments are each, within a sphere, co-ordinate and independent.'[17] He then becomes concerned primarily with classifying systems as federal or non-federal and with examining the constitutional provisions which define central and regional powers. He is less concerned with processes of adjustment. Whatever the dependence of constitutional and institutional arrangements on broad social and cultural factors, it is certain that in the short run at least the former do provide the framework within which decision-makers operate. They are an essential part of the environment, and should therefore help to shape the behaviour of decision-makers. It is in this sense that I shall be concerned with these arrangements: does the constitution, for example, give advantage to one level of government or another? how does it define the channels through which decision-makers operate?

Another group of institutional writers focuses on the effects of such organizations as the party system and the national legislatures. William Riker writes: 'there is one institutional condition that controls the nature of the [federal] bargain ... This is the structure of the party system.'[18] Grodzins, Truman,[19] and others have all pointed out the close relationship between federalism and a decentralized party system in the United States. The dominance of centralized parties in Germany appears to be a major reason for the relative weakness of the Land governments. The operation of political institutions such as the national legislature may play an important role in the relationship among the governments. If legisla-

16 'Approaches to the Study of Federalism,' reprinted in Wildavsky, *American Federalism in Perspective*, p. 76.

17 *Federal Government* (4th ed., New York, 1964), p. 10. He reiterates and defends his position in 'Some Theoretical Questions about Federalism,' paper presented to the Oxford Round Table Meeting, International Political Science Association, 1963.

18 *Federalism: Origin, Operation, Significance* (Boston, 1964), p. 136.

19 For example, David Truman, 'Federalism and the Party System,' and Morton Grodzins, 'American Political Parties and the American System,' both reprinted in Wildavsky, *American Federalism in Perspective*.

tures act as arenas for the expression and accommodation of local and regional interests – as in the United States – *intergovernmental* adjustment may be less important.

It seems clear that neither sociological nor institutional factors alone can account for the actual performance of political systems or for their policy-making processes. More likely there is a subtle interplay between three sets of factors: (*a*) broad social and cultural characteristics, (*b*) institutional and constitutional factors, and (*c*) the particular norms, attitudes, goals, and perspectives of decision-makers and the particular demands and problems facing the system at a given time. Each level is logically independent, but each interacts with the others. What R.L. Watts has said of the newer federations is equally true of the older: 'It is in the interplay and the interactions of the social foundations, the written constitutions and the actual practices and the activities of government that an understanding of the nature and effectiveness of the recent federal experiments is to be found.'[20] I shall explore some of this interaction by examining how some basic social and institutional factors help to determine the basic pattern of federal-provincial negotiations and how they shape the conditions within which the decision-makers operate. They are an essential part of the 'strategic environment.'[21]

Looking at this link between these underlying factors and the behaviour of decision-makers should also permit some exploration of another important question: what accounts for differences in the relationship of central and regional governments in federal countries?

Another underlying question concerns the relationship of federalism to conflict and conflict management. A major rationale for federalism is that it helps to minimize conflict by permitting local majorities to satisfy their goals without requiring consent of national majorities which may be hostile,[22] and without overloading the national system with too heavy a burden of issues. Vile makes the point that the very complexity of the American federal system diffuses conflict throughout the system.[23] S.M. Lipset suggests federalism may lessen conflict by adding yet another cleavage line; but, he adds, when state boundaries coincide with religious, linguistic, or other cleavages this reinforcement will increase conflict.[24] On the other hand, William Riker and Richard Schaps argue that federalism can act as a source of conflict by setting governments of different

20 *New Federations: Experiments in the Commonwealth* (London, 1966), p. 15.
21 The term is used by Polsby and Wildavsky; see *Presidential Elections: Strategies of American Electoral Politics* (New York, 1968), chap. 1.
22 R.A. Dahl, *Pluralist Democracy in the United States* (Chicago, 1967), p. 180.
23 Vile, *The Structure of American Federalism*, p. 93.
24 *Political Man* (Anchor ed., Garden City, 1963), p. 81.

parties at state and national level against each other.[25] These comments suggest that federalism can have quite different effects in different circumstances. One purpose of this book, therefore, will be to try to sort out this relationship, by examining the bases of conflict and sources of disagreement between governments and by observing the way the system handled actual disputes. The two prime questions are: does the federal system itself foster some kinds of conflict which would not arise were the system unitary; and, given disagreement among major groups, does the federal system provide mechanisms through which differences can be reconciled?

A particularly intractable type of conflict, in both developed and underdeveloped nations, is that between different subcultures.[26] Few countries have been able to resolve such differences. Canada is an excellent site to examine the effectiveness of federalism in managing subcultural conflict since the existence of the province of Quebec as the national home of the French Canadians has given this question a particular salience throughout Canadian history. Whether both ethnic groups can continue to operate successfully within the Canadian federal system remains an open question. All cases dealt with here involve relations between French and English Canada and they should shed some light on the nature of this conflict, and its relation to the federal system.

The examination of federal-provincial negotiations in Canada, then, should provide some useful insights into some broader questions about federal systems. It should also contribute to a greater understanding of the general process of decision-making and negotiation. Federalism is, in a sense, just one form of a decentralized system, one decentralized on a territorial basis rather than on a functional one.[27] As such, processes of decision in federal systems have much in common with those in other decentralized systems, which share many of the same problems of co-ordination.

In contrast to many federal countries which appear to be becoming more centralized with the development of nationally oriented interest groups, nationally experienced needs, and so on, Canada in recent years has moved in the opposite direction. It is not alone. Yugoslavia and India, for example, have experienced a resurgence of localism. Canadian ob-

25 'Disharmony in Federal Government,' *Behavioral Science* 2 (1957), p. 277. For a sharp critique of their position, see Roland Pennock, 'Federal and Unitary Government – Disharmony and Frustration,' *Behavioral Science* 4 (1959), pp. 147–57.

26 See R.A. Dahl, *Political Opposition in Western Democracies* (New Haven, 1966), pp. 357–8.

27 See Arthur Maas, ed., *Area and Power: A Theory of Local Government* (Glencoe, Ill., 1959), p. 10, and Harold Lasswell and Abraham Kaplan, *Power and Society* (New Haven, 1963), p. 225.

servers in the immediate postwar period were unanimous in pointing to the growth of the federal power;[28] today they are almost as unanimous in describing 'the attenuation of federal power.'[29] Canada's ten provinces are vigorous, activist units, jealous of their powers and anxious to use them. Related to this is the crucial – and growing – role federal-provincial interaction plays in the development and implementation of major national policies. In short, Canada is interesting because the system is a changing one. The cases I shall examine both reflected and contributed to this change, and so hold the promise of suggesting some reasons for it.

Three cases provide the main focus for the analysis of federal-provincial negotiations. In April 1963 a newly elected Liberal government in Ottawa proposed the establishment of a universal national pension plan based on payroll contributions and paying wage-related benefits. The plan would supplement the existing flat-rate pension paid to all persons over seventy years old. There followed two years of complicated negotiations between Ottawa and the provinces, during which the plan underwent major changes. In 1965 two identical pension plans were finally enacted: the Canada Pension Plan,[30] to be run by Ottawa and serving all English-speaking provinces, and the Quebec Régime des rentes,[31] which was to operate in that province. These were a major addition to the welfare state in Canada and were among the most complex pieces of legislation passed in recent years.

The second issue concerns a problem central to all federal systems: the division of financial resources among the units. 'The problem of finance,' says Birch, 'is the fundamental problem of federalism.'[32] The allocation of taxing powers and financial resources directly affects the abilities of the governments to develop and carry out programmes. It is therefore an area of continual intergovernmental conflict. Canada has evolved a flexible system of dividing the most lucrative sources of revenues through a series of federal-provincial agreements, negotiated each five years.[33] I shall examine closely the round culminating in the fall of 1966, in which the agreements for 1967 to 1972 were debated.

28 See J.A. Corry, 'Constitutional Trends and Federalism,' in A.R.M. Lower, ed., *Evolving Canadian Federalism* (Durham, NC, 1959), pp. 95–123. See also other articles in this volume and Birch, *Federalism, Finance and Social Legislation*, p. 290.
29 D.V. Smiley, *The Canadian Political Nationality* (Toronto, 1967), p. 45 ff.
30 13–14 Eliz. II, c. 51, assented to 3 April 1965.
31 13–14 Eliz. II, c. 24, assented to 15 July 1965.
32 *Federalism, Finance and Social Legislation*, p. vi.
33 For a detailed history of these agreements, see A. Milton Moore, J. Harvey Perry, and Donald I. Beach, *The Financing of Canadian Federation: The First One Hundred Years* (Toronto, 1966).

Finally, an issue which goes to the heart of the structure of the federation itself will be examined. In 1967 the eleven governments began the process of re-evaluating and revising Canada's written constitution, the British North America Act. In doing so, they confronted many of the issues of intergovernmental relations which had been implicit in the first two cases. They began to look at the most basic rules which would govern federal-provincial interaction in the future. The discussion of the constitution was, by 1971, still going on; it gave every promise of continuing into the indefinite future. This poses some problems for description and analysis which are unavoidable: we shall have to content ourselves with a tentative and incomplete examination. The writer is well aware that he risks, even more than is usually the case with topical studies, being outrun by events.

The case study method permits an intensive examination of the actual operation of the decision-making process. But it also has its dangers. Too often analysis is subordinated to exhaustive description; the unique takes precedence over the general. In this study the cases are valuable not in themselves but only as they serve as a springboard for analysing the more general process of federal-provincial negotiation. Therefore, I shall draw on insights and examples from several other issues, which were dealt with at the same time as the three chief cases. More important, interviews were aimed not simply at eliciting the 'how, what, when, why, where' of the two issues, but instead were directed more broadly to the respondents' perceptions of the general nature of the federal-provincial negotiations and their attitudes towards the process.

These are the major questions and concerns which animate the study. We must now sketch a framework within which to organize the analysis. The similarity of federalism to other decentralized systems suggests that models of bargaining in other arenas, especially the international, will provide a fruitful approach.

The student of policy-making looking for a conceptual framework faces a difficult dilemma. He wants a neat, simple framework which highlights a few critical factors, but at the same time he does not want to sacrifice the richness and complexity of the data to an arbitrary set of *a priori* categories. The dilemma is the more difficult because there is no consensus on what factors are crucial for decision-making. The result is that models have proliferated. I shall not try to solve this puzzle here, but rather outline a brief set of categories which promise a useful way of organizing the material.

The framework can be stated like this: there is a set of interdependent *actors*, or partisans; they operate within a certain *social and institutional environment*; they share some *goals* but differ on others – it is a 'mixed-motive game';[34] they have an *issue* or set of issues on which they must negotiate; none has hierarchical *control* over the others; they have varying *political resources*; they use these resources in certain *strategies and tactics*; they arrive at certain *outcomes*; and these outcomes have *consequences* for themselves, for other groups in the society, and for the system itself. The problem now becomes how each of these elements is related to the others, and how together they provide a 'satisfying' explanation of the adjustment process. As Edward Banfield puts it: 'what is the system of influence?'[35]

The framework also focuses on the interplay between (*a*) antecedent or background factors, which include the social and cultural characteristics of the federal system as well as the political institutions which define the environment for the decision-makers; (*b*) concurrent or immediate factors, including the nature of the issues, the goals, and resources of the actors; and, (*c*) consequent factors, such as the implications for the participants. It will be useful to examine how the background factors influence the actual operation of the process, and then how the consequences feed back to affect both the process and some of the underlying factors.[36] This conception stresses the dynamic quality of the process and helps to make explicit the relationship between the federal structure and the operation of policy-making.

The framework can be described in more detail:

## 1 The social and institutional context

How do some of the basic characteristics of Canadian society and of its institutional arrangements shape the form the negotiation process takes? Do they encourage some forms of interaction and discourage others? Do they condition the ways actors behave and affect the nature of the outcome in particular cases? These underlying social and institutional factors should be expected to play a major role in determining the overall pattern

34 The term is Thomas Schelling's; it refers to a situation in which there is 'a mixture of mutual dependence and conflict, of partnership and competition.' *The Strategy of Conflict* (New York, 1963), p. 89.

35 *Political Influence: A New Theory of Urban Politics* (New York, 1961), p. 3. The paradigm given here draws on Banfield's outline, developed in chap. 11, as well as on Morton Deutsch's paradigm for the study of conflict. 'Conflict and Its Resolution,' paper prepared for the 1965 meeting of the American Psychological Association.

36 See Jack Sawyer and Harold Guetzkow, 'Bargaining and Negotiation in International Relations,' in Herbert Kelman, ed., *International Behavior* (New York, 1965), pp. 467–8.

of relations between the governments. They should also affect the issues that arise and the goals, tactics, and resources of individual participants as they debate the issues. Among the elements to be considered here are the degree of regional diversity and the pattern of loyalties, and the functioning of legislatures, courts, the party system, and constitutions.

## 2 Actors

Canada's eleven governments are the actors. For most purposes each will be considered as a single unit. But it is their political leaders and civil servants who formulate, express, and fight for their government's interests. Their perceptions, attitudes, and behaviour are my main concern. These governments follow the British – as contrasted to the American – model of strong central control. This has important implications for intergovernmental relations. Nevertheless intragovernmental differences are often important and their effects on the negotiations will be examined.

Moreover, the governments do not operate in a vacuum. They must bear in mind other groups – audiences – which form their environment and on which they depend for support. Audience behaviour will be examined as it impinges on the participants themselves. The most important audiences are the governments' respective legislatures and interested pressure groups. More generally, the electorate may be considered an audience and the actors may be expected to condition their behaviour on what they conceive (rightly or wrongly) to be the 'popular will.'

## 3 Issues

Issues are seldom neat and clear-cut; they seldom arise alone or spring full-blown into the political scene. But they represent the stakes[37] in the negotiation process; their nature affects the way it works.

Issues can vary in several important ways, all of which may be expected to affect the way they are negotiated and resolved. For example, is the issue a new and unfamiliar one or is it a recurrence of an older one? The latter case raises the possibility that the nature of the outcome is largely determined by previous experience, that the terms of argument and the actor's goals are reasonably stable and well known and that regularized procedures have been developed for handling the issue. Different issues may also affect different groups. In particular, we might expect an issue which directly involved a wide range of active pressure groups to be

37 Wallace Sayre and Herbert Kaufman, *Governing New York City* (New York, 1965), p. 39 ff.

discussed differently from one which involved only the governments themselves. Finally, the relations of one issue to others being discussed at the same time may affect the negotiations, for example, by increasing the possibility of log-rolling. A given issue may also come to be defined as representing some other broader issue. This implies that the student courts disaster if he stands outside the process and ascribes his own views about the significance of issues to the participants. Instead, he must ask how the actors themselves perceive and define the issue and the stakes.

Several other dimensions of issues may also affect the negotiations. How are they raised? Are they perceived as being divisible – that is, capable of being sliced into smaller more manageable parts – or indivisible? Are they seen as either zero-sum, in which there must be a winner and a loser, or as providing the possibility for all to gain? Again these qualities depend more on perceptions than on 'objective' characteristics.

### 4 Sites and procedures

Where do the negotiations take place? How are they conducted? Do the rules and procedures favour some actors at the expense of others? Who gets included in the discussion? These are important questions for understanding the nature of the negotiation process. We will ask first how the traditional political institutions – Parliament and cabinet – serve as arenas for adjustment, and then examine the role played by extra-constitutional arenas for negotiation, notably the federal-provincial conference. In addition to the places where interaction occurs, we are interested in the rules and procedures that have been developed. How is the debate organized: what effect does structure have on process?

### 5 Goals and objectives

What values and interests do the participants bring to the negotiations? As Fred Iklé points out, for fruitful negotiation to take place there must be both a common interest and conflicting interests.[38] It is thus important to examine the bases and dimensions of conflict and consensus in the system. What are the roots of disagreement, what kinds of issues provoke federal-provincial conflict? How widely do federal and provincial interests diverge? Here I shall depart from pensions, finances, and the constitution and consider some of the more basic causes of tension. I shall be concerned with the participants' overall view of the nature of the federal system, and of the proper roles of the two levels of government. In this

38 *How Nations Negotiate* (New York, 1964), p. 2.

vein, goals on specific issues can be seen as intimately bound up with a broader set of overall goals. To understand conflict in particular cases we must understand these wider, or 'superordinate,' interests.[39]

## 6 Political resources

'A resource,' says Robert A. Dahl, 'is anything that can be used to sway the specific choices or strategies of another individual.'[40] The allocation of political resources is therefore a crucial dimension of the negotiating process. How are political resources distributed among the governments, and what explains differences in the resources available to different actors? The answers involve one of the central questions about federal systems: what is the relative strength of central and state governments?

Several sources of political resources will be examined. Despite its importance, the concept of resources has received relatively little attention and I shall suggest several hypotheses about the nature of resources in general.

In addition we must consider political constraints. They may be defined as those factors which serve directly to limit the ability of actors to persuade others and to engage in certain tactics and strategies. They are not merely the absence of sanctions, but positive deterrents.

## 7 Strategies and tactics

Given a set of objectives, a certain strategic environment, and available political resources, the actors engage in various strategies to gain their ends. Those they choose will depend heavily on these prior factors. The range of possible tactics is wide – from persuasion to log-rolling to, ultimately, violence. In much writing about bargaining the actors are treated as perfectly rational Machiavellians, who choose strategies solely on the basis of what would be most effective in the circumstances. But a description of strategies and tactics simply in these terms produces a distorted picture of the motives of the actors. My concern, rather, will be with the factors which shape the tactics available to the actors, including particularly the norms and rules which define some tactics as legitimate and others as illegitimate. I shall ask what is the nature of the 'game' the actors see themselves as participating in, what are the terms of the discussion, and what norms govern it.

39 Sawyer and Guetzkow, 'Bargaining and Negotiation,' p. 469.
40 *Who Governs? Democracy and Power in an American City* (New Haven, 1961), p. 226.

### 8 Outcomes and consequences

The end point of the process may not be a decision at all – it may be simply an agreement to disagree.[41] But whatever it is, the outcome has consequences. The simplest question is 'who won?' Which actors achieved their goals and which failed? It is more important to ask whether the result was a creative solution which allowed all participants to find a mutually satisfactory solution. The nature of the solutions produced by the process provides a useful basis for judging its success and the prospects for future successful resolution of conflicts.[42]

The consequences have several dimensions. For the actors themselves: how are their bargaining positions for future issues affected? For audience groups: how were they taken into account? For the system itself: how does it affect the overall relations among governments, how does it meet the needs of the wider society, how will it affect future negotiations? Answers to such questions can only be tentative, but they should be attempted.

This framework constitutes the basic outline of the chapters to follow. Throughout I shall stress the way the various factors interact with each other. By examining the operations of a federal system from an unfamiliar viewpoint, fresh light may be shed on some traditional questions about federal institutions and their consequences for society. The framework is a useful tool for examining intergovernmental relations in policy-making in Canada. It may be equally useful for those studying other federations; the lessons learned from study of the processes of coordination in this country will yield some suggestions for examining similar problems in other settings.

## RESEARCH DESIGN AND DATA

The chief subjects of the study are primarily those who were involved in the pension, finance, and constitutional issues. There is considerable overlap between the two groups, especially in the provincial governments.

Rather than study all provinces, five were selected for intensive examination: Quebec, Ontario, Manitoba, British Columbia, and New Brunswick. The other provinces enter the story, but the prime focus is

41 Roger Hilsman points out that 'few, if any, of the decisions of government are either decisive or final.' *To Move a Nation* (New York, 1967), p. 5. See also Iklé, *How Nations Negotiate*, p. 17.

42 Ernst Haas, for example, suggests three levels of decision, each denoting a higher degree of integration. 'International Integration: The European and Universal Process,' *International Organization* 15 (1961), p. 367.

these five. Together they account for sixteen million of Canada's twenty million population.

Several factors account for the selection of these provinces. First was the need for a regional distribution. The five provinces are well distributed in an intensely regional country, but it should not be thought that this implies that the concerns and interests of Manitoba are exactly the same as its prairie cousins, or that New Brunswickers are exactly the same as Nova Scotians.

The second criterion was a distribution by party differences. The federal government, though with two prime ministers, was Liberal for the whole period under examination. British Columbia, with Premier W.A.C. Bennett's Social Credit government, and Ontario, with the Conservative government of John Robarts, both avoided changes in government. New Brunswick was Liberal until the election of a Conservative government in 1970. Manitoba was Conservative until the New Democrats won in 1969. Quebec had the most changes: the Liberals under Jean Lesage were replaced by the Union Nationale in 1966, and it in turn was defeated by the Liberals in 1970. The sample thus includes governments of both major parties and of three smaller ones. But, as we shall see, the same party label for different governments by no means indicates they think and act alike or in concert.

The third criterion was for a distribution based on size and relative wealth. The sample includes the three largest provinces – Ontario, Quebec, and British Columbia – and two smaller ones. British Columbia and Ontario are the two wealthiest provinces, as measured by per capita personal income, while Manitoba ranks fifth, Quebec sixth, and New Brunswick, with a per capita personal income in 1965 only a little more than half that of British Columbia or Ontario, ranks eighth.

Thus, the five provinces are in many respects broadly representative of all. Considerable attention was also paid to the other provinces, both in the interviews and in study of written sources.

The prime source of data for the study is interviews with government personnel in the six units, plus interviews with some others close to the process. Most were senior officials and cabinet ministers; almost all were in the 'executive branch.' The interview data are most complete for the pension and financial issues. Interviews were conducted in the summer of 1967 for these two cases. The discussion of the constitutional issue depends much less on interviews, though twenty-five additional interviews were conducted in the summer of 1969, and less formal conversations were held since then. Time and resources, together with the inherent difficulties in getting officials to discuss on-going negotiations, dictated the decision to rely primarily on written sources for the constitutional issue. In this sense, my discussion of the constitutional issue must be considered rather more tentative.

All issues obviously involved in a greater or lesser degree many persons in all governments, ranging from premiers and prime ministers to civil servants who prepared statistical material. The universe is thus a large and poorly defined one. No attempt, therefore, was made to draw a representative sample. Rather, as many as possible of those involved were interviewed – a very high proportion of the most important participants, especially in the first two cases. The sample includes 129 persons, distributed as in Table I.

TABLE I
Participants in the interviews

| | Number | Officials | Ministers |
|---|---|---|---|
| Federal | 37 | 34 | 3 |
| Ontario | 30 | 29 | 1 |
| Quebec | 19 | 18 | 1 |
| British Columbia | 11 | 9 | 2 |
| Manitoba | 11 | 10 | 1 |
| New Brunswick | 12 | 10 | 2 |
| Other | 9 | | |
| Total | 129 | 110 | 10 |

The variation in number of interviews by province reflects two factors: first, the scale of the government establishments in British Columbia, Manitoba, and New Brunswick is much smaller than in the others; and, second, in the smaller provinces there is much greater overlap between those concerned with each of the issues. The 'other' category includes five representatives of interest groups. The remaining four are a federal opposition member of Parliament, an academic expert on pensions who acted as an adviser to the Ontario government, a private accountant who acted on behalf of a province throughout the financial discussions, and a former deputy provincial treasurer who has remained close to the process.

The interviews, all carried out by the author, were unstructured, although many questions were common to all. Each interview was tailored to the position and experience of the respondent. They lasted from twenty minutes, with one premier, to five and one-half hours. The average was just over two hours, and many respondents were interviewed twice. Particularly gratifying was the fact that some of the most extensive interviews were with persons most deeply involved. Notes were taken during the interview, which was recreated afterwards on tape. Richard Fenno, in his interviews with United States congressmen, decided that there might be better rapport, so crucial when interviewing élites, if no notes were taken.[43] This course was rejected. I felt that the respondent, expecting to be interviewed, would find *not* taking any notes through a two- or three-hour session even more disturbing and strange than taking them. In such long interviews, failing to take notes would also create the danger of loss of information.

The interviews had two main objects. The first was to find out what went on in the negotiations. The second was to explore the respondents' attitudes about these events and about the negotiation process in general. The relative emphasis on these two goals varied from interview to interview. The experience indicated that a discussion of their own role in concrete events is a useful way of leading respondents to generalize and express their personal attitudes.

Apart from the interviews, documentary sources were examined. These included several Canadian newspapers, at least one from each province studied; published government documents, including parliamentary and legislative debates; briefs to federal-provincial conferences; and some unpublished confidential sources, including summaries of debates at federal-provincial conferences.

Research on live political issues, especially given the Canadian tradition of official secrecy, obviously has many pitfalls. Much documentation remains hidden to the researcher until long after the event. Respondents, naturally, are tempted to tell their side of the story. In conducting the research I tried to ensure accuracy by cross-checking information from different respondents and searching for published accounts wherever possible. I trust few glaring inaccuracies remain, though no doubt there are many small ones.

43 *The Power of the Purse: Appropriations Politics in Congress* (Boston, 1967), p. xxviii.

CHAPTER TWO

# The social and institutional context

The basic social and institutional underpinnings of federalism in Canada have many implications for the pattern of negotiation. In the previous chapter I suggested that the broad pattern of adjustment in federal systems is a product of the interaction of three levels of factors: first, the basic social structure of the system (is it what W.S. Livingston calls a 'federal society'?[1]); second, the institutional arrangements in the system – to a large extent these are products of the social structure, but they also have an independent life and effect of their own; finally, the particular goals, perceptions, and attitudes of individual decision-making élites, particular demands on the system, and so on. Both the social and the institutional elements are essential determinants of this third layer, which will be my chief concern. But in this chapter I shall look at some of the ways the social and institutional environments help to shape the pattern of federal-provincial relations.

## THE SOCIAL ENVIRONMENT

The basic elements of the 'federal' basis of Canadian society have been described many times. We need only summarize them.

The most salient characteristic of Canadian society is its regional diver-

1 'A Note on the Nature of Federalism,' in Aaron Wildavsky, ed., *American Federalism in Perspective* (Boston, 1967), p. 37.

sity – geographic, economic, cultural, and historical.[2] Geographic differences stemming from long distances and a scattered population persist even after the barrier of distance itself has been reduced by modern technology. This simple geographic distance appears to be one factor accounting for the great sense of remoteness and isolation from Ottawa found in British Columbian respondents. 'Victoria is only some 2,700 miles from Ottawa,' said one BC official, 'but Ottawa is 27,000 miles away from Victoria.'

But added to geography are much more important regional influences. Great economic differences among the regions persist – in wealth, income, and the nature of regional economies.[3] These differences have led to great variations in outlook, with, for example, the central provinces more interested in tariff protection of secondary manufacturing and the west stressing free trade. Regional economic interests have been an important source of conflict in Canadian history, from battles between protectionists and free traders over the tariff to the rise of third party movements on the prairies, which based much of their appeal on resisting the exploitation of the bankers and manufacturers of the east.[4] These regional differences remain a prime source of conflict.

Coupled with economic influences are differences in historical tradition between the various regions. Ontario, Quebec, the Maritimes, and British Columbia all had an independent existence as British colonies long before Confederation. Many of the distinctive characteristics engendered by the pre-Confederation experience have persisted, especially in Quebec and the Maritimes. As a result it appears reasonable to conceive of Canada as a collection of regional cultures rather than one 'national' culture.

The most salient and historically most important basis of social diversity in Canada, of course, is the existence of what is commonly referred to as the 'two cultures' of French and English Canada.[5] The French-

2 See essays in Mason Wade, ed., *Regionalism in the Canadian Community, 1867–1967* (Toronto, 1969).

3 See, for example, H.A. Innis and W.T. Easterbrook, 'Fundamental and Historical Elements,' in John Deutsch, Burton Keirstead, Kari Levitt, and Robert Will, eds., *The Canadian Economy: Selected Readings* (rev. ed., Toronto, 1965), pp. 440–8.

4 See C.B. Macpherson, *Democracy in Alberta: Social Credit and the Party System* (2nd ed., Toronto, 1962); S.M. Lipset, *Agrarian Socialism: The Cooperative Commonwealth Federation in Saskatchewan* (Anchor ed., Garden City, NY, 1968).

5 There are many analyses of French-Canadian society. A good general introduction is found in Edward M. Corbett, *Quebec Confronts Canada* (Baltimore, 1967). See also Ramsay Cook, *Canada and the French-Canadian Question* (Toronto, 1967); Philippe Garigue, *L'option politique du Canada*

Canadian minority, about 30 per cent of the population, is highly distinctive in its language, history, religion, and culture. It is heavily concentrated in Quebec, where 81 per cent of the population is of French-speaking origin. New Brunswick, where 35 per cent of the population is of French origin, is the only other province with a large proportion of French Canadians.[6] In all other provinces the proportion is less than 10 per cent.

Quebec is the home of a distinct subculture. It has an autonomous educational system, code of civil law, and a distinctive pattern of institutional and associational life. In addition it has its own political voice, the provincial government. Moreover, French Canadians have been imperfectly integrated into national life. The province's economy has been dominated by English-Canadian–owned industry. Nationally, French Canadians are underrepresented in professional and financial occupations. Only 6.7 per cent of the Canadian 'economic élite' are French Canadian; only 13 per cent of higher federal bureaucrats are French Canadian; and there has been less, but still significant, underrepresentation in a 'political élite' defined to include federal cabinet ministers, provincial premiers, and senior members of the judiciary.[7] Official policies to increase French-Canadian participation both in government and in national life generally are recent developments. Thus, not only are French Canadians a highly distinctive minority but also they are a disadvantaged one.

As a result French-English relations have been a central problem facing the Canadian system since before Confederation. Indeed, a major reason for federation itself was the political deadlock which developed when what are now Ontario and Quebec were combined in the united province of Canada. Since 1867 there have been recurrent conflicts between French and English Canadians, over language and religious rights, education, conscription during both world wars, and other matters. The 'crisis' of the 1960's, while different in many ways from previous conflicts, is only the most recent. Relations with Quebec have been a central preoccupation of national leaders since 1867.

The effect of these widespread regional differences in Canada has been

*français : une interprétation de la survivance nationale* (Montreal, 1963); D. Kwavnick, 'The Roots of French-Canadian Discontent,' *Canadian Journal of Economics and Political Science* 31 (1965), pp. 509–23; Marcel Rioux and Yves Martin, *French-Canadian Society* (Toronto, 1964); Mason Wade, ed., *Canadian Dualism / La dualité canadienne* (Toronto, 1960); Royal Commission on Bilingualism and Biculturalism, *A Preliminary Report* (Ottawa, 1965); André Siegfried, *The Race Question in Canada* (New York, 1908).

6 *Census of Canada, 1961*, catalogue number 92-549, vol. I, part 2: 'Population: Official Language and Mother Tongue.'

7 John Porter, *The Vertical Mosaic: An Analysis of Social Class and Power in Canada* (Toronto, 1965), pp. 87, 286, 441, 389.

to make regional and ethnic cleavages the most important source of conflicts within the system. The 'great issues' of Canadian politics have revolved around questions of national unity and survival rather than around class and economic problems.

These factors have also had a profound effect on Canadian political behaviour. Thus, electoral cleavages are largely regional, religious, and ethnic. 'Class voting,' Robert Alford has found, is lower in Canada than in any of the other Anglo-Saxon democracies, and there is no evidence that it is increasing,[8] or that regionalism in electoral behaviour is on the decline.[9] Another consequence (when combined with some more institutional factors, as we shall see later) has been the recurrence of regionally based parties, like Honoré Mercier's Parti National in nineteenth century Quebec, the Cooperative Commonwealth Federation and Social Credit in the west, and the Union Nationale in Quebec. Regionalism has also affected the structure and behaviour of national parties, forcing them to become loose coalitions of diverse elements. Even so, the national parties have traditionally drawn disproportionate strength from different regions. The Liberals, for example, are the most nearly 'national party' with support in all sections. But their strength has come primarily from Quebec and, to a lesser extent, Ontario.

Thus the social basis for Canadian federalism is strong. Even without Quebec regional diversities would persist. But how does this affect the relationship of provinces and central government? At a minimum the great diversity, organized largely along regional or territorial lines, means that Canadian political institutions will give great weight to regional interests. More particularly, the degree of regionalism, both in mass publics and various élite groups, will be a central factor in determining the relative weights of central and provincial governments. But at the same time the nature of the federal society is not sufficient to explain the particular patterns of adjustment between central and regional interests. Given the

8 *Party and Society* (Chicago, 1963), passim, and his 'The Social Bases of Political Cleavage in 1962,' in John Meisel, ed., *Papers on the 1962 Election* (Toronto, 1964), pp. 203–34. For a more detailed examination of the relation of class, religion, and ethnic factors to voting, see John Wilson, 'Politics and Social Class in Canada: The Case of Waterloo South,' *Canadian Journal of Political Science* 1 (1968), pp. 289–309. Wilson suggests class may be becoming more important, and that while religion and ethnicity continue to be important, working class voters are becoming more homogeneous. We may expect these patterns to vary considerably from constituency to constituency. National patterns of cleavage can obscure great variations in the patterns from area to area.

9 The most careful analysis of electoral regionalism is by Donald E. Blake. 'The Measure and Impact of Regionalism in Canadian Voting Behaviour,' paper presented to the Canadian Political Science Association, 1971.

Canadian social structure one would expect that regional interests in national policy-making will be strong, but one could still imagine a variety of institutional and operational forms within which the adjustment process could take place. The United States also has much regional diversity, but its federal system operates very differently from Canada's.

Another basic characteristic of Canadian society, which operates in the same direction as regionalism, is a weak sense of national identity.[10] This is, of course, related to regional diversity. In particular, the Quebec government provides a very important focus of loyalty for Quebec citizens. In that province it is still unclear whether the crises of legitimacy and integration, to use LaPalombara's and Weiner's terms,[11] will be resolved in favour of the Quebec or national polities. But this lack of a strong sense of national identity has other causes as well. Canada lacks a central national myth around which a strong sense of national identity could form. Until recently the country has had few of the common symbols of nationhood. Lipset and others suggest that this is related to the lack of a revolutionary tradition.[12] Formal independence in 1867 was followed by a gradual and relatively conflict-free weaning from imperial ties, of which vestigial elements remain. Many Canadians maintain emotional ties to Britain. The economic and cultural influence of the United States adds to the diffusion of loyalties and identity and to the lack of a single distinctive Canadian social or political culture. This situation may be changing. D.V. Smiley, for example, suggests that English Canadians are forming a distinct national identity oriented around the federal government.[13] But this sense of community is clearly not shared by many French Canadians. The effect of the weak sense of identity, of strong and persisting regional identities,[14] and of the divergent French and English identities, is to deny

10 See Mildred Schwartz, *Public Opinion and Canadian Identity* (Berkeley and Los Angeles, 1967), esp. chaps. 1 and 2.

11 Joseph LaPalombara and Myron Weiner, eds., *Political Parties and Political Development* (Princeton, 1966), pp. 15–17.

12 S.M. Lipset, *The First New Nation: The United States in Historical and Comparative Perspective* (London, 1964), p. 87. Lipset finds many other traits of Canadian political culture traceable to the lack of revolutionary tradition; see *Revolution and Counter-Revolution: Change and Persistence in Social Structures* (New York, 1968), pp. 47–52.

13 'The Two Themes of Canadian Federalism,' *Canadian Journal of Economics and Political Science* 31 (1965), pp. 88–93.

14 Many writers have suggested there are inevitable 'nationalizing' forces in modern society, which would tend to weaken more parochial regional identities. Such forces as a 'national' economy with 'national' interest groups, urbanization, development of the mass media, and so on are expected to promote national feeling. However, this does not seem to be happening – regional identities do not appear to be weakening significantly, and, indeed, it has been argued that such factors as urbanization have actually enhanced

the federal government a large measure of authority and legitimacy. It is reasonable to assume that if a stronger sense of national community developed Canadians would be more hostile to local and particularistic interests, so that the long-run influence of provincial governments would decline.

This brief discussion suggests that some basic characteristics of Canadian federal society underlie the relationship between federal and provincial governments and help to determine the relative balance between the two. The effects of these broad factors can be detected, as we shall see, even in the day-to-day discussions of federal and provincial officials. They are reflected in the goals of the actors, the degree of conflict between them, their political resources, and even their tactics.

## THE INSTITUTIONAL FRAMEWORK

Canadian political institutions help to account for the distinctive pattern of direct negotiations between the executives of federal and provincial governments in several ways. This framework – including the nature of the national and provincial legislatures, the party system, and the courts – provides some of the fundamental parameters to which the decision-makers must accommodate themselves as they work out their differences. It helps to channel and direct political activity, and in large measure has made the Canadian pattern of federal-provincial relations both necessary and possible.

Where will the interaction of federal and regional or unit interests take place? Two alternatives suggest themselves: these interests may be adjusted *within* the central government, or they may be adjusted in relations *between* the levels. In most federations both forms are likely to exist, but broad differences are apparent. Thus in the United States the party system, the role of the states in national political recruitment, and the decentralized nature of the Congress and bureaucracy facilitate a high level of federal-state accommodation within national political institutions. In Canada the second pattern dominates: accommodation takes place not within but between governments.

### *National political institutions as arenas for adjustment*

Canada's Parliament represents an interesting grafting of British parliamentary forms onto the highly diverse federal society already described.

regional orientations. See J.M.S. Careless, '"Limited Identities" in Canada,' *Canadian Historical Review* 50 (1969), pp. 1–10.

The Canadian Parliament was a direct transplant rather than an indigenous creation of Canadian political requirements.[15] The result, S.M. Lipset suggests, is a basic incompatibility between the logic of the British model and the requirements of federalism. 'Contemporary Canadian politics should be seen as the product of the failure of British Parliamentary institutions to work in a complex North American federal union.'[16] Lipset and others see the existence of many regionally based third parties as one consequence of this incompatibility. But another consequence is that the Canadian Parliament, unlike the American Congress, has failed to provide an important arena within which local and provincial interests are worked out.

The reason for this failure is that a fundamental requirement of British parliamentary or cabinet government is party unity and discipline. Crossing party lines is extremely rare in Canada. Legislative party unity, says Hugh McD. Clokie, is expected by both politicians and public as 'the very condition of party government of the cabinet variety.'[17] In such circumstances it is almost impossible for members of Parliament to push for policies favourable to their regions if they clash with government policy. Similarly, members from different parties are unlikely to form powerful regional blocs or caucuses.[18] Even within the general party caucus there is little evidence that regional groups play an important role in overall policy formation,[19] though there are some intra-party regional caucuses. A Manitoba MP summed up his relationship to the provincial government: '[Being a provincial spokesman] is a pretty minor role for MPs. You hardly ever hear from the provincial government. Lines are all party down here.'

There are, of course, exceptions. Thus members of the Ralliement des créditistes, based entirely in Quebec, have been vocal spokesmen for their interpretation of Quebec's interests, but it seems highly unlikely that they have ever been a channel for communication between the federal and Quebec governments. For most MPs, especially those in the government party, the political environment within which they operate and the struc-

15 See Leon Epstein, 'A Comparative Study of Canadian Parties,' *American Political Science Review* 58 (1964), p. 48.

16 'Review of *Democracy in Alberta*,' *Canadian Forum* 34 (1954–5), p. 196.

17 'The Machinery of Government,' in George W. Brown, ed., *Canada* (Berkeley and Los Angeles, 1950), p. 307. See also Epstein, 'A Comparative Study of Canadian Parties,' p. 52.

18 For the New Brunswick example, see H.G. Thorburn, *Politics in New Brunswick* (Toronto, 1961), pp. 172, 178.

19 See Allan Kornberg, 'Caucus and Cohesion in Canadian Parties,' *American Political Science Review* 60 (1966), pp. 84–7.

ture of incentives that surrounds them stress loyalty to the party leadership. They have few debts to provincial governments. Thus, while they may act as provincial spokesmen on minor matters of local interest, on overall policy questions, such as I am considering, contact with the province is negligible. In these circumstances it is impossible for the legislature to act as an important forum for federal-provincial adjustment. 'Because of the discipline imposed by cabinet government in Canada and Australia, regional interests cannot express themselves as freely in the national Parliaments as they do in the United States.'[20]

But what of the cabinet? As the central policy-making body, does it serve to accommodate provincial interests? To some extent it does. The cabinet, says R. MacGregor Dawson, is federalized. Strong norms dictate that all provinces will be represented, as will major religious and ethnic groups: 'The cabinet has, in fact, taken over the allotted role of the Senate as the protector of the rights of the provinces and it has done an incomparably better job.'[21] R. Gordon Robertson, secretary to the cabinet, suggests that: 'It is behind the closed doors of the cabinet, and in the frankness of its confidence, that we achieve much of the vital process of accommodation and compromise that are essential to make this country work.'[22]

Thus the cabinet is an important element in the adjustment process. But it has some important weaknesses. First, like Parliament, it is governed by norms of unity and solidarity, which may make it hard for members to act as regional spokesmen. Second, provinces represented by weak or very junior ministers may find 'their' members are not effective. Or a federal minister may be a political opponent of the provincial premier.[23] Quebec, which traditionally has several members in the cabinet, has suffered from a 'hidden underrepresentation' because Quebec ministers have received lesser cabinet posts and have had less political experience.[24] Vincent Lemieux suggests that Quebec ministers have much less power

20 J.A. Corry, 'Constitutional Trends and Federalism,' in A.R.M. Lower, ed., *Evolving Canadian Federalism* (Durham, NC, 1958), pp. 120–1. See also Leon Epstein, *Political Parties in Western Democracies* (New York, 1967), p. 62.
21 *The Government of Canada*, revised by Norman Ward (5th ed., Toronto, 1970), p. 179. See also Paul Fox, 'The Representative Nature of the Canadian Cabinet,' in Fox, ed., *Politics: Canada* (Toronto, 1962), pp. 140–3.
22 R.G. Robertson, 'The Canadian Parliament and Cabinet in the Face of Modern Demands,' paper presented to the Institute of Public Administration of Canada, 1967, p. 18.
23 See Paddy Sherman, *Bennett* (Toronto, 1966), esp. pp. 135–8.
24 Richard Van Loon, 'The Structure and Membership of the Canadian Cabinet,' report prepared for the Royal Commission on Bilingualism and Biculturalism, 1966, pp. 56–7. This point was frequently made by Quebec respondents.

and status than the senior federal ministers on the one hand and provincial cabinet ministers on the other.[25] With a French-Canadian prime minister and a strong Quebec delegation in the cabinet this underrepresentation does not appear to exist today, though it is impossible to tell whether the change is permanent.

But some other fundamental factors appear to weaken the ability of the cabinet to act as a forum for adjustment. Federal ministers operate in the federal environment. They are oriented to winning national office, to formulating national policies in areas of federal jurisdiction, and to survival in the House of Commons. Provincial governments are only a part of that environment. It would therefore be unrealistic to view the minister's chief role as that of regional spokesman. This is not to say they never play this role. In fact, the example of Forestry Minister Sauvé in the pension negotiations and Manpower and Immigration Minister Marchand in the manpower negotiations provide two examples of Quebec ministers playing crucial roles as intermediaries between the governments. It is also clear that much tacit negotiation takes place within the cabinet. Policies, such as the education and equalization proposals of 1966, will often be drawn up to meet provincial objections in advance. Trudeau, Marchand, Sauvé, and other French-Canadian ministers played a very important part in shaping the 1966 federal proposals to accommodate Quebec's position on shared-cost programmes and on federal involvement in educational matters. In this sense, then, the cabinet is an arena for adjustment, but that is only one of its functions.

Its success in this task will also depend greatly on the number and seniority of ministers from any region, their perceptions of their role, and the kinds of problems competing for their attention. But, in sum, the cabinet's activity in adjustment, according to R.B. Bryce, former deputy minister of finance, is unprofessional, sporadic, overlain by personal and partisan differences; it 'consequently has not been by any means an effective channel.'[26]

Finally, and perhaps most important, if cabinet ministers do represent regions and have important regional bases of support, that is not at all the same thing as saying they represent *governments*. The distinction is vital. Thus federal ministers from Quebec and Quebec government ministers

25 'Les partis et le pouvoir politique,' *Recherches sociographiques* 7 (1966), p. 51. See also Jean-Charles Bonenfant, 'L'évolution du statut de l'homme politique canadien-français,' *ibid.*, p. 117.

26 Bryce, 'Discussion,' Canadian Institute of Public Administration, *Proceedings*, 1957.

have very different views about the nature of the federation and Quebec's place in it, but both groups can argue they equally represent Quebec, seen as a region. Provincial governments have few claims on ministers from the province. Indeed, during the pension negotiations the partisan complexion of seven of the ten provinces differed from Ottawa's. Two federal ministers from Ontario – Judy LaMarsh and Walter Gordon – were the chief opponents of the Ontario government. Federal-provincial disagreements are differences between governments as much as if not more than between the regions the governments represent. Therefore cabinet success in adjusting regional interests does little to resolve intergovernmental conflicts. 'In no way are the cabinet ministers spokesmen for provincial governments,' said one respondent.

The cabinet, then, is one forum for the adjustment process. But it is far more concerned with federal policy-making and execution than with expression and accommodation of provincial interests. Similarly the bureaucracy is organized primarily on functional or interest-group lines rather than regional ones.

A third element in the national Parliament is the Senate, which does provide for fixed representation from each province. However, any role it might have played was vitiated because senators are named by the federal government. A bicameral legislature with one House effectively representing the states is virtually impossible to reconcile with responsible cabinet government on the British model.[27] As a result the Senate has been primarily a retirement home for party warhorses, with little policy-making significance and even less function in federal-provincial relations.[28] Changes in the Senate's makeup – and hence in its role – may emerge from the constitutional discussions.

A fourth potential site for the working out of federal-provincial conflicts is the Supreme Court, whose equivalents have played an important role in other federations. Until 1949 final judicial review of Canadian legislation rested with the Judicial Committee of the British Privy Council, one of the last appendages of Canadian colonial status. Its decisions had a fundamental effect on the meaning of the British North America Act, the written part of the constitution.[29] 'The just-short-of-unitary state that [Sir John A.] Macdonald thought he had achieved,' says A.R.M. Lower, 'was

27 Carl J. Friedrich, *Trends of Federalism in Theory and Practice* (New York, 1968), p. 100.
28 See Dawson, *The Government of Canada*, pp. 279–303.
29 For a thorough description of the workings of the process of judicial review, both in the JCPC and later, see W.R. Lederman, ed., *The Courts and the Canadian Constitution* (Toronto, 1964).

cut down to something just short of a Confederacy.'[30] The Judicial Committee drastically reduced federal powers through its interpretation of sections 91 and 92 which described federal and provincial powers.[31] Although its position moderated somewhat after 1935, one product of the committee's line of constitutional interpretation appears to have been a reluctance by the Canadian governments to submit conflicts to the courts for judicial review. Thus, after the war Ottawa took massive initiatives in fields of social policy, basing its activity on the federal spending power and using shared-cost programmes. Their constitutionality has seldom been tested in the courts, at least partly because no government has been willing to risk the programmes' being shot down. The Canadian Supreme Court has been Canada's final court only since 1949, and has so far not established itself as an important factor in federal-provincial relations. It is not – unlike the American court – enshrined in Canadian political life and tradition, and, in fact, it has frequently been criticized in French Canada as an English-dominated institution which should not play the role of constitutional court.[32] It appears unlikely the court will play a much larger part in the future. When Ottawa referred a federal-provincial dispute about who controls mineral resources located off Canada's shores, it was widely interpreted as a violation of the rules of the game since the matter was a political conflict which should be settled politically.[33] Thus the Supreme Court is not an important arena for federal-provincial discussion. Quebec has suggested a constitutional court with fairly wide powers and membership appointed by both federal and provincial governments, but the idea has little support from other governments which share a suspicion of a political judiciary and the danger of limiting parliamentary sovereignty.

This discussion suggests that the traditional institutions of the central government have been relatively ineffective as sites for federal-provincial negotiation. This is not to say these institutions never act as arenas for

30 'Theories of Canadian Federalism: Yesterday and Today,' in his *Evolving Canadian Federalism*, p. 40.

31 See, among many others, A.H. Birch, *Federalism, Finance and Social Legislation* (Oxford, 1955), pp. 158–62.

32 For example, the famous Tremblay Commission investigating Quebec's constitutional problems declared that in creation, jurisdiction, and personnel the Supreme Court is a creature of the federal government, which made it 'fundamentally repugnant to the federative principle.' See Royal Commission of Enquiry on Constitutional Problems, *Report*, vol. III (Quebec, 1956), pp. 289–96. Prime Minister Johnson of Quebec has repeated this contention in his *Egalité ou indépendance* (Montreal, 1965), p. 77. See also Quebec's 'Propositions' to the Constitutional Conference.

33 Edwin R. Black, 'Oil Offshore Troubles the Waters,' *Queen's Quarterly* 72 (1966), p. 592.

accommodation, but they do so only rarely. The result has been that the adjustment process has grown up in an *ad hoc* fashion outside traditional institutional forms, notably in the federal-provincial conferences. The inadequacy of the institutions at the national level is one reason why intergovernmental negotiations have taken the form of direct confrontations between governments. Were regional interests accommodated better within Parliament, as they are within the United States Congress, there would be less need for governments to negotiate directly with each other, or for new institutional arrangements to be built.

*Political parties: separate political systems*

The Canadian party system also fails to provide an adequate mechanism for federal-provincial coordination in policy-making. On the face of it, one might expect parties to be a frequent channel of provincial demands. The major parties have small and weak national organizations, nominations are made at the constituency level, and, parties are in large measure federations of provincial associations. 'The Canadian party structure,' writes Leon Epstein, 'resembles that of Republicans and Democrats in its federative character.'[34]

But this local dominance is not translated into provincial influence at the national level. There are several reasons. First, partly because they are diverse the major Canadian parties are non-doctrinal and play little policy-making role in any case. Indeed, John Meisel suggests that the growth in importance of federal-provincial intergovernmental negotiation has weakened still further the parties' policy-making concerns.[35] The locus of party *policy-making* is in the disciplined parliamentary party, which, as I have suggested, is not dominated by provincial interests.

Another reason is that the logic of federal-provincial negotiations means provincial governments must be able to deal with governments of a different political stripe in Ottawa, and vice versa. Conservative Ontario must negotiate with Liberal Ottawa. There is little point in trying to influence the federal government through the Conservative opposition in Ottawa, because the parliamentary system gives little policy-making importance to the opposition. Hence, just as it may be dangerous for interest groups to become too closely identified with one party, so it is unwise for provincial governments to stress party differences in the negotiations.

A broader reason seems to lie in what appears to be a high degree of

34 'A Comparative Study of Canadian Parties,' p. 50.
35 John Meisel, 'Les transformations des partis politiques canadiens,' Cahiers de la Société canadienne de science politique, no 2, 1965, pp. 11–12.

separation between federal and provincial branches of the same parties. '[I]n provincial politics one cannot understand the Canadian political system *except* as a series of discrete compartments contained by political boundaries.'[36] Again, this is because the parties operate in different environments with different perspectives: 'The national party structure is designed to help provide leaders and decisions in Ottawa; the provincial party structures help to perform these functions in the various provincial governments.'[37]

There are many indications of this apparent separation of federal and provincial party systems. In few provinces is the national party pattern reproduced; in British Columbia, the most extreme example, the two major provincial parties are both minor parties at the national level. Provincial electorates frequently return members of different parties to provincial and federal legislatures. One study of an Ontario constituency suggests 38 per cent of the voters voted for different parties at the federal and provincial levels in recent elections.[38] Stephen Muller suggests that Canada has a 'two-layer' party system of provincial and national levels.[39] He goes on to postulate a cyclical pattern by which voters elect a national party and then, because it does not adequately reflect provincial viewpoints, the voters gradually become disaffected and elect governments of opposing parties in the provinces. The federal government eventually finds itself faced with hostile governments in most provinces, and finally it is replaced by the opposition and the cycle begins over. There is little evidence for this view, which seems to imply an exceedingly calculating electorate, but it does seem clear that election of minor parties at the provincial level, especially in Quebec and the west, is in a sense a safety valve for the expression of regional disaffections from the major parties.[40] Another possible explanation for provincial electorates' returning different parties at different levels is simply that, since federal and provincial elections are held at different times, many voters approach each separately, reacting to a different set of issues, candidates, parties, and concerns.

The relative separation of federal and provincial parties takes other

36 David E. Smith, 'The Membership of the Saskatchewan Legislative Assembly: 1905–1966,' in Norman Ward and Duff Spafford, eds., *Politics in Saskatchewan* (Don Mills, Ont., 1968), p. 178.

37 F.C. Engelmann and M.A. Schwartz, *Political Parties and the Canadian Social Structure* (Scarborough, 1967), p. 143.

38 Patti Peppin, 'Split-Ticket Voting,' unpublished undergraduate honours essay, Queen's University, Kingston, 1969.

39 'Federalism and the Party System in Canada,' in Wildavsky, *American Federalism in Perspective*, pp. 144–62. Similar points were made earlier by Dawson in *The Government of Canada*, p. 486.

40 See Lipset, 'Review of *Democracy in Alberta*,' passim. The Union Nationale in Quebec, he suggests, is the functional equivalent of a United States primary.

forms. Federal parties do not attempt to control nominations in provincial parties; seldom do national parties play an active role in provincial elections[41] or try to influence the policies of provincial parties.[42] Much more than in the past, provincial parties have their own sources of funds.[43] In some provinces federal and provincial party organizations are quite distinct,[44] though there appears to be wide variations between provinces and informal relations may still provide important links. In July 1964 the federal and provincial wings of the Quebec Liberals formally separated. Premier Lesage said at the time: 'It has become evident that the Canadian reality demands more and more that the political parties which work on the federal level be distinct from provincial parties and vice versa ... In effect ... the interests are too divergent between federal and provincial governments at the high political level, so that the members of the [party] executive and those on the committees are constantly in a dilemma which I describe as almost insoluble for them.'[45]

It is clear, therefore, that the party system does not often serve as a channel for intergovernmental adjustment. Partisan factors are little help in understanding or explaining either federal-provincial conflict generally or the particular conflicts examined here. Like the operation of the traditional institutions, the Canadian party system does not greatly integrate politics at the provincial and national levels. The party subsystems are largely separate and distinct, and again this fosters the pattern of government-to-government negotiation, more analogous to that between nation-states than that between units in the same political system. The governments are interdependent, but truly autonomous.

This may be broadened to a more general hypothesis about federal and provincial political systems, although there is only fragmentary and im-

41 The Quebec election of October 1939 is the most famous exception. Premier Duplessis threatened to make it a referendum on Canadian participation in the Second World War and was defeated after a massive invasion of the province by federal ministers who warned that to so cut off Quebec from the rest of Canada could be disastrous.

42 Engelmann and Schwartz, *Political Parties and the Canadian Social Structure*, pp. 198–9. More often provincial governments run 'against Ottawa.' That is standard election fare in Quebec, British Columbia, and other provinces. For a good description of a campaign in Nova Scotia by the Conservative government of Premier Robert Stanfield against alleged unfair treatment at the hands of federal Liberals, in a federal election, see J. Murray Beck, 'The Electoral Behaviour of Nova Scotia in 1965,' *Dalhousie Review* 46 (1966), pp. 29–39.

43 Khayyam Z. Paltiel, 'Federalism and Party Finance: A Preliminary Sounding,' in Committee on Election Expenses, *Studies in Canadian Party Finance* (Ottawa, 1966), pp. 5–6.

44 Engelmann and Schwartz, *Political Parties and the Canadian Social Structure*, p. 143.

45 Speech to la Fédération libérale du Québec, 5 July 1964.

pressionistic evidence. Federal and provincial political systems are to a high degree separate and distinct, with few connecting links. Not only parties but also electoral behaviour, political leadership, and dominant political traditions, culture, and issues distinguish politics in the provinces from national politics and from each other. In the matter of political leadership, for example, there is very little mobility between federal and provincial governments. Between 1919 and 1971 only three of the eleven national leaders of the two major parties have been provincial premiers. All were Conservatives; none has become prime minister. In the United States, however, nine of twenty-two first-time presidential candidates since 1896 were at one time state governors.[46] Another indication is that among English-Canadian cabinet ministers appointed between 1948 and 1965 only 4 per cent were premiers, 7.5 per cent provincial cabinet members, and 19 per cent members of provincial legislatures. No French-Canadian ministers had been provincial premiers or cabinet ministers, and only 8 per cent had been MLAs.[47] Of twenty-six Liberal cabinet members in January 1966, none had been in a provincial cabinet and just two had been MLAs, but ten had once worked in the federal civil service.[48] By contrast 22 per cent of United States senators were state governors immediately before election to the Senate.[49] About 13 per cent of Canadian MPs have prior experience in provincial government and legislatures; in the United States the comparable figure is 38 per cent, in Australia 27.4 per cent. Immediately prior to election to the lower house of the national legislature, 27 per cent of American, 17.5 per cent of Australians, and only 8 per cent of Canadians served in state or provincial positions.[50] Similarly, since Confederation, only nine federal cabinet ministers have returned to provincial politics.[51]

Some data on the individual perspectives of members of the Ontario

46 Paul David, 'The Role of Governors at the National Party Convention,' in Daniel J. Elazar *et al.*, eds., *Cooperation and Conflict: Readings in American Federalism* (Itasca, Ill., 1969), p. 373.
47 Van Loon, 'The Structure and Membership of the Canadian Cabinet,' p. 111.
48 Calculated from biographical material in the *Canadian Parliamentary Guide*.
49 Donald R. Matthews, *U.S. Senators and Their World* (New York, 1960), p. 55.
50 Joseph A. Schlesinger, 'Political Careers and Party Leadership,' in Lewis Edinger, ed., *Political Leadership in Industrialized Societies* (New York, 1967), pp. 266–93; calculated from tables on pp. 277 and 279. The data is based on the 1957 Canadian election, 1956 American elections, and 1964 Australian elections. Only 4 per cent of a sample interviewed by David Hoffman and Norman Ward reported provincial experience. *Bilingualism and Biculturalism in the House of Commons*, Documents of the Royal Commission on Bilingualism and Biculturalism, 3 (Ottawa, 1970), p. 63.
51 Van Loon, 'The Structure and Membership of the Canadian Cabinet,' p. 123.

and Michigan legislatures, collected by E.J. Heubel, also indicate the separation of provincial and national politics. Asked which level of government best met its responsibilities, 76 per cent of the Ontario legislators said the province; only 4 per cent felt the federal government did. But 42 per cent of the Michigan legislators opted for the federal government, and only 19 per cent for the state government.[52] Three times as many Michigan representatives often mentioned national issues in speeches (27 per cent to 9 per cent); twice as many planned to run for national office (19 per cent and 9 per cent); and, while two-thirds of the Michigan respondents would run for national office if asked, only a fifth of the Ontario ones would. Michigan legislators, Heubel concludes, are 'clearly supportive of a nation-centred polity,' but in Ontario 'national sentiment, though expressed, is heavily discounted by provincial regard and interests.'[53] If, as seems likely, these orientations can be generalized to other provinces, they should have important implications for federal-provincial relations. They reinforce the impression of relative separation of provincial and federal political systems. They also suggest that in dealings with Ottawa provincial representatives are unlikely to identify with the interests and concerns of federal negotiators, are unlikely to perceive them as potential colleagues or to see themselves as future incumbents of federal roles, and are more likely to see disputes in the form of 'your government versus my government.' Thus, at many different levels, what evidence there is suggests that the two levels of government are clearly differentiated from each other. Party, Parliament, and other institutions provide few channels between them, and few ways of meshing activity at one level with that of another. As a result, the adjustment process takes the form of separate, distinct, and autonomous organizations dealing directly with each other, rather than a diffuse pattern of relations through parties, the Congress, and the bureaucracy as in the United States, or rather than a pattern in which centralized programmatic parties serve to greatly integrate politics at the two levels as in Germany.[54]

### *Internal organization: centralization*

So far I have suggested a pattern of separation *between* governments. Equally important as a determinant of the shape of federal-provincial

52 E.J. Heubel, 'Michigan and Ontario Legislators: Perspectives on the Federal System,' *Canadian Journal of Economics and Political Science* 32 (1966), p. 450.
53 *Ibid.*, p. 454.
54 See Arnold J. Heidenheimer, 'Federalism and the Party System: The Case of West Germany,' *American Political Science Review* 52 (1958), pp. 809–28.

relations is internal organization within governments. Here the pattern is one of relative centralization, and the principal explanation, again, seems to lie in the transplantation of British governmental forms, together with a tradition of strong executive authority. All provincial governments, like the federal, are organized after this model. In Ontario, for example, 'There can be no denying the fact of cabinet domination over the whole of government operations.'[55] Provincial legislatures have little impact on policy-making, and, with the exception of Quebec, appear to spend very little time discussing federal-provincial relations. One consequence of this cabinet dominance, and the absence of separation of powers, is that premiers and prime ministers can firmly commit their own governments, since there is very little chance of their being repudiated by a recalcitrant legislature.

In the United States, says William Anderson, the 'splitting up of the political authority of the states and the national government has the effect that no one in the national government can promise the states what the national government will do for them; and no one in the state government can commit the state in advance to any agreement with the national government.'[56] In contrast, the Australian and Canadian premiers 'have been able to speak with the full authority of their states and to drive hard bargains with the prime minister and cabinet of the central government.'[57] This greatly simplifies the bargaining process by making it possible for agreements to be worked out in face-to-face meetings of relatively few persons. It is also one reason why federal-provincial conferences have been able to become such important sites for negotiation.

The centralization of governments also means that development of horizontal relations between ministers or officials with similar interests at both levels will be inhibited. Edward Weidner finds such relationships to be a central characteristic of intergovernmental relations in the United States.[58] Similar 'collaboration' is common in Canada as well, particularly among officials sharing common professional values in particular programme areas. The extensive federal reliance on shared-cost programmes in the postwar period fostered its development.[59] Federal and provincial

55 Fred Schindeler, 'The Organization and Functions of the Executive Branch in Ontario,' *Canadian Public Administration* 9 (1966), p. 431. For a more extended discussion, see his *Responsible Government in Ontario* (Toronto, 1969), pp. 28–55.

56 *Intergovernmental Relations in Review* (Minneapolis, 1960), p. 15.

57 *Ibid.*, p. 139.

58 'Decision-making in a Federal System,' in A.W. Macmahon, ed., *Federalism Mature and Emergent* (New York, 1955).

59 See D.V. Smiley, *Conditional Grants and Canadian Federalism* (Toronto, 1963), esp. pp. 37–42.

officials often made common cause to promote and protect their programmes against the interference of federal and provincial central agencies like finance departments, treasury boards, and prime ministers' offices; they knew that if they failed to resolve conflicts among themselves, then it would be done by outsiders who did not share their programme concerns.[60]

By the 1960s, however, the significance of such horizontal relationships, especially in matters of broad policy like those discussed here, began to weaken. In part, this is because provincial premiers and other central officials began to make greater use of the hierarchical controls at their disposal to exert greater dominance over programme departments. Several provincial governments became much more committed to their own long-term planning and to developing their own priorities, and recruited officials with general concerns less tied to particular programmes.[61] Thus Quebec centralized all federal-provincial relations within a new Department of Federal-Provincial Affairs; Ontario gradually strengthened its Treasury Board, increased the role of the cabinet secretariat, and established the Office of the Chief Economist with major responsibilities in federal-provincial relations;[62] Manitoba strengthened the Treasury Board and developed a personal staff for the premier centred in the cabinet secretariat;[63] New Brunswick greatly strengthened its Treasury Department. In addition, the strong personal control exerted by such premiers as Bennett in British Columbia contributed to increased centralization within provincial governments. Wrote a senior Ontario official: 'These agencies will all tend to diminish the independence of specialist relationships between operating departments, by attempting to develop common policies for all federal-provincial relationships.'[64] Ottawa also moved in the direction of centralization, especially after the 1968 election. A cabinet committee on federal-provincial relations expanded its role, and a strong Federal-Provincial Relations Division was set up in the Privy Council Office. A greatly decreased emphasis on shared-cost programmes also promised to weaken cross-governmental officials' relationships.

60 D.V. Smiley, 'Public Administration and Canadian Federalism,' *Canadian Public Administration* 7 (1964), p. 378.
61 *Ibid.*, pp. 380–1.
62 Schindeler, 'The Organization and Functions of the Executive Branch in Ontario,' pp. 410–28. See also H. Ian Macdonald 'The "New Economics" and the Province of Ontario,' *Ontario Economic Review* 4, no 4 (1966), pp. 4–9.
63 M.S. Donnelly, *The Government of Manitoba* (Toronto, 1963), p. 99.
64 Don Stevenson, 'Federalism and the Provision of Public Services: A Canadian Viewpoint,' paper presented to seminar on federalism, Indiana University, June 1967, p. 8.

These developments, while not eliminating horizontal relationships, do reduce their significance for federal-provincial relations. The most important consequence of centralization within governments is to channel conflicts through to the cabinets and senior central officials of the governments. Instead of being diffused throughout the bureaucracy, and settled in adjustments at lower levels, many issues will emerge at the political level. If it is assumed that political leaders of the governments have fewer areas of common interest than officials concerned with particular programmes, then such channelling of disagreements to the political level should increase the level of conflict. The values of the central officials predominate over those of programme officials and the values of the two groups often differ.[65] More important, this channelling gives a certain shape to the conflict. The participants are not scattered through the system in the form of federal cabinet members, members of Parliament, bureaucrats, and party leaders; rather they are concentrated and limited largely to provincial premiers, senior cabinet members, and senior officials on the one hand, and their federal counterparts on the other. Being thus expressed as *intergovernmental* conflicts, it seems more likely that considerations of institutional status and prestige become inextricably intermingled with more substantive programme differences. The concentration also makes it less likely that alliances in policy-making will cut across governmental lines. Thus the institutional arrangements of the constituent governments are a fundamental factor shaping intergovernmental relations in Canada. Combined with the inadequacy of national political institutions as arenas for adjustment, and the apparent isolation of federal and provincial political systems, they provide an essential reason for the overall pattern of direct negotiations between senior executives as the dominant form of adjustment.

A final, very simple, institutional factor also facilitates this pattern: the relatively small number of units in the federation. This may have two effects. First, it might help to explain the degree of provincial influence, since the smaller the number of units, presumably, the greater the influence of each. However, the German case, for one example, shows that this is by no means a sufficient condition. Second, the small number of units facilitates the pattern of direct relations between governments by keeping the number of participants at a manageable level. It is hard to imagine decision-making in a body like the federal-provincial conference with five times as many units. Coordination among eleven governments, we shall see, is hard enough; to coordinate fifty would be much more difficult. At the least, one would expect more tacit or indirect bargaining,

65 See J.A. Corry, *Difficulties of Divided Jurisdiction* (Ottawa, 1939), p. 16.

and many more relationships between the central government and groups of a few states. It would be a much more complex and diffuse process, and this very diffuseness should be expected to change not only its outward form but also its results.

Thus the coexistence of British models of governmental organization at both federal and provincial levels with the diverse social and economic environment of Canadian federalism is a crucial determinant of the nature of federal-provincial relations. Both sets of factors help to create a characteristic form of decision-making, one narrowly focused in direct relations between distinct governments, which have relatively few links with each other except through direct contacts between their political leaders. The institutional arrangements do not, of course, completely explain the pattern of negotiation: underlying them are the great regional differences, differences in perspectives of different governments, the nature of the problems facing the system, and the activism of provincial governments. But it does seem clear that these institutional arrangements have had a significant independent effect: the contrast of the Canadian pattern with that in the United States, which does not differ greatly in social characteristics but does have a very different set of institutions, is adequate illustration of the point.

## THE CONSTITUTION

Just as the institutional environment sets some basic parameters for the decision process, so too does the constitutional framework. The Canadian constitution lies partly in the written British North America Act, which established the Dominion in 1867, and its later amendments and judicial interpretation, and partly in unwritten custom and tradition, like the British model.[66] As already mentioned the BNA Act originally envisioned a highly centralized union, but its judicial interpretation has made it highly decentralized. What are some of its effects on federal-provincial relations?

First, the interplay between constitutional provisions and problems raised in the system helps to shape the kinds of issues the governments negotiate. Thus, if the constitution allocated both functions and the resources to perform them unambiguously, then presumably there would be less interdependence. But to the extent that problems cut across constitutional provisions, or the allocation of revenue sources and the allocation

66 For a good brief summary of the principal features of Canadian constitutionalism, see R.I. Cheffins, *The Constitutional Process in Canada* (Toronto, 1969).

of legislative responsibilities do not match, or functions are shared among governments, then the need for interaction increases. All three conditions obtain in Canada. The BNA Act is vague or silent on many of the important issues of modern times, requiring the development of new forms and procedures to handle them. Similarly, a chronic imbalance between revenues and responsibilities has dogged federal-provincial relations since 1867, especially since the constitution gives Ottawa very broad taxing powers while at the same time consigning such areas as health, education, and welfare, which have assumed crucial importance in the twentieth century, to the provinces. Moreover, many important matters are shared between governments. For example, both levels have the right to impose personal income taxes.[67] As a result of a 1951 amendment to the BNA Act, which gave Ottawa authority to establish the Old Age Security programme, pensions became a matter of shared jurisdiction. Therefore when the issue arose in 1963 it was immediately a federal-provincial one. Finally, rigidities in the constitution, or its failure to permit resolution of important questions, may lead to attempts to circumvent its provisions and develop new mechanisms. Thus, in response to widespread demands, including some from the provinces, Ottawa became deeply involved in many provincial responsibilities, partly through constitutional amendment, as in the pension case, but even more through extensive use of the spending power.[68]

One factor preventing a major reallocation of functions to Ottawa in the postwar period of relative centralization was the extreme difficulty of amending the British North America Act. Amending procedures were not spelled out in the act and have themselves been the subject of extensive and continuing federal-provincial negotiations.[69] This difficulty has partially prevented the removing of some issues from the federal-provincial arena, and has so fostered a continuing high level of interaction.[70] Thus,

67 For an exhaustive analysis of constitutional provisions concerning taxation, see Gerard V. La Forest, *The Allocation of Taxing Power under the Canadian Constitution* (Toronto, 1967).

68 See D.V. Smiley, *The Canadian Political Nationality* (Toronto, 1967), pp. 39–43.

69 See W.S. Livingston, *Federalism and Constitutional Change* (Oxford, 1956); and Department of Justice, *The Amendment of the Constitution of Canada* (Ottawa, 1965); see also Alexander Brady, 'Constitutional Amendment and the Federation,' *Canadian Journal of Economics and Political Science* 29 (1963), pp. 486–94, and articles in the section on 'Constitutional Amendment' in Fox, *Politics: Canada*, pp. 81–98. For a description of one noted attempt to develop a formula for amendment, see Agar Adamson, 'The Fulton-Favreau Formula: A Study of Its Development, 1960–1964,' paper presented to the Canadian Political Science Association, Ottawa, 7 June 1967.

70 Smiley, 'Public Administration and Canadian Federalism,' p. 372.

one basic effect of the constitutional provisions is to shape the kind and degree of federal-provincial relations as well as to affect what sorts of issues arise. It does so not by itself but rather as it interacts with the goals and objectives of governments, the demands of other élites, and basic problems facing the system.

The constitution has other effects on the process. It is a crucial element in the allocation of political resources and hence also in strategies and tactics. Constitutional factors will help to shape outcomes. The form of federal aid to higher education proposed in 1966 is an example. It was designed partly to reconcile widespread demands for federal involvement in an area with provincial constitutional jurisdiction. The pension outcome would almost certainly have been different had the provinces not had precedence in the pension field. More broadly, Birch suggests 'the complications of federalism,'[71] in particular the inappropriateness of the constitution to contemporary problems and the inflexibility of amendment, slowed progress in the development of social legislation in Canada, despite widespread demands, by giving veto power to reluctant provincial governments and by giving provinces jurisdiction in such fields without giving them sufficient financial resources. Without assessing the goodness or badness of such 'complications,' it is clear, however, that while the constitutional provisions did make agreement on such welfare programmes more protracted and difficult to attain, it did not, as the pension case shows, prevent the establishment of a welfare state in Canada.[72]

None of this is to suggest that the constitution is fixed or immutable. Its omissions and ambiguities are often as important as its more definite provisions. Federal-provincial relations are often attempts to get around constitutional strictures, and in doing so they may result in *de facto* constitutional changes. The whole structure of federal-provincial conferences, to mention one example, is now an essential part of Canada's governmental structure, though unmentioned in the British North America Act. Piecemeal adjustments such as the development of shared-cost programmes, the contracting-out legislation of 1965 which implied a special status for Quebec, and the more recent federal attempt to draw a fairly strict line between federal and provincial responsibilities and revenues all have implications for the operating constitution. The frequency of constitutional discussions, especially since 1968, is a good indicator of the

71 *Federalism, Finance and Social Legislation,* p. 204.
72 For a strong argument that the BNA Act provides a flexible form for change in the federal system, see Barry Strayer, 'The Flexibility of the BNA Act,' in Trevor Lloyd and Jack McLeod, eds., *Agenda 1970: Proposals for a Creative Politics* (Toronto, 1968), pp. 197–216. See also Cheffins, *The Constitutional Process in Canada.*

importance of constitutional matters in shaping relations among governments.

This discussion has shown that institutional and constitutional arrangements play their part in directing not only the overall pattern of federal-provincial negotiations but also the operation of the process in specific cases. They provide some of the basic parameters within which the decision-makers operate. They provide both constraints on behaviour and opportunities which can be exploited.

Together, the social and institutional foundations of the system help to determine the broad outlines of the relationship between federal and provincial governments, and the patterns of decision-making they have evolved. Alone, neither provides sufficient explanation. Thus, Australia has many institutional characteristics, especially parliamentary government and party discipline, which are much like the Canadian ones. As in Canada, conferences of premiers and prime ministers are an important mechanism for adjustment.[73] However, the overall degree of centralization appears to be much greater in Australia, and the reason seems to lie in differences in social structure. Australia is a much less 'federal society.'[74] Together, the social and institutional patterns in Canada facilitate a pattern of federal-provincial relations which not only gives great weight to regional interests in national policy-making but also takes the form of direct negotiations between the executives of different governments. The following chapters describe three major examples.

73 J.D.B. Miller, *Australian Government and Politics* (London, 1954), pp. 137–8.
74 Alexander Brady, *Democracy in the Dominions: A Comparative Study in Institutions* (3rd ed., Toronto, 1958), p. 178.

CHAPTER THREE

# 'Better pensions for all'

Development of the Canada and Quebec pension plans, working out the federal-provincial financial arrangements in 1966, and the constitutional debates are three of the most important issues for intergovernmental negotiation in recent years. Together these examples span a critical period in Canadian political history, therefore providing valuable insights into the operation of the negotiation process and, more broadly, the dynamics of the Canadian federal system. Before analysing the principal elements of the process in detail we need to set the stage by describing how the negotiations unfolded.

Broadly, each negotiation proceeds through several stages. First the issue is raised and the participants formulate their goals and objectives. Next the participants engage in the exchange of information, either directly or indirectly, about each other's positions, political resources, and the like. Third, they reassess their own positions and resources in light of this communication. Fourth, they make decisions about what concessions or compromises to offer and what alternatives to accept as they move towards some outcome. Finally, the outcome is ratified in the various legislatures. The process is dynamic and fluid; the participants must continually make complex calculations about their own behaviour and that of others in an often uncertain environment. This chapter examines development of the two pension plans; the following ones describe finances and the constitutional debate.

The pension negotiations[1] really began when a Liberal federal government, pledged to introduce a national contributory pension plan before the end of 'Sixty Days of Decision,' was elected on 8 April 1963. They ended on 23 June 1965 when the Quebec legislature gave final reading to a bill establishing the Régime des rentes du Québec. The discussions were intimately tied up with the whole range of contentious issues facing the federal and provincial governments in the period.

## FORMULATION AND INITIATION: EARLY STAGES TO JULY 1963

'Better Pensions for All,' read the headline on a Liberal election pamphlet in 1963. The plan was a major plank in the Liberals' election platform. It had been spelled out in great detail as part of a general campaign strategy to stress 'issues' rather than personalities. As described in the pamphlet it would include benefits for orphans and widows and a maximum contributory pension of $165 a month at age seventy. The Liberals narrowly won the election, with 129 out of 265 seats, four short of a majority. But they formed the government after five years of the Progressive Conservatives under John Diefenbaker.

A few days after the election the new government appointed a twenty-eight man interdepartmental task force[2] to translate the election promise into a concrete plan. It was a difficult job.[3] Not only was the issue complex and the time pressure great but also the Liberals' campaign promise quickly proved to be unworkable. It had been developed by party advisers who had little expertise in the complexities of pension legislation. The result was that the task force worked frequently until the early morning, first seeking agreement among themselves and then getting cabinet approval. But by 19 June, just before the government's needlessly self-imposed deadline, a resolution was on the Commons order paper.[4]

1 The best published account of the pension negotiations is found in Peter Newman, *The Distemper of Our Times* (Toronto, 1968), chap. 22. For a personal account by a participant, see Judy LaMarsh, *Memoirs of a Bird in a Gilded Cage* (Toronto, 1969), chaps. 5 and 6.

2 The task force was headed by the deputy minister of welfare, Dr Joseph Willard, and included representatives from the departments of national health and welfare, national revenue, finance, justice, insurance, and labour and from the Prime Minister's Office, Unemployment Insurance Commission, and Comptroller of the Treasury. See Department of National Health and Welfare, *Annual Report, 1965* (Ottawa, 1966), p. 100.

3 See Peter Stursberg, 'Judy's Punch with Pensions,' *Saturday Night*, Sept. 1963, pp. 9–10. The 'Sixty Days of Decision' deadline was a piece of election strategy which came to haunt the new government.

4 For the text of the resolution, see *H. of C. Debates*, 1963, p. 2340.

It envisioned a national, federally operated contributory pension plan, voluntary for the self-employed but compulsory for all employees, providing wage-related pensions of up to 30 per cent of the contributor's lifetime average income up to $4,000, for a maximum of $100 per month. Employer and employee would each contribute one per cent of income (also up to $4,000), and from the initial surplus of contributions over benefits the existing Old Age Security (OAS) pension, paid to everyone over seventy, would be raised by $10 to $75 per month. Both benefits and contributions in the 'Canada Pension Plan' (CPP) would rise automatically as wages and prices rose. Because of administrative difficulties and the constitutional problem, the plan would pay simply a retirement pension, without 'supplementary benefits' for widows, orphans, and the disabled as originally expected.[5]

On 20 June Prime Minister Lester B. Pearson wrote to the premiers suggesting discussion on the measure 'as soon as possible.'[6] A month later Judy LaMarsh, minister of national health and welfare, opened Commons debate on the resolution and a white paper was released. The new government had many inexperienced ministers, it was preoccupied with problems like unemployment, committed to its own social programme, and worried about survival in the House of Commons with a minority government. Its members therefore had little attention to spare for the provinces. Federal planners did not expect any major objections either from Quebec or other provinces.[7]

Meanwhile, Quebec had set up an interdepartmental study committee on pensions in 1962. Its main effort had been to follow closely Ontario's development of legislation to regulate private pension plans; but pensions were low on the provincial agenda. The federal initiative changed all that and catapulted the matter to the highest priority. Asked to report on the Ottawa proposal the committee sent a memorandum to Prime Minister Jean Lesage on 8 July rejecting the Ontario approach of regulating and

5 For additional details, see white paper reprinted in *ibid.*, pp. 2431–6; also Laurence Coward, ed., *Pensions in Canada: A Compendium of Fact and Opinion* (Don Mills, Ont., 1964), appendix 1.

6 A copy of the letter is included in House of Commons, Sessional Paper 202C, 6 March 1964.

7 'Quebec's insistence on its own plan came as an unpleasant surprise,' said one official. Even after Prime Minister Lesage had said Quebec would have its own plan, Ottawa planners were unconcerned: 'I thought he knew darn well he could not have a plan, and that he was going to make a lot of noise just in order to get another concession. But I learned my lesson. I said to Lesage once, "I don't think you are serious." He said, "Sure I'm serious; the trouble with you fellows is that you never understand when we are serious."'

expanding private pension plans and calling the federal proposal an infringement of Quebec's jurisdiction. It recommended that Quebec set up its own plan, more suited to Quebec's needs, with broader and more generous coverage and benefits and, most important, with a financing system which would build up a large fund to help channel Quebecers' savings into provincial economic development. This idea was to become a trump card. A few days later the cabinet approved the recommendation and instructed the committee to prepare such a plan.[8]

Late in June Lesage wrote to Prime Minister Pearson demanding that no legislation be dealt with in Parliament before federal-provincial discussions. 'Any unilateral action in these areas,' he wrote, 'would not facilitate the necessary agreement.'[9]

Ontario said it welcomed the chance to discuss pensions, stressing the need for careful study, but withheld substantive comment.[10] The province had intensively studied pensions for several years and had recently passed legislation to extend private pension coverage and to provide minimum standards and protection to contributors.

In the federal Parliament the opposition quickly found a weak spot in the federal plan: making the ten-dollar OAS increase contingent on passage of the whole CPP. Opposition Leader John Diefenbaker introduced a resolution calling for the increase immediately. An acrimonious debate followed, but the admissibility of Diefenbaker's resolution was still being debated when Parliament adjourned for the summer. Meanwhile, opponents of the pension plan began to mobilize. The Canadian Life Insurance Officers' Association, consisting of more than one hundred companies, issued a detailed attack on the proposal: 'A serious misfortune for Canada and Canadians.'[11] It favoured the Ontario approach. Others spoke out against the plan and letters, mainly from insurance and trust company executives, began to arrive on cabinet ministers' desks.[12] Criticism centred on the proposal's economic effects, its generosity, its effect on private plans, the likelihood of rapid cost increases, and the like.[13]

8 Interviews and private sources. Henceforth only published references will be footnoted.
9 27 June 1963, in Sessional Paper 202C.
10 18 July 1963, in *ibid.*
11 Canadian Life Insurance Officers' Association, 'Memorandum,' 26 July 1963, p. 2.
12 For copies of all letters from 'life insurance companies, private pension firms or consultants, private actuarial consultants, investment houses and Chambers of Commerce,' to cabinet members between April 1963 and May 1964, see Sessional Paper 202I, 22 May 1964. Thirty-eight letters are included: most were strongly critical of the plan and commonly suggested 'a full public enquiry' before legislation was passed.
13 See, for example, 'The Pension Plan,' *Financial Times*, 29 July 1963, p. 3.

## INFORMATION EXCHANGE: THE JULY AND SEPTEMBER 1963 CONFERENCES

The first direct federal-provincial discussion on pensions – and the first encounter between the new government and the premiers – was at a Federal-Provincial Conference held on 26 and 27 July 1963. Ottawa hoped it would set the stage for a new cooperative relationship among the governments. Two issues dominated the agenda. On the first, a federal proposal to establish a Municipal Loan Fund to make low-cost loans available to local governments as one way to ease unemployment, the provinces triumphed completely.[14] The proposal was rewritten on the spot to permit a wider range of eligible projects, to divide the fund among the provinces proportionately to population, and to allow provincial administration of the programme.[15]

The pension discussion was less conclusive. Many provinces, lacking interest and expertise in the area, had not yet formulated their positions, and for them the meeting was a learning experience. 'It was an information conference,' said a federal official. 'We let them officially have our position, and they could ask questions.' For several provinces information exchange was a necessary prelude to formulation of their own goals. The provinces were unanimous in demanding, as the opposition in Parliament had, the separation of the OAS increase from the CPP. There was a tactical reason: as long as the two proposals were tied together Ottawa could blame the provinces for delaying aid to the elderly if they objected to the wider plan.

Saskatchewan quickly set up a pressure on the left; Premier Woodrow Lloyd said the proposal corresponded closely with his government's own views and urged quick passage and broader benefits.[16] Ontario had not yet formulated a definite position. It wanted to delay the plan as much as possible, and Prime Minister John Robarts raised a host of questions. Some Ontario officials felt Ottawa 'would never be able to pull it off' anyway, and that it was easier to 'sit on the side-lines and snipe at the proposal' than to present an alternative. Ontario officials also felt constrained about the criticisms they could make because they wanted to avoid the charge that they were 'tools of the insurance companies.' Manitoba's Premier Duff Roblin followed Ontario's lead and urged delay and

14 *Globe and Mail*, Toronto, 27 July 1963.
15 Observed Mr Lesage in the conference room: never had he been at a conference where Ottawa showed so much goodwill.
16 Saskatchewan, 'Statement by the Hon. Woodrow Lloyd on the Canada Pension Plan,' 1963.

more study. British Columbia, reacting like any other employer, wanted to ensure that provincial employees would be exempted from the plan.[17]

Prime Minister Lesage reiterated Quebec's intention to go it alone, and warned that Quebec would agree to an amendment to the British North America Act, necessary if Ottawa was to be able to include the politically attractive supplementary benefits, only if Quebec were allowed to opt-out of the plan.

The meeting ended with agreement to discuss pensions again in September. The participants agreed the conference had been a success; it seemed to presage a new era of cooperation and goodwill, and of equality between Ottawa and the provinces. Relations between Quebec and Ottawa seemed to have warmed considerably.[18]

Nevertheless, Ottawa had to reassess its pension position. Its concessions on the loan fund had demonstrated its vulnerability to provincial pressure. The disastrous 'Gordon Budget' in June had been followed by an ignominious retreat.[19] Both events reinforced an image of federal weakness, which was felt by federal leaders themselves. Quebec had firmly announced its intention to stay out of the federal pension scheme, and had made this commitment crystal clear with a unanimous resolution of its legislature on 23 June.[20] Ontario and some other provinces were obviously cool to the federal plan, but their criticisms were of an entirely different nature from Quebec's.[21] Finally, there was increasing criticism from the press and interest groups.

The federal government decided to push ahead. A senior adviser recommended that it try to woo Quebec in by making substantial concessions, including making the federal plan funded, but it was decided

17 British Columbia, 'The Statement of the Hon. W.D. Black on Behalf of the Province of British Columbia,' 26 July 1963, p. 1.

18 'Everybody is happy,' said Premier Smallwood of Newfoundland; 'I mean everybody.' *Globe and Mail*, 29 July 1963. See also Maurice Western in the *Winnipeg Free Press*, 29 July. Said a writer in *Le Devoir*, Montreal, 29 July: '[The provinces] will deal with the representatives of the federal government as equals, and the solutions to common problems will not be proposed or rejected unilaterally; they will arrive at them together in a spirit of understanding and collaboration' (my translation).

19 For a description, see John T. Saywell, ed., *Canadian Annual Review for 1963* (Toronto, 1964), pp. 53–7, 195–204.

20 See *Le Devoir* and the *Globe and Mail*, 23 Aug. 1963. Shortly after the session, on 23 August, Lesage wrote to Pearson: 'Given the intention clearly expressed in this resolution and in virtue of the text of Article 94A of the constitution, Quebec considers that it previously occupies the field of pension plans' (my translation). In Sessional Paper 202C.

21 See letters from Premiers Roblin and Robarts to the prime minister, 12 and 22 Aug. 1963, in Sessional Paper 202C.

instead to fight it out with Ontario. The problem of Quebec could be postponed.

Federal officials, especially Miss LaMarsh, whose occasionally belligerent behaviour caused much resentment among Ontario officials, aggressively pushed the plan in Ontario. On her return from a European trip, ostensibly to study foreign pension arrangements, Miss LaMarsh suggested that if Ontario failed to support the plan it would be blamed for the failure of the project.[22] In August a provincial election campaign opened and the provincial Liberals made support of the CPP a major issue. Miss LaMarsh and others campaigned vigorously, though late in the campaign it was reported that Mr. Pearson tried to stop them. In any event the tactic failed; Prime Minister Robarts' Conservatives were re-elected handily. The episode generated considerable friction; after the election Miss LaMarsh was to play a diminished role in the negotiations.

In the midst of the Ontario campaign the second conference, this one chaired by Miss LaMarsh, began on 9 September. It opened with the first important federal concession: the OAS increase would be separated from the CPP and financed from general revenue.[23] The federal statement also recognized that Quebec would have a separate plan, but expressed hope the two could be coordinated.

Prime Minister Robarts, citing the 'misinformation and misconceptions that are floating around,'[24] because of the campaign, was the only premier to attend. He was conciliatory, announcing Ontario's approval in principle of a federal plan and offering his support. But the plan must not disturb the sanctity of private plans, must safeguard the flow of savings and investment capital, and must adhere to the principle of individual equity, meaning benefits must be closely tied to actual contributions.[25] Quebec's delegates, attending as 'observers,' said the province would not try to prevent Ottawa's establishing a pension plan for the rest of Canada. But just a few days before, Natural Resources Minister René Lévesque,

22 *Globe and Mail*, 27 Aug. 1963. Miss LaMarsh had an unfortunate knack for saying the wrong thing. After the September conference she told reporters there might be a 'vast exodus' from Quebec if it went ahead with its plan, and why didn't they just translate her plan into French (Saywell, *Canadian Annual Review for 1963*, p. 69). Later she was to suggest in an interview with Jean Howarth in the *Globe and Mail* (27 Sept. 1963) that the concentration of funds in the hands of the Quebec government had overtones of national socialism.

23 *Globe and Mail*, 9 Sept. 1963.

24 *Ibid.*, 6 Sept. 1963.

25 Ontario, 'Statement by the Prime Minister at the Federal-Provincial Conference on Pension Plans,' 9–10 Sept. 1963.

who was to become leader of the separatist Parti québécois, had made a strong attack on the federal proposal: 'The two systems are incompatible,' he said. 'One excludes the other. We will not give in. Ottawa must renounce.'[26]

At the end of the conference, where information exchange had still been dominant, Miss LaMarsh informally polled the delegates about the willingness of their governments to approve the constitutional amendment necessary if the plan were to provide for supplementary benefits. Two small committees, one of Ontario and federal the other of Quebec and federal officials, were set up to see if differences could be resolved.

The Ontario officials went to Ottawa in November and again voiced their concerns about the cost of the plan and its effect on private companies. A week later Quebec officials met their federal counterparts. The federal officials informally sounded out Quebec on a proposal to reduce the age at which the flat-rate OAS pensions could be paid, financing the cost out of the CPP. Would Quebec do the same out of the fund in its, as yet unrevealed, plan? The reply was 'no' because it would be too heavy a drain, and why should Quebec pay for a programme decided in Ottawa? The episode is a nice example of how officials can informally and privately explore proposals without committing their governments to it, as would happen at a formal conference. Both meetings were inconclusive.

Meanwhile Parliament reconvened, and the ten-dollar increase in OAS was quickly passed. The original pension resolution, however, was tabled without a vote, and on 4 November Mr Pearson announced that no bill would be introduced before the New Year. Pressure from private interests continued. Most of the effort was directed at the federal level. All the group activity seems to have had little effect. Whatever misgivings Liberal MPs and cabinet ministers had – and many were concerned – the plan was a central part of the government's programme and it was too late to turn back. The government also had the support of unions and other groups, which, while not so vocal, tended to balance criticism from insurance companies and chambers of commerce. Most criticism was a root and branch attack on the plan; few proposals for more minor modifications, which might have stood a better chance of success, were offered.[27]

26 *Le Devoir*, 7 Sept. 1963 (my translation).

27 The most vocal critic of the pension plan was D.E. Kilgour, president of the Great West Life Assurance Company of Winnipeg. He travelled to most provinces talking to government officials, and delivered a clarion call for businessmen to unite. 'Let's raise a storm! Let's make it a good one – the strongest, most lightning packed, angry wind that has blown around Parliament Hill for a long, long time ... Let's get militant ... There will have to be political pressure with teeth in it.' Speech to the Canadian Institute

## THE NOVEMBER 1963 FEDERAL-PROVINCIAL CONFERENCE

The next major consideration of pensions came at the Federal-Provincial Conference of 26 to 29 November 1963. Again pensions were only one subject of discussion. In fact the conference was widely seen as a crucial event in the evolution of Canadian federalism. 'This conference can shape the direction of Canadian federalism for a generation,' said Mr Pearson in his opening statement.[28]

Two matters dominated the agenda: finances and Quebec's demands for a fundamental reshaping of the federal union. Almost all provinces were most dissatisfied with the 1962–7 financial agreements worked out under the Conservative government of John Diefenbaker, and the Liberals had promised to review them. Saskatchewan, Manitoba, and the Maritimes focused on improving equalization, the unconditional federal payments to the poorer provinces. British Columbia (which asked for 100 per cent of the major tax fields) and Ontario wanted more tax-shares, in which Ottawa would turn over, or abate, a greater share of personal or corporate income taxes. The figures are expressed in percentage 'points.' Quebec wanted both equalization and '25-25-100' – one quarter of personal and corporate income taxes and all succession duties.

In addition Quebec's detailed forty-eight-page brief called for full federal-provincial consultations on such matters as economic, tariff, transportation, and monetary policy, the right for Quebec to opt-out of shared-cost programmes with complete compensation, and other matters.[29] 'Jean Lesage,' wrote a reporter, 'took his axe to the foundations on which federal power is built.'[30] Quebec, with its strong demands, carefully designed proposals, and forceful presentation was effectively setting the agenda for federal-provincial discussion.

of Chartered Accountants, Winnipeg, 9 Nov. 1963, privately printed, pp. 13–14. The vehemence of this attack could well have backfired.

In addition the Life Underwriters' Association of Canada was reported to be planning a lobbying campaign and at the annual meeting of the Canadian Pension Conference, a forum for the private pension industry, speaker after speaker roundly condemned the federal plan. See *Proceedings*, vol. III, no 4 (Toronto, 1964).

For labour's views on the CPP at this stage, see Gordon Milling, 'Labour's Interest in Pension Planning,' in Coward, *Pensions in Canada*, pp. 185–92; and J.H. Craigs, 'Labour Looks at the Canada Pension Plan,' in Laurence Coward, ed., *Symposium of Views on the Canada Pension Plan* (Don Mills, 1964), pp. 55–60.

28 *Federal-Provincial Conference*, Nov. 1963 (Ottawa, 1964), p. 9.

29 Quebec, 'Statement by the Hon. Jean Lesage,' Federal-Provincial Conference, 25 Nov. 1963.

30 *Globe and Mail*, 27 Nov. 1963.

Ottawa made a modest financial offer – a small adjustment in the equalization formula and an increase in the provincial share of succession duties to 75 per cent, but no increase in the provincial share of personal or corporate income taxes. The offer was worth an estimated $87.4 million in new funds to the provinces.[31]

The meeting ranged over many aspects of pension legislation. Prime Minister Pearson listed eight 'essential principles' Ottawa was committed to, but stressed there was much room for flexibility. Since the OAS increase had been separated from the CPP, the plan would now build up a small fund, and Mr Pearson hinted Ottawa might turn half over to the provinces, a major lure. The idea of a partially funded plan was gradually becoming more and more popular among the provinces, as they began to see its implications. The premiers ranged over many other aspects of the plan, discussing pros and cons of such things as the length of the transition period before full benefits became payable. Ottawa officials informally sounded out Quebec officials on the possibility of Quebec coming in if the plan were suitably modified. Quebec's answer: we are bound by our August resolution. In the full meeting Lesage made a powerful threat: Quebec would now agree to the British North America Act amendment only if the contribution rate in the federal plan was 4 per cent of contributory income, twice that Ottawa suggested.[32] Although Ottawa still had no provisions for the added benefits for which the amendment would be required, the threat had force because Ottawa knew that the Quebec plan would have such benefits and to compete Ottawa would have to have them too.[33]

All discussions, especially among the premiers, were complicated by the extreme complexity of many of the issues. The politicians were unversed in the arcane world of the actuaries. Both Ontario and Ottawa had

31 At the time, the provinces were receiving seventeen points of personal and nine of corporate income tax, and 50 per cent of succession duties. Equalization was based on this, but half of natural resource revenue was also included in the base. Ottawa proposed to raise equalization to the level of the top two provinces (rather than the national average), and also to change the way natural resource revenues were included. Now equalization would be reduced if a province made more than the average in natural resource revenues but not increased if the province received less. This feature particularly annoyed Saskatchewan's delegates who sat up most of one night to prepare a blistering attack. For details, see A. Milton Moore, J. Harvey Perry, and Donald I. Beach, *The Financing of Canadian Federation* (Toronto, 1966), p. 74.

32 The threat was revealed after the conference by Jean Howarth in the *Globe and Mail*, 16 Dec. 1963.

33 Quebec's brief also suggested that Quebec take over the whole field of social security, including old age security. Federal officials had held their breath that Quebec would not push that point.

their actuaries, both groups gave equally persuasive figures – and both disagreed. But the conference ended with Ottawa promising to consider the provincial views, and to submit a revised proposal soon. There was still no agreement, but on 3 December Pearson told the House there was no need for further discussions with the provinces. He was wrong.

After the November meeting, as after previous conferences, all governments re-evaluated their positions. Ottawa still needed to get Ontario's agreement. 'We did not at that time think we could ever bridge the gap with Quebec,' said an official. But if agreement could be reached with the other nine provinces, 'then Quebec would have had a choice – either to change its mind and go along with this, or to introduce a very different plan of its own.' Accordingly, Ottawa reconsidered. Officials prepared one proposal which went a long way to meeting Ontario's criticisms. But the cabinet rejected it as too much of a retreat, and a new proposal with fewer changes was drawn up and sent to the provinces on 11 January 1964.[34]

The major effect was to reduce somewhat the scale of benefits in the CPP. In addition, payment of the reduced OAS pension at sixty-five instead of seventy, which had caused the earlier difficulty with Quebec, would be introduced gradually and financed from general revenue. Half the CPP fund – now estimated at $2.5 billion in the first ten years – was offered to the provinces. Most other major provisions were unchanged.

The revisions were immediately attacked from both sides. To Ontario they were not nearly enough. To Saskatchewan they were a lamentable retreat. Robarts said in a letter to Pearson that the changes were 'far short of what we had hoped' and 'little in accord with the representations we had made.' He repeated again his earlier criticisms. Manitoba was also wary of the new proposal and again called for a full impartial study of the whole proposal. On the other hand, to Premier Lloyd the revisions were a 'retrograde step.'[35] Most provinces, scenting federal retreat on the disposition of the fund, wanted 90 to 100 per cent turned over to the provinces. Thus, the revisions pleased no one.

But Ottawa decided to push ahead. In February Pearson told the Commons that legislation would be passed and the Canada Pension Plan in operation before the end of the session. On 14 March Bill C-75, embodying the new proposals, was introduced – partly as a tactical device to get something firm on the table with which to confront the provinces. In the

34 For details of the revised proposal, see Coward, *Pensions in Canada*, appendix 2.
35 These letters, and other provincial reactions, are found in Sessional Paper 202H, 13 May 1964.

House the New Democratic Party took much the same position as its fellow NDP government in Saskatchewan, and the Conservatives made many of the same criticisms as Ontario. But nothing was done until new developments changed the situation entirely.

## IMPASSE: THE QUEBEC CONFERENCE

In November the premiers had agreed to meet again at Quebec City in March. It promised to be a difficult conference. Many provinces wanted further financial concessions – and time was running out on Quebec's ultimatum for '25-25-100' which had been made the previous April. Ottawa had two other proposals on the table – one an extension of Family Allowances to those aged seventeen and eighteen if they remained in school, and the other a programme of federally guaranteed loans to university students. Both were interpreted by Quebec as federal intrusions into its jurisdiction. As well, Quebec was still pressing the demands, especially for opting-out, it had made in November.

Added to all this was the atmosphere of the meeting itself, the first recently held outside Ottawa. Separatist feeling in Quebec was growing and English-French relations was clearly the most threatening and fundamental issue of the day. Extraordinary security precautions were taken and thousands of students demonstrated on the Quebec Parliament's lawns. This atmosphere lent an air of crisis to the proceedings. 'We all went with a certain amount of trepidation,' said a Manitoba official. 'We did all have the feeling that perhaps the chips were pretty close to being down on Confederation.'[36]

The meeting justified the worst fears. Ottawa decided beforehand it would make no financial concessions. 'We had no money to give,' said a cabinet minister, 'and even if we did, we were not going to give it anyway.' The provinces saw the November proposals as only the first stage of federal concessions, with more to come later; and some things Pearson said at the meeting had encouraged that belief. 'But now the cabinet had decided that was it,' said a federal official. '[It] went to the conference with a fiscal position that was not negotiable.' Thus after an acrimonious debate only one concession was announced; it had been 'dreamed up' late one night without even consulting Finance Department officials. It was a proposal to establish a Tax Structure Committee, composed of

36 'It was a pretty nasty situation,' said an Ontario official; 'it gave Quebec a huge amount of leverage.' Said a New Brunswick official: 'Behind them they had the bomb threats and so on of the separatists ... There were police everywhere, and outside the students from Laval [university] were chanting demanding Lesage to come out and talk to them, and you could hear it right in the meeting room.'

ministers of finance, to review the whole financial question. Quebec threatened not to participate. Nor was there any agreement on student loans and family allowances. Ottawa was ready to negotiate about contracting-out for Quebec, but many English-speaking provinces were opposed to the idea. To Robarts, coercing some provinces into line while exempting others was a violation of the 'cardinal principles' of federalism, and opting-out by one province would isolate that province, 'drive a wedge between us,' and 'make for disunion rather than union.'[37] Premier Roblin of Manitoba echoed these views.

But the most dramatic developments at the conference concerned pensions. First, Ontario appeared to make a major shift in its position. Prime Minister Robarts strongly hinted that unless the federal plan were truly national (meaning unless it included Quebec) his province would not participate. Ontario might develop its own plan instead.[38] Mr Pearson put a brave face on it outside the conference, but it seemed clear that without Ontario the federal plan had little chance of success.

The second dramatic development was the unveiling of Quebec's pension plan. The provincial interdepartmental committee had worked on the plan since July and had delivered its report to the government just a few days before the conference. It had not yet even been considered by the cabinet. But, faced with a failing conference, Prime Minister Lesage decided to describe it. Federal officials were warned the night before, but none had expected such a well-prepared, fully developed proposal.

The plan caused a small sensation. It had much wider benefits than Ottawa's plan, with provisions for widows and orphans. It covered more people, and was compulsory for the self-employed. It was more generous – paying a quarter of the participant's average income up to a ceiling of $6,000. Contributions were twice that of Ottawa's plan and were paid on a wider wage base (up to $6,000), but the contributor could exempt the first $1,000 of his earnings thus making the plan one which would in effect help to redistribute income. The transition period before full payments would be made was twice Ottawa's – twenty years. Most appealing of all, it would create a reserve fund worth, in Quebec alone, over $8.3 billion by 1996 – a powerful instrument of provincial development.[39]

37 'Statement by the Hon. John Robarts at the Federal-Provincial Conference, Quebec City, March 31, 1964,' pp. 10–11.

38 Robarts said: 'Ontario is prepared to enter a national plan which is truly national and embraces all of Canada. Whether we are to have such a plan is a matter of some doubt. In the event that we do not, then we reserve our right to make the decision as to our future action in providing pension benefits for our people in Ontario until we see the ultimate form of Bill C-75 and the position of our sister provinces.' *Globe and Mail*, 2 April 1964.

39 For details, see Quebec, Interdepartmental Study Committee on the Quebec Pension Plan (Quebec, 1964), vol. I, passim.

This new alternative changed the whole debate. Premier Smallwood – and Prime Minister Pearson – both quipped that they would like to 'opt-in' to Quebec's plan.[40] The provinces immediately saw its advantages. 'It made an absolutely enormous impression,' said one official. Another said: 'It introduced a whole new dimension to the argument.' All participants would now have to modify and re-evaluate their positions.

For Ottawa the Quebec plan, together with Ontario's threatened withdrawal, seemed to spell the end of its scheme. 'My God, this makes ours look sick,' one official told another as he heard Lesage outline the Quebec proposal. Said another: 'The federal plan as it then stood was dead. It was obvious at that point if there ever was to be a pension plan, it would be Canada joining the Quebec plan.'

The conference ended with no agreement. It was generally felt that a nadir had been reached in federal-provincial relations. Prime Minister Lesage refused to accept the traditional post-conference communiqué, drafted by federal officials.[41] 'We were on the brink of the abyss at that moment,' stated a federal official.[42] Said a minister: 'I think we suddenly realized that, by God, the country might break up.' Quebec officials had told Ottawa that the upcoming budget speech – a year after the '25-25-100' ultimatum – would be a bitter attack on Ottawa. A major collision, with frightening consequences, seemed to be in the offing. 'Confederation was in the balance that week.' It was clear something had to be done, and again Ottawa had to reassess its position.

## RESOLUTION: THE POST-CONFERENCE NEGOTIATIONS

The conference broke up on 2 April; eleven days later the crisis was over.[43] Both sides had powerful incentives to find agreement. Ottawa

40 Saywell, *Canadian Annual Review for 1964*, p. 66.
41 Newman, *The Distemper of Our Times*, p. 310.
42 He continued: 'If things had gone on from there, Lesage would have attacked the federal government with enormous venom and to great effect. It would have prevented any possibility of recovery. It would have been done on an issue [finances] where all the provinces were agreed. The federal government would be forced into a general retreat.' A Quebec official added: 'The questions were flying – would there be an election on the whole issue, and might it lead to separation?' Mario Cardinal wrote in *Le Devoir* on 3 April: 'Never at such a high and public level has Confederation seemed so menaced. For the first time the efforts which are habitually made to create an atmosphere of harmony at the Federal-Provincial Conference have been in vain' (my translation).
43 Published accounts of this period include Peter Desbarats, *The State of Quebec* (Toronto, 1965), pp. 125–32; Peter C. Newman, 'The Secret Deal That Saved the CPP,' *Toronto Star*, 12 Nov. 1964; and 'Five Days in April,'

most feared an irrevocable split which would imperil national unity and could lead to fatal weakening of the Liberals in Quebec. It was deeply committed to the pension plan. The only way to rescue it was to reach a compromise. In addition, officials knew Quebec's budget speech would soon be delivered. Quebec too wanted to avoid potentially disastrous conflict and was by now firmly committed to its pension plan. The planners realized that politically it might be difficult for Quebec's plan to have a contribution rate twice that of Ottawa's so some agreement was vital. Finally, Quebec wanted to use the pension plan to gain leverage on the other disputed issues. But Quebec was in the stronger position. 'It was [Ottawa's] move now,' said a Quebec minister. 'We knew the pressure was against them. If they failed they would have to go to the country.'

Shortly after the Quebec conference ended two senior federal officials, Tom Kent, Liberal policy planner and chief aide to Pearson, and Gordon Robertson, secretary to the cabinet, drafted memoranda recommending that Ottawa move towards Quebec's position on pensions and reassess its financial position. Forestry Minister Maurice Sauvé, the most junior French Canadian in the cabinet but one who had maintained the best relations with the Quebec government, was also concerned. On Monday, 6 April, Sauvé and Kent both telephoned Claude Morin, Quebec's deputy minister of federal-provincial affairs, to find out if Quebec would be willing to talk.

The answer was yes. Tuesday evening, after some persuasion, Kent and Sauvé got Pearson's permission to talk to Quebec representatives, and that night the two flew in great secrecy to Quebec. Not even the other Quebec ministers were informed. If the attempt failed the federal decision-makers did not want it to become known.

Wednesday morning the two federal emissaries met Morin at the Chateau Frontenac in Quebec City. By noon it was clear something could be worked out. Kent called Pearson, who gave permission for a meeting that afternoon with Lesage and another Quebec minister. Kent, Sauvé, and Morin presented the ministers with the results so far,[44] and all agreed a tentative settlement would be drawn up and presented to both cabinets. Lesage agreed to postpone his budget speech.

The two federal representatives telephoned Ottawa with this news and

*Time* (Canadian ed.), 1 May 1964. My reconstruction differs in some detail from these sources. My description also follows that given by Miss LaMarsh in her *Memoirs of a Bird in a Gilded Cage*. See also Newman, *The Distemper of Our Times*, chap. 22.

44 While permission had been given by Pearson to meet only one Quebec minister besides Lesage, actually Education Minister Paul Gérin-Lajoie and Natural Resources Minister René Lévesque were both present.

Pearson told them to return straight to his residence. They flew back in a Quebec government plane (a good sign) and went straight to 24 Sussex Drive. Now the most delicate part of the whole operation began: persuading the federal cabinet to agree to a major shift in policy. Miss LaMarsh felt her pension plan was being torpedoed; Finance Minister Walter Gordon was worried about a new drain on the federal treasury; several other English-Canadian ministers resisted a federal retreat or giving in to Quebec. Some of the Quebec ministers resented having been bypassed. Lining up cabinet support began at Pearson's house and continued through the week. Gordon, initially unenthusiastic, agreed on Thursday, on condition that the final settlement included agreement on the major details of the pension plan. The leading role in these internal negotiations was played by Pearson himself. 'He was the real hero of this period,' said one minister.

After the initial meetings in Quebec there was still only agreement to work out a settlement. Many details, especially on the pension plan itself, remained. On Wednesday and Thursday there was a flurry of phone calls between the capitals as both sides firmed up their positions, and on Friday night Morin and Claude Castonguay, Quebec's chief expert on pensions, flew to Ottawa. They met Kent, Sauvé, Dr Joseph Willard, deputy minister of welfare and chairman of the federal task force, and D.S. Thorson, associate deputy minister of justice, on Saturday, to work out the pension settlement. By three in the afternoon the two sides were still far apart. Finally, Kent and Sauvé, after retiring to a washroom to consult alone, proposed that two plans would operate – but they would have identical provisions and be fully coordinated. After this breakthrough, agreement came fast. At seven in the evening the meeting ended and the participants retired to the Chateau Laurier for a congratulatory drink. The spirit of the discussion was later summed up by Kent: 'To reduce large questions to manageable proportions and then work out the details.' But this could not have happened without consensus on one fact: conflict must be avoided.[45]

Now all that remained was to tidy up the loose ends and get formal approval from both cabinets. On Wednesday, 15 April, the final federal proposal arrived in Quebec. On Thursday remaining details were settled and the next day Pearson sent a telegram to the premiers outlining the accord.[46] Prime Minister Robarts knew of the meetings, but neither he nor other premiers had played any part.

45 Miss LaMarsh played very little part in these discussions. She was not optimistic about a settlement, and spent the crucial weekend at home in Niagara Falls.

46 The telegram is reprinted in Ontario, Legislative Assembly, *Debates*, 1964, pp. 2220–1. See also *Le Devoir*, 19 April, and the *Globe and Mail*, 21 April 1964.

The settlement was a victory for Quebec, a solution to most of the outstanding issues. Quebec would get fiscal equivalence payments instead of the federal family allowance and student loan plans. All provinces would get a greater share of personal income taxes. Under the existing arrangement they were to get 19 per cent in 1965–6 and 20 per cent in 1966–7; now they would get 21 per cent and 24 per cent.[47] Quebec now agreed to take part in the Tax Structure Committee. Ottawa agreed to negotiate the details of Quebec's opting-out of a wide range of shared-cost programmes.

The pension plan was a compromise. Quebec and any other province that wanted could have its own plan. Quebec agreed to the amendment to the British North America Act so Ottawa too could provide supplementary benefits. Benefits and contributions were a compromise, though the result was closer to Quebec's position. Quebec was deeply committed to an exemption of the first $1,000 of earnings from contributions; both sides compromised at $600, which virtually everyone later agreed retained all the administrative difficulty Ottawa feared and little of the redistributive benefit Quebec wanted. Ottawa was most committed to a short transition period, and Quebec conceded this point. Finally, the settlement offered to turn over 100 per cent of the fund – now much larger than previously envisioned because of the higher contribution rate – to the provinces.

It had been an exhausting two weeks. Prime Minister Lesage told the legislature: 'I have lived for the past month a terrifying life. I have worked for my province as no man has ever worked for it. I have made use of all the means which Providence granted me ... so that Quebec, finally, could be recognized as a province which has a *statut spécial* in Confederation, and I have succeeded.'[48] 'It was incredible,' said a senior federal official. 'At the time I was almost numb, because you could see the whole thing could blow up at any moment.'

When details of the accord was unveiled simultaneously by Lesage and Pearson the reaction was enthusiastic. Pearson 'appears to have pulled a political triumph out of the teeth of disaster,' said a writer in the Toronto *Globe and Mail.* Lesage 'is generally being credited with pulling off a minor political miracle,' said the Montreal *Gazette.* And Claude Ryan in *Le Devoir* said the real beneficiaries were old people and the federal system.[49]

The provincial governments reacted as enthusiastically. All liked the broader coverage, the averting of conflict, and most of all their gains from

47 The increase would produce an extra $60 million in the first year according to government estimates. *Globe and Mail,* 21 April 1964.

48 Québec, Assemblée législative, *Débats,* 1964, p. 2650.

49 Bruce Macdonald, *Globe and Mail,* 20 April; Gordon Pape, Montreal *Gazette,* 22 April; and Claude Ryan, *Le Devoir,* 21 April 1964.

the pension fund and the boost in their share of income taxes. These benefits tempered any resentment at their being left out of the negotiations. Ontario, however, now had to re-evaluate its goals and resources. Would it approve the settlement – which was attractive on many grounds – or would it continue to make the kinds of criticisms it had made earlier? The new plan was even worse from the conservative point of view than its predecessor. But it now seemed clear that the new situation ruled out Ontario's being able to force any change in the conservative direction. The province felt it could not wreck the agreement; thus it welcomed the settlement and dropped its earlier criticisms. It was to return to them later, but in a *pro forma* fashion.

## PUTTING IT ALL TOGETHER: APRIL TO SEPTEMBER 1964

The Canada Pension Plan did not finally appear for another year. Bill C-75 had to be scrapped and a new one prepared; Quebec had to prepare its own legislation; many more details had to be agreed on; and Parliament had to act.

Following the agreement Quebec and Ottawa collaborated extraordinarily closely in drafting the bills. Throughout May they discussed various aspects of the pension plan and the wording of the amendment to the British North America Act. In early June Pearson again wrote the premiers providing more information and later in the month the Commons officially approved an address to the Queen calling for the constitutional amendment. On 15 June the Quebec legislature passed a resolution setting out the major features of the pension plan.[50]

But the discussion continued right through the summer. Many questions remained to be decided. Some were trivial; others dealt with substantive provisions of the pension plan like the size of widows' pensions and rules governing disability pensions. Still other questions had symbolic importance for Quebec, such as the design of the joint identification card which would be carried by participants in both plans and the wording of the section in the federal act which made employees in Quebec of companies regulated by Ottawa participants in the Quebec plan. Finally, arrangements had to be worked out for making sure the schemes functioned together, including a joint appeal board to prevent divergences through future interpretation, and ways to handle contributions and benefits for participants who moved between Quebec and the other provinces.

50 Québec, Assemblée législative, *Débats*, 1964, pp. 4074–89. The revised section 94A of the BNA Act ends with the words: 'but no such law shall affect the operation of any law, present or future, of a provincial legislature in relation to any such matter.'

All these matters had to be agreed among the officials, then cleared with the respective cabinets. As the bills went through several drafts, clauses were exchanged and modified. By the final meetings in September the bills were virtually complete.

This work was done in great secrecy. Federal officials were afraid of the storm the opposition might create if it were known that such major legislation was being prepared in such close collaboration with another government. It seemed to threaten the parliamentary norm that new legislation should be discussed first in Parliament. 'But really who could doubt that this was the only way to proceed in a case like this,' said one federal participant. 'I suppose we did observe the amenities [of parliamentary norms] but in spirit we certainly violated them."

Participants were unanimous in stressing the high degree of cooperation in this process. The reasons are clear: first, the political heads were strongly committed to protecting the agreement and, second, those working on the details saw themselves as pension experts sharing the same values and committed simply to preparing the best plans. Each side did want its view to prevail, but on many issues there was complete agreement from the start, and on others both sides were willing to trade.[51]

There were additional negotiations with the other provinces. Partly to mollify insurance interests who felt they had been abandoned and partly to assert that all provinces had the same rights as Quebec, Ontario wanted two important safeguards. One was some provincial control over future amendments and the other was the right for any province to pull out of the plan later if it desired. Ottawa still wanted Ontario in the federal plan. If not there would be great administrative difficulties in coordinating three separate plans. Ottawa did not want to restrict its own resources for future changes, and realized there would be parliamentary opposition to this apparent violation of the norm that Parliaments cannot bind future ones;[52] but they felt they had to agree to the Ontario demand. Thus the final plan specified that a province could pull out when it wanted and that agreement of two-thirds of the provinces with two-thirds of the population was required for future substantive changes in the plan. This gave Ontario a virtual veto.

At a conference of officials in July 1964 federal and Quebec represen-

51 Quebec had an initial advantage in these discussions because it had thought out more thoroughly the supplementary benefits. But Ottawa moved ahead quickly, and in May a senior Quebec official wrote a memorandum urging Quebec to organize its operation more fully and speed up its planning to prevent federal officials gaining the advantage.

52 The federal memorandum written at the time said, 'the constitutional and political facts are – as this whole business has shown – that federal freedom to move on pensions is limited by the provinces. The proposal merely recognizes facts.'

tatives outlined the complete plan. Ontario now returned to many of its earlier criticisms.[53] Its representatives expressed frustration at the fait accompli which really meant that no important changes could be made since they would bring the whole fragile agreement with Quebec crashing down. One other matter to be resolved was regulations for the disposition of the fund which was to be, in effect, a massive source of borrowing capital. Manitoba and British Columbia – which prided itself on being 'debt-free' because all provincial borrowing was in the form of provincially guaranteed securities for other agencies rather than in direct provincial debt – wanted to make provincially guaranteed securities eligible as well as direct provincial securities. After some discussion the provinces won the point.

## RATIFICATION: PARLIAMENTARY ACTION, 1964–5

It remained for Parliament to pass the plan. On 9 November 1964 a new resolution on pensions was passed. A new bill, C-136, was introduced and referred to a joint committee of House and Senate for study. This was the first time interest groups had formal access to the decision-making process. The committee heard 116 witnesses and filled two thousand pages of *Hansard* with its hearings.[54]

But the committee, and indeed Parliament, worked under a vital constraint: few major changes could be considered because the agreement with Quebec could not be jeopardized. 'If the committee had come up with basic changes, we would have had to go back and start all over again with Quebec,' said an official. 'Nobody relished that idea.' This constraint led to frustration both among opposition parties and among interest-group representatives. Said one witness: 'They were quite certain they weren't going to change, they didn't want to hear constructive criticism.' And Conservative pension critic Gordon Aiken had this exchange with Judy LaMarsh:

Aiken: I am told we are sitting here to rubber stamp this Bill, and I am wondering if we are sitting here to any purpose.

53 Among its suggestions were: that the $600 exemption should be abolished; the automatic escalation of contributions and benefits should be removed; the 'retirement test' for persons electing to take their pensions before age seventy should be modified or abolished; some officials wanted to permit companies providing private plans meeting CPP standards to be permitted to opt-out; the CPP and OAS programmes should be integrated so the true total cost of old age security would be visible; a different method should be used for calculating widows' pensions; and so on.

54 For details, see Department of National Health and Welfare, *Annual Report, 1965*, pp. 102–3.

LaMarsh: I cannot imagine you being a rubber stamp for anything in this government.

Aiken: There is an agreement between the federal government and Quebec that the basic parts of the plan won't be changed ... If we do make recommendations in this committee regarding the broad nature of a principle, is the government going to be able to bring in such a change?[55]

But this frustration was only part of the reason for the committee's impotence. Clearly it was late in the day for any major changes, and parliamentary committees generally have little effect on legislation, especially when it is a central part of the government's programme.

Ontario was still critical. Federal planners got a shock when in January Laurence Coward, Ontario's chief negotiator, telephoned the committee and said Ontario would submit a brief.[56] It was a strong attack on the Ottawa-Quebec plan. It demanded reconsideration of the financial impact, doubling the transition period, abolition of the $600 exemption, and other changes. Most important, it said the plan did not provide anything for the presently retired and recommended a $25 increase in the OAS pension, financed by the CPP. These criticisms were the same as those being made by the federal Conservatives. To Ottawa it looked like 'mischief' and 'a political gambit.' 'It would have reintroduced the whole question of Quebec again.'

But simultaneously with the brief Ontario announced it would participate in the federal plan. A committee of Ontario officials had been studying the pros and cons of Ontario having its own plan and had gone so far as to produce a draft bill. There were good arguments on both sides. Having its own plan would give Ontario political credit, allow Ontario to make its own improvements, give it unequivocal control over the fund and future changes, and make Quebec's status less 'special.' On the other hand the machinery would be costly to establish; it would be extremely difficult to devise a plan which both met the conservative viewpoint Ontario had espoused and gave benefits comparable to those in the Ottawa-Quebec plan; and Ontario's participation in the national plan could be interpreted as a contribution to national unity. The debate illustrates the way goals must be continually balanced against each other, and how the actions of Ottawa and Quebec put a great constraint on Ontario's freedom of action. The committee recommended Ontario join the CPP, and the

55 Special Joint Committee of the Senate and of the House of Commons to Consider and Report on Bill C-136, *Minutes of Proceedings and Evidence*, 1964–5, p. 28.

56 Ontario, 'Submission to the Joint Committee on the Canada Pension Plan,' Toronto, 21 Jan. 1965.

cabinet agreed. But, Robarts told his colleagues, it was one of the most difficult decisions he ever made.

After the Ontario brief was received federal planners invited Quebec and Ontario representatives to Ottawa. The federal officials felt that Ottawa might have to concede on the exemption question in Parliament. Quebec refused, and said if Ottawa did so, Quebec would return to its $1,000 exemption. But it was agreed the plans could still work together if one had the exemption and one did not. It was soon clear that Ontario would not push its criticisms further and the threat was over.

The joint committee reported on 16 February. It recommended relatively minor changes.[57] Only one had serious implications for the Quebec-Ottawa agreement. That was a proposal to increase the number of years the beneficiary could exclude or 'drop-out' in his calculation of average lifetime earnings for pension purposes. This meant if the worker had been unemployed or had received low wages for a few years his pension would not suffer. The committee wanted to double the number of drop-out years.[58] Before accepting the recommendation Ottawa consulted with Quebec, which agreed to a compromise. Quebec had purposely delayed introducing its bill to the provincial legislature to allow for just such developments, since it could then make changes without having to admit publicly it was altering its bill because of federal pressure.

On 22 February the Commons began clause-by-clause debate on the bill. The discussion, often acrimonious, lasted twenty-six days. The government beat back Conservative and NDP amendments to increase the OAS by $25.[59] It had been a long and bitter session, characterized by difficult wrangling and divisive issues like a new Canadian flag. The Conservatives wanted to adjourn before the pension plan was finally dealt with; so did some Liberals. But the New Democratic Party had forced a commitment from the government to get the bill through. The pressure was welcome to the bill's managers – and Miss LaMarsh later held a small luncheon for Stanley Knowles, the chief NDP spokesman, in gratitude. The bill finally passed the House on 29 March by a vote of 159 to 12 (seven Social Credit members and five Conservatives voted against). It quickly passed the Senate and on 3 April 1965 received royal assent. The Canada

57 It suggested that consideration be given to improving pensions for those presently retired, removal of a ceiling on the total amount of orphan's benefits payable to one family, inclusion of members of the armed forces and Royal Canadian Mounted Police, and so on.

58 Of the forty-seven-year contribution period from ages eighteen to sixty-five.

59 In 1966, however, the government introduced legislation to ensure a guaranteed income of $104 per month for those over sixty-five.

Pension Plan came into operation on 1 January 1966, when Canadians found a new deduction on their pay-cheques.

Debate was shorter in the Quebec legislature. Bill 50, the Quebec pension plan, received first reading 21 May, and it, together with bills to regulate private pensions[60] and to establish the Quebec pension board to administer the legislation, was passed on 23 June.

60 This act was the product of an interesting example of interprovincial cooperation. Ontario, whose original pension legislation was primarily regulatory, still felt that despite the CPP action was needed to ensure proper running of private pension plans. It took the lead in urging other provinces to develop legislation along the lines of its own, and most have done so.

CHAPTER FOUR

# The financial negotiations

'The holy spirit seems to have a marked horror for those mortal men who occupy themselves with the tax system,' wrote a Quebec journalist during the confused Federal-Provincial Conference in October 1966.[1] Many would agree with him. The conference was the climax of the negotiations for the 1967–72 federal-provincial financial arrangements. They had begun, in a sense, with the hasty proposal to establish the Tax Structure Committee at the Quebec Conference in 1964.

## A NEW FEDERAL APPROACH

Negotiations on pensions and other issues in 1964 had shown how vulnerable Ottawa was to provincial pressures. The status of the federal government had been weakened, especially by Quebec's opting-out. Ottawa had been on the defensive. Even among the Liberals there was a pervasive dislike of the opting-out arrangements. Many felt it was time for Ottawa to reassert itself. These views were shared in the wider environment. 'Almost without exception the major Canadian newspapers called for an assertion of federal power against the alleged rising tide of provincialism.'[2] There was also a feeling that part of the reason for

1 *Le Devoir*, Montreal, 27 Oct. 1966 (my translation).
2 John T. Saywell, ed., *Canadian Annual Review for 1966* (Toronto, 1967), p. 48.

provincial success was that Ottawa had not developed a coherent, thought-out position – it had simply been reacting to the provinces.

Thus several groups in Ottawa began to think about a new federal position. A response to the Quebec revolution had to be developed. The financial discussions were approaching and Ottawa should be prepared for them. 'The federal government was on the ropes,' said a senior official, 'and the time was ripe for some rational move. We had to develop a position that would be strong and viable.'

This rethinking began in 1964, at first mostly among officials like Tom Kent, Gordon Robertson, and R.B. Bryce, deputy minister of finance. But the chief architect of the new fiscal approach was Dr A.W. Johnson, formerly deputy treasurer in Saskatchewan, who was appointed assistant deputy minister of finance, with special responsibilities for federal-provincial relations, in September 1964. His thoughts were to fit in well with the ideas of an influential group of federal cabinet ministers. There was little action at the cabinet level before the Liberals called a federal election for November 1965.

The government hoped – and expected – the election would produce a comfortable majority, but the Liberals received only 131 seats, two short of the magic number.[3] The election did, however, have important consequences for the coming negotiations. Most important, three strongly federalist French Canadians entered the government, including Pierre Elliott Trudeau, who was to become justice minister and, in 1968, prime minister; Jean Marchand, a labour leader, to become minister of manpower and immigration; and former newspaper publisher Gérard Pelletier. All were to become strong proponents of the new federal approach. In addition, Finance Minister Walter Gordon resigned and was replaced by Mitchell Sharp, who was in 1966 to defend tenaciously the federal treasury against provincial 'inroads.'

Following the election a series of papers outlining a proposed new strategy was submitted to the cabinet. There was considerable debate both within the civil service and the cabinet, and final agreement on some aspects did not come until a few days before the October 1966 conference.

The approach had several elements. First, Ottawa must respect the constitution. A firm line should be drawn between federal and provincial responsibilities. Ottawa would retain its initiative and resources in matters of federal jurisdiction – especially in economic policy. But it would not get involved in provincial areas. This meant, for one thing, much less re-

3 For a good summary of the election and its results, see J. Murray Beck, *Pendulum of Power: Canada's Federal Elections* (Scarborough, Ont., 1968), pp. 374–98.

liance on shared-cost programmes. Another element of the strategy was to reverse the trend towards special status for Quebec.[4] Third, a clear line should be drawn between federal and provincial revenue sources; no longer should Ottawa turn over tax sources to the provinces as it had done steadily since the war. Fourth, Ottawa would continue to support the poorer provinces through an expanded and more rational equalization formula. Much of the debate within the government stemmed from the belief of some leaders that by stressing the need to prevent special status, and therefore reducing federal involvement in provincial matters, Ottawa was abandoning its historic role of national leadership. The counter-argument was that only by respecting the constitution could Ottawa get away from its continuously defensive posture of recent years.

Thus, by 1966 Ottawa had tried to develop a viable approach to the provinces. The first comprehensive statement of the position came in Finance Minister Sharp's statement to the Tax Structure Committee in September 1966.

## THE TAX STRUCTURE COMMITTEE PROJECTIONS

A potentially important form of information exchange between the participants is the creation of new information out of the negotiation process itself. The Tax Structure Committee, which first met in October 1964, was an attempt to do just that. It was to undertake a synoptic study of the whole field of federal-provincial fiscal relations including future revenue and expenditure needs, the effectiveness of the current division of revenues, means of reconciling federal and provincial priorities, and so on.[5] The committee was made up of three federal ministers and the provincial treasurers or finance ministers. Its working arm was the Continuing Committee on Financial and Economic Matters, made up of senior officials from both levels, and its working secretary – nominated by Prime Minister Lesage – was A.W. Johnson. At its first meeting the TSC commissioned a series of studies,[6] by far the most important of which was the projection

4 Said Justice Minister Trudeau after a meeting of the federal Quebec Liberal Federation in April 1966: 'We rejected any kind of special status for Quebec. In essence the meeting was an affirmation that federalism cannot work unless all the provinces are in basically the same relation toward the central government.' Quoted by Peter Newman, *Toronto Star*, 2 April 1966. The whole question was to become a major issue in the 1968 federal election campaign.

5 *Federal-Provincial Tax Structure Committee*, 14–15 Sept. 1966 (Ottawa, 1966), pp. 4–5.

6 Some were subsequently published by the Canadian Tax Foundation. See A. Milton Moore, J. Harvey Perry, and Donald I. Beach, *The Financing of Canadian Federation: The First Hundred Years* (Toronto, 1966); and Marion Bryden, *Occupancy of Tax Fields in Canada* (Toronto 1965).

of federal and provincial revenues and expenditures for coming years. This project was to be an interesting example of negotiation in itself and a major influence on the later discussions.[7]

Most provinces welcomed the study because they felt certain it would show a large gap between federal and provincial revenue needs, and thus back up and legitimize provincial demands for a greater share of resources. 'We thought "This is it, now we've got them," ' said an Ontario official. To the provinces the purpose of the projections was to find out how big the revenue gap was, with the obvious implication the findings would be the basis for the 1966 settlement. 'Otherwise, why the hell would you go through all that work,' said one official.

The result was that the projections themselves became a subject of negotiation. It was an exceedingly complex task. Complicated assumptions about economic growth rates, population trends, and particular programmes had to be agreed on – and in many cases the assumptions chosen would greatly influence the result. A common statistical basis for each government's figures had to be devised and much new data collected. Much of the information needed was material that governments were traditionally secretive about, and rules had to be set up to prevent them leaking out. All these matters were discussed in the continuing committee, and the work was coordinated by a small secretariat. Each government prepared its own figures, using the common (negotiated) guidelines, set out in regular 'bulletins.'

The most difficult questions had to do with what programmes could be included in the projections. Did one have to be enacted before it could be included, or just set forth in a white paper, or what? Both Quebec and the Maritimes wanted a 'catch-up' element to be included in their projections of such programmes as education since they were currently well below the national average in these services. All these questions had to be negotiated. The provinces wanted to estimate expenditures as high and revenues as low as possible, to best make their case. Some padding did take place. 'The provinces threw in everything but the kitchen sink,' said a former BC official. One province made expenditure projections which, according to a federal official, 'were so huge they just couldn't have done everything they said they were going to do.' Said another: 'For many provincial officials this was a negotiation, not an attempt to work out the most objective technical study possible ... This was ammunition for the [later] negotiations, and I don't blame the officials here. I suppose I would have done the same thing myself.'

7 The only published account of the work of the TSC is found in Robert A. McLarty, 'Organizing for a Federal-Provincial Fiscal Policy,' *Canadian Tax Journal* 15 (1967), pp. 416–18.

Despite this, most provinces were careful, and it was generally agreed that even though there were many 'hairy assumptions' the results were generally valid. 'They were in the right ball-park.' Careful provisions were made to ensure accuracy. Thus bulletins were regularly issued, and the continuing committee often discussed the matter.[8] Then, in August 1965 representatives of all provinces except British Columbia and Newfoundland met in Ottawa to put the figures together. Small teams went through each provinces' figures to make sure they had not been too liberal and that they had included everything they decently could. It was a two-week 'blood-bath.' 'You had to be able to look the other fellow in the eye.' Shortly after, a small group of federal officials made the compilation of the final figures and sorted out last minute differences. Some of Quebec's figures were still open to question, and a Quebec official went to Ottawa where he and a federal official sat down and went through them all, striking compromises, and clearing them with senior officials back home by phone. British Columbia was suspicious of the whole exercise. It supplied – unofficially – expenditure figures, with the warning that if they ever came out they would be disavowed. But it gave no revenue figures, so they were estimated by a member of the secretariat. Newfoundland supplied no figures, and they too were estimated.

But more important than these external controls, the governments had their own incentive to be relatively honest. As an Ontario official said, 'If the figures had been open to question, then they would not have been a useful bargaining tool.' Another added: 'We had the feeling let's be really conscientious about the facts, then we can argue about them.' The governments also wanted to use the figures for their own budgetary planning purposes. Moreover, the projections soon took on a life of their own. Those involved saw the project as a major step in intergovernmental collaboration. Trust and honesty were among their norms, and 'There was a sense of professional ethics here.'

The results were submitted to the full Tax Structure Committee in November 1965. They showed broadly what everybody had expected, and meant that 'this time the provinces could say: the projection proves we need money. Before that they could voice their demands but without any real rationale behind them.'

At the same time, the results showed that spending and revenue needs by all governments were going up far faster than expected. No redistribution would solve that problem. 'The primary feeling was "Oh my God, do we really need that much proportion of GNP just to keep doing what we are already doing." ' said one official. Thus another – unanticipated –

8 The Revenue bulletins alone totalled more than three hundred pages, and at one point included an entire PH D thesis as an appendix. *Ibid.*, p. 417.

effect of the exercise was to sharpen the conflict over revenues by making the needs of all much clearer. The projections thus did not lead to a solution of the basic problem. All they could do was provide the figures; the implications of the figures were still open to disagreement. To Ottawa they meant one thing – everyone must tax more; to the provinces another – Ottawa must transfer revenues to us. As a Quebec official put it, 'It remains a question of politics. Before the TSC tax-sharing was purely a political question. Now it is a little less political. The projections really change nothing.'

This illustrates one of the basic difficulties inherent in attempts at synoptic consideration of policy problems. But the projection exercise did represent a potentially important new development in federal-provincial relations. Its success, of course, depended on mutual trust, and on the belief by most participants that important advantages stem from the effort. Unfortunately, both these beliefs were weakened when Ottawa appeared to ignore the projections in October 1966. The reaction of many of those most involved was 'to hell with it.' There was much less enthusiasm when another, more modest, attempt at projections was begun after the 1969 Constitutional Conference.

## THE PRELIMINARIES: TO AUGUST 1966

Several developments in 1965 and early 1966 affected the later negotiations. First was a growing demand, from the provinces, universities, and the Economic Council of Canada, for much greater federal assistance to higher education.[9] Ottawa responded by raising the existing per capita grant programme from two to five dollars per capita early in 1966; but it was called an 'interim solution'[10] and a federal-provincial conference on education was scheduled for the summer. Because of several provincial elections it was postponed until October when it would be held simultaneously with the conference on finances.

One of the elections was in Quebec. In June the Liberals called an election, hoping 'to obtain from the population a precise mandate,'[11] to guide the government in the forthcoming financial negotiations. National-

9 The most important of these was the Bladen Commission on Financing Higher Education, sponsored by the Association of Universities and Colleges of Canada. It recommended a great increase in federal aid to higher education, better federal-provincial cooperation, and an increased federal role. For a summary, see Saywell, *Canadian Annual Review for 1965*, p. 418. The Economic Council of Canada also recommended a massive increase in public investment in higher education.

10 Secretary of State Judy LaMarsh in *H. of C. Debates*, 1967, p. 13689.

11 Quoted in Saywell, *Canadian Annual Review for 1966*, pp. 57–8 (my translation).

ism played an important role in the campaign. Despite its demands the Liberals campaigned against separatism and argued Quebec must work within the Canadian framework. The Union Nationale, led by Daniel Johnson, used the slogan 'Québec d'abord' and implied the Liberals were Ottawa's captives. Its programme included fundamental constitutional reform, 100 per cent of the major taxes, greater international competence for Quebec, and other demands. The Union Nationale insisted separatism was an alternative worth considering.[12] The party won fifty-six seats to the Liberals' fifty, even though the Liberals won more votes. Virtually every commentary on the election, however, agreed it was not nationalism but resentment at the speed and cost of social change led by the Liberals that was responsible for the defeat. Nevertheless, the election meant a new cast to Quebec's demands. There would be a period of testing between the two governments. None of the new Union Nationale ministers had much experience outside Quebec; federal policymakers were nervous about the apparent nationalism of Johnson and his colleagues. Ottawa expected less free communication between the two governments. On the other hand it would probably be easier politically to stand up to Johnson than to the Liberal Lesage. Thus the election meant a re-evaluation of both goals and resources.

Most of the early discussions of the new fiscal arrangements took place at several meetings of the continuing committee and were occupied with the exchange of information. In February 1966 the discussions began in earnest. The first major topic was equalization.

For several years provincial officials, especially in Saskatchewan, New Brunswick, and Manitoba, had urged that equalization be expanded and that it be based on a more complete measure of provincial fiscal capacity than simply the three 'standard taxes' – personal and corporate income taxes and succession duties. As early as 1960 A.W. Johnson and his colleagues in Saskatchewan had developed an alternative formula for the continuing committee. Federal officials had also worked on the problem, and New Brunswick was working along the same lines. After the Saskatchewan government changed in 1964, with the Liberal government of Ross Thatcher replacing the CCF-NDP, Johnson left for Ottawa, together with several other officials. One, James Lynn, went first to the Royal Commission on Taxation, where he did a study of federal-provincial financing, and then later to the Finance Department where he continued his work

12 In his book, *Egalité ou indépendance* (Montreal, 1965), p. 105, Daniel Johnson wrote: 'There remain to us only two solutions: equality or independence, a new constitution or separation ... Me, I am ready to save the autonomy of Quebec even at the price of Confederation' (my translation).

with other federal officials. Another, Thomas Shoyoma, went to the Bank of Canada and in 1968 succeeded Johnson as assistant deputy minister of finance. Two other Johnson colleagues went to New Brunswick: D.D. Tansley as deputy treasurer and Robert McClarty as economic adviser. All members of this group favoured the 'tax-indicator' or representative tax method of calculating provincial need.[13] It would base equalization on the overall per capita yield from all tax sources. This became the basis of the federal position in 1966. The experience nicely illustrates the role chance can play in negotiations. If the Saskatchewan government had not fallen, so that many of its senior officials moved into strategic positions in other governments where they could much more effectively advocate their approach, 'we might never have had the new formula.' By 1966 the question was not would equalization be changed but how much?

At the February continuing committee meeting federal officials presented papers outlining the tax-indicator approach and its chief rival, the 'total income approach,' which used per capita income as the basis for measuring a government's fiscal capacity. Both were given without figures to promote non-partisan discussion. 'We got a great blast from the provinces; they wanted to see it in dollars and cents,' said a federal official. At this and later meetings there was wide-ranging discussion of most major aspects of equalization. By the July meeting Ottawa had firmly decided on the indicator approach. Provincial reaction was best indicated by how they fared under the new formula.[14] Saskatchewan, ironically, stood to lose its whole payment; Manitoba and Prince Edward Island also did poorly. All three attacked the new proposal. Quebec was the biggest gainer, in absolute amounts, but it played little part in the discussions, primarily because there was no point wasting scarce political resources to make marginal improvements in an already attractive proposal. Mani-

13 See James H. Lynn, *Comparing Provincial Revenue Yields: The Tax Indicator Approach* (Toronto, 1968), for an excellent description of the rationale of the new approach by one of its architects. Much of the theoretical basis for this approach was drawn from work done by the American Advisory Commission on Intergovernmental Relations. See *Measures of State and Local Fiscal Capacity and Tax Effort* (Washington, 1962).

14 Based on 1966–7 figures, Ottawa estimated the new formula would increase total equalization payments by $138.7 million. The estimated per capita *increases* for each province were: Newfoundland, $44.93; PEI, $1.85; Nova Scotia, $24.77; New Brunswick, $25.08; Quebec, $14.96; Manitoba, $1.66; Ontario, British Columbia, and Alberta would continue to receive nothing; and Saskatchewan's payment would decrease by $6.30 per capita. *Federal-Provincial Tax Structure Committee*, 14–15 Sept. 1966, p. 17. When the 1966–7 figures under the old formula were compared with the 1967–8 figures under the new, the estimated total increase in equalization was $194 million. See *H. of C. Debates*, 1967, p. 9291.

toba stressed past federal 'commitments' to equalize to the top province, and wanted to retain the old 'standard taxes' measure. Ontario and British Columbia both felt that higher costs of providing services in high-wage areas partially offset the poverty of the poorer provinces, and that this should be taken account of in the formula. Ottawa was sympathetic to the claim, and Ontario experimented with different formulae which would work, but was never confident enough of any to formally present them. Ottawa argued that leaving municipal revenues out of its formula and equalizing only to the level of the national average was in effect compensation, but the chief reason for these provisions was to keep the total cost of equalization down.

Nova Scotia, even though it did well under the new formula, argued strenuously for the 'income approach' which would yield more money for it and several other provinces. But it got little support. New Brunswick officials, natural allies here, had of course played a central role in developing the indicator formula and anyway felt that on tactical grounds it was better to settle for it than to risk losing all.

By July equalization was generally settled. There would be further complaints, but the only changes would be marginal.

The next major question was tax-sharing. It is not, however, greatly suited to discussion at the official level since it is a relatively cut-and-dried political question, with few complexities to sort out. 'Tax-sharing had to be deferred pretty much,' said one official. 'It was the minister's job; officials don't discuss the amount of tax-shares as such, though they do indicate what their ministers are probably going to ask for.'

There were more tactical reasons for not discussing tax-sharing at length. Ottawa needed the support of the richer provinces for its equalization formula, and, said one federal official, 'They undoubtedly would not have agreed if they had known they were going to get nothing in tax-sharing.' The equalization-receiving provinces agreed with Ottawa's agenda, but Ontario, Manitoba, and British Columbia wanted tax-sharing discussed first, and only then equalization.

There was nevertheless some discussion. At an early meeting Ottawa outlined its principle that each government should tax independently – and Ontario immediately started preparing its objections. In May an Ontario economist presented a paper to the committee arguing that Ottawa could fulfil its economic management role with much less than 50 per cent of the personal income tax.

At the July continuing committee meeting, Ottawa confidentially outlined its formal proposals for the financial agreements. This made it possible for the provinces, then engaged in preparing their own positions for the September TSC meeting, to take account of the federal proposals in their own briefs, and to prepare their arguments. Ottawa, of course, could also anticipate the line of provincial argument in the political level meetings to come.

### THE POLITICIANS TAKE OVER

So far, all the discussions, including the projections, had gone on in secret, and had mainly involved senior officials. In August the negotiations became more public. The occasion was the two-day Interprovincial Conference of Premiers in Toronto. The agenda was primarily concerned with such innocuous matters as coordination of interprovincial trucking. But coming immediately after the presentation of the federal proposals to the continuing committee, and only a month before the formal opening of negotiations, federal-provincial financial relations were bound to arise. Premier Thatcher of Saskatchewan, incensed at the new equalization formula, precipitated the discussion. The formula, he told the press, 'would wipe us out.' Saskatchewan citizens were being treated as 'second-class citizens' to benefit Quebec.[15] The federal government was naïve to hurt Saskatchewan when 'After all we're the only Liberal government out there [in the west].'[16] Prime Minister Robarts, too, gave some details of the proposed equalization formula. Federal representatives and some provincial officials felt the discussion was unfair, especially since the proposal had been outlined in confidence. What was important was not that the provinces discussed the matter at the conference but that Thatcher used the forum thus provided – including the attention paid to it by the press – as a platform to get national attention. Perhaps the most important function of the conference was to give the premiers a chance to do what their officials had done in the continuing committee: get to know each other's positions. It also put Ottawa on notice of provincial objections and introduced the issue to public discussion.

Saskatchewan's pressure seems to have had an immediate effect on its equalization payment. Thatcher continued to paint a dire picture of his province's finances if it lost the payment and threatened: 'If Mr. Pearson persists in this proposal, I'll pull out of the National federation [of the Liberal party].'[17] A week later Pearson wrote Thatcher that the matter was still open for discussion, and soon after Sharp and Thatcher met for sixty-five minutes at Toronto International Airport. Thatcher was pleased

15 *Winnipeg Tribune*, 3 Aug. 1966.
16 *Globe and Mail*, 3 Aug. 1966.
17 *Ibid.*, 6 Aug.

– and indeed when the federal proposal formally appeared it included a transitional payment for Saskatchewan, meaning the province would lose only about $6 million rather than the whole payment of about $35 million. Whether this pressure accounts for the concession is unclear. Certainly it is to be expected Ottawa would have made a transitional payment, and federal officials claimed they had already planned one.

The next move was Ottawa's. On 8 September Mr Sharp, worried about inflationary pressures in the economy, delivered a major speech in the House which was billed as a 'mini-budget.'[18] He announced a cutback in federal programmes – including the delay of introduction of medicare by a year (which pleased most provinces) and ending the shared-cost programme for forestry, which, though not large, particularly annoyed some provinces like British Columbia. Sharp made a public commitment in the speech that there would be no more tax-shares transferred by Ottawa to the provinces.[19]

Not all provinces shared Mr Sharp's reading of the economic climate, and, more important, Ontario and others were worried that Ottawa's focus on short-term economic conditions was going to divert attention from the real issue as they saw it: a redistribution of resources.

## THE SEPTEMBER TAX STRUCTURE COMMITTEE MEETING

On 14 September the Tax Structure Committee reconvened, this time to open the negotiations formally. The meeting's importance is indicated by the presence of eight of the ten premiers.

Mr Sharp's brief was the first full statement of the new federal objectives. No longer would Ottawa 'make room' for the provinces by abating taxes as in the past.[20] Henceforth each government should be responsible to its own taxpayers for its own revenues. Ottawa, largely to reduce Quebec's special status, would move away from shared-cost programmes. It offered to turn over three of the largest such existing programmes – hospital insurance, health grants, and the Canada Assistance

18 The text is reprinted in *ibid.*, 9 Sept.

19 'I thought this was a matter to be discussed at the Conference,' said Prime Minister Robarts. *Ibid.*, 15 Aug.

20 All briefs are included in *Federal-Provincial Tax Structure Committee*, 14–15 Sept. 1966. Said Mr Sharp: 'It is time to recast the whole question of tax-sharing in broader and more comprehensive terms ... We must get away from what is tending to become a conventional notion that the federal government can and should be expected to give greater tax room to the provinces when they find their expenditures rising more rapidly than their revenues. This has been possible, and has been done, in the past decade, but it cannot be accepted as a general duty' (p. 23).

Plan – to the provinces in return for seventeen points of the income tax plus adjustment payments to make up the difference between actual programme costs and the value of the seventeen points. Sharp outlined the new equalization formula and a stabilization plan to ensure that in case of economic trouble, provincial revenues would not fall more than 5 per cent.

Prime Minister Johnson's brief was a nationalistic one, calling for massive reallocation of both functions and resources to the province, fundamental constitutional change to recognize the presence of two nations in Canada, and a provincial share of 100 per cent of all the major shared taxes. Rather than turning the shared-cost programmes over to the English-speaking provinces, which was a roundabout way of solving the problem, Ottawa should admit Quebec was different and not try to force all provinces into the same mould. The brief ended with an implied threat: 'As of September 1966, this is Quebec's attitude to Canadian Confederation; in short, it is a waiting attitude. It is up to this gathering – particularly the federal government's representatives – to decide whether waiting is worthwhile.'[21] The brief seemed to presage severe conflict. But it did not come. Inside the meeting, Johnson did little to push for immediate approval of these demands.

For all governments the briefs were important policy statements. Prime Minister Robarts pinned his argument to the projection results which showed the need 'for an immediate additional abatement.'[22] He said independent taxing would carry the danger of intergovernmental tax competition and conflict, and make coordination of fiscal policy more difficult. He called for greater federal assistance to higher education, and criticized the shared-cost proposals. Most important he insisted that Ontario was not prepared to agree to the new equalization formula until 'tax-sharing has been satisfactorily determined.'[23]

Other provinces rang similar themes. Premier Roblin of Manitoba, taking a much stronger position than he had before, wanted an interim one-year agreement during which Ottawa should abate twenty-six more personal income tax points, raising the provincial share from 24 to 50 per cent. He particularly lamented failure of the TSC to solve the problem of reconciling federal and provincial priorities. He attacked the shared-cost proposal – the compensation was inadequate, and it was precisely in those areas that programme costs were rising fastest. Mr Bennett wanted an additional two points a year of personal income tax and one point of corporate income tax, rejection of the new equalization formula, and 'fair and equal treatment' for British Columbia. Thatcher returned to his

21 *Ibid.*, p. 57. 22 *Ibid.*, p. 38. 23 *Ibid.*, p. 46.

criticism of equalization. But, like the Maritimes, he did not want more tax-shares, which would only weaken Ottawa's ability to make grants to the poorer provinces. New Brunswick welcomed the federal proposals. Nova Scotia strongly criticized Ottawa's unilaterally choosing the tax-indicator equalization method (it should have been the responsibility of the whole TSC) and made a vigorous critique of the federal proposal and defence of the 'income approach.' Prince Edward Island also criticized the equalization proposal for not meeting the needs of the poor island province with its tiny resource base. Alberta felt the existing arrangements should be continued to allow fuller consideration of the issues. It also proposed a novel equalization formula, by which a federal-provincial tax commission would distribute funds from a 'basic revenue fund' supported by specially earmarked taxes. The idea had been raised before in the continuing committee, but had never received serious attention.

These were the basic provincial positions. Each government tailored its position closely to its own particular needs. There was no coordinated provincial position.

The two-day debate centred primarily on tax-sharing and equalization. The provinces were not interested in discussing the shared-cost proposals, since the programmes in question did not expire until 1970. 'Politicians like to talk about immediate problems.' And it was hard in 1966 to know how attractive the federal proposal might look in 1969. In addition, many provincial officials thought the whole proposal a red herring to make it look as if Ottawa were giving the provinces seventeen points, when really they were not. These seventeen points would bring the provincial share of personal income taxes to 41 per cent – dangerously close to Ottawa's symbolic '50 per cent line.' Most provinces therefore withheld committing themselves when Mr Sharp informally polled them on the proposal.

It was clear that few changes would be made in equalization despite the arguments of Manitoba and Nova Scotia. Similarly, it was becoming clear that Ottawa was adamant about tax-sharing. Outside the meeting Sharp said what he repeated over and over again inside: 'It is not possible for the federal government to go further than it has.'[24]

Thus the conference ended with no movement on any side. Many provinces, led by Manitoba, now felt a shorter interim agreement should be signed but Ottawa still wanted five years.

The provinces continued to attack the federal proposal outside the meeting. Johnson, who had hinted at a press conference before the conference that separation might be the only alternative if Quebec's demand was refused, reminded Ottawa at the end that he had political support: in

24 *Globe and Mail*, 15 Sept. 1966.

a referendum, he told the press, 80 per cent of Quebecers would support his view of 'deux nations.'[25]

The next change came at a continuing committee meeting in September. The provinces by now realized little would be forthcoming in tax shares, but still hoped for some 'sugar-coating' to the bitter pill. These hopes were raised when Ottawa officials initiated a discussion of alternative means of making a fiscal transfer. The meeting also updated the TSC projections. Ottawa officials apparently believed that new figures would reduce the gap between federal and provincial revenues, but if so they were disappointed.

## THE OCTOBER 1966 FEDERAL-PROVINCIAL CONFERENCE

The climax of the negotiations came at the October Federal-Provincial Conference. It was really three conferences in one extending from 24 to 28 October – first the postponed education conference, then another TSC meeting, and finally the plenary conference of prime ministers and premiers. It was to last from Monday to Friday, and in practice the three meetings were hard to distinguish from one another.

As the delegates arrived in Ottawa on Sunday evening, 3 October, they received a thirty-page mimeographed federal statement.[26] It was completely unexpected. In it Prime Minister Pearson announced a major new approach to education. First, Ottawa would meet demands for federal assistance to higher education by paying half the operating costs of institutions of higher learning. But the form of payment was to be an *unconditional* abatement of four points of income tax and one of corporate tax, or, if a province wanted, a cash payment of $14 per capita. The existing per capita grants to universities would end. The chief reason for this formula – which had been the subject of intense debate within the federal government – was to get around the constitutional problem and ensure the plan would be acceptable to Quebec. Another reason was that Ottawa could give the impression of meeting provincial demands for an abatement while simultaneously meeting demands for aid to education. 'We hoped we could get off the hook by doing that,' said a federal official. 'We hoped maybe we could kill two birds with one stone.'

Second, Ottawa proposed not to renew the shared-cost programme by which the federal government had paid up to 75 per cent of the capital cost of vocational high schools, trade schools, and the like. The pro-

25 *Ibid.*, 16 Sept.
26 Reprinted in *Federal-Provincial Conference*, 24–29 Oct. 1966 (Ottawa, 1968), pp. 6–23.

gramme had provided the provinces with about $600 million over the past five years. The original need, said Mr Pearson, had abated, and Ottawa should reduce this involvement in provincial education. To ease the blow provinces would still have until 1970 to claim the $480 per capita[27] allotted to them under the agreements. If by then a province still had not spent the average per capita amount, it would have three more years to draw at a 50 per cent sharing rate. Federal operating assistance to these technical and vocational training institutions would end. Under another shared-cost programme Ottawa had paid up to 97 per cent of the cost of training allowances for those undergoing adult training in provincial manpower programmes. That would end, and Ottawa itself would become fully responsible for paying both the allowances and training costs, but only for *adults*. It would now be a federal programme, with Ottawa in effect buying training services from the provinces. The provinces were to become fully responsible for the costs and allowances of all *non-adults* in vocational training, defined by Ottawa as those who had been in the labour force less than three years – the 'three-year rule.' Thus the existing manpower training system, working through shared-cost programmes, would be dismantled. The provinces would be solely responsible for all 'regular' education, including vocational education. But adult manpower training – defined by Ottawa as an economic matter, and therefore federal – would be a federal responsibility. The total education package would give the provinces an estimated $360 million a year, but they would lose $270 million through the ending of existing programmes.[28]

The provinces had had no warning of such massive proposals. 'It was like a bolt from the blue,' said one official. Ottawa had decisively gained the initiative and had determined the agenda. It had reaped a publicity coup, since Pearson had explained the federal proposals on television at about the same time as the provinces were reading them for the first time.

This meant the provinces had to reassess their goals and strategies to react to the federal move. In many cases key officials and information had been left at home. 'We had to try to open up the phone lines back here to Winnipeg and roust our deputy ministers out of bed, to try to get the figures to find out what kind of effect all this would have on us.' Everyone had known the shared-cost agreements in manpower training were to

27 Of the 1961 population in the fifteen to nineteen age group.
28 *Federal-Provincial Conference*, 24–29 Oct. 1966, p. 22. The best description of the new policy is by Tom Kent (who became deputy minister of manpower and immigration), 'Intergovernmental Responsibility for Manpower Training,' paper delivered to the Institute of Public Administration of Canada, Hamilton, 7 Sept. 1967.

expire, but most had taken for granted they would be extended. Robarts, for example, had been briefed for a renegotiation. Now briefs had to be scrapped or modified. Officials worked most of the night to formulate a response before the official conference opening the next day. 'How can you expect people to come here and discuss such a problem,' asked a member of Ontario's delegation, 'when they throw this sort of thing at you on your arrival?'[29]

The problem was complicated by the vagueness and ambiguity of the federal proposals. Partly that was because in the end they had been put together hastily after final cabinet approval late Friday afternoon before the conference opened. The brief was a surprise to many federal officials. Many questions were still unanswered, and the federal position was unprepared. A second reason for the vagueness was a desire to make it possible to make later concessions without it looking like a defeat. But this too increased provincial difficulties and annoyance. 'I don't recall when the federal position was so badly prepared,' said a BC minister. 'It was thoroughly bad staff work ... They could not provide answers to even the most simple questions.'

A breakfast meeting of officials on Monday morning tried to sort out some of the confusion but with little success. How would operating costs be defined? How to define post-secondary education? The answers were crucial, but missing. Calculating the effect of the proposals was almost impossible. The result was that 'the provinces were really annoyed at the federal proposal being pulled like that.'

All provinces – especially their education departments – were greatly disturbed at ending the shared-cost manpower arrangements which had served them so well. They particularly objected to the 'three-year rule' because most provincial programmes were oriented to younger students rather than to retraining older members of the work force – which was one reason for Ottawa's introducing the new system.[30] Provincial premiers and finance departments were less concerned about ending the shared-cost programmes in manpower training and more worried about the total financial effect. Ontario was particularly hard hit by the end of capital grants because it had used up its $480 per capita quota and had recently embarked on a community college programme, for which it counted on federal help. In addition, Ottawa was 'giving with one hand and taking with the other,' with the result that Mr Robarts, for one, estimated On-

29 *Globe and Mail*, 25 Oct. 1966.

30 Kent, 'Intergovernmental Responsibility,' p. 11, notes that about two-thirds of the federal contributions under the old system went for youth training, and relatively little to the retraining of adults displaced by technological change.

tario would suffer a net loss from the overall federal proposals of $7 to $13 million, and others estimated little overall gain. Mr Johnson called Ottawa's proposal 'ill-prepared nonsense,'[31] and rejected Ottawa's claim that adult manpower training was an economic matter and therefore a federal responsibility.

The debate began on Monday. After a statement by Prime Minister Pearson the premiers made a few remarks, but the session broke up early to allow more study of the proposal. That afternoon provincial officials met in small groups to sort it all out. That night federal Manpower Minister Jean Marchand and his officials drafted a new statement which was submitted on Tuesday to clarify Ottawa's position.[32] But Ottawa was impressed by some of the provincial arguments. Tuesday's meeting adjourned early. The federal delegation met during the afternoon to reconsider its position and a full cabinet meeting was held that night to decide what concessions would be made. Next day Mr Pearson announced an extra $320 per capita would be available for capital grants for technical schools to provinces which had reached the previous $480 limit. If all provinces took the full amount it would mean an additional $275 million over the next several years.[33] The original $14 per capita offer on higher education was raised to $15 – a particular boon to Newfoundland and Prince Edward Island.[34] On Tuesday federal and provincial officials again broke off from the main meeting to discuss details.

A potentially acrimonious dispute between Ottawa and Quebec over the federal manpower training proposals was avoided by the intervention of Jean Marchand. Prime Minister Johnson had denied the validity of Ottawa's distinction between education (provincial) and manpower training (economic, and therefore federal). However, Marchand drew up a new statement of the federal position, which, while not changing the policy, did make the distinction much clearer. After a private meeting between the two men on Tuesday, Johnson announced Quebec would accept the federal proposal on an experimental basis. The Quebec prime minister said he was impressed by Marchand's explanation, and that he did not want to make Quebec a 'ghetto.'[35] Many Quebec officials were

31 *Globe and Mail*, 25 Oct. 1966.
32 In *Federal-Provincial Conference*, 24–29 Oct. 1966, pp. 48–52.
33 *Ibid.*, pp. 53–5.
34 For all but three provinces the 50 per cent option would yield more than the per capita payment option, but for Newfoundland the latter would be worth almost twice as much as half the operating costs. Newfoundland and PEI also gained from the rise to $15 per capita. For data see *H. of C. Debates*, 1967, p. 13719.
35 *Le Devoir*, 27 Oct. 1966.

surprised at this concession, but it seems clear that Quebec 'was not ready for a showdown at this point,' and that it badly needed the financial assistance involved. Marchand's intervention provided Quebec with a graceful way to concede, without provoking conflict and without giving the appearance of defeat.

The education conference ended with some modifications but with many questions still to be answered. The federal programme, though, was largely intact. On Wednesday the Tax Structure Committee met, with Mr Sharp in the chair. The topic was finances.

Since September each government had been re-evaluating its position. But little had changed. The federal brief[36] offered two minor concessions: an extra $3.5 million in equalization for Prince Edward Island, and an offer to renegotiate the overall financial agreements at the end of two years rather than five, which at least held out the possibility of some future adjustment. Otherwise, Ottawa stood firm. Ontario now offered to trade support of the transfer of the shared-cost programmes for five more tax points.

Quebec, however, took an entirely different approach than it had the previous month. Gone was the nationalism. Instead were the same economic arguments – tied largely to the TSC projections – that were used by Ontario, British Columbia, and Manitoba.[37] This new emphasis was continued in Mr Johnson's conduct in the conference room – we will examine the reasons at a later point.

The debate at the Tax Structure Committee meeting achieved little. Positions were fixed: 'There was little give and take ... One stressed the same arguments over and over. The general shape of the new arrangements was nailed down ... Practically everything had been said in September.' Tax-sharing was the chief issue. Most of the beneficiaries of equalization were happy, and they played little role. The chief protagonists on the provincial side were Roblin, Robarts, and Johnson. Much argument centred on the TSC projections, which the provinces rightly felt Ottawa had ignored. This angered the provinces, for whom they were 'the only real weapon we had.' The provinces hoped that the results would provide the basis for the new settlement, and said that Ottawa had implied as much in earlier statements. They had been coaxed into the study, only to find it ignored. Ontario, Quebec, and Manitoba wanted the projection results released to the public; Ottawa and several other provinces refused, but that argument became pointless when the overall figures were leaked

36 *Federal-Provincial Conference*, 24–29 Oct. 1966, pp. 60–5.
37 Prime Minister Johnson's statements are found in *ibid.*, pp. 24–7 and 68–71.

to the Toronto *Globe and Mail.*[38] That caused more bad feeling, but it was not surprising, since 150 copies were in various hands.

The provinces repeated over and over the arguments they made in September: provincial priorities were more important than federal ones; provincial tax resources were relatively inelastic at a time of rapidly rising costs; Ottawa could borrow more easily; independent taxing would lead to a 'tax jungle'; and so on. Mr Sharp reiterated his arguments: why should Ottawa raise taxes for provinces; it had its own spending requirements; if you want more money, raise it yourself. The sense of the meeting was conveyed by one New Brunswick official:

It was an acrimonious meeting. On Wednesday and Thursday everybody was sitting there saying to Sharp: 'Surely you must understand what our problems are. Don't you appreciate we have terrible problems, and must have the money.' And the feds would say: 'Well, we too have problems, and the money just isn't there.' Then Roblin would jump up and start talking about priorities, making his priorities speech. And Sharp would say: 'Yes, I know you have priorities, but that is not good enough. No one disagrees with your priorities ... But what is your last priority? What are you willing to sacrifice? There's just no more money in the till.'

On Thursday night the federal cabinet met again to discuss whether it would make any further concessions. The answer was no.

The plenary conference opened Friday morning and provincial anger and frustration came to a head. Because of the sudden introduction of education and manpower, the whole conference had been confused. The projections had been ignored. Ottawa was firm. By Friday most participants were impatient to get home. With Mr Pearson in the chair the provinces continued to push for more concessions. Robarts, Roblin, and others 'were in a pretty nasty mood.' They felt the conference had never touched the really important questions. Robarts suggested it was perhaps time that the provinces took the initiative in doing some fundamental rethinking of the nature of the federation, and introduced his idea of the Confederation of Tomorrow Conference. Though denied later, the implication at the time was that it would be a weapon against current federal policies. At another point Premier Bennett, with a huge smile, said that perhaps something could be worked out if only the premiers and

38 *Globe and Mail*, 28 Oct. 1966. The figures showed that the anticipated federal surplus would rise from $13 million in 1966–7 to $323 million by 1971–2. In the same period provincial-municipal deficits would rise from $1 billion to $2.5 billion.

the prime minister had a private lunch together – in the obvious belief that Pearson was a softer target than Sharp. After a hurried consultation the federal delegation declined the suggestion.

In this atmosphere federal officials had prepared a draft communiqué. Mr Pearson thumbed through it, but it did not seem satisfactory. Finally one premier said: 'Why should we agree when we don't.' Others concurred and the conference dissolved. 'Everybody just got up and left without any formal end at all,' said one official. 'Pearson just said, "Well, I suppose the conference is adjourned." He looked like death warmed over.' A senior federal official gave a poignant description of the final moments, which well illustrates how goals and objectives may clash with each other: 'I had a glimpse of the prime minister as he sat at the table, and all the others had left, and the meeting had broken up in some disarray. He knew he could go no further in the interest of Canada in yielding to provincial demands. But he also knew that the interests of Canada were not best served by this kind of conflict, and he was deeply moved. I felt very much for him. I don't think I would have been able to resist those pressures.' An Ontario official summed up the meeting another way: 'It was a disaster.' Another added: 'We could as well have left on the morning of the first day.'

## RATIFICATION: PARLIAMENTARY ACTION, 1967

In contrast to the pension plan, parliamentary action was little more than a formality. There was a short discussion when Mr Sharp tabled the federal briefs immediately following the October conference. Spokesmen of both New Democratic and Conservative parties criticized Ottawa for relinquishing its responsibility in its shared-cost and education financing proposals. But legislation putting the new arrangements into effect was passed on 10 March 1967 after a very short debate.[39] On 26 April Bill C-278, implementing the new federal manpower programme, was passed after slightly longer debate.

Further federal-provincial discussions continued on both higher education and manpower. The education meetings were mainly to clarify details. More substantial changes were made in the manpower proposal. Shortly after the October conference Ottawa agreed to modify the 'three-year rule' so that it would pay the training costs (but not the allowances)

39 For example, Conservative Alvin Hamilton said: 'We in the federal Parliament do have responsibility for this whole nation and for good government of the whole nation, and we should be reluctant at all times to give away power or initiative.' *H. of C. Debates,* 1966, p. 9293.

for those in the labour force for only a year. Later, when the bill was before Parliament, Quebec succeeded in having a joint federal-provincial committee established to oversee the programme. But the main discussion came after Ottawa distributed proposed contracts with the provinces. These would govern the operation of the programme, since the provinces were still providing most of the training services, which Ottawa was in effect purchasing. The provinces – now really convinced the old régime was over – felt the agreements implied too much federal control of matters like curriculum. Led by Quebec, the deputy ministers of education and ministers of education had several meetings, and they sent a joint brief to Manpower Minister Marchand.[40] There was then a meeting with Marchand and several relatively minor changes were made.

## AFTERMATH: TO 1968

One of the few federal concessions in October 1966 was the agreement to review the financial arrangements in two years. But when financial discussions were reopened in 1968 little had changed, and indeed the bitterness was renewed. The negotiations were made more difficult by two other factors. First, Ontario and several other provinces had been waging a campaign against the federal medicare programme, which was seen as a costly and unwarranted federal involvement in provincial priorities. Second, in October 1968, just before the negotiations were to begin, Ottawa announced that it would impose a 2 per cent income tax surcharge, to raise money primarily for medicare. It would not be shared with the provinces.

Announcing the Social Development Tax almost on the eve of financial negotiations was no way to encourage fruitful negotiations, said Ontario. The form of the tax was an elaborate device to avoid sharing the proceeds with the provinces, and effectively pre-empted tax sources from the provinces. At a meeting of finance ministers in November Ontario Treasurer Charles MacNaughton led the provincial attack. Federal policies were characterized as 'effrontery,' 'unacceptable,' 'irresponsible,' and 'unjust federalism.' If Ottawa really wanted coordination, why did it present its budget immediately before negotiations? The form of the Social Development Tax was just a subterfuge to avoid sharing. Does the federal government believe in a 'spirit of partnership,' MacNaughton asked in a series of rhetorical questions. 'Will the federal government continue to insist that

40 'Memorandum on Occupational Training of Adults, prepared for the Minister of Manpower and Immigration by the Provincial Ministers of Education,' 1967.

the provinces should go their own way, raise their own taxes and concern themselves only with their own responsibilities without regard to the needs and requirements of governments as a whole? Is this what you really want? Is this your view of Canadian federalism ... Do you really wish to have a tax jungle? Do you really wish to have a Balkanized economy? Do you really wish to have ten economic principalities in Canada?'[41] The strong tone of the speech represented an important change in Ontario's tactics; it would now make much more open attacks on Ottawa and appeal more directly for public support.

Other provinces voiced the same points of view – in much the same language – that they had voiced in the 1966 negotiations. Several also called for sharing the Social Development Tax and a federal reconsideration of medicare.

To no avail. In November, and again in December, the federal government held to its position. It would not share the Social Development Tax although 'undoubtedly that would have been helpful to you.' Said Finance Minister Edgar Benson, who had replaced Mr Sharp: 'We did not feel we could ask Parliament to take this action to raise revenue for the provinces.' He pointed out that the original tax structure projections were no longer applicable. 'Our own forward estimates, assembled for internal planning purposes, now suggest a completely different prospect ...'[42] The federal government's position on all other financial issues was unchanged. And that, despite provincial protests, was how it was left. Again, the idea that Ottawa would turn over more funds at each round of discussions had been confounded.

That was not the end of the matter, of course. Economic and financial questions were raised by many provinces in the constitutional discussions, especially in February 1969 when the frustration arising from the 1968 discussions spilled over, almost destroying the Constitutional Conference. Long and difficult financial negotiations were in prospect, as the governments considered the constitutional division of resources and a series of controversial proposals for tax reform, which had many implications for federal-provincial relations.

41 'Statement' by the Hon. Charles MacNaughton to the federal-provincial meeting of finance ministers, Ottawa, 4–5 Nov. 1968.

42 'Statement' re fiscal arrangements by the Hon. Edgar Benson to ministers of finance and provincial treasurers, 19 Dec. 1968. This statement represents a strong federal rebuttal to provincial positions.

CHAPTER FIVE

# The constitution

Both pensions and finances involved fundamental constitutional principles and basic questions about the sharing of responsibility in a federal state. By 1967 an explicit discussion of these problems could no longer be ignored and the process of constitutional review became the chief preoccupation of federal-provincial negotiation. Four years later the Constitutional Charter, 1971, emerged from the constitutional conference in Victoria. For a brief moment a limited consensus appeared imminent. A few days after it appeared, the charter was rejected. The discussions seemed certain to continue, but much less intensively. The eventual outcome seemed as distant and shadowy as ever. The reassessment of Canada's constitution originated in federal-provincial conflict and remained almost entirely a federal-provincial issue with little wider involvement. This fact decisively structured the issues, the language, and the procedures of the review.

## THE PRELIMINARIES

During the tenure of the Lesage government in Quebec it appeared as if there were a tacit agreement between Ottawa and Quebec not to raise the constitutional issue directly, for fear the conflict in basic goals revealed would be unsolvable. But, as we have seen, constitutional change was a central objective of the new Quebec government elected in 1966. The Union Nationale reactivated the legislative committee on the constitution.

The throne speech in December 1966 said: 'In accordance with the mandate granted to it by the people the government intends to strive to the utmost to achieve a new constitutional order which will be the instrument, not of an artificial unity, but of a true alliance between two co-equal peoples.'[1]

Piecemeal adjustments were no longer acceptable to Quebec; the demand for constitutional review could not be denied. 'Quebec has brought the constitution to the centre of the stage,' wrote D.V. Smiley, 'and it seems likely that Ottawa and the provinces could resist her demands for discussions only at very great peril.'[2]

Quebec was the only government for whom constitutional change was a central goal. The federal government agreed to a full-scale review of the constitution very reluctantly, and only because Quebec was so insistent. Federal officials feared that the only outcome of a constitutional review would be a continued diminution of their role, and an increase in the level of conflict. Any review must be a slow and cautious process.

Ontario's attitude towards the constitution was ambivalent. On the one hand Ontario was broadly satisfied with the existing document and felt little need to change it; on the other hand Prime Minister Robarts felt that constitutional adjustment might be the price of keeping Quebec in the federation – and that Ontario might be able to play the mediator. The 1966 negotiations had also left Ontario dissatisfied with developments in federal-provincial relations, and Robarts had said on the last day of the October meeting: 'I'm tired of the cart going before the horse. We have got to get down and talk about the fundamental problems of federalism first.'

Most other governments were either opposed to constitutional review or simply uninterested, even though many current grievances over such matters as finances and shared-cost programmes had a constitutional dimension. Most felt there was little wrong with the British North America Act and preferred piecemeal adjustment to a full-scale review. Some western provinces saw the review as one more example of pandering to Quebec, and felt there were far more immediate and important problems to discuss. Only Quebec, the *Globe and Mail* reported on 3 January 1967,

1 *Montreal Star*, 2 Dec. 1966.

2 'Towards Constitutional Reform,' address to the 14th winter conference of the Canadian Institute of Public Affairs, Toronto, 26 Jan. 1969, p. 9. Discussing the genesis of the negotiations later, Justice Minister John Turner gave a similar interpretation: '... in order to face up to a very serious lack of confidence, it became absolutely necessary to start discussions at the constitutional level.' Special Joint Committee of the Senate and House of Commons on the Constitution of Canada, *Minutes of Proceedings and Evidence*, no 1 (1970), p.23 (hereafter noted as Joint Committee, *Proceedings*).

had any commitment to changing the constitution. Hostility and indifference by other governments were to characterize the whole process of reviewing the constitution.

The pressure to do *something* about the constitution grew with political events in 1967. Ironically, the centennial year saw increased federal-Quebec conflict on several fronts. With some avowed separatists in his cabinet Prime Minister Daniel Johnson had to steer a difficult course between moderates and nationalists. Within the Liberal party, too, there was a strong separatist contingent. René Lévesque and his supporters were rebuffed when they proposed a motion calling for an independent Quebec at a party meeting, and they left the party to form the Mouvement souveraineté association, which later became the Parti Québécois. Nevertheless, the Liberals remained far closer to the Union Nationale's position than to Ottawa's. They called for a new constitution, in which Quebec would have special status and broader powers. Reacting to Ottawa's proposed charter of human rights, Opposition Leader Lesage rejected it as an infringement on provincial jurisdiction and appealed for internal unity on the question: 'For the love of the French Canadians, for the love of Quebec, I ask the leader of the Union Nationale for a truce between us on partisan politics on the constitutional question ... We French Canadians must stop fighting among ourselves.'[3]

Thus, with substantial unity among the major parties, and growing pressure from the nationalists, Quebec was in an assertive mood. At the same time the federal government, especially under the influence of French Canadians like Pierre Trudeau and Jean Marchand, was no longer content to leave Quebec the initiative or to let the nationalist doctrine go unchallenged. For example, Justice Minister Trudeau, speaking at a press conference, said: 'I think particular status for Quebec is the biggest intellectual hoax ever foisted on the people of Quebec and the people of Canada.'[4] Quebecers responded in kind.

Thus, there was increasing friction during centennial year. Quebec's strategy was apparently to test continually the limits of federal patience. The most significant tensions were in foreign affairs, as Quebec asserted an independent provincial role in foreign relations concerning matters of provincial jurisdiction, and Ottawa asserted federal primacy. All this culminated in French President Charles de Gaulle's visit to Canada in

3 John Saywell, ed., *Canadian Annual Review for 1967* (Toronto, 1968), p. 78.
4 Quoted in Don Peacock, *Journey to Power: The Story of a Canadian Election* (Toronto, 1968), p. 160. Chapters 5–7 are particularly useful for understanding the evolution of the federal position and its relationship to internal Liberal party politics.

July, with his call for 'Québec libre' from the Montreal city hall. The event helped to shatter the euphoric centennial mood, and may have increased the realization of the need for some sort of constitutional debate.

This was the inauspicious background to formal constitutional discussions. The dilemma was clear: the demand for the constitutional change stemmed from deep conflict; this conflict in turn meant that consensus on any new constitution would not soon develop, at the same time as the existing one was at least partly discredited. Four years later the dilemma had not been resolved.

## THE CONFEDERATION OF TOMORROW CONFERENCE: NOVEMBER 1967

Despite a growing federal realization that negotiations on the constitution were inevitable, the first concrete initiative came from Ontario. The idea of Ontario's sponsoring a conference where the governments could discuss the basic issues of federalism, free from immediate negotiating concerns, had occurred to Ontario decision-makers even before 1966; but the idea crystallized at and immediately after the October 1966 Federal-Provincial Conference. There were several motives: in part, it was to assert provincial strength after Ottawa's perceived intransigence; in part, too, it stemmed from a feeling that Ottawa was not providing effective leadership on the central issue of Quebec – and a belief that Ontario's position would make it an effective leader. The conference, Robarts felt, might help French Canadians feel that English Canadians took their grievances seriously, and might help English Canadians gain a better understanding of the problem. With these feelings in mind the Ontario throne speech in January 1967 announced the Confederation of Tomorrow Conference, to be held that November. It would not discuss specific proposals, but would '... examine Confederation as it is today, to take stock after 100 years, to examine the areas of agreement and disagreement and to explore what can be done to ensure a strong and unified Canada.'

Federal leaders strongly opposed the Ontario initiative. 'They impressed on us with greatest vigour that the federal government felt it would be totally inappropriate to discuss constitutional matters at this time in any form.' It violated the federal prerogative of calling federal-provincial conferences, and could set an embarrassing precedent in which federal dominance in calling and running conferences would be challeged. More substantively, the time was not right for constitutional discussion: this would be one more forum for the expression of Quebec's demands.

Robarts and his advisers also had doubts about the success of the conference. 'We could flop very easily.' Open discussion of highly charged constitutional issues could exacerbate conflict. Too high expectations of the results could be disappointed. The province was also afraid of getting caught between Quebec and other (especially western) provinces hostile to Quebec's linguistic and constitutional goals. It was also sensitive to fears of a Quebec-Ontario 'axis' and of a province's usurping of federal leadership. Throughout this period Mr Robarts was consciously playing the role of mediator – between Quebec and the other provinces, and between Quebec and Ottawa. He felt he must remain on good terms with all sides as he was the only link.

At the same time Ontario felt that the issues of Confederation must receive wider public discussion. Hence, the decision, taken with great nervousness, to have the meetings televized, the first open interprovincial conference in history.

The Confederation of Tomorrow Conference, held in plush surroundings at the new Toronto-Dominion Centre in Toronto, was exceedingly carefully staged.[5] It was to be a place for discussion, not decision. The agenda was to try to steer clear of contentious issues. Short sessions and congenial surroundings were to ensure harmony. Before the conference Ontario officials visited other provinces, explaining the purposes and methods of the conference, and circulating theme papers. It had been feared some premiers would refuse to attend; in the end all did except Mr Bennett. Ottawa sent four official observers, but it was a provincial affair.

'We are here ... to determine the measure of our consensus and, perhaps, the range of our differences,'[6] said Robarts as the conference opened before the television cameras. The two central questions were to be: 'the place of French Canada in Canadian society' and 'the relationship between federal and provincial governments.'

The conference clearly made a full-scale constitutional review inevitable. The feared confrontation never appeared – Prime Minister Johnson calmly and succinctly stated Quebec's goals, but at the same time stressed the common interests of all provinces. Several premiers – for example, Robarts, G.I. Smith of Nova Scotia, and Alex Campbell of Prince Edward Island – while not fully agreeing with Quebec's positions, stressed the need for sympathetic understanding and dialogue. Premier Robichaud of New Brunswick made a dramatic appeal for the delegates to under-

5 See Murray Edelman, *The Symbolic Uses of Politics* (Urbana, Ill., 1964), chap. 5, for a discussion of the importance of setting in structuring political events.
6 Confederation of Tomorrow Conference, *Proceedings* (Toronto, 1967), p. 3 ff.

stand Quebec's aspirations and the problems faced by Johnson at home.[7] Here lay the chief contribution of the conference: it showed that complex constitutional issues could be discussed amicably, and served to educate both the politicians and the public about the issues involved.[8]

Nevertheless, there was little consensus even on the need for the constitutional review – let alone on the substance of changes. Three basic positions emerged. Quebec said the constitution must be changed. British Columbia, Alberta, Saskatchewan, and Newfoundland said there should be no changes. Premier Smallwood was 'absolutely opposed not only to a new constitution, but to any change whatsoever in the existing constitution.'[9] For Saskatchewan, said Premier Thatcher, '... if we had a hundred problems, the constitution would be the hundred and first.' And Premier Manning of Alberta raised the basic question: 'It is my sincere belief that in the present context it is not realistic ... to think that a sufficient measure of agreement could be attained among the Canadian people to make possible at this time the writing of a new constitution for Canada.'[10] To try – and fail – would be far worse than not trying at all. Premier Bennett of British Columbia did not personally attend, saying before the conference that the whole issue was not very important, the country was working well anyway, and that to open up the discussion would only invite dissent.[11] Finally, Ontario, New Brunswick, Nova Scotia and Prince Edward Island all took the position that, as Premier Smith said, 'many of us ... do not feel any great need for a new constitution ... if developing a new constitution will help [to preserve and improve Canada], then surely it is worth trying.'[12] Said Robarts: 'We don't see a necessity for a complete revision of the constitution ... On the other hand, Ontario has no fear or trepidation about change ... If changes are necessary ... then we are quite prepared to play our part.[13] As long as one member of the federation was deeply dissatisfied, change must be considered. These three positions continued: change: yes; change: no; and, change: if necessary.

The conference discussed many other issues such as language rights for French Canadians. Quebec and French Canada did dominate the proceedings, but, also setting a pattern to be followed at later conferences, several governments made clear there were other real problems which should have equal priority in constitutional discussions – like regional

7 *Ibid.*, pp. 94–5; *Globe and Mail*, Toronto, 29 Nov. 1967.
8 See commentary in *Le Devoir*, Montreal, 28, 30 Nov. 1967.
9 Confederation of Tomorrow, *Proceedings*, p. 81.
10 *Ibid.*, p. 149.
11 *Globe and Mail*, 25 Nov. 1967.
12 Confederation of Tomorrow, *Proceedings*, p. 73.
13 *Ibid.*, pp. 141–2.

disparities and other economic issues. They must not be pushed aside in the constitutional debate.[14]

Conference discussions were wide-ranging and general. No substantive decisions were made, but the premiers did set up a Continuing Committee on Confederation (the prime ministers of Ontario, Nova Scotia, and Alberta) to plan further efforts.[15] By the end of the conference the premiers seemed more willing to discuss basic constitutional issues than they had previously, and some observers detected a greater sympathy for and understanding of Quebec's position.[16] Both participants and the press echoed Robarts' assessment of the meeting: 'A firm and meaningful beginning.'[17]

The provinces had taken the initiative; like it or not, Ottawa would now have to respond with constitutional initiatives of its own. 'I am quite sure that if the conference had not taken place, the federal government would not have allowed the constitutional issue to get going as it did,' said a senior federal official. 'After that we had no alternative.'

Just like Quebec's, Ottawa's position in 1966 had contained an implicit constitutional doctrine. In 1967, under pressure from Quebec and Ontario, the federal government moved towards accepting the inevitability of some form of constitutional review. In May 1967 Prime Minister Pearson announced that a constitutional task force had been established in the Justice Department, now headed by Pierre Trudeau. Early in July, in a private meeting after he and the premiers had met the Queen, Pearson proposed a constitutional conference for early 1968. On 4 September then Justice Minister Trudeau told the Canadian Bar Association: 'The time is ripe. The federal government declares itself ready to discuss any constitutional changes that are proposed.'[18]

In December 1967 a cabinet committee and a committee of officials were established to formulate the federal position for the February Constitutional Conference. Ottawa was now committed not just to examining some aspects of the constitution but to 'a process of constitutional review

14 'What really matters in Canada,' said Premier Smallwood, 'is a standard of private living and a standard of public services.' *Ibid.*, p. 80. Similarly, Premier Thatcher argued that Saskatchewan's concerns were more 'economic than cultural.'
15 *Globe and Mail*, 1 Dec. 1967.
16 See editorials in *Le Devoir*, 29, 30 Nov., 1 Dec. 1967.
17 *Globe and Mail*, 1 Dec. 1967.
18 In the speech Trudeau also stressed the initial federal concern with language and civil rights as a first step, and, as in later speeches and press conferences, he continued the attack on the 'two nations,' 'associate states,' and 'special status' doctrines of federalism; this attack became the cornerstone of federal policy after he became Liberal leader and prime minister. See Peacock, *Journey to Power*, pp. 156–66.

that will be both broad and deep.'[19] A new set of constitutional rules of the game, said Trudeau in 1969, was necessary because 'the federal and provincial governments were stumbling over each other, completely out of kilter, like characters in one of those Chinese plays.'[20]

But, having agreed to have a constitutional conference, there remained the question: what to discuss? What were the issues to be debated, and in what order? For Quebec the first order of business should be the basic question of the distribution of legislative responsibilities and financial resources. The federal government disagreed. Instead, it suggested the first concern should be the development of a constitutionally entrenched Canadian charter of human rights, which would place limitations on both levels of government and which, in addition to traditional civil rights, would help to guarantee language and cultural rights.[21] Not only did such an approach fit in well with the federal government's own thinking but also it would be less contentious: consensus should be relatively easily achieved, and this experience would thus 'open the door wide to necessary constitutional change.' For Prime Minister Johnson the issue was little more than a red herring; the other provinces evinced little excitement.

## THE FIRST CONSTITUTIONAL CONFERENCE: FEBRUARY 1968

The Constitutional Conference of February 1968 promised to be a dramatic one. Canadians were to watch their 'first ministers' on live television debating the great issues of the day. Prime Minister Pearson was to make his last major appearance on the political stage before retirement, not as a lame duck, he said, but as an 'elder statesman.'[22] Pierre Trudeau, as the articulate defender of 'One Canada' was to help cement his claim to the Liberal leadership in his debates with Prime Minister Johnson. And the stakes involved seemed high: 'Let me repeat: what is at stake in my opinion is Canada's survival,' said Mr Pearson in his opening remarks.[23]

But it soon became clear the constitutional review would be a long, in-

19 See testimony by R.G. Robertson, clerk of the Privy Council, Joint Committee, *Proceedings*, no 2, pp. 6–9. See also *Federalism for the Future* (Ottawa, 1968), p. 4.
20 Quoted in Edith Eglauer, 'Prime Minister/Premier ministre,' in *New Yorker*, July 1968, pp. 36–60.
21 *Federalism for the Future*, p. 8. Canada already had a bill of rights passed by the Diefenbaker government in 1960. It was, however, only an ordinary federal statute, subject to revision or revocation, and not thought to apply to those rights affected by provincial action.
22 *Globe and Mail*, 15, 16 Dec. 1967.
23 Constitutional Conference, First Meeting, *Proceedings* (Ottawa, 1968), p. 7.

volved, and, ultimately, very tedious business. In its policy statement, *Federalism for the Future*, the federal government spelled out its conception of the purposes and procedure of a 'total review' of the constitution. The first concern must be the rights of individuals; next must come an examination of the roles of some of the institutions of federalism, notably the Senate and Supreme Court; next would be the study of the basic goals of the federation and revision of the BNA Act in light of this – and only then would the distribution of powers be dealt with. This February conference, said the government, should concentrate on Ottawa's proposal for an entrenched charter of human rights and on ways of implementing the recently received proposals of the Royal Commission on Bilingualism and Biculturalism concerning the status of French and English languages in Canada. The other opening statements revealed great diversity in approaches to the constitutional review, in attitudes towards the role of Quebec and French Canada in Confederation, in conceptions of the importance of the federal government, and in views on the specific issues.

Ottawa's concern with promoting French language rights was central to its goal of strengthening unity through ensuring French Canadians could be at home anywhere in the country; at the same time it rejected any special role for Quebec as a political unit. But for Quebec the root of the problem lay in the allocation of powers and in the need for a constitution which recognized a Canada made up of both ten territories and two nations. So Prime Minister Johnson, both at and before the conference, urged that, to get at the root of Canada's constitutional problem, priority be given to 'a new distribution of powers' and that the review should begin with the fields of 'immediate urgency' – social security, foreign relations, and so on.[24]

Nevertheless, discussion at the conference focused primarily on Ottawa's agenda, though it was already considerably expanded from an earlier proposal. But little progress was made towards agreement on entrenching a bill of rights in the constitution.[25] Most governments, including Quebec, Ontario, Nova Scotia, British Columbia, Alberta, and Saskatchewan,[26] expressed serious reservations on various grounds. These

24 *Ibid.*, p. 69; *Globe and Mail*, 2 Feb. 1968. British Columbia also took a stand before the conference opened. Its throne speech declared its opposition to a charter which would limit provincial jurisdiction.

25 The most complete collation of governmental views on the charter of human rights is found in Joint Committee, *Proceedings*, no 3, appendix B, pp. 45–143. Also see Secretariat of the Constitutional Conference, 'A Briefing Paper on Discussions within the Continuing Committee of Officials,' pp. 25–43.

26 Quebec would agree to constitutional entrenchment of certain collective language rights, but had reservations about other rights. A bill of rights should

included fears that such a charter would seriously restrict the principle of legislative sovereignty, and that it infringed on existing provincial jurisdiction. Premiers Bennett, Manning, and Thatcher pointed with some horror to current law and order problems in the United States and suggested a link between increased crime and the dangers inherent in a written bill of rights open to interpretation by judges. Newfoundland, Prince Edward Island, and New Brunswick were all in basic agreement with an entrenched charter, but showed little real enthusiasm for it. It was clear that no government was really interested in the matter, and that agreement could not easily be reached; so the question, like others, was left to a committee of attorneys general, in which, apparently, occasional and desultory discussion continued.

Perhaps more significant was that there was some consensus – if fragile – on the need to secure French-language rights. There was little dispute with the basic ideas: that as a matter of equity French and English should have equal rights across the country, and that governments should do what they could to implement the recommendations of the B and B Commission. The Maritimes and Ontario were Ottawa's allies. But some governments, again the western provinces in particular, were reluctant to embody these ideas in a constitution. Premier Manning of Alberta was their leader. Thus agreement on a statement embodying these principles was achieved only after a fascinating public exercise of revision, as the federal delegates sought agreement on some kind of a statement of consensus on language rights. Ottawa originally suggested a five-point statement, which embodied a novel form of constitutional amendment in which Ottawa and other governments would bind themselves to constitutional entrenchment of language rights, and other governments could 'opt-in' to this amendment as they saw fit.[27] This was designed to secure the agreement of the governments which Ottawa knew beforehand would not agree to immediate amendment. But Alberta, British Columbia, and Saskatchewan objected both to the principle of entrenching such rights and to the back-door method of constitutional amendment proposed. Even Prime Minister Johnson undermined the federal position by noting

be the 'last part' added to a new constitution. It could infringe on provincial jurisdiction over property and civil rights, and would need to be adapted to the differing traditions of Quebec and English Canada. Constitutional Conference, First Meeting, *Proceedings*, pp. 289–301. Ontario also raised the problem of provincial powers, as well as that of parliamentary sovereignty, but took a generally non-committal position (pp. 281–7). Alberta expressed much stronger objections (pp. 301–15), as did British Columbia (pp. 129–31) and Saskatchewan (pp. 151–3). Nova Scotia did not 'oppose the idea' but stressed the need for careful study (p. 315).

27 *Ibid.*, pp. 253–7.

that several governments were already moving to improve the status of French-speaking citizens, so an amendment hardly seemed urgent. To preserve unanimity the proposal was dropped, and constitutional entrenchment made just one of several alternatives to be considered as a means of promoting French.[28] Finally, there was a flurry of concern as British Columbia's delegates quibbled about the basic premise: the draft declaration stated agreement that French Canadians 'should' have the same rights as English Canadians. Mr Bennett had already left, but the remaining BC delegates thought 'should' was perhaps too strong and that 'desirable' would be better. Prime Minister Pearson argued that 'should' meant the same thing, and that it did not 'impose any obligation on British Columbia at all.' Unanimity was his chief concern at this point – 'unless we can get agreement from British Columbia on that, I don't know what we will do'[29] – and Pearson said he would be willing to telephone Premier Bennett to ensure British Columbia remained in. The episode reflects the great tenuousness of the consensus: a unanimous statement was achieved, but it was a weak one, expressing the lowest common denominator. It expressed recognition that there 'should' be equal rights; suggested the 'desirability' of implementing the bilingualism and biculturalism recommendations 'in ways most appropriate to each province'; and established a committee to consider the commission's and others' views on implementation of language rights. Constitutional amendment would be only one alternative considered.[30]

Through a strategy of continual modification of its proposals the federal government had achieved its symbolic goal, while demonstrating in full view of the public the difficulty of achieving agreement. Unanimity was crucial for Ottawa, if the statement were to be an effective signal to Quebecers. Nevertheless, even the minimal result was shaky: the consensus largely broke apart in 1969.

The conference discussions also touched on many other subjects which were to arise time and again in the future. Thus, the problem of poorer regions – and the differing views about equalization and the role of the federal government held by the richer and poorer provinces – was aired at length. Regional disparities was not originally on the agenda – it was

28 Thus the third point of the federal draft of a 'Possible Consensus on Language Rights' contained agreement on constitutional amendments to guarantee rights along the lines suggested by the Royal Commission on Bilingualism and Biculturalism, and these amendments would apply to the federal government and those provinces which agreed. The fourth point established a committee which would consider the form of the amendment. *Ibid.*, p. 465.

29 *Ibid.*, p. 503.

30 *Ibid.*, appendix A, p. 545.

put there at the request of Nova Scotia. Economic issues, which many premiers felt were both more important and more comfortably discussed, were to continually vie for attention with the more remote, abstract and confused questions of constitutional purpose and principle.

Nor could the fundamental question of the role of Quebec in the federation be avoided. Quebec's opening statement reiterated the demand for a new constitution recognizing a 'two-nation' Canada. The stage was set for a dramatic confrontation between Justice Minister Trudeau and Prime Minister Johnson, which was the television highlight of the conference, and which is widely regarded as the single most important event leading to Trudeau's winning the Liberal leadership. Trudeau developed the theme he had expressed in his writings before, and was to use to such effect in the 1968 federal election campaign: special status for the province would lead to weakening of the authority of Quebec's members in Ottawa, would progressively cut ties between Quebec citizens and the national government, and would thus lead inexorably towards separation in fact if not in name. 'This extension of Quebec's jurisdiction must have some limits.' For Johnson special arrangements for Quebec were a prerequisite to continuing Confederation, and it was a serious error to believe that strengthening language rights would satisfy French Canadians. 'This problem cannot be solved with an aspirin tablet.'[31] Pearson ended the exchange with a strategic call for a coffee break, but the debates continued in later press conferences and elsewhere. It was hard to see, even if one granted these to be partly only bargaining positions, how such profound differences in purpose and assumption could produce agreement on constitutional provisions.

Nevertheless, despite wide differences about the goals of the constitutional review, the principles to be embodied in a new constitution, or the specific procedures to be followed, the conference did agree to continue the review and to establish some machinery to do it.

Here there had been considerable prior discussion and agreement between Quebec and Ottawa. Both governments made similar proposals to the conference, and these were coordinated in informal private talks. The agreement formally established the continuing constitutional conference, made up of the first ministers and assisted by a continuing committee of senior officials, which was chaired by Gordon Robertson, clerk of the Privy Council and cabinet secretary. A secretariat – independent of any one government – would be established to assist the conference and the continuing committee. The agenda for future discussion would include official languages; fundamental rights; the distribution of powers;

31 *Ibid.*, pp. 227–37, 241.

the reform of institutions like the Supreme Court and Senate; regional disparities; that old bugbear of constitutional discussion, amending procedures; and – at Ontario's suggestion – mechanisms of federal-provincial relations. It was an imposing list of closely interrelated problems – which ramified even further in the later discussions.

Most observers felt the conference was a success, and that Pearson's swan song as prime minister had been a 'dazzling' performance.[32] It did reach agreement on language rights; and it did agree to undertake a wholesale review of the constitution. It had also shown that Ottawa, with new leadership, was to take the offensive. At first reluctant, it was henceforth to take the lead in encouraging reluctant governments to participate, and in advancing well-argued proposals to which the provinces would have to react. Nevertheless, the agreement to review the constitution was still tenuous; most governments had yet to take it seriously. The issues and positions had been stated: but it was most unclear whether it would be possible to reconcile them all.

## THE PROPOSITIONS

How was the constitutional review to proceed? The scope and methods, and the issues to be dealt with, were still highly unclear. These questions were considered by the continuing committee of officials which met for the first time in May 1968 at Mont Gabriel in Quebec. There was a long discussion of how best to go about the review. 'It became apparent early in the exercise that this would prove a very complex task.'[33] The federal government suggested that the most appropriate way to begin was to have each government submit a series of 'propositions' or statements on matters which should be included in a new or revised constitution. These propositions could then be grouped and collated, to lay bare areas of agreement and disagreement. The propositions were intended to 'give an indication of the thinking within the several governments concerning the views, needs, and aspirations of Canadians across the country; they were not intended to be firm or final positions.' Some provinces were reluctant to engage in this exercise, partly because such a procedure implied not just an examination of parts of the constitution, but a really total review; but in the end all agreed on the approach.

There was also some discussion of the role of the secretariat. The federal government proposed that Edgar Gallant, well known and liked in

32 *Globe and Mail*, 8 Feb. 1967.
33 Henry F. Davis, secretary of the constitutional Conference, in Joint Committee, *Proceedings*, no 1, p. 75.

the provinces from his previous position in the Department of Finance, be named secretary of the constitutional conference and head of the secretariat. He was immediately accepted. Several provinces were concerned that the autonomy of the secretariat be assured and that it not be another federal arm.[34] For example, Ottawa had assumed that Gallant would sit in on federal planning sessions, but this was vetoed as inconsistent with his independence. The secretariat was to play a major role both in preparing a report on the propositions submitted and in trying to stimulate the provinces to take part.

At the first meeting of the continuing committee a recurrent problem became clear: several governments were neither very interested in the review nor willing or able to contribute much effort to the task. Ottawa, Quebec, Ontario, and New Brunswick were the only ones that appeared really interested. A few others indicated that they saw their role as little more than observers. This problem stemmed partly from the membership of the committee itself. It contained many officials who had had little previous contact with federal-provincial negotiations. But much more important was the lack of interest of their parent governments. 'There was no input from some governments and limited input from others. Most of the provinces were not yet too keen on the review.' In addition, some governments were reluctant to establish subcommittees because their staff resources were too thin.

But by December the continuing committee had met four times. Originally only Ontario, Quebec, Ottawa, and New Brunswick submitted propositions. Quebec's propositions, contained in a fifty-two-page document, were by far the most comprehensive; they developed in great detail a systematic vision of a decentralized federation. Other governments gradually contributed their own ideas, partly in reaction to those already submitted; they were much less elaborate than the original submissions.[35] By early 1969 all provinces had submitted at least some proposals. They

34 However, none but Ontario, which contributed two token payments to the cost of the secretariat, saw fit to back up the demand for impartiality with proposals for sharing costs and personnel. *Ibid.*, p. 92.

35 All the propositions, after Quebec's became public, were released for public use. They are published by the governments concerned or by the secretariat of the constitutional conference. The federal propositions are contained in *The Constitution and the People of Canada* (Ottawa, 1969).

Some governments submitted their propositions by the summer of 1968; others not until the late fall. The documents varied greatly in length, comprehensiveness, and amount of argument and documentation. For example, New Brunswick submitted 59 propositions, Ontario 40, British Columbia 19, Alberta 11, Saskatchewan 14, and so on. Many of these were of the order of 'Canada should be a federal state of which the Queen is head of state' (Saskatchewan, proposition 2), and were without any supporting material.

were grouped under nine headings, including matters like 'objectives of Confederation,' 'general principles of the constitution,' 'official languages,' 'constitution of the central government,' and so on. Before the February 1969 Constitutional Conference the secretariat prepared a sixty-eight-page 'briefing paper' for the premiers summarizing the extensive discussions within the continuing committee of officials.[36] It showed a wide variety of opinion both on the purposes of the constitutional review and on specific proposals. Many propositions were simply platitudes: that Canada should be a federal state and so on. 'Sharp differences' appeared over the objectives of Confederation itself; when they did agree on basic goals, governments often gave them different meanings.[37] The briefing paper reflected long hours of wrangling within the continuing committee, much of which had only an uncertain relationship to immediate problems. For example, should the constitution state the 'primacy' of the federal government; if it did, what did the word mean? The debate, moreover, revealed the expected wide disagreement in both basic conceptions of federation and in specific proposals between Quebec and most other governments. Most participants in this exercise suggest it was not very productive. The proposition method did imply a review of the whole constitution; but it also meant that the discussion ranged extremely widely, making it hard to pin down areas of agreement and disagreement. 'It did not work too well,' said a federal official. 'It meant that much of the initial discussion was very abstract. The time spent delayed getting down to the concrete issues.' It was hard for governments to perceive what this very general debate implied in terms of the more concrete and immediate problems that interested them. On the other hand, it could be argued that the debate over the propositions did get the review started, and gave all governments a sobering indication of the complexities of the issues involved. However, there was little evidence when the first ministers reconvened in February 1969 that their discussions were much enlightened by the continuing committee's efforts.

In general, most of the discussion in the continuing committee revolved around the same points the heads of governments had enunciated in February. Most delegations stuck closely to the official views of their governments. There were a few efforts to introduce more flexibility and develop more of a seminar style of discussion, but they failed. No consensus among officials emerged which could then be presented to the governments. Thus little real progress was made in the four continuing committee meetings between May and December 1968.

36 Secretariat of the Constitutional Conference, 'A Briefing Paper on Discussions within the Continuing Committee of Officials,' 1969.
37 *Ibid.*, p. 7.

In the meantime, political events with major effects on the negotiations were taking place. First, Pierre Trudeau became leader of the federal Liberals and in June 1968 led them to a decisive victory. After six years of minority government the Liberals were now in power with a clear majority of 155 seats. Trudeau had campaigned strongly on a 'united Canada' platform, which was widely interpreted as a 'stop Quebec' stand; while the Conservatives were saddled with a vague 'two-nation' position. While it is unclear how much Trudeau's stand on federalism and Quebec affected the election results, there is no doubt the election could be – and was – seen as a mandate for a strong federal government. Moreover, the federalist Trudeau had maintained and extended French-Canadian Liberal support, and clearly the Quebec federalists were reinforced. This was to greatly strengthen Ottawa's resolve and its bargaining position in the later negotiations.

While the federal government was gaining more strength the Quebec government appeared to be losing it. Daniel Johnson had been the articulate spokesman for Quebec and for the 'two-nation' concept of Canada. Throughout much of 1968, however, illness took him out of political life. Then, only a week after he returned to work, on 26 September, he suddenly died and Quebec was left without a leader. These problems were compounded by Quebec's considerable internal difficulties which left less time available for discussion of constitutional matters.

Johnson was replaced by Education Minister Jean-Jacques Bertrand, who had a reputation for being much more moderate than his predecessor. Moreover, at first he was only interim leader of his party: he could not speak with the authority of a confirmed leader. At the February Constitutional Conference, which was delayed because of Johnson's death, Bertrand made clear he was simply carrying on Johnson's position, and would await his confirmation by the party before he moved to put his own stamp on Quebec's goals. By mid-1969, while he had been confirmed as the Union Nationale's leader, that policy had hardly begun to emerge. These changes in Quebec meant to some extent a vacuum of power. The sustained pressure from Quebec slackened and, while still active, the province began to play a much less visible role in the debates.

## THE SECOND CONSTITUTIONAL CONFERENCE: FEBRUARY 1969

These events conditioned the preparations for the next meeting of the premiers and prime ministers in February 1969. The initiative now lay with Ottawa. It had a self-confident government and a prime minister with a clear and consistent policy about federalism and Quebec, and a firm control over his own members. Unworried about defeat in Parliament,

Ottawa could devote more effort and energy to the constitutional review, which was high on its agenda. Federal machinery for constitutional review had been considerably strengthened with the shift of the working group on the constitution to the Prime Minister's Office and the Privy Council Office from the Justice Department. A secretariat had been established in the latter, and a talented group of special advisers to the prime minister, including former assistant deputy minister of finance A.W. Johnson and constitutional lawyer Carl Goldenberg, had been appointed. From having been a reluctant participant in the constitutional review, Ottawa had become its leading advocate.

It was clear from the beginning that the provinces had other things than the constitution on their minds and were determined to raise them when they convened for the second Constitutional Conference. The result was little progress. The previous fall, Ottawa had again held firm on the financial question, and had added insult to injury by refusing to share with the provinces its new 2 per cent Social Development Tax, which was ostensibly to pay for medicare – itself opposed by several provinces. Many of the latter, led by Ontario, were therefore in an angry mood[38] and used the opportunity to sharply attack recent federal policies, as Robarts did in attacking medicare as a 'Machiavellian scheme ... one of the greatest political frauds that has been perpetrated on the people of this country.'[39] Moreover, the consensus on language rights seemed to be falling apart. Before the meeting the three prairie premiers sent telegrams to the government calling for submission of the federal Official Languages Act to judicial review.[40] Federal firmness – seen by some as inflexibility and intransigence – on other issues inevitably spilled over into the constitutional discussions.

Much of the debate at the conference, therefore, was given over to a recitation, before the television cameras, of provincial grievances over financial and other questions. Indeed, the federal government was prepared at one point simply to adjourn the conference. That was unneces-

38 See, for example, statement by Provincial Treasurer Charles MacNaughton to the Conference of Finance Ministers, 4–5 Nov. 1968; and his statement 'Ontario's Position on Medicare' at the same conference. See also statements by other governments.

39 Constitutional Conference, Second Meeting, *Proceedings* (Ottawa, 1968), p. 161.

40 The Official Languages Act, implementing on Ottawa's part some of the recommendations of the Royal Commission on Bilingualism and Biculturalism, was of course not itself a constitutional matter, though some questioned its constitutionality. But it was regarded with great suspicion in many areas, notably on the prairies, where ethnic minorities who were neither French nor English made up a large proportion of the electorate, and where distrust of Quebec and French Canada was high. The prairie premiers especially seemed to express these feelings.

sary, but the provinces did force a major change in the future agenda: they wanted to get down to concrete 'bread and butter' issues. The bill of rights was largely forgotten, and the question of the taxing and spending powers was brought forward. The provinces had a bargaining advantage here: if Ottawa wanted agreement on such matters as language rights it had better listen to the provinces on the economic issues. Alberta, and to a lesser extent, Ontario, were quite explicit on that point.[41]

Finally, it appeared that rather than forging a new national consensus, regional cleavages were emerging more sharply. The western provinces took positions reflecting both their economic position in Confederation and their suspicion or hostility towards granting any 'special' language rights to French Canadians. 'Western alienation' was as much an issue as French-Canadian alienation, and the federal government must deal with western problems rather than concentrate on Quebec and the east.[42] The maritime provinces pressed their concerns for a concerted attack on regional disparities and for a strong central government to lead it.

The conference took up the financial issues on the second day. British Columbia said the federal government had usurped provincial taxing powers and should lose all powers of direct taxation. Prime Minister Robarts argued that Ottawa had used the federal spending power to coerce the provinces and to effectively alter the constitution, and he demanded that the revenues from the special Social Development Tax be shared. Premier Smith of Nova Scotia, and others, attacked Ottawa for not adequately consulting the provinces about medicare. Other premiers commented in the same vein. Later the delegates spent considerable time discussing regional disparities, which was primarily an opportunity for the poorer provinces to voice their needs.

The debate on French-language rights showed that there was considerable opposition, both to the federal Official Languages Act and to entrenchment of language rights in the constitution, coming from Alberta, Manitoba, Saskatchewan, and British Columbia. Ontario, Quebec, and the Maritimes generally supported the federal position on these matters. On the other hand, the earlier discussion of French-language rights had probably played an important part in stimulating most governments to expand French-language schooling, recognize French as an official language, and so on through their own legislative powers. The result was a far greater official recognition of French than had been true previously.[43]

41 See opening statement by Prime Minister Robarts in Constitutional Conference, Second Meeting, *Proceedings*, pp. 16, 18.

42 These viewpoints were expressed forcefully by all four western governments.

43 See statement by Prime Minister Trudeau, *ibid.*, p. 216.

Ottawa agreed to have further meetings with provincial attorneys general on the constitutionality of Bill C-120, the official languages bill, and to consult the provinces about its implementation and about proposed amendments.[44]

As for the entrenched bill of rights, only three of the smaller provinces – Newfoundland, Prince Edward Island, and New Brunswick – supported the idea without more or less serious reservations, and it was clear they did not feel very strongly about the matter. Spokesmen for all the others emphasized the need for careful study about such matters as what rights to include.

Despite the largely successful diversion of debate to immediate problems and economic matters and a generally acerbic tone to the debates, the first ministers did agree to an accelerated process of constitutional review. The conference also established a series of ministerial committees to pursue further the questions of official languages, fundamental rights, regional disparities, and reforms of federal institutions, including the Senate, judicial system, and national capital region. The conference recognized 'as a matter of priority the study of the distribution of powers, in particular the taxing and spending powers,' and reconstituted the Tax Structure Committee to pursue further study.[45] Prime Minister Trudeau professed to see in these results a 'remarkable degree of consensus on a large number of issues,' and suggested the conference was 'an educational exercise of considerable importance.'[46]

Several governments had become frustrated by the lack of progress in meetings open to the press. Various delegates felt the participants were 'grandstanding' for the benefit of the folks back home; others felt it was impossible to talk frankly and negotiate easily in public. So it was decided to hold 'informal' closed-door meetings – 'working sessions' – at which specific proposals would be discussed, in addition to further open meetings. The first closed conference was to be held in June.

## GETTING DOWN TO BRASS TACKS: THE JUNE 1969 MEETING

The procedure for constitutional review had now changed. No longer were the governments to submit scattergun 'propositions.' Instead, there would be working papers on each of the major questions. There would be less discussion of general matters and more on specific areas of disagree-

44 *Ibid.*, pp. 254–5.
45 *Ibid.*, appendix A, pp. 395–400.
46 *H. of C. Debates*, 14 Feb. 1969, pp. 5523–4.

ment and friction in federal-provincial relations. The first to be discussed – reflecting the changed priorities forced by the provinces – was the distribution of taxing and spending powers. These and other matters were taken up at two meetings of the continuing committee before the premiers met in June's 'working session.'

The federal government structured the discussion with the presentation of two working papers at the preliminary officials meetings. This allowed the federal government to make minor changes before making its proposals public, and permitted the provinces to prepare their responses. The first federal paper dealt with taxing powers, *Taxing Powers and the Constitution of Canada*, the second with the spending power of the national Parliament, *Federal-Provincial Grants and the Spending Power of Parliament*.[47] There was basic agreement, in principle at least, with Ottawa's position on taxing power. The regular fiscal bargaining was concerned with how joint tax fields should be shared, not with constitutional disputes about who had rights to which fields. Ottawa rejected as a possible solution the idea that the various tax fields should be constitutionally divided up among the governments, and instead suggested the 'principle of access'[48] by which all governments would have access to all major tax fields so long as mechanisms were developed to prevent barriers to interprovincial trade or double taxation. This was a formalization of the move away from the coordinated division of revenues as represented by the postwar tax-sharing arrangements and implied little constitutional modification. It did mean that the provinces could use the politically attractive indirect sales tax which they were presently denied by the British North America Act.[49] Only British Columbia seriously advocated splitting up the tax fields. It had suggested that Ottawa leave to the provinces all personal and corporate income taxes and estate taxes, except for an amount necessary to finance a guaranteed minimum income.[50] The other governments had little basic disagreement. Ontario argued for a much more comprehensive federal-provincial coordination of tax policy and administration, with more projections like those of the Tax Structure Committee.[51] Ottawa

47 Both (Ottawa, 1969).

48 *Taxing Powers and the Constitution of Canada*, p. 16.

49 Discussion of means by which this could be done without setting up interprovincial trade barriers or leading to double taxation was pursued in continuing committee meetings. See Joint Committee, *Proceedings*, no 6, pp. 14–15.

50 This proposal was elaborated at the 1969 Constitutional Conference. See Constitutional Conference, Second Meeting, *Proceedings*, pp. 152–8. See also British Columbia, proposition 9.16, 14 Feb. 1969.

51 Ontario, 'Intergovernmental Finance and Ontario's White Paper on Provincial-Municipal Taxation Reform,' working paper submitted to the Constitutional Conference, 6 June 1969, pp. 9–15.

rejected such cooperative decision-making in favour of independent government decision-making. New Brunswick reiterated its concern that nothing weaken Ottawa's power to tax for the benefit of the poorer regions.[52]

But the federal government's proposals concerning the spending power represented a more dramatic departure. Federal use of the spending power involved some of the most contentious federal-provincial issues. On one hand federal assistance to the needy provinces, through both equalization and shared-cost programmes, depended on the federal power to spend. It was through the spending power that Ottawa had become involved in many areas of provincial jurisdiction, and had come to supply large proportions of the budgets of several provinces. And it was of course the spending power that was involved in the arguments about federal intervention, federal skewing of provincial priorities, federal failure to consult, and all the other grievances about shared-cost programmes. Next to tax-sharing, shared-cost programmes had probably provoked more federal-provincial acrimony since the Second World War than any other aspect of federal-provincial relations.

Perhaps in response to these feelings – and in accord with Trudeau's conception of a limited federal government – Ottawa proposed a strong set of limitations on its own spending power. Ottawa would retain the right to make unlimited unconditional grants to provincial governments, thus providing a constitutional basis for equalization payments. But it would limit its power to make conditional grants in areas of provincial jurisdiction: it could do so only if there was a 'national consensus' as indicated by the votes of provincial legislatures.[53] Obviously, Ottawa had always been preoccupied with getting provincial agreement for programmes in areas of provincial powers; this would be a formalization, in the constitution, which would establish clear rules to replace the much more indeterminate process of before. Moreover, governments not agreeing could 'opt-out' of a shared-cost programme, thus avoiding the 'fiscal penalty' of having citizens paying for a programme they would not benefit from. Instead of these *governments* receiving direct compensation, as in the earlier opting-out arrangements of 1964, the compensating payments would be made to individual citizens of the provinces.

52 New Brunswick, 'Taxing Powers, Spending Powers and the Constitution of Canada,' working paper submitted to the Continuing Committee of Officials, 29 Sept. 1969, p. 2. Manitoba also insisted on federal dominance in the major tax fields: 'Only the federal government can effectively employ taxation for the crucial functions of stabilizing the economy and redistributing the wealth among the provinces.' Constitutional Conference, Third Meeting, *Proceedings* (Ottawa, 1970), p. 36.

53 *Federal-Provincial Grants and the Spending Power of Parliament*, pp. 38–48.

Ottawa proposed a complicated formula for determining the 'consensus' based on the votes of legislatures of a majority of the provinces in each of the four existing Senate regions. The consequences of these proposals, if adopted, would be difficult to assess, but they had some fascinating implications. It would presumably be much harder for Ottawa to engage in anything like the massive extension of its efforts as it had through shared-cost programmes after the Second World War (and, indeed, it was clear the present government had no inclination to do so). The notion of a national consensus, represented and determined not by the elected members of the national legislature, nor by individual citizens, but by provincial governments raised interesting questions about the nature of representation. So did the strong 'regional' rather than population-based component of the federal formula. The idea of compensating individuals instead of governments was obviously designed to make opting-out seem less attractive, but it seemed inconsistent with the procedure for determining consensus, as well as being extraordinarily difficult to administer. Moreover, could not 'opting-out,' especially if Ottawa were forced to give in and compensate governments, lead to a reintroduction of 'special status' for Quebec, which Ottawa was so opposed to? The proposal, embodying as it did a limited federal role, produced a great deal of 'agonizing discussion' within the federal government.

Again, there was wide agreement with the principles, but very little about mechanisms. British Columbia was the only province to reject federal unconditional grants to provinces; Quebec also had serious reservations about whether Ottawa should be permitted to continue to make direct payments to individuals.[54] Few accepted Ottawa's compensation formula; compensation should go to the provincial government directly, or, as Ontario suggested, Ottawa would raise taxes to finance the programme only in participating provinces.[55] There would be much debate over the particular formula for attaining the national consensus, as governments based their calculations both on the weight it would give them in the voting and on the expected effect on the role of the federal government. For example, the federal formula would allow Ontario and Quebec to veto any programme.

Not all governments approved a constitutional requirement for a national consensus. Some, indeed, felt it was a frivolous proposal, advanced only as a tactical ploy. Manitoba and New Brunswick argued it would mean the end of shared-cost programmes of national scope, that

54 See remarks by Prime Minister Bertrand, Constitutional Conference, Third Meeting, *Proceedings*, pp. 17–18.

55 'The Ontario Position on the Spending Power,' presented to the Constitutional Conference, 3 June 1969. Ottawa replied this would be undesirable because it would lead to varying federal income tax levels from province to province.

the federal government should have unrestricted power to spend in the national interest, that any formula might be quickly outdated, would be very hard to change, and would prevent speedy action on urgent problems.[56] New Brunswick argued that the main problems with shared-cost programmes had to do with federal failure to consult adequately, and with administrative difficulties – problems which could be resolved more simply through development of better consultative machinery. 'Political bargaining in each case' was a more appropriate strategy.[57] Various alternative formulae were suggested in which a consensus would be considered to exist if: seven out of ten provinces with 60 per cent of the population agreed (Ontario's suggestion, which, it was pointed out, would mean Ontario plus any of several provinces could provide a veto); six provinces, one from each region, representing 51 per cent of the population agreed; a majority of provinces agreed; the legislatures of three of five regions agreed; and so on.[58] Such possibilities again implied many assumptions about representation (by region or population, for example), but the discussions turned primarily on the perceived advantages and disadvantages of different alternatives for each of the governments. There were similar debates over compensation formulae.[59]

Again, no final details or agreements were worked out, and several questions were referred to the continuing committee of officials. All governments recognized the interconnectedness of taxing and spending powers and the division of legislative responsibility, so final agreement on the former must await discussion of the latter.[60] But the conference had begun to get down to more concrete matters and most participants felt the discussion, away from the reporters' pens, had been far more productive than earlier talks. 'The debate in June was more pointed than at the previous conferences. This time there were specific proposals and papers to discuss. There was less posturing or political speech-making at

56 See New Brunswick, 'Further Observations on the Matter of Shared-Cost Programs and a National Consensus Formula,' working paper submitted to the Continuing Committee of Officials, 10 Nov. 1969. Manitoba suggested as an alternative 'priority option grants,' by which Ottawa would make funds available for a list of purposes, from which the provinces could choose. See remarks by Premier Schreyer in Constitutional Conference, Third Meeting, *Proceedings*, pp. 146–52.

57 New Brunswick, 'Further Observations,' p. 2 and passim. See also New Brunswick, 'Taxing Powers, Spending Powers and the Constitution of Canada.'

58 For a full discussion, see Secretariat of the Constitutional Conference, 'A Briefing Paper on Constitutional Review Activities and Discussions within the Continuing Committee of Officials,' Dec. 1969, pp. 8–13.

59 *Ibid.*, pp. 13–19.

60 Secretariat of the Constitutional Conference, First Working Session, 'Report on the Conclusions of the Meeting,' 1969.

this conference,' said one federal participant. But at the same time, 'I think the conference gave further evidence that, for the most part, the English-Canadian premiers have not yet got around to taking the whole thing seriously.'

During 1969, in addition to meetings of the continuing committee and the June conference, the committees of ministers established in June began their work. The committees on fundamental rights, the judiciary, and official languages each met twice; the committee on the Senate, once. None had made much progress. For example, the committee on official languages had done little more than look at federal proposals for financial assistance to provinces in implementing the language recommendations of the Royal Commission on Bilingualism and Biculturalism.[61] The committee on the judiciary had discussed Quebec's proposal for the establishment of a separate constitutional court, without coming to any conclusions.[62] The committee on fundamental rights had reached the striking conclusion that the constitution should guarantee the right of free elections at maximum intervals of every five years, but there were some reservations about constitutional guarantees of political rights such as freedom of expression and assembly. And there was no agreement as to legal rights, such as those of presumed innocence or of security against unreasonable search. Some felt that all these rights should be enshrined in the constitution; others felt that some basic rights should be entrenched while others were left as presently to federal and provincial legislation; still others rejected any entrenchment. The discussion seemed to have advanced nowhere since February 1968.[63]

## THE THIRD CONSTITUTIONAL CONFERENCE: DECEMBER 1969

The third meeting of the full, open Constitutional Conference took place from 8 to 10 December 1969. This time the discussion centred around the federal working paper, *Income Security and Social Services*,[64] as well as around taxing and spending powers. The emphasis had moved decisively away from language and civil rights. As in earlier conferences, governments used the opportunity to raise other more immediate problems, as when the three westernmost premiers issued a press release in December

61 Secretariat of the Constitutional Conference, 'Progress Report of the Committee of Ministers on Official Languages to the Constitutional Conference,' 1969.
62 Secretariat of the Constitutional Conference, 'Progress Report of the Committee of Ministers on the Judiciary to the Constitutional Conference,' 1969.
63 Secretariat of the Constitutional Conference, 'A Briefing Paper on Discussions within the Committee of Ministers on Fundamental Rights,' 1969.
64 (Ottawa, 1969.)

1969 condemning the federal white paper on taxation proposals. Before the meeting Prime Minister Trudeau had suggested that the negotiations were moving ahead well, and that the end was in sight. More accurate seemed to be Prime Minister Robarts' comment after the first day's discussion; he suggested it might be ten years before a new constitution was written: 'We won't come to any rapid conclusions ... It just is not possible, with the great variation of opinions among governments. Some of our differences may never be reconciled and we may, in fact, never be able to reach agreement.'[65] There was still disagreement about where the review was going. Westerners complained about the concentration on abstract matters and on the preoccupation with the problems of Quebec and the Maritimes; Quebec delegates on the other hand wanted to get back to the fundamental constitutional problems, and felt they had to fight the hostility and indifference of other governments.[66]

The federal working paper on income security and social services suggested few changes in existing patterns. Both levels of government should, as now, have equal and concurrent powers to make direct payments to individuals, as with family allowances and other measures. It justified a federal role on grounds such as the need for Ottawa to redistribute income from richer to poorer areas, the need for interprovincial portability of benefits, the need for coordinated economic policy, and the desire to build a sense of community in Canada. This position, of course, conflicted directly with Quebec's often expressed desire to transfer such services, including the existing family allowances, manpower training, and old age pensions, to the province. In June Ottawa had taken the position that discussions of the Quebec proposals to restrict federal payments to individuals and private institutions must await receiving *all* propositions concerning the distribution of powers.[67] Prime Minister Bertrand repeated his position firmly at the December conference.[68] The Quebec-Ottawa conflict on this question, which had been downplayed in earlier discussions, thus re-emerged, as fundamental and intractable as ever.

As for 'income insurance' programmes, Ottawa proposed no changes in responsibility for unemployment insurance (as an economic matter it should remain solely a federal field) or in workmen's compensation programmes (they should remain provincial). But in order to ensure continued 'portability' of benefits from province to province it did propose that the federal government should gain 'paramountcy' on matters to do

65 Canadian Press dispatch, 8 Dec. 1969.
66 *Le Devoir*, 9 Dec. 1969.
67 *Federal-Provincial Grants and the Spending Power of Parliament*, pp. 18–20.
68 Constitutional Conference, Third Meeting, *Proceedings*, pp. 6–18.

with retirement insurance, ending the provincial superiority worked out in the pension negotiations. There was strong opposition to this proposal; and it was referred to the continuing committee of officials for further study.[69]

Social services and health insurance Ottawa would leave with the provinces, though with the appropriate discovery of a national consensus shared-cost programmes in these fields would still be possible.[70]

Except for Quebec there was little provincial disagreement with the basic federal position. Again the division between richer provinces and poorer ones primarily concerned with federal ability to redistribute income and assist them in their programmes emerged. Several governments, therefore, wished to make social services a concurrent matter.[71] For example, Premier Robichaud of New Brunswick called for a 'new partnership for unity' which would include concurrent powers in education and social services, and others agreed with him. Edward Schreyer, the new premier of Manitoba, a New Democrat, argued that Ottawa had an 'excessively modest' conception of its role in these fields.[72] Mr Schreyer adopted a very different tone from that of his predecessor, Walter Weir. He was much more sympathetic to French language rights and much more 'national' in outlook, especially in his appeal for a powerful central government.

The conference also returned to the questions of taxing and spending powers which had been discussed privately in June. Again, there was no agreement on a 'national consensus' formula, and Manitoba and New Brunswick, concerned once more with the danger of a weak federal government, argued there should be no formula, only a federal obligation to consult with provinces.[73] Nor was there any resolution of the question

69 'Conclusions of the Third Meeting,' in *ibid.*, p. 242. For the conference discussion of the matter, see *ibid.*, pp. 101–16. Premiers Bertrand, Robarts, and Bennett were the most vocal.

70 The distinction between 'income support' programmes involving payments to individuals and social services was unclear. Ottawa suggested it would have to be left to the courts to draw the line, deciding whether any given programme which involved both direct payments and associated social services was primarily an income support programme, and hence within federal powers, or mainly a social service programme, and hence outside federal powers. *Income Security and Social Services*, pp. 104–6.

71 See Constitutional Conference, Third Meeting, *Proceedings*, p. 243.

72 Premier Schreyer significantly changed the emphasis of Manitoba's position, taking a much more accommodating position towards extension of language rights and showing much greater concern for the necessity of federal financial strength, federal control of the major tax fields, and federal involvement in areas of provincial jurisdiction than had his predecessor, Conservative Walter Weir. *Ibid.*, pp. 232–3, 239.

73 See *ibid.*, pp. 243–4.

as to how to compensate provinces not participating in shared-cost programmes. Taxing powers and regional disparities were once again left to officials' discussion.[74] No one disagreed with writing into the preamble of a new constitution the general objective of relieving regional inequalities, which had been proposed by Nova Scotia with the support of the other maritime provinces, but more specific provisions were another matter.

Two years after the constitutional debate had formally begun, the discussions had taken a very different turn. Fundamental rights and the official languages were barely mentioned in December 1969. They had not been resolved; they had simply been pushed aside. The emphasis now was on much more concrete issues of federal and provincial powers in taxing and spending. But here, too, agreement seemed remote. The governments continued to participate in very unequal ways. Ontario, Quebec, New Brunswick, and, after the Schreyer government was elected, Manitoba responded fully to the federal proposals with working papers of their own. The others tended to react off the cuff, with little prior preparation or detailed analysis. There was a growing sense, shared by some participants, and many outside observers, that the purpose and direction of the review was more unclear than ever. It was difficult to see when, if ever, the process would be terminated.

Moreover, criticisms of the process were beginning to mount. Delegates themselves felt the constant preoccupation with constitutional matters was postponing consideration of other more immediate federal-provincial matters, such as the economic grievances of western farmers. To meet this problem it was decided to hold some non-constitutional federal-provincial conferences, the first in February 1970. From outside came criticisms that, despite the innovation of public meetings, the process was too restricted to the representatives of the eleven governments, who tended to be preoccupied with their own particular institutional concerns. Thus spokesmen for municipal governments protested strongly that they should have some more formal role in the discussion. Similarly, opposition members in Parliament felt they had little role to play. A joint Senate–House of Commons committee was established in 1970, and held public hearings, but this was more than two years after the first of the constitutional conferences.

But, in May 1970 Justice Minister John Turner listed six areas in which 'substantial agreement had been reached.' The most important included recognition that French-speaking Canadians outside Quebec should have the same language rights as English-speakers in Quebec; that the preamble to the constitution should contain a declaration that reduction of regional disparities is an 'essential objective' of Confederation; that future shared-

74 See the *Globe and Mail*, 11 Dec. 1969.

cost programmes would require a provincial consensus and permit compensation for non-participating provinces; that both levels of government should have equal access to all tax fields; and that medical and welfare services should be provincial, 'subject to the spending power of Parliament to support such services.' Mr Turner suggested these covered 'some of the most contentious issues ... and they augur well for the future of the constitutional review.'[75] Similarly, when the conference summed up its activities at the second working session in September 1970, it reported discussion at an advanced stage on many issues but little formal agreement.[76]

## 'A FEASIBLE APPROACH': FEBRUARY AND JUNE 1971

By early 1971 impatience with the dilatory and inconclusive progress of the review was growing. The demand for some tangible result was being made with increasing urgency. Growing separatist strength, together with the October crisis, perhaps impressed on federal leaders the need to come to a decision. Other governments, and the public too, seemed simply fed-up. Moreover, in April 1970 a staunchly federalist Liberal government led by Robert Bourassa came to power in Quebec – though with strong opposition from the Parti Québécois. Bourassa, it appeared, was far more concerned with economic than constitutional matters and would likely be considerably more moderate and tractable (from a federal point of view) than his predecessors.

These views were uppermost as the governments met for another working session in February 1971. The result was, as Mr Trudeau put it, an apparent 'breakthrough' in the constitutional log-jam. Most important, the conference turned its attention to the matter of developing an amendment formula, which had been attempted so many times before. Now there was agreement on 'a feasible approach' to such a formula, which would also permit the patriation of the constitution. 'Bringing the constitution home' would indeed be a popular symbolic achievement. The conference also agreed on 'such other changes as could be agreed on quickly,' including such matters as civil rights, regional disparities, and the Supreme Court.[77] Another full-dress constitutional conference was to be held in June to work out the final details. Most observers seemed optimistic that some concrete results were imminent.

But there were some difficult roadblocks ahead. The proposed agree-

75 Joint Committee, *Proceedings*, no 1, pp. 43–5.
76 Secretariat of the Constitutional Conference, Second Working Session, 'Statement of Conclusions,' 1970, appendix.
77 Secretariat of the Constitutional Conference, 'Process of Constitutional Review,' 1971, pp. 6–7.

ment contained little of substance dealing with Quebec's central concern, the division of powers. Gradually it became clear that the price of Quebec's acceptance of an amending formula would be some real concession towards its goal of increased jurisdiction over social policy; it was no longer greatly concerned with the amending formula itself. Thus Quebec insisted that social policy be placed on the agenda for the June conference, and regained the initiative by submitting a major new proposal. The real debate in Victoria, wrote Claude Ryan of *Le Devoir*, would not be the Turner-Trudeau amending formula but social policy.[78]

Quebec's proposal stemmed in part from a massive study of welfare policy undertaken by Claude Castonguay, who had been one of the chief negotiators of the pension settlement and who was now minister of social welfare in the Bourassa government. Quebec now envisioned a comprehensive and integrated programme of social security to replace the scattered federal and provincial programmes currently in effect. To do so, Castonguay argued, Quebec required clear constitutional supremacy in these fields. This would be achieved through modification of section 94A of the British North America Act, which, as we saw in chapter 3, gives concurrent jurisdiction over pensions, with provincial paramountcy. Quebec would add to 94A family and youth allowances, occupational training grants, unemployment insurance, and the guaranteed income supplement to old age pensions, while retaining provincial primacy. New provincial legislation concerning family allowances, manpower training, and the guaranteed income supplement would displace federal legislation. New programmes adopted by Ottawa in the other fields would not affect existing or future provincial legislation. Equally important, Ottawa would pay compensation to a province whose own legislation displaced federal programmes. Finally, Ottawa would be constitutionally required to consult the provinces before introducing any new legislation in these fields. The new section would give clear constitutional sanction for federal involvement in these policy areas, rather than forcing it to use the general spending power; but at the same time it would limit federal powers and subordinate them to provincial powers.[79]

This was a far cry from the position Ottawa had adopted in 1969. The federal government had accepted concurrency but had argued for retention of occupational training and unemployment insurance as purely federal matters, and had requested paramountcy in the pension field.[80] Its formula for compensation for non-participating provinces was to apply only to federal programmes in areas of provincial jurisdiction, and was to

78 *Le Devoir*, 8 June 1971.
79 *Ibid.*, 15, 19 June 1971.
80 *Income Security and Social Services*, passim.

involve payment not to governments but to individuals.[81] Against Quebec's emphasis on provincial primacy were Ottawa's commitments to maintain a federal role in assuring comparable services across the country, in achieving redistribution of wealth, in retaining sufficient financial power to manage the economy, and in maintaining direct federal ties with individual citizens.

Thus the stage was set: a detailed, concrete proposal from Quebec; a federal position asserting a far different conception of the powers of governments; and a commitment from Quebec that unless some compromise was reached on this issue agreement on the other issues would be impossible. The June conference would not simply be the triumphal ratification of the tentative agreement of February; rather, it would involve some very hard bargaining.

The bargaining began long before June 14. Justice Minister Turner toured the provinces, and the attorneys general met at the end of May to go over constitutional texts. Soon after, the welfare ministers met to discuss Quebec's proposals as well as new federal initiatives on family allowances and other matters. Mr Bourassa and Mr Trudeau held several long private meetings, at which Trudeau apparently stressed the compelling need to achieve some progress and Bourassa stressed that to defend any agreement in Quebec there must be some advance on matters of substance. Both leaders appeared anxious to reach agreement.[82] Bourassa, though continuing to express with only slight alterations the remarkably consistent views of all Quebec governments since the early sixties, was a committed federalist. If agreement with him could not be reached it was impossible to conceive of agreement with any Quebec political leader.

But when the first ministers convened in the British Columbia legislative chambers, the impasse remained. For three days politicians and officials – sometimes together, sometimes separately – debated the draft constitutional texts which had emerged from the discussions since February. Most of the talks involved social security, but other issues also proved contentious. Quebec made a special effort to explain its proposals and to garner support, including a special briefing session held by Mr Castonguay. The conference ended, not with the originally planned televised final session, but with a marathon negotiating session, in private, lasting from ten in the morning on June 17 until after midnight. The result was tentative agreement on a 'Canadian Constitutional Charter, 1971' – the Victoria Charter. For a moment it looked as if the impasse was broken, that the British North America Act, substantially revised, would be transformed into the Constitution Act.

81 *Federal-Provincial Grants and the Spending Power of Parliament*, passim.
82 *Le Devoir*, 1 June 1971.

But the agreement was still tentative. Formal approval by the governments, then legislative ratification, was still required. To secure approval the conference decided on a novel procedure: the governments would have until June 28 to make up their minds. They would have to accept or reject the charter as a whole;[83] there was to be no more discussion, 'no more deals.' It was now or never, take it or leave it.[84] Quebec, said *Le Devoir*, went to Victoria to propose a bargain and returned with an ultimatum. This procedure indicated strong reservations remained, but ensured that the governments would be under maximum pressure to agree.

The charter contained sixty-one articles in ten parts. First, it constitutionally entrenched some political rights – the rights to freedom of thought, conscience, religion, expression, assembly, opinion, and association. The misgivings expressed earlier by some provinces had been partly overcome. But the statement of rights omitted many of the legal rights commonly found in bills of rights and included in the original federal proposal. It also embraced a very large hedge: the political rights were subject to 'such limitations ... as are reasonably justifiable in a democratic society in the interests of public safety, order, health or morals, of national security, or of the rights and freedoms of others.'[85]

Second, the charter guaranteed the right of suffrage, annual legislative sessions, and a maximum of five-year terms for legislatures.

Nowhere was the real lack of consensus more evident than in the articles on language rights. Again, Ottawa had fallen far short of its aims. The charter declared English and French as official languages. It entrenched the right to use either language in Parliament and the provincial legislatures – but the three western provinces were excluded. It declared statutes and other official documents to be authoritative in either language – but only in Ottawa, Quebec, New Brunswick, and Newfoundland. When a province failed to publish its documents in one of the languages, the federal government would do so. It declared equal language rights in the courts – but only in federal courts and those of Quebec, New Brunswick, and Newfoundland. It gave citizens the right to communicate with their governments in either language – except in Nova Scotia, Manitoba, Saskatchewan, Alberta, and British Columbia. It did not mention minority education rights. Canada was still a long way from a linguistic consensus and faced the anomalous situation of having constitutionally entrenched rights which applied in some parts of the country but not in others. However, provinces left out of the charter provisions could decide later to

83 Constitutional Conference, 14–16 June 1971, 'Statement of Conclusions.'
84 *Globe and Mail*, 18 June 1971.
85 'Canadian Constitutional Charter, 1971,' Art. 3.

opt-in, with a procedure similar to that Mr Pearson had suggested in 1968.[86]

Fourth, after long discussion the conference agreed on a compromise statement of provincial participation in the naming of judges for the Supreme Court, suggesting a cumbersome and lengthy procedure giving the provinces a large role but not a veto. The charter also guaranteed that at least three of the Supreme Court judges must be appointed from Quebec, and that in cases involving Quebec's civil code at least three of the four or five sitting judges should be trained in the code.[87]

Fifth, the charter dealt with regional disparities by declaring that the governments were committed to promoting the equality and well-being of all Canadians, to assuring that 'essential public services of reasonable quality' are available to all, and to promoting economic development so as to reduce disparities. It was simply a moral injunction, specifically noting that the provision committed no government to do anything. Perhaps because of British Columbia's insistence, it focused on individual inequalities rather than on regional disparities and assistance to governments.[88]

Sixth, the charter presented an amendment formula. For most changes passage would require the approval of the federal government, plus: all provinces with 25 per cent or more of the population (assuring Quebec and Ontario a veto, even if Quebec's population were later to fall below 25 per cent); at least two of the Atlantic provinces; and at least two of the western provinces, with at least 50 per cent of the region's population (thus assuring British Columbia a strong position). Amendments concerning some but not all provinces could be approved by Ottawa and the affected provinces. Ottawa and the provinces could amend their own constitutions alone.[89] Unlike the ill-fated Fulton-Favreau formula, which had also won approval only to be turned down by Quebec, the new formula contained no provision for the delegation of powers between governments.

Seventh, there was a compromise on social policy reflected in a new section 94A. It added family, youth, and occupational allowances to pensions and retained provincial primacy. It also required the federal government to inform the provinces of any proposed legislation in these fields at least ninety days before presentation to Parliament.[90] It represented a substantial concession by Ottawa and some of the provinces (indeed, it was reported that Minister of National Health and Welfare John Munro threatened to resign if further concessions were made[91]).

86 *Ibid.*, Arts. 8–16.
87 *Ibid.*, Arts. 22–42.
88 *Ibid.*, Arts. 46–7.
89 *Ibid.*, Arts. 49–57.
90 *Ibid.*, Arts. 44–5.
91 *Le Devoir*, 18 June 1971.

But it fell short of Quebec's wishes, since the new list of concurrent powers was shorter than Quebec's and since no mention of compensation was included. There was also some ambiguity about the extent of provincial paramountcy: would new provincial legislation displace existing federal law? Ottawa and its allies and Quebec had made substantial compromises, but social policy was to prove the rock on which the charter foundered.

Finally, the charter recognized the importance of federal-provincial negotiation, but only to the point of requiring yearly meetings of first ministers. It also contained a final section revising some of the language of the BNA Act.

## REJECTION: SEVEN DAYS IN JUNE

That the document emerged at all might be counted as a breakthrough. It bore all the earmarks of a desperately sought compromise. No government could be completely happy with it. It did not touch on many of the points at issue; in places it was vague and awkward. It represented very little change from the constitutional status quo. But here at last was a tangible, if somewhat uninspired, result representing some minimal degree of consensus. Agreement on the amending formula, and with it on a means to make the constitution a truly Canadian document, would be an important and undoubtedly popular symbolic accomplishment. Few participants could expect to find agreement on anything more substantial. So most governments seemed certain to accept the charter despite many misgivings. Who, after all, would wish to be responsible for sabotaging what had been so painfully achieved? Ontario, British Columbia, and Alberta quickly announced their acceptance.

The question mark was Quebec. Widespread opposition mobilized almost immediately after the charter was revealed. The Confederation of National Trade Unions, the Federation of St Jean Baptiste societies, the Quebec wing of the New Democratic Party, and other groups formed a common front to mount a campaign against acceptance. All three opposition parties and the Quebec Federation of Labour demanded rejection. Acceptance of the charter would mean protesters on the streets once again, and a major political crisis, including defections from Liberal ranks. 'The days of conscription have returned,' proclaimed newspaper advertisements, 'the answer must be NO to Ottawa's ultimatum ... There must be a general mobilization of the people of Quebec.'[92] The opposition came from all quarters. It was not, said *Le Devoir*, the ranting of a small group of reactionary intellectuals, as Trudeau had suggested.[93] The opposition

92 *Ibid.*, 22 June 1971.

93 *Ibid.*, 25 June 1971.

condemned not only the social policy provisions but many other aspects of the charter as well. They bitterly attacked the 'ultimatum.' The constitution could not be wrapped-up behind closed doors, but must receive thorough public discussion, and perhaps even a referendum.

The Bourassa government was in a painful dilemma. On the one hand greater control of social policy had become the irreducible minimum of Quebec's demands; on the other hand Ottawa was most unlikely to go any further and rejection would almost certainly bring the whole review to a halt. 'If there isn't agreement, then that is the end of the matter, for now, or for a while, I hope,' Mr Trudeau had said.[94] It is impossible to know what Mr Bourassa's own inclinations were, but after extensive consultations with his caucus, cabinet, and the extra-parliamentary party, he announced the decision: 'No.' His rejection statement left the door open for further talks: it was not so much the charter itself, but the uncertainties and ambiguities in social policy that determined Quebec's answer, he said.[95] But clearing up the uncertainty would certainly mean real change, not minor alterations in wording. The 'non' expressed the profound conviction of the whole Quebec people, said Claude Ryan. The other governments, not Quebec, were responsible for the stalemate. Quebec's discontent had led to the review in the first place. How, he asked, could one possibly imagine that a return to the status quo could make these feelings disappear?[96]

The constitutional review had thus reached a hiatus. More discussion there would certainly be, but the momentum had dissipated. The other governments were in no hurry for another round. 'This puts us back to square one,' said Alberta's Premier Strom.[97] Mr Trudeau recalled his original position on a constitutional review: 'If we open the constitution, it will be a can of worms. That is exactly what happened.' He added: 'I do not see many more conferences unless Quebec can suggest a way out of this impasse.'[98] But that would be difficult: the disagreement stemmed from the fundamentally different views of Confederation held by Quebec and Ottawa and the English-speaking provinces. That is what led to the debate; that is what prevented agreement. It would continue to do so unless there were major revisions in the objectives of either side.

Yet the problem remained. In Quebec disaffection from the federal régime was more widespread than ever. The internal debate was between those who argued that English Canada would never permit the province to negotiate for itself a special status or a much expanded provincial role,

94 *Globe and Mail*, 18 June 1971.
95 *Montreal Star*, 23 June 1971.
96 *Le Devoir*, 25 June 1971.
97 *Montreal Star*, 23 June 1971.
98 *Globe and Mail*, 24 June 1971.

and those who argued that new arrangements could be worked out. The outcome could only strengthen the argument of the Parti québécois, as it was quick to point out.

The constitutional negotiations were not over. They promised to continue, at least sporadically, but the major focus of federal-provincial relations would return to the traditional concrete problems of the moment. Mr Trudeau professed himself to be not very worried about the outcome. There were always more important things than the constitution, he said, and the setback did not mean the end of the world.[99] Many agreed – and several premiers had made that point all along. But, once opened, the can of worms could not be capped so easily. Those who argued the danger and difficulty of the review in the first place seemed proven right. The original disagreements were clearer than ever. English Canadians might cheerfully tolerate a constitutional limbo; it is very doubtful French Canadians would. The matter could not simply be dropped.

## CONCLUSION

The constitutional review was thus the most drawn-out and so far least successful of the three cases. For almost four years it was the central preoccupation of federal-provincial relations. Since February 1968 there had been seven meetings of first ministers, nine meetings of ministerial committees, fourteen of the continuing committee of officials, fifteen of officials' sub-committees, and innumerable informal discussions at all levels.[100]

The chief reason for the protracted and inconclusive talks was the profound difference between the views of Quebec and most other governments, exacerbated on one hand by increased support for separatism within Quebec and on the other hand by the Trudeau government's firm belief that there could be no special status because Confederation would not survive if Quebec had special powers. However much the participants tried to steer the discussion to less contentious matters, it always came back to this central issue.

There were other factors contributing to the length of the debate. Until 1971 there was little external pressure to reach a conclusion. The bargainers faced no deadlines; there was little public pressure. Few outside Quebec sensed great crisis or felt there were many vital issues which could not be dealt with without solution of the constitutional puzzle. So the pressure to

99 *Ibid.*
100 Secretariat of the Constitutional Conference, 'Process of Constitutional Review,' p. 8.

decide was low, and the costs of delay were hard to measure. Many participants thus decided that the costs of forcing matters to a head and making a decision were greater, and that it was best simply to keep talking. These views had changed by 1971: the Victoria Charter and its rejection were the result.

Moreover, discussion was complicated by the ambiguity of the procedures to be followed. Issues were raised, debated, and dropped with no concrete result. There were few rules for determining what constituted a decision. As Premier Bennett pointed out in 1970: 'It is impossible to determine whether a subject matter under review has been satisfactorily resolved unless we know what degree of unanimity is necessary to constitute agreement. If it is to be 100 per cent unanimity, then I do not think it is unfair to say that we have made literally no progress to date.'[101]

Finally the great number and complexity of the issues made discussion difficult. Each item on the long agenda was related to each of the others, and to issues arising outside of the immediate constitutional context. Many of the questions were vague and abstract. 'All concerned underestimated how long and difficult it would be,' Gordon Robertson, the senior federal official involved, told the parliamentary committee. 'I think it is a good deal more difficult than had been realized at the outset.'[102]

It might be argued, as some federal officials did, that the chief goal was not so much a revised constitution at all. More important was that the debate should provide an opportunity to expose both the problems and the potential of Canadian federalism, and thus be part of an exercise in national consensus-building. It would educate English Canadians in the needs and goals of French Canadians. It would help to convince French Canadians of the benefits of continued union, and of the willingness of English Canadians to make suitable accommodations. If anything, the opposite effect seems to have been produced by 1971.

The three cases differ greatly from one another, but they also have many characteristics in common. Each illustrates some important elements of federal-provincial negotiation; each is an important event in the evolution of Canadian federalism. Together they provide a base for examination of the negotiating process in more detail, this time from an analytical rather than a chronological or historical perspective.

101 Secretariat of the Constitutional Conference, 'British Columbia's Proposals to the Working Session of the Constitutional Conference, September 1970,' p. 2.
102 Joint Committee, *Proceedings*, no 2, p. 9.

CHAPTER SIX

# Sites and procedures

The Canadian constitution did not envisage the need for extensive federal-provincial negotiations. It was not expected that the various governments' functions would overlap much; and, in case they did, the constitution tried to make sure there was no doubt who would win by granting Ottawa the power to disallow provincial legislation, to appoint senators, and to appoint lieutenant governors.[1] But with the demands of the modern state and the resulting increase in federal-provincial interaction, the need to develop a set of institutions within which adjustment could take place became crucial. This was especially true because of the failure of parliamentary institutions to provide a satisfactory forum for the adjustment of differences. Hence there has developed – 'growing gradually like a coral reef' – a set of extraconstitutional and extraparliamentary institutions which provide the sites for most federal-provincial negotiations. These institutions, as well as the rules and norms which govern the discussions, will be examined in this chapter.

By far the most important sites for negotiations are federal-provincial conferences, which bring together representatives of all governments to discuss matters of mutual concern. The number of such meetings has increased enormously in recent years. In 1939 a total of seven federal-provincial meetings was reported;[2] in 1957 sixty-four federal-provincial

1 British North America Act, 1867, 30 & 31 Vict., c. 3, ss. 24, 58, 90.
2 The figure was calculated from data supplied in House of Commons, Sessional Paper 245B, 18 May 1966.

committees met; in 1965 the figure was 125;[3] in 1967, 119,[4] some more than once. This does not include a myriad of informal meetings between officials and ministers of different governments. The conferences cover a wide variety of subjects, from agricultural statistics and coal research to major policy matters like fiscal relations and the Canada Pension Plan.[5] They also involve representatives from many different levels, from the Federal-Provincial Plenary Conference involving the premiers and prime ministers and their chief advisers, to ministerial meetings dealing with one subject area, to meetings of relatively minor officials concerned with technical details. In 1965, for example, there were two prime ministers' conferences, fourteen at the deputy ministers' level, twenty-seven at the division directors' level, and sixty-five at the professional and technical levels.[6]

Some of the meetings are annual affairs; others are established as the need arises. Table II summarizes the meetings planned for 1967. Not only the wide variety of federal-provincial conferences but also the great variation among departments is shown. The bulk of the meetings include representatives from all governments, but many – such as semi-monthly meetings to ensure coordination of the Canada and Quebec pension plans – are between federal representatives and those of individual provinces or groups of provinces to deal with matters of particular interest to them.

## FEDERAL-PROVINCIAL PLENARY CONFERENCE

The capstone of the system is the Federal-Provincial Plenary Conference of Premiers and Prime Ministers, which has also gone under names like the Dominion-Provincial Conference and, more recently, the Constitutional Conference or Conference of First Ministers. The importance of the plenary conference stems from its membership. A British Columbian cabinet minister explained why: 'They represent almost a totality of power in Canada and the reason for that is that each premier and head of government can commit his own government.' Thus the conference brings together the top political leaders of the eleven governments – each of whom has a high degree of control over his legislature and cabinet.

3 Edgar Gallant, 'The Machinery of Federal-Provincial Relations, I,' *Canadian Public Administration* 8 (1965), p. 3.

4 Gerard Veilleux, 'The Machinery for Intergovernmental Cooperation in Canada,' unpublished MPA thesis, Carleton University, Ottawa, 1968, p. 17 and appendix A, pp. 94–100.

5 The most complete listing of federal-provincial committees is found in a report by the Institute of Intergovernmental Relations, Queen's University, *Intergovernmental Liaison on Fiscal and Economic Matters* (Ottawa, 1969), appendix D.

6 Gallant, 'The Machinery of Federal-Provincial Relations,' p. 11.

TABLE II

Meetings of intergovernmental conferences and committees by levels and areas of activity, 1967

| Area | Ministerial | Administrative | Total |
|---|---|---|---|
| General government | 3 | 23 | 26 |
| Protection of persons and property | 1 | 15 | 16 |
| Transportation and communications | 1 | 1 | 2 |
| Health | 1 | 20 | 21 |
| Social welfare | 1 | 17 | 18 |
| Recreation and cultural services | 4 | 6 | 10 |
| Education | | 5 | 5 |
| Natural resources and primary industry | 5 | 54 | 59 |
| Trade and industrial development | 1 | 1 | 2 |
| Totals | 17 | 142 | 159 |

SOURCES: Gerard Veilleux, *Historical Development of the Machinery for Intergovernmental Cooperation in Canada, 1867–1967* (Ottawa, n.d.) appendix A, p. 52. The figures are approximate, since they are compiled from departmental reports to the Privy Council Office. Some meetings may therefore have been left out. The list is based on proposed meetings rather than those actually held, and it excludes purely interprovincial meetings.

The core of each delegation generally consists of the premier or prime minister, two to five other ministers and a group of officials. The selection of the members will depend largely on the topics for discussion. The delegations can be large. The total membership at a typical conference, in November 1963, was 203 persons;[7] at the third meeting of the Constitutional Conference in December 1969 there were 140 delegates – fifty-one ministers and eighty-nine advisers – and twenty-eight observers.[8] The federal delegation in 1963 included ten cabinet ministers and thirty-three officials. Ontario, with a total representation of thirty-four, and Quebec, with twenty-one, sent the largest provincial delegations. Other provincial delegations ranged from nineteen for New Brunswick to seven for Prince Edward Island. Federal officials have generally constituted the conferences' secretariat; the chief exception is the constitutional conference.

7 Prepared from list of participants in *Federal-Provincial Conference*, Nov. 1963 (Ottawa, 1964).

8 Secretariat of the Constitutional Conference, 'List of Delegates, Advisers and Observers,' 1969.

Despite its importance the conference is more a forum for discussion than a formal decision-making body. Votes are never held and few clear-cut decisions are taken. Rather the conference provides an arena in which all governments can inform each other of their positions and attempt to persuade each other. Each government must return to its legislature for formal approval of any positions taken at the conference. While positions may be changed at the conference itself – as when Ottawa rewrote its Municipal Loan Fund legislation in July 1963 or modified its education proposal in 1966 – more often the governments will reassess their policies in the light of the discussions at the conference and any changes will be revealed later. The federal-provincial conference is – formally, at least – not a legislature.

The federal government is responsible for calling a conference and plays a dominant role in setting the agenda. Both factors give Ottawa a great advantage, allowing it to call meetings at its own political convenience to discuss whatever it wishes. Part of the federal objection to Ontario's calling the 1967 Confederation of Tomorrow Conference was that Ontario was infringing on a federal prerogative, and some provincial officials agreed.[9] Before the meeting, however, Ottawa will correspond with the provinces, which will often suggest matters for discussion. It may send officials on the rounds of provincial capitals to outline approaching federal proposals and prepare the groundwork. Increasingly cabinet

9 See exchange of letters between Prime Ministers Robarts and Pearson, 26 Jan. and 1 Feb. 1967. Ontario, press release, 1967.

Mr Pearson's comments are instructive. There were, he said, no precedents for a premier's calling a federal-provincial conference, and he asked if a new precedent would be wise 'especially in present circumstances.' He continued: 'Normally when a Provincial Premier wishes to have a matter of common concern discussed at a Federal-Provincial Conference, he has suggested to the Prime Minister of Canada that a conference should be assembled, or that a particular item should be called ... Therefore, I wonder whether it would be wise or desirable, to move to a situation in which the Premier of any Province might initiate a Federal-Provincial Conference that could be awkward or untimely for one of the other governments, or unhelpful to the country as a whole.' As the quotation indicates, another reason for federal opposition to the conference was a fear that debate on the most contentious issues of Canadian federalism might reveal the depths of the conflict and open a dangerous Pandora's Box. There is finally a bargaining consideration: the responsibility for calling conferences and setting agenda gives Ottawa an advantage it would not want to relinquish.

Mr Robarts' defence was that his conference would not infringe on federal prerogatives, and that it was not a conference designed to consider immediate policy matters nor to rewrite the constitution but rather one to explore generally some fundamental questions. 'No one can justly deny the provinces, nor prevent them from asserting, the right to assume their proper place and play their proper role in the evolvement of the governmental process of our country.'

ministers have been used for this purpose. The provinces may bring up new subjects at the conference itself, and in effect pre-empt the agenda, as Quebec did in 1963 and 1964, or as several provinces did during the constitutional debates. The federal dominance over both timing and agenda seems to have weakened considerably in recent years.

With few exceptions the conferences have been held in Ottawa.[10] The meeting is almost always chaired by the prime minister; in his absence or for the discussion of particular topics another federal minister presides. Most comments are directed at the federal government; there is little cross-talk between provinces. The general pattern is for the federal government to make the opening statement, explaining its own proposals. Each provincial premier then states his position. Until 1963 each delegation would read its brief to the conference. This generally took up a good part of the time available, so it was decided the briefs, which represent a major policy statement by each government, would usually be distributed but not read. The practice, however, varies greatly from meeting to meeting. Following the opening statements there is usually less structured discussion.

The meeting is dominated by the prime ministers and premiers. Other ministers will speak when a matter of their direct concern is being discussed, and occasionally an official will be asked to explain a technical point. When the conference breaks up into subcommittees, however – as happens frequently – individual ministers do play a more important role, and an official might be the only representative of his government present. The chief role of the officials is to prepare material for their ministers and to keep them well briefed. They also meet informally with representatives of other governments. Federal officials will meet with provincial representatives to clarify technical details or discuss administrative aspects, as in October 1966.

Discussion inside the conference generally follows the correct style of parliamentary debate, though there have been a few notable exceptions. Most of the premiers have met each other many times before and understand each other's positions. 'It is like an Old Boy's league,' said a Manitoba official. A set of informal rules governs the discussion. For example, the participants are expected to respect each other's confidences; even

10 For a description of the setting for most meetings, see Robert A. McLarty, 'Federal-Provincial Relations: Machinery and Policy,' unpublished paper, Fredericton, n.d., pp. 6–7. Material throughout this section is based primarily on interviews with participants. In 1969 Ottawa converted the Centennial Centre, formerly a railroad station, into an elaborate site for federal-provincial meetings.

when they disagree, provincial governments will seldom attack each other; the language of direct bargaining and 'power politics' is avoided. At the same time, because the meetings are usually held *in camera*, and because they are dealing with people in similar positions with similar problems, the premiers can often be very frank, discussing matters they would be reluctant to discuss publicly. The nature of the discussion also depends greatly on the conduct of the chairman. Respondents from all provinces agreed that Prime Minister Pearson's conciliatory manner and flexible chairmanship had made discussion much easier. 'It was a whole new world,' said one New Brunswick cabinet minister. Trudeau has equally impressed the participants. 'Despite the differences and antagonisms,' said a long-time observer of the conferences, 'it's really very friendly. It's rather like belonging to a club and they have the rules they all play by.'

Individual personalities also play differing roles. Thus Prime Minister Lesage often dominated the meetings. Premier Roblin of Manitoba, for another example, was often very active. On the other hand, some other premiers participate little in the substantive discussion. Premier Smallwood tells the story of how he led Newfoundland into Confederation in 1949 at every conference, at least at private ones, but often says little beyond that. 'I certainly know the details of how Newfoundland got in better than any other province, so I suppose there's some value in it,' said one respondent.

Much of the important work of the conference is done outside the formal session, at dinner, in the lobbies of hotels, and so on. Formal dinners hosted by the federal prime minister may give the first ministers a chance to get down to brass tacks alone.

Discussion at the meetings often covers a wide variety of questions. Thus, in November 1963, in addition to new fiscal arrangements and the Canada Pension Plan, delegates discussed conditional grant programmes, employment and economic policy, Indian and Eskimo affairs, lotteries, and other subjects. Often subcommittees of ministers or officials will discuss particular topics, as when Minister of National Health and Welfare Judy LaMarsh chaired a discussion of the CPP in November 1963. Generally, discussion of different matters is well compartmentalized so that there are few attempts in the conference itself to trade support on one issue for support on others. Creation of subcommittees to discuss different aspects of the constitutional issue helped to institutionalize this. Particular governments take advantage of the conference to discuss matters of special concern to their provinces with federal representatives.

Federal-provincial conferences have until recently been held *in camera*.

Only the opening briefs and the final communiqué are officially released to the public. At the same time, however, as the focal point of federal-provincial relations they attract a great deal of attention from the press and the public. The result is that much of what transpires does find its way, more or less accurately, into the press. Of course leaks may be used as a tactical device as well, as when the results of the Tax Structure Committee were given to the Toronto *Globe and Mail*.[11] Delegates may also give a different impression outside the conference than they gave inside. Thus Quebec delegations have taken a more militant stand when talking to Quebec reporters than they took in the conference. Prime Minister Lesage, according to respondents, on occasion apologized to federal officials that he would have to denounce them outside the conference room. This is a manifestation of the difficulty for the actors caused by their participating in several simultaneous games.

Despite the fact that much of what is said at the meetings becomes public, secrecy has conditioned the negotiations in some important ways. It would, for example, have been almost impossible to conduct the Tax Structure Committee projection exercise in public, since no provincial government wanted to risk revealing its taxing and spending plans for the future. There has been a pervasive feeling among the participants that were the meetings always open the nature of the discussion would change greatly. Said a BC cabinet minister: 'When the meeting is open, there is more of a tendency for people to strike attitudes and poses and they may or may not lead to useful decision-making. It's not easy to change a position once you've struck an attitude. That's why many of the opening statements are so bland. There has got to be some place in the governmental system where you can be frank and where you will not be held publicly accountable.' 'I don't think they would be so effective if they were publicized,' said a Manitoba official. 'There would be an awful lot of grandstanding.' A New Brunswick official agreed: 'We'd have speeches made purely for home consumption.' To return to the analogy of the participants' playing in many games at once, this emphasis on secrecy can be seen as an attempt to keep the games separate. Mingling them might increase the problems of reaching agreement. And, as Jack Sawyer and Harold Guetzkow point out, the more openness the more people involved, and hence the more restrictions on the negotiator.[12] In addition, the emphasis on secrecy is consistent with norms of secrecy which are strong within other areas of Canadian government, and which seem to

11 See 'Secret Source Leaks TSC Projections,' *Globe and Mail*, 27 Oct. 1966.
12 'Bargaining and Negotiation in International Relations,' in Herbert Kelman, ed., *International Behavior* (New York, 1965), p. 492.

stem from an emulation of British governmental practices and from a suspicion of public involvement in policy-making. Respondents often likened the conferences to cabinet meetings. Just as the cabinet decides its policies in secret but is responsible for them to Parliament, so the governments are responsible to their legislatures for the outcomes of federal-provincial conferences.

With this background it was therefore a major innovation when the constitutional conference was opened to television cameras and the press. The experience of these meetings modified many of the evaluations just discussed. It is now assumed that open meetings will continue to be part – but only a part – of the federal-provincial negotiating machinery.

Nevertheless, open meetings clearly altered the function of the conference. Their purpose was largely to stimulate public interest and concern, and to provide a public forum for the participants. The delegates now distinguish clearly between 'discussion' meetings – which can be public – and 'decision-making' meetings which, like the working sessions of the constitutional conference, will remain private. The actual behaviour of the participants at the public conferences has differed in some important ways from conduct in private meetings. Said one participant: 'It was obvious with the speakers playing to the TV cameras that we were not going to get a good conversational meeting. They [the first ministers] tend to make resounding statements and to be very careful about what they say. In a closed meeting there is a freer exchange. They will say things in one or two sentences rather than make a speech. And they can talk as if they are searching for the truth rather than pretending they must be an oracle of wisdom.' Said another: 'The public meetings can be regarded as educational meetings; the private meetings are the working sessions.' That was clear at the June 1969 meeting where the delegates discussed in detail specific proposals in a way very different from the more partisan generalities of the previous open meetings. At a public meeting the delegates are speaking to a different audience – the press and public – than they are in a private meeting where the audience is restricted to their colleagues. The open meeting may even – if only briefly – make a national political figure out of someone who has previously not been well known. The effect of Trudeau's performance in February 1968 and Manitoba Premier Walter Weir's intervention in 1969 are good examples. Presumably this characteristic of the meetings gives the premiers an advantage, since the federal prime minister always does have a national platform. On the other hand, of course, the provincial voice is divided among ten – which are often not agreed among themselves. Ottawa also has the advantage of the chair. Thus both the conduct and function of the open constitutional conferences are different from the traditional closed meetings. They are likely to remain a part of the process but still in a limited fashion.

Another innovation started by the constitutional conference is the development of committees of ministers to examine particular problems. Their activity and effectiveness appears to have been very uneven.

Respondents differ in their assessment of the overall role of the Federal-Provincial Plenary Conference. At one extreme was the Ontario official who felt little is accomplished: 'Well, there is nothing done at the conferences that could not be done by letter for the price of a postage stamp.' Provincial criticisms centre on the federal advantage in the procedures: Ottawa dominates the agenda, has the advantages of chairmanship, makes the basic proposals (sometimes with little prior warning); and the procedures give the provinces no formal sanction (in the form of a vote). On the other hand, federal critics take the opposite view. One cabinet minister, for example, felt there were 'too damn many' plenary conferences because the provinces got ten-to-one publicity and Ottawa got no political benefit. Said one cabinet minister: 'When you have a federal-provincial conference, you are giving the premiers a national platform and a national audience ... We should not have too many conferences at the premiers' level. It just builds the premiers up and you build up more opposition to federal policies.'

But most respondents felt the plenary conferences are the central arenas for federal-provincial policy-making. They provide a forum where 'the principals meet with the principals' to influence, bargain with, and persuade each other. They can discuss the fundamentally political questions which can be discussed at no other level. The purpose is not to make 'executive decisions' but rather to 'influence and enlighten each other, and develop common knowledge.' And, while it is not a place where *formal* decisions are made very often, 'it is a place where I think the stuff of decisions is put forward and digested. Decisions may be made effectively there, even if the actual decision is made somewhere else.'

Thus the pension plan was discussed at four premiers' conferences, and at each of them important new developments took place. At the October conference in 1966 the governments agreed on the new equalization formula, achieved modifications in the federal educational proposal and its plan for phasing out capital grants for technical and vocational schools, and, while not agreeing, did lay the basis for the new financial arrangements. The outcome of the constitutional conferences is still unknown, but few would deny their importance in the process of constitutional change. The federal-provincial conference, then, is the 'summit' meeting. It plays a vital role in the adjustment process, and for both public and participants is the focal point of federal-provincial negotiations.

## MINISTERIAL MEETINGS

Meetings of ministers are more frequent than premiers' conferences. In 1965 thirteen such meetings were held,[13] including conferences of ministers of finance and provincial treasurers, ministers of social welfare, ministers of labour and education, ministers of health, and others. Some, like the welfare ministers' and resource ministers' conferences, are regular affairs; others, like the meeting to discuss the Canada Pension Plan in September 1963, are *ad hoc*.

Two ministerial meetings play an important role in financial relations: the Conference of Ministers of Finance and Provincial Treasurers, and the Tax Structure Committee. The first meeting of the finance ministers was held in 1959 and the conference was re-established permanently in 1964. Since then it has been held each November or December. Its chief purpose is to discuss economic and fiscal policies in the light of economic trends, with the object of permitting the various governments to coordinate their fiscal policies. It has met with mixed success.[14] The meeting is chaired by the federal finance minister. Membership overlaps considerably with the premiers' meeting since several provincial premiers are their own provincial treasurers. The conference's main purpose is not to discuss tax-sharing arrangements, but at the 1966 meeting, which occurred soon after the October Federal-Provincial Conference, several provinces tried to reopen the question of tax sharing, but without success. This tendency to turn the meeting into another forum for debate on tax sharing has continued. Generally, the finance ministers' conferences do help to increase the various governments' understanding of the interests and problems of their colleagues, but their success in achieving harmonious fiscal policies depends largely on agreement on more contentious matters.

Closely related to the finance ministers' conference is the Tax Structure Committee, which was established after the Quebec Conference in 1964 'to carry out background studies and prepare proposals for the future financial structure of Canadian Confederation.'[15] We have already seen its role in the 1966 financial negotiations. It was revived, with consider-

13 Gallant, 'The Machinery of Federal-Provincial Relations,' p. 11.

14 For a discussion of the role of the finance ministers' conference, see Robert A. McLarty, 'Organizing for a Federal-Provincial Fiscal Policy,' *Canadian Tax Journal* 15 (1967), esp. pp. 414, 415–16. See also R.M. Burns, 'The Machinery of Federal-Provincial Relations, II,' *Canadian Public Administration* 8 (1965), esp. pp. 17–18.

15 For a description of the terms of reference and historical background of the Tax Structure Committee, see *Federal-Provincial Tax Structure Committee*, 14–15 Sept. 1966 (Ottawa, 1966), pp. 5–6. For a brief description of the projection study, see McLarty, 'Organizing for a Federal-Provincial Fiscal Policy,' pp. 417–18.

ably less enthusiasm, as a committee of the constitutional conference in 1969.

In reality formally separate conferences overlap considerably. This is especially true when the subjects to be discussed have such crucial consequences as financial questions – in such negotiations the premiers will inevitably be involved. The distinction between meetings may easily become blurred. The three separate meetings in October 1966 were in fact one long conference, and the participants sometimes had to remind themselves which one they were actually in at a particular moment. Ministerial meetings are thus an important component of federal-provincial relations. But while they are often held, the Canadian system does not provide for the continuing contact at the ministerial level like that in the Common Market where the Council of Ministers meets two or three times a month.[16]

## OFFICIALS' MEETINGS

By far the greatest number of conferences – about 90 per cent – take place at the official level. Most are concerned with relatively minor technical coordination, but some play a vital role in negotiations on broader policy issues.

The significance of officials' meetings can be illustrated by examining the role played in the financial negotiations by the Continuing Committee on Fiscal and Economic Matters.[17] In 1955, at the suggestion of Ontario Premier Leslie Frost, a preparatory committee of financial advisers was set up to prepare for the negotiations for the 1957–62 financial arrangements. Following the 1955 conference the committee was established permanently as the continuing committee. Its formal membership is the eleven deputy ministers of finance or provincial treasurers, but other senior officials regularly attend. 'In this room,' said an Ontario official, 'we have just about all the people in Canada who know anything about federal-provincial finance.' The committee's formal role is to prepare the way for negotiations at the political level by collecting information and studying technical aspects of policy for presentation to the federal-provincial conference and the members' own governments.[18] It takes no votes,

16 W. Hartley Clark, *The Politics of the Common Market* (Englewood Cliffs, NJ, 1967), p. 17.

17 The most complete study of the continuing committee, written by a participant, is A.R. Kear, 'Cooperative Federalism: A Study of the Federal-Provincial Continuing Committee on Fiscal and Economic Matters,' *Canadian Public Administration* 6 (1963), pp. 43–56.

18 *Ibid.*, p. 50.

has no executive responsibilities, makes no independent decisions, and does not lobby as a group. Between 1956 and 1966 it met thirty-one times.[19] It is most active close to renegotiation of financial agreements: five meetings were held in 1961 (for the 1962–67 agreements) and nine in 1965 and 1966 (before the 1967–72 agreements).

Continuing committee members interact very frequently and know each other personally very well. They also share many of the same professional values, stemming from similar backgrounds and similar jobs. The result is that the committee forms a tight-knit group with an esprit of its own. A few quotations illustrate this sense:

We have developed a kind of ethic. It is rather like a profession. We feel we belong to a group, sometimes more than to a provincial government. I do think it is a useful cement for Confederation. [Quebec official]

There is a sort of esprit among the officials – an esprit about the future of the country and a feeling that we are doing an important task and that we're an important group in keeping the country together. We speak very freely and frankly, if not in formal discussions, then over drinks and in private discussions. There has built up this sense of rapport. [federal official]

The continuing committee is terribly valuable because we have people here with the common professional backgrounds. The politician just does not have the time to have the kind of discussion we do. It facilitates very, very free discussion. It provides great opportunity to view the positions of others very clearly and honestly. [Manitoba official]

Such comments were offered by all those who have attended committee meetings. This sense of community has some important consequences for the negotiations. First, the officials are highly motivated to find agreement, hence minor disagreements can be settled before they fester and burst out at the political level. Second, it facilitates free and easy communication – each government is made fully aware of the positions of others. Said a Quebec official: 'There are no secrets at these meetings.' This communication has meant fewer misunderstandings, and better preparation for the first ministers' conferences. The underbrush is cleared away. Federal officials often brief the provinces on proposals to be presented at later ministerial meetings. The informal discussion also permits wide-ranging discussion far beyond specific technical details about upcoming federal-provincial conferences. This may help to build consensus on future policies and again help to minimize conflict.[20]

19 Sessional Paper 245B.
20 See comments by Leon Lindberg for a similar development with permanent

This does not imply that delegates to the continuing committee have no disagreements. They have a dual loyalty, to the committee and to their own governments, and there can be no doubt which is most important. 'When an official forgets that his full responsibility is to his own government,' said an Ontario official, 'it's time to quit.' Officials of most governments are given much freedom to discuss their government's policy at the meetings, but a few are greatly restricted. In addition, some questions which are purely political have received little attention in the committee.

The influence of the continuing committee is not based on its own decisions. Rather it is dependent on the influence of its individual members within their governments, and on the results of the technical studies which it carries out. It was, for example, the working arm of the Tax Structure Committee, and its members carried out the projection of governmental revenues and expenditures which was to be so important a part of the financial negotiations. They provide much of the information on which strategies in other sites will depend.

The continuing committee is, therefore, an important element in fiscal negotiations. It does not eliminate conflict, but does affect the nature of the negotiations by bringing many of the participants into close and continuing contact, and by improving the flow of information. It lessens misunderstandings, and by providing objective data makes for more objective debate.[21] It is not a 'political' body, but its activity greatly influences how the political adjustment process operates.

The constitutional conference also established a continuing committee of officials to do preparatory work for the first ministers. In 1968 it met four times, usually for two or three days, concentrating mainly on discussing the 'propositions' submitted by the various governments. In 1969 the federal position papers on the taxing and spending powers were first discussed in a continuing committee meeting allowing the federal government to make some modifications and the other governments to formulate their positions before the June Constitutional Conference. However, the constitutional continuing committee does not appear to have developed the closeness of contact and openness of the financial committee. There appear to be several reasons. The committee has not had time to develop

committees within the Common Market system. *The Political Dynamics of European Economic Integration* (Stanford, Calif., 1965), pp. 77–9.

21 It can be argued that perfect information, rather than making agreement easier, makes it more difficult by revealing the real depth of disagreement. See Sawyer and Guetzkow, 'Bargaining and Negotiation in International Relations,' p. 495. Certainly the high degree of information affects strategies and tactics, as we shall see in a later chapter.

strong personal relationships; on the financial committee members have dealt with each other more or less continuously over a long period. There is much more diversity in professional interest and backgrounds within the constitutional committee. Finally, the common suspicion of and lack of interest in the whole constitutional exercise on the part of some premiers was reflected in the behaviour of their officials. 'For many of them, appearing at the meetings was little more than an "acte de présence,"' said one delegate. At least one group of delegates announced they were there simply as 'observers.' Delegations at the fourth meeting in November 1968 ranged in size from twelve (Ottawa) to eight (Ontario) to six (New Brunswick) to one each from Newfoundland, Prince Edward Island, and the four westernmost provinces. As a result, discussions within the constitutional committee have tended to be formal and stilted. There was little flexible discussion of alternatives; rather officials stuck to their governments' stated positions. The committee has played little of the creative role that the financial committee has, for example, in developing the Tax Structure Committee projections. Nevertheless, with growing familiarity and growing interest by the governments, the constitutional committee may become more important, especially as the debate moves further towards discussion of concrete proposals.

## INTERPROVINCIAL CONFERENCES

A potentially important site for bargaining is the interprovincial conference, especially if used to develop coordinated provincial positions, which would then be pressed on Ottawa. In 1960 Premier Lesage urged that interprovincial conferences, which had occasionally been held in the past, be re-established on a continuing basis. The first premiers' conference was held that year in Quebec City.[22] Since then they have been held yearly, usually during the summer. A federal observer attends but takes no part.

Discussion at the conference covers a wide variety of topics of interest to the provincial governments. In 1966, for example, the agenda included twenty-three items, including such matters as regulation of mutual funds and investments, interprovincial competition in incentives to industry, consumer protection legislation, university financing, and uniform legislation for road safety and trucking. Some important legislation – includ-

22 For a discussion of the origin and role of the interprovincial conference, see J.H. Aitchison, 'Interprovincial Co-operation in Canada,' in Aitchison, ed., *The Political Process in Canada: Essays in Honour of R. MacGregor Dawson* (Toronto, 1963), pp. 153–70.

ing regulation of private pension plans and securities legislation – has largely been the product of interprovincial discussions.

But federal-provincial conflicts have until recently received little attention. The statement released after the first conference in 1960 was at pains to stress that the interprovincial conference in no way represented a threat to Ottawa. The premiers agreed to discuss only 'subjects which are purely provincial and interprovincial in their effects and which would in no way impinge on the area of federal-provincial collaboration and action.'[23] Two reasons account for this position: first, the provinces are seldom agreed in their goals; more important is a pervasive norm against provincial 'ganging-up' against Ottawa. This norm finds frequent expression in the press; it is just as strongly held by the participants themselves.

However, the interprovincial conferences are becoming much more important in federal-provincial negotiations. At the 1966 conference the delegates reported a 'frank exchange of views' on equalization, medicare, shared-cost programmes, tax sharing, and other federal-provincial matters. They agreed that high priority should be given to federal assistance in educational financing. Premier Thatcher of Saskatchewan bitterly attacked the new federal equalization proposal and later revealed some of its details. The other premiers discussed the subject briefly but soon dropped it, though Prime Minister Robarts also gave out some details of the equalization formula and attacked the federal medicare proposal. But, significantly, many of the delegates considered Thatcher's statement a violation of the rules of the game. A New Brunswick official called it 'boorish.' Premier Roblin, said a Manitoba official, 'was very annoyed at this break in confidence.' Several respondents suggested that a major reason for the revelation of federal-provincial matters was that reporters covering the conference were more interested in federal-provincial conflict and the approaching financial negotiations than in the more mundane matters the premiers were discussing. The federal government, too, felt the disclosures were a violation of the rules. Mr Pearson said it would be impossible to negotiate if every proposal was made public. 'Surely, this is not the way to conduct negotiations among governments,' he added.[24] But even though there was considerable discussion of the coming negotiations and despite the conference being on the eve of the negotiations 'there was still no "let's take a united front" movement.'[25]

23 Quoted in *ibid.*, p. 155.
24 *Globe and Mail*, 4 Aug. 1966.
25 This is echoed by another observer who for many years participated in federal-provincial negotiations. See R.M. Burns, 'The Machinery of Federal-Provincial Relations,' p. 19.

However, at both the 1967 and 1968 conferences delegates discussed the federal medicare proposal and other federal-provincial issues at length. At the ministerial level, the provincial ministers of education, dissatisfied with the federal manpower programme, met in July 1967 and drew up a joint statement for the federal government. In 1968 the premiers passed resolutions calling on Ottawa to consult the provinces before introducing tax reforms, to reopen financial discussions, and to permit provincial variations in the medicare scheme. Thus the non-federal-provincial character of interprovincial conferences has changed somewhat. Because of the 'anti-ganging-up rule,' Robarts said at the Confederation of Tomorrow Conference, 'we have, to some extent at least, not developed to the full, the potential that that ... Conference has.' The validity of the rule had 'long since gone.'[26] However, reservations about such use of the interprovincial conferences remain and it is likely provinces will use it to develop coordinated positions only on those federal-provincial matters where the provincial oxes have all been equally gored, and when feelings, as in 1968, are running high.

In addition to formal interprovincial conferences, the provinces may cooperate in other ways. For example, the three prairie premiers have taken joint positions on several issues. So have the premiers of the Atlantic provinces. Officials of various governments, especially Ontario and Quebec, often discuss their respective positions with each other both before and at federal-provincial conferences. Again, however, there is little evidence that such meetings have led to coordinated joint provincial positions.

Interprovincial conferences, then, are potentially important sites for negotiation, but far less important than federal-provincial conferences themselves.

## TOWARDS AN INTERGOVERNMENTAL BUREAUCRACY: THE CONSTITUTIONAL SECRETARIAT

Participants in the federal-provincial negotiating process have traditionally been suspicious of creating a 'third level' of federal-provincial machinery, such as an independent secretariat or clearing house. Such bodies – like the Common Market's Commission and its body of Eurocrats committed not to their own governments but to the process of European integration itself – can play a major role in proposing policy initiatives, suggesting compromises, and the like. But in the Canadian context it has been feared that they would unnecessarily complicate the process and would infringe

26 Confederation of Tomorrow Conference, *Proceedings* (Toronto, 1967), pp. 182–3.

on the freedom of action of the various governments. A separate bureaucracy would not be directly accountable to any electorate and there would be problems of how to oversee and finance it.

Several small steps in the direction of establishing independent secretariats have been made. The Council of Resource Ministers (really an association more than a federal-provincial body) has its own secretariat, as does the Council of Education Ministers. The Tax Structure Committee had a small secretariat to assist in the projection exercise. In February 1968 the Constitutional Conference moved another large step by establishing a secretariat to serve the conference and the continuing committee of officials.[27] It too is a limited body, dealing with only one subject area, and with a small staff. But some of its members suggest it may be the nucleus for a permanent federal-provincial body serving all eleven governments.

The secretariat's role is still in the process of evolution. Its basic jobs are administrative – arranging meetings, providing background papers, translation services, secretarial help, and preparing summaries of the various meetings. It coordinates communications among the various committees and helps to provide documentation. In addition, it can carry out some special assignments – such as collating and summarizing the various constitutional propositions submitted by the governments. So far its work has not gone much beyond these basic secretarial functions.

The secretariat has been more cautious in moving towards other roles, but its members suggest it has a potentially central position in intergovernmental affairs. For example, it could engage in independent research projects. Here the danger is that research is seldom neutral; any conclusions would likely favour the positions of some governments over others. 'And the Secretariat is and must be seen as the servant of all governments.'[28] Another still largely potential function is to serve as 'a source of communication and interpretation to facilitate the development of understanding between governments.'[29] If its members have well-established contacts within all governments, and are trusted by them, it can exchange information about policies and attitudes, help to prevent misunderstandings, and encourage governments to take into account others' points of view when formulating their positions. It could be an 'honest broker.' The secretariat has also seen its role as helping to stimulate interest and activity in the constitutional review, to act as 'an inspirer, a catalyst.' Particularly for

27 Material for this section is drawn from Edgar Gallant, speech to Toronto Chapter of the Institute of Public Administration of Canada, 22 Jan. 1969, and from interviews.
28 Gallant, *ibid.*, p. 17.
29 *Ibid.*

the smaller provinces with few resources and little expertise of their own, the secretariat may provide information and assistance so they have to rely less on initiatives from the federal government. The secretariat could also play a larger part in the preparation of conference agenda, and perhaps even in chairing meetings at the official level, although, as one secretariat official put it, 'it is illusory to believe the federal government will abandon its primacy in these matters.' But these functions are still largely potential. In its first years the secretariat moved cautiously to avoid building up resentments and suspicion. It concentrated on building confidence in its probity and impartiality. In this it has been successful. 'We've had no complaints about our objectivity,' said one official; 'in fact we have have had a number of compliments.'

In organizing the secretariat several governments insisted on safeguards to ensure that it would be truly a servant of eleven governments, not one. But in fact the secretariat remains largely staffed and funded by the federal government. The original initiative for establishing the body came from Quebec and Ontario: they and Ottawa had informally agreed on its basic set-up before the first Constitutional Conference. The federal government appointed the original secretary, Edgar Gallant, an official with a long experience in federal-provincial relations, who was welcomed by the provinces. Gallant appointed a staff, primarily from among federal officials. Even while on the secretariat they are still technically federal employees. The secretariat was removed physically from the Privy Council Office, and attempts have been made to ensure it is effectively independent. Provision was made for provinces to second staff to the secretariat, but Ontario is the only province to have done so, and then in little more than token fashion. 'In principle we would be staffed by people seconded from the governments,' said a secretariat member, 'but in practice the provinces really cannot spare them, especially the people who are experienced enough to come here.' Similarly, despite some discussion about methods of financing the secretariat, the funds come not from all governments but from Ottawa. Again, only Ontario has made a token payment of $10,000 a year. This very limited provincial participation is only partly a matter of available resources: it also appears to indicate a general lack of interest in developing a strong independent secretariat, as well, perhaps, as some trust in the determination of the federal government not to use the secretariat for its own purposes. Some suspicions arose when in May 1969 Ottawa promoted Gallant to an important planning post in the Privy Council Office and proposed a federal diplomat with little experience in domestic federal-provincial diplomacy to replace him. However, the appointment was quickly ratified at the June Federal-Provincial Conference and the new secretary appears to have built up the confidence of provincial governments.

The secretariat, then, is something of an experiment in intergovernmental relations. It is a first, small, tentative step towards the creation of an independent federal-provincial bureaucracy serving all governments, and towards greater institutionalization of the negotiating process. Whether it serves as a model for other areas and whether it expands its role greatly beyond the purely secretarial, depends greatly on its initial success and perhaps on the outcome of the constitutional debate itself.

### OTHER SITES

Not all the bargaining is face-to-face and explicit. All the parties take positions in their own legislatures, in speeches, and so on which affect their bargaining position and which are designed to influence others. In addition, governments frequently correspond by letter, telegram, and telephone. Between June 1963 and May 1964 about sixty letters referring to the pension plan were exchanged. Most were from premier to prime minister, or vice versa.[30]

### BILATERAL NEGOTIATIONS

When Quebec and Ottawa negotiated a solution to the pension impasse after the Quebec Conference, the other provinces were left out. Similarly, discussion of Quebec's opting-out proposals went a long way before the other provinces were brought in. In 1966 Finance Minister Sharp and Premier Thatcher of Saskatchewan met alone and worked out a compromise saving Saskatchewan from having its equalization grant totally cut off under the new formula. Provincial and federal officials often discuss matters of particular interest to their governments, without involving the other provinces. Bilateral diplomacy is a common feature of federal-provincial relations.

But it is limited. Provinces are deeply concerned that they be involved. Thus, there was some resentment about the bilateral Quebec-Ottawa negotiations in April 1964 – but since the outcome benefited everyone, it did not go far. In the opting-out negotiations, the other provinces insisted on being present. An Ontario official said: 'We did share some of the resentment at special relations between Quebec and Ottawa. This feeling was running quite high in the later years of the Lesage period. We thought

30 The correspondence was tabled in Parliament in a series of sessional papers in response to members' questions. See Sessional Papers 216A, 216B, 202, 202A, 202C, 202H, 202J, all in 1964.

too many things were being decided just between those two.' A New Brunswick official said: 'We resent that kind of negotiation [on opting-out]. Although we weren't involved, everyone went. It was really pretty funny. The federal government was on one side and Quebec was on the other, and the rest of us were just sitting there, like in a jury box.' The incident demonstrates that bilateral negotiations, while common, are often resented, and that it is difficult for any government to negotiate alone with the federal government without the nine others becoming concerned except on a purely local issue. It also shows that the other provinces are reluctant to permit 'special status' for Quebec to result in a secondary status for them.

## CONFERENCE DIPLOMACY

The focal point of federal-provincial negotiation is the federal-provincial conference. The conferences provide the chief arena within which executives of the eleven governments deal with each other. As more and more important national policies become matters for federal-provincial concern, so the federal-provincial conference has become a more and more crucial element in the Canadian federal system. Despite its importance, the position of the conferences remains fluid. They have no legislative sanction, have few formal rules or procedures, and, most important, have little institutional life of their own. They are gatherings of the executives of the eleven governments, and are dependent on the decisions and goals of these executives for their continued existence. There is no body of officials, like the Commission of the European Common Market, which has an existence separate from that of the participant governments themselves. No 'federal-provincialcrats' correspond to the Common Market's 'Eurocrats.' Nor is there a central federal-provincial bureaucracy yet established. While, especially at the official level, participants may share many common interests,[31] they are more analogous to ambassadors than to members of a single unit.

The lack of an independent institutional character means that the federal-provincial decision-making machinery is far less extensive and less institutionalized than that of the European Economic Community, despite the high degree of interdependence. Federal-provincial coordinating machinery is heavily dependent on the attitudes of the participating

31 For an excellent description of the sharing of common interests (occasionally in opposition to their respective political heads) by officials in certain departments with similar programme and professional interests, see D.V. Smiley, 'Public Administration and Canadian Federalism,' *Canadian Public Administration* 7 (1964), pp. 377–80.

governments. The system is fragile. It operates differently from issue to issue and the machinery of collaboration is far more elaborate in some fields than others.[32] New machinery and procedures were easily created when constitutional discussions began. There is thus a proliferation of federal-provincial bodies but no really coherent 'system' of federal-provincial consultation, despite the many calls for one.[33] Part of the reason seems to be that, in a continually changing federation, few governments are willing to institutionalize a system which may limit their own freedom to bargain or give formal recognition to a status they would not accept.[34] It does appear to have been easier to develop cooperative machinery in the less 'political' areas like welfare administration than in the more contentious areas like tax sharing.[35] Competitive governments, jealous of each other's authority, are unlikely to be able to agree easily on the rules and procedures for their negotiations. Appeals for better machinery often assume coordination is a technical-administrative process, not a political one.

Another characteristic of federal-provincial bargaining machinery is its centralization. Meetings take place at all levels of the government services, but policy questions defined as important are dealt with primarily at the top political level. This stems from the high degree of centralization within governments themselves and from the desire of premiers and prime ministers to retain their own authority. It has the effect of channelling and focusing disagreements to the senior level instead of diffusing it through the system. It may make for easier resolution of conflicts because the political heads can make firm commitments of their own governments, but it may also mean that conflicts become much more sharply defined and therefore more intractable. American bureaucrats operating federal-state programmes try to keep their respective political heads out of things. Their Canadian counterparts have not been able to do so.

The machinery also limits the participation of interest groups in the bargaining process. Affected groups are not invited to participate or make their views known. The relative secrecy of debate means group leaders may often be unaware of developments in federal-provincial negotiations which might involve them. To the extent that the mechanisms we have

32 R.M. Burns, 'Cooperation in Government,' *Canadian Tax Journal* 8 (1959), p. 7.

33 Veilleux, 'The Machinery for Intergovernmental Cooperation,' pp. 37, 44.

34 In this connection it is interesting to note that most proposals for more extensive machinery in fiscal matters have come from the provinces, which, presumably, have had most to gain. See R.M. Burns, *Intergovernmental Liaison on Fiscal and Economic Matters* (Ottawa, 1969), pp. 32, 35–9.

35 *Ibid.*, pp. 45–56.

described become a central arena for policy formation and form the major preoccupation for both federal and provincial policy-makers, the process thus limits the number and scope of participants in policy-making.

Canadian observers from the authors of the Rowell-Sirois Report[36] to the present have frequently lamented the lack of formal procedures for coordination, and have advanced a number of suggestions for improved machinery. But it seems clear that the smooth operation of the decision process depends more on the attitudes and perspectives of the participants than on the existence of formal machinery. It may also be argued that the existing fluid sites for negotiation, centred in the federal-provincial conference, provide a flexible forum for accommodation in a system which is continuing to undergo major changes. It remains to be seen whether a much more extensive and integrated intergovernment machinery will emerge from the constitutional discussions.

36 Royal Commission on Dominion-Provincial Relations, *Report* (Ottawa, 1941). This report, generally known as the Rowell-Sirois Report, was a product of the royal commission enquiry into problems of federalism in Canada brought about by the depression crisis. It remains one of the most important studies of Canadian federalism.

CHAPTER SEVEN

# The issues

Pensions, dollars, and the constitution represent just three of many issues that have arisen for negotiation in the federal-provincial arena in recent years. We have already touched on a few of these. Others include the development of a comprehensive welfare programme (the Canada Assistance Plan), comprehensive medical insurance, and even some foreign policy questions. Why do such issues arise? What do they have in common? What are the stakes and how are they defined? Along what dimensions do the issues vary, and what consequences do these variations have for the operation of the negotiations and for the results? In this chapter I shall examine some of these questions.

While it is true that many issues facing the Canadian political system become grist for the federal-provincial mill, it is also true that many issues are raised and resolved without becoming involved in intergovernmental negotiations. This prompts the question of what kinds of issues do become 'federal-provincial'? As the examples have shown, the range is a wide one. Pensions, hospital insurance, and medicare are all social welfare issues and this category is perhaps the most important, both in numbers and in significance for Canadian citizens. The most obvious explanation for the raising of such issues lies in the imbalance between the constitutional allocation of responsibilities and resources on the one hand, and the demands and problems facing the system on the other. The provincial governments, constitutionally responsible for most such social concerns, have lacked the finances to develop the desired programmes alone. As a result such problems have often been defined as 'national problems' and demands have been made to the national level for their resolution. But because provincial governments have been unwilling to give up their own positions in these fields, and because of the inflexibility of constitutional amending procedures,[1] these tasks have not often been transferred to the central government; rather, they have remained shared. The imbalance between responsibilities and resources is of course also at the root of the fiscal problem. Since governmental activities are always changing it is well-nigh impossible for a 'final' solution to be developed. Thus the question has bedevilled federal-provincial relations ever since Confederation in 1867, despite the optimistic claim in the British North America Act itself that its financial provisions were 'in full settlement of all future demands on Canada.'[2] Subsequent 'final' settlements have been just as short-lived.[3]

Economic and fiscal questions also frequently arise. One reason is that in such a regional economy, federal fiscal and monetary policies have important, varying, and easily visible effects on the different regions. Hence the provinces have an interest in ensuring that federal policies take regional needs into account. In addition, partly because of the failure of federal regional development policies to do so, the provinces themselves have become deeply involved in their own regional economic development programmes, which have obvious implications for national economic policy.[4] Finally, the provinces have come to control a greater proportion of total governmental expenditure, and have come to control a greater

1 Canadians have not been able to agree on procedures for amending the British North America Act, which is a statute of the British Parliament. Formally, most amendments require an address to the Queen from both houses of the Canadian Parliament, but informally it is agreed that for most amendments some form of provincial government approval is required. A 1949 BNA Act amendment did permit the Parliament of Canada to make some constitutional changes without reference to Westminster. The debate has revolved around when provincial approval should be required, and what forms of majorities are needed for different types of amendment, such as those affecting only the federal government, those affecting the distribution of powers, and the like. For further reading on the problem, see sources given in n. 69, chap. 2.

2 R. MacGregor Dawson, *The Government of Canada,* revised by Norman Ward (5th ed., Toronto, 1970), p. 100.

3 The most complete summary of federal-provincial financial arrangements is found in A. Milton Moore, J. Harvey Perry, and Donald I. Beach, *The Financing of Canadian Federation: The First Hundred Years* (Toronto, 1966). See also A.H. Birch, *Federalism, Finance and Social Legislation* (Oxford, 1955), chap. 3.

4 For a discussion of this problem, see Jacques Parizeau, 'Prospects for Economic Policy in a Federal Canada,' in P.-A. Crépeau and C.B. Macpherson, eds., *The Future of Canadian Federalism/L'avenir du fédéralisme canadien* (Toronto, 1965), pp. 52–4.

share of the major taxes (notably income taxes) used by governments in the management and regulation of the economy. Thus the fiscal impact of the provinces has made both levels recognize the importance of some coordination if effective economic management is to take place. In 1947 federal expenditures as a per cent of Gross National Product was 15.6 and together the provincial and municipal governments spent an amount equal to 10.3 per cent of GNP. By 1960 the shares were nearly equal: 18.4 per cent of GNP for Ottawa and 17.3 per cent for the provincial-municipal sector. By 1966, however, the figures were reversed: Ottawa expended only 16.6 per cent of GNP, while the provinces and municipalities together spent 21.3 per cent.[5] Similarly, in the 1962 tax year the provincial share of personal income taxes collected was 16 per cent, but by 1966 it was an estimated 33.5 per cent, excluding taxes earmarked for social security. (Table III shows the estimated division of total personal income tax revenue between the provinces and the federal government in 1962 and 1966.) By contrast, in the United States state income taxes represented only about 6 per cent of the total income taxes collected.[6] Thus, quite apart from the immediate financial question of how the total revenue pie should be divided among governments, economic policy becomes a shared field.

A third group of issues arises primarily because of lack of consensus concerning some of the basic structural characteristics of the system. When large groups come to feel that the existing system works to their disadvantage, or that they cannot satisfy their aspirations within it, then there will be demands for change. This is at the root of recent demands by the Quebec government as the political expression of the French-Canadian subculture. The demands involve basic questions about the nature of Canadian sovereignty and the relative roles of the various governments. And because constitutional arrangements are to a large degree the legal expression of the relations between governments, such demands are a major reason why the nature of the constitution itself has become a subject for negotiation.

Constitutional issues are also much more likely to emerge when the existing constitution lacks the sanctity and legitimacy possessed by such long-lived constitutions as the American one. A striking feature of the recent debate on the constitution has been the extremely pragmatic approach taken by officials at all levels. The British North America Act

5 Calculated from the Canadian Tax Foundation, *The National Finances: 1967–1968* (Toronto, 1967), Table 12, p. 8.

6 Advisory Commission on Intergovernmental Relations, *Federal-State Coordination of Personal Income Taxes* (Washington, 1965), Table 10, p. 62.

TABLE III

Share of total personal income taxes, 1962 and 1966

| | 1962 | 1966 |
|---|---|---|
| | (per cent of total) | |
| Federal share | 83.62 | 66.48 |
| Provincial share | 15.93 | 26.33 |
| PLUS: | | |
| Quebec, abatement for opting-out | | 6.68 |
| Manitoba, surtax above abatement | .26 | .26 |
| Saskatchewan, surtax | .20 | .24 |
| Total provincial | 16.39 | 33.51 |

SOURCE: Marion Bryden, *Occupancy of Tax Fields in Canada* (Toronto, 1965), Table 5, p. 20.

lacks any mystique; no participants have felt moved to make ringing appeals to its glories. As a result, while in a country like the United States the constitution itself, because of its prior legitimacy, may foreclose some subjects from conflict, the opposite is true in Canada. Not only do these conflicts emerge, but also they frequently call into question the constitution itself.

Federalism is one way in which many societies, including Canada, have tried to reduce conflict between different subcultures. But the logic of this solution is one of disengagement, permitting each group to make its own majority decisions without involving the other. But when (as in the conscription crises of both world wars)[7] the goals of the majority group imply demands or claims on the minority, or when the aspirations of the minority imply claims on the majority (as in the recent Canadian crises of the sixties), the federal solution works less well, and conflicts will inevitably arise. Because the Quebec government is the chief political instrument of the French Canadians, these become federal-provincial issues, and an important way of dealing with them is the negotiation process.

A final reason why issues arise in the federal-provincial arena is that constitutional rules may be ambiguous or non-existent. This arises partly because constitutional planners of an earlier day did not anticipate recent problems, and partly because divergent lines of interpretation have grown up. Is the constitution what the original document said, or what judicial bodies have said it is? When the two differ as much as they do in the

7 See Mason Wade, *The French-Canadians, 1760–1945* (Toronto, 1955), p. 734, for a discussion of the First World War crisis, and R. MacGregor Dawson, *The Conscription Crisis of 1944* (Toronto, 1961), passim.

Canadian case there is rich ground for disputes. The recent argument about control of offshore mineral rights is a good example.

Thus there appear to be several basic reasons why issues arise in federal-provincial relations, the most basic being the interdependence of governments and the lack of correspondence between the incidence of substantive policy questions and the more procedural lines drawn by constitutions. In general they stem from an interplay between rigidities and inflexibility in the constitutional arrangements, the problems facing the system, and the demands and goals of the various élites, particularly those of the leaders of the federal and provincial governments. When the constitutional allocation of both responsibility and the requisite resources is clear, when the respective government leaders feel this allocation is legitimate, when social problems do not cut across constitutional categories, and when the actions taken by the governments do not have spill-over effects to the other governments which are perceived as important by their leaders, issues will not arise for negotiation. But when these conditions are not met, they will. In spite of desires to 'simplify the system through constitutional change,' it seems clear that some overlapping is inevitable and that 'water-tight compartments' will always leak.

This raises the question of who initiates issues? It is often difficult to pinpoint the origin of an issue. Pensions had been debated in the federal Parliament as early as 1907.[8] More recently, many groups such as the Canadian Labour Congress (CLC) had advocated improvement of the existing social security system. Conservative leader John Diefenbaker made a major issue of pensions in the 1957 federal election. At its founding convention in 1961 the New Democratic Party urged raising the Old Age Security pension to $75, payable at age sixty-five, and called for an additional wage-related contributory pension plan.[9] In 1960 Ontario had established a six-member Ontario Committee on Portable Pensions,[10] which was most concerned with protecting the rights of workers participating in private pension plans, and with making it possible for workers to keep their pension benefits when changing jobs. Based on the committee's work, the Ontario Pension Benefits Act was passed in the spring of 1963. It seems clear that this Ontario initiative, together with the other demands for improved pensions, helped to stimulate the federal Liberal government to formulate and initiate its 1963 pension

8 Birch, *Federalism, Finance and Social Legislation*, provides the best description of the development of social legislation in Canada up to the 1950s.

9 Robert Gordon, 'The Canada Pension Plan,' Ottawa, 1964, p. 1; and New Democratic Party, *The Federal Programme of the New Democratic Party* (3rd ed., Ottawa, 1967), pp. 14, 44, 67.

10 See Ontario Committee on Portable Pensions, *Second Report* (Toronto, 1961).

proposal. Resolutions calling for a contributory pension plan had been passed at Liberal party meetings in 1958 and 1961, and the proposal became part of the Liberal election platform in 1962. It was an even more important plank in the 1963 campaign. Liberal strategists saw it as a potent vote-getter, which, being financed by contributions, would not require a tax increase. Thus while the immediate proposal for negotiation, the Canada Pension Plan, was initiated by Ottawa, it had roots in other arenas. Similarly, there had been widespread demands for an increase in federal aid to education, but the immediate formulation of the issue in the federal-provincial context was done by Ottawa.

In these two cases Ottawa was the chief initiator of proposals for federal-provincial discussion, and the same is true for a large number of important national policies developed since the war. The provinces, however, have also been frequent initiators. Most striking has been the example of Quebec with its demands for fundamental changes in the federal system. Constitutional negotiations such as the attempts to develop an amending formula are not new. But without Quebec's dissatisfaction with the federal system it seems certain the present full-scale review would never have come about. Saskatchewan, which developed a comprehensive compulsory government-operated medical care scheme, can be viewed as the real initiator of the later federal proposal for a shared-cost programme to achieve the same goal on a national scale. But in general provincial initiatives appear to be less concerned with national policies and more concerned with matters of particular regional or provincial interest. These may be important issues, but they do not concern us greatly here.

Who initiates the issue has some important consequences for the operation of the negotiating process. The initiator has substantial control over the timing of the debate and in determining the agenda. In formulating the issue he also has a great deal to do with defining how the issue will be perceived, and what will be regarded as the stakes. In many ways once the issue is defined then the range of possible outcomes is also defined. Other participants in the process must react to the proposal as put forward by the initiator. Hence the initiator has an immediate advantage in the negotiations, though the longer the discussions are drawn out the less advantage he has.

Another crucial question about the issue is: what is at stake? Different issues will have different meanings to different people. Therefore it is impossible for the observer to stand outside the process and decide what the stakes are; they depend on the interests and perceptions of the participants themselves. How the stakes are defined, moreover, may have important consequences for the ways they are negotiated. An example is provided by the pension plan. The interests of many of the provinces were primarily in what implications the plan would have for their own financial positions. Several provinces, like Manitoba, Saskatchewan, and New Brunswick, designated officials from treasury departments rather than from, say, welfare departments to carry out most of the work on pensions. These groups were much less concerned about the details of actual provisions of the pension plan; they looked at the legislation not as pension or welfare experts but as government finance experts. This meant that in the federal-provincial negotiations there was relatively little attention paid to many important aspects of the plan, and more paid to such matters as disposition of the fund, which was largely irrelevant to the goodness or badness of the plan from the point of view of the contributor. Similarly, the question of federal aid to education in 1966 became defined primarily as a financial issue. The discussion revolved not around how to develop educational policy, but around the amount of money Ottawa would give the provinces to help pay the costs of higher education.

The governments differed greatly in the conceptions of the nature and seriousness of the stakes involved in the constitution. Their differing definitions help to account for differences in their interest and level of participation. For Ottawa, the stakes are national unity and the authority of the federal government; for Quebec the achievement of distinct national goals. For both the stakes are very high. But many English-speaking provinces were not convinced that the crisis in Confederation was as great as Ottawa or Quebec felt – hence their lack of participation and willingness to introduce other issues into the debates. The federal and Quebec governments, with an assist from Ontario and New Brunswick, spent considerable effort in trying to encourage other governments to perceive what was involved and to take the matter seriously.

In addition, an issue may be regarded as having two levels of interest. First is what might be called the manifest stakes, the particular immediate policy questions to be decided. Second, a given policy may become a symbol or a surrogate for other broader issues. Thus in the pension plan the manifest stakes revolved primarily around questions about what sort of a pension plan would there be, if indeed there was to be one. Who would be covered; what would the benefits be; how would the plan be financed; would there be a single federal plan or several plans; how would the plan be integrated with the existing public and private pension system; and so on? Within these questions were a host of others, even more detailed. Only a few of these actually got discussed at great length.

On such a complex issue the participants must simplify their calculations and one way to do so is to take the proposal as initiated and concentrate the discussion only on the most obvious important points of difference.

Many of these points of difference had to do more with the broader underlying stakes than with the manifest ones. Thus, for conservatives, like many of the Ontario advisers, the real issue was one of conservatism versus the welfare state. For Quebec, the province's economic development was one of the broader stakes. More important, for Quebec it was a case of provincial autonomy versus federal interference, and a test of 'special status' for the province.

Similarly, on the financial issue the immediate manifest stakes included three main questions: tax-sharing, equalization, and shared-cost programmes.[11] In the first, the question revolves primarily around how revenue sources will be divided among the governments. Both levels of government jointly occupy or share most major fields of taxation, but the main question concerns the most lucrative and elastic of these – personal and corporate income taxes. Since the beginning of the 1957–62 tax-sharing arrangements, Ottawa had 'abated' or reduced its own income taxes to allow the provinces to impose their own painlessly, with Ottawa offering to remain the collection agent.[12] By 1966 the question really was how many more points would Ottawa turn over. Equalization – to what degree will Ottawa act as a transfer agent to provide special assistance to the poorer provinces so they can provide a level of services roughly comparable to that of the other provinces without having to impose abnormally high taxation[13] – was also a well-established programme by 1966. The manifest question, then, was how equalization would be extended or improved? What revenue sources would be included in the calculation of provincial fiscal capacity,[14] how much would the total equalization amount to, would provinces be equalized to the level of the top two provinces or the national average, and so on? The third question

11 For an excellent summary of the main issues, see Tom K. Skoyama, 'The New Federal-Provincial Fiscal Arrangements,' paper presented to the Ottawa Chapter, Canadian Political Science Association, 22 Nov. 1966, passim.

12 See Moore, Perry, and Beach, *The Financing of Canadian Federation*, for discussion of recent arrangements.

13 For a good statement of the basic problem and some of the theoretical questions associated with it, see J.F. Graham, A.W. Johnson, and J.M. Andrews, *Intergovernmental Fiscal Relationships* (Toronto, 1964), pp. 3–31. See also James H. Lynn, *Federal-Provincial Fiscal Relations*, studies of the Royal Commission on Taxation no 23 (Ottawa, 1967), pp. 4–8, 23–33.

14 For an analysis of this problem, see J.H. Lynn, *Comparing Provincial Revenue Yields: The Tax Indicator Approach* (Toronto, 1968).

was less important. Shared-cost programmes have been a vital element in Canadian federalism[15] and most of the major programmes making up the welfare state in Canada have been developed through the shared-cost device. But there had been many criticisms of them for skewing provincial priorities, for administrative duplication and complexity,[16] and so on. These criticisms came to a head with Quebec's demands to be able to refuse to participate in such programmes and to receive full compensation in unconditional grants or abatements instead. This meant a rethinking of the whole role of shared-cost programmes which was evident in the 1966 federal position.

As with pensions these issues involved many broader questions. As federal control over the major taxes decreases, the whole question of how governments can manage the economy through monetary and fiscal tools becomes involved.[17] More important, the division of financial resources is a basic factor in determining the relative importance and impact of the various governments. Control of finances is a prerequisite to the formulation and execution of policies. Therefore the sharing of resources is also intimately, if indirectly, linked to the kinds of policies which get made, since the different governments have different constitutional responsibilities, goals, and perspectives. Thus, a basic underlying issue is the deciding of overall national priorities. Both what will get done and who will do it are involved. Finally, to the extent that electoral success depends on the ability to produce and market policies, then even the electoral positions of the governments are at stake. The pension plan also involved some of these broader issues about the relative importance and status of the governments.

Even more clearly the manifest stakes of the constitutional issue – would there be an entrenched bill of rights, would the Senate and Supreme Court be changed, how could coordinating machinery be improved – fundamentally involved far more basic issues such as national unity, ethnic relations, and the status of governments. The participants were extremely conscious of these broader questions.

These underlying issues can have important consequences for the degree of conflict and for the operation of the process. Thus, if it is defined as one which involves very basic values, on which the participants

15 Federal contributions through shared-cost programmes amounted to over $1 billion in 1965–6. For a list of such programmes, see Moore, Perry, and Beach, *The Financing of Canadian Federalism*, appendix A.

16 The best general discussion is found in Donald V. Smiley, *Conditional Grants and Canadian Federalism* (Toronto, 1963), esp. chap. 4.

17 See Jacques Parizeau, 'Federal-Provincial Fiscal Developments,' Eighteenth Tax Conference, *Proceedings* (Toronto, 1965), pp. 222–30.

feel they cannot easily compromise, then conflict should be greater and resolution more difficult. But whether the issue does come to be defined as one involving basic underlying concerns depends only partly on the objective nature of the issues (what do pensions on the surface have to do with provincial autonomy?). More important are the perspectives and attitudes of the élites who must deal with the issue. In many cases the stakes become clear only as the negotiation develops.

Charles Lindblom suggests that decision-makers who disagree on fundamentals can still often find agreement on lesser issues, even if they agree, so to speak, for quite different reasons.[18] Whether in fact this happens depends on the decision-makers' perceptions. The converse may indeed be the case: disagreement on fundamentals or a general atmosphere of distrust may prevent agreement even when on the smaller issue there are no obvious differences in goals.

The definition of the nature of the issue and of the stakes involved is a crucial element in the decision process. A great deal of the discussion and negotiation in fact revolves around these questions. If an actor can get others to accept his definition of the situation he is well on the way to getting him to agree with his solution. On all three issues the discussion focused heavily on such matters. As Raymond A. Bauer points out, 'a key skill of leadership is that of formulating policy so that a winning coalition can be mobilized behind it.' It also involves 'spelling out to the potential members of the ... coalition the ways in which the policies will serve their interests.'[19]

Another way in which issues can vary is in the degree of involvement of what we have called audience groups. The pension case provoked widespread public debate. Many pressure groups were deeply involved and Parliament played a significant role, at least if measured by the time spent discussing the issue. On the financial question, by contrast, there was perfunctory parliamentary consideration and very few interest groups were active. The reason is that the pension issue had direct and immediate consequences for all citizens. They would be paying a new payroll deduction and all would eventually benefit from the plan. Many interest groups were directly affected, especially those which at the time provided private pension plans for individuals and firms. Trusteed plans operated either by individuals or trust companies covered one million employees in 1961. Contributions totalled $436 million and assets were over $4

18 *The Intelligence of Democracy: Decision-making through Mutual Adjustment* (New York, 1965), chap. 14.

19 'The Study of Policy Formation: An Introduction,' in Bauer and Kenneth J. Gergen, eds., *The Study of Policy Formation* (New York, 1968), p. 16.

billion. Group annuities provided by insurance companies covered another half million employees.[20] Thus a large and lucrative business field was directly threatened by a government move into pensions. In addition, pension funds provided a good part of the flow of investment capital in Canada – about 20 per cent of the new capital raised annually, according to one pension company executive.[21] The financial issue had none of this immediate impact. The policy consequences of shifts in revenue were difficult to assess or predict both for individuals and groups; the outcome would have no immediate effect on the voters' pocketbooks. This difference meant the course of the deliberations would be different. Pensions were debated widely outside the federal-provincial arena; finances were not. In finances, third parties had very little role to play; they did in the pension issue. This suggests that different tactics would be called for, and that in the financial case the federal and provincial governments would operate with fewer constraints. But even in the pension case, the governmental participants were remarkably successful in defining the issues in terms important to them, rather than in the terms used by such groups as insurance companies.

Given its long-term importance and the centrality of constitutions in federal systems, one would expect the constitutional issue to have involved a high degree of public interest. In Quebec, to some extent it did. But the overwhelming impression is that in English Canada the discussion provoked extraordinarily little public or group involvement. The televized constitutional conferences in 1968 and 1969 did receive much attention, but it appears to have been transitory. Some aspects of the discussion – like language rights, especially in the west – provoked wide concern. But these seem to be exceptions. This is not surprising. Outside Quebec there was little apparent dissatisfaction with the constitutional status quo. The discussion itself has tended to be remote, abstract, and legalistic. The implications of proposed changes are often unclear. The relevance of the debate to particular individuals or groups, or for substantive issues like pollution or housing, are at best obscure. And despite the televising of the conferences the participants in the exercise themselves have made few efforts to stimulate public interest, enlarge the scope of participants in the constitutional review, or discuss matters which go beyond the institutional concerns of governments themselves. They have been unsympa-

20 W. Leonard McBridge, 'The Growth and Coverage of Insured and Trusteed Pension Plans in Canada,' in Laurence Coward, ed., *Pensions in Canada: A Compendium of Fact and Opinion* (Don Mills, Ont., 1964), esp. tables, pp. 143–4.

21 Graham Towers, address to 117th annual meeting of the Canada Life Assurance Company, 30 Jan. 1964, p. 8.

thetic to the few attempts – by the Canadian Federation of Mayors and Municipalities, for example – to attain wider participation.

Another characteristic of the issues with implications for the operation of the process is the extent to which they are new issues, facing the system for the first time, or old, recurring issues. Pensions, to be sure, had faced the Canadian political system several times before. In 1927 the Old Age Assistance Act – the first federal-provincial venture into the welfare field[22] – was passed. Then, at the end of the war, Ottawa unveiled, as part of a wider programme, a proposal for the federal government to take full responsibility for providing pensions to those over seventy and to assist provinces in providing pensions[22] for the needy between sixty-five and seventy. Eventually, the federal Old Age Security programme providing flat-rate pensions for those over seventy was established.

But federal-provincial discussions on pensions before 1963 had been sporadic. Pensions had last been extensively discussed in the federal-provincial context in the negotiations prior to passage of the 1951 amendment to the British North America Act which made the federal OAS programme possible. A wage-related contributory plan was a new proposal.[23]

By contrast, finances are a familiar issue. Since the Second World War a pattern of five-year financial agreements between the federal and provincial governments has been developed, with occasional renegotiations during those periods, as we saw in 1963. The agreements have been the vehicle for a progressive fiscal decentralization, seen in both the increasing provincial revenue share and in the weakening of federal control over tax rates and bases. The issues are thus familiar ones. The arguments have all been made before and positions are well established. Precedent plays an important role. Rules and procedures have been well defined. These differences between the two issues greatly affected how they were negotiated. Thus, on the pension plan much time was spent exchanging basic information and defining what the stakes really were. In finances this is not as necessary. Governments will have more internal resources of personnel, expertise, and experience when dealing with a familiar and recurring issue than with a new and unfamiliar one. All governments are likely to have much better defined goals when they have evolved over a long period. Tactics are likely to differ as well, since, for example, it is harder to bluff and dissemble when you have debated the same issue before than when it is being discussed for the first time. Officials will have

22 Smiley, *Conditional Grants and Canadian Federalism*, p. 2.

23 The Conservative government of John Diefenbaker had informally polled the provinces about their willingness to consent to the constitutional amendment necessary if Ottawa was to develop a plan with supplementary benefits for widows and orphans, but nothing came of it.

dealt with each other before. Finally, on a recurring issue we should expect the possible outcomes to be much more circumscribed than on a new one. It is more likely that outcomes will simply be marginal incremental adjustments to on-going programmes. Rather than an issue like finances being viewed anew each time it comes up, the pattern should be more like that of United States government agencies when they go to Congress for their appropriations: the existing situation is taken as the starting point.[24]

Constitutional questions had been implicit in many recent federal-provincial issues, and the governments had only recently completed unsuccessful debate on an amending formula. It was thus not a wholly new issue; but an attempt at a synoptic review of the whole constitutional base was a new and unfamiliar idea. There was, as we saw, considerable doubt and debate about the appropriate rules and procedures for carrying out the review, about what the issue really involved, about what officials and ministers should participate, and about how the debate could be terminated. These questions, therefore, occupied a good deal of the negotiators' time. Two responses to this uncertainty were particularly important for the conduct of the debate: first, the attempt to bring the focus around to those old, familiar issues like tax-sharing; and, second, to rely largely on already established mechanisms and procedures.

A related characteristic of the issues is the extent to which they lend themselves to simple compromise. Are they zero-sum games or can all parties gain something? Again the actions and beliefs of the participants are crucial in this sort of definition. But some objective characteristics of the issues are also important. Thus finances are much closer to a zero-sum situation than pensions, since on finances it is hard for the provinces to gain dollars without Ottawa losing them – though it is possible governments could arrange mutually beneficial arrangements with the cost being borne by taxpayers. At a time of taxpayer resistance, of course, such schemes are less likely. It is therefore difficult to imagine a 'creative' solution in which everyone benefits. In addition, the financial issues are relatively clear-cut and easy to define, although the formulae used to express the settlements may be anything but simple. It is relatively easy for each participant to measure exactly what he gains or loses from different alternatives. This may make the conflict more visible and therefore more sharp. On the other hand, dollars are easily divisible units, making it easy

24 Aaron Wildavsky, *The Politics of the Budgetary Process* (Boston, 1964), p. 15. See also Otto Davis, M.A.H. Dempster, and Aaron Wildavsky, 'A Theory of the Budgetary Process,' *American Political Science Review* 60 (1966), pp. 529–47.

to develop 'splitting the difference' solutions, rather than global 'all or nothing' solutions.

Some characteristics of the pension issue appear to have made it easier to reach agreement. It was one of the most complex pieces of legislation to be developed since the war. This very complexity, with its myriad of sub-issues, appears to have made resolution easier by permitting extensive trading within the issue itself. A participant's position on one question, like the contribution rate, could be traded for another's position on another sub-issue like the length of the transition period. The complexity of the pension issue also meant that some elements of the conflict were less clear, simply because it was more difficult for the participants to grasp and discuss fully all the details and ramifications. The complexity also makes it more possible for participants to suggest new formulations or new alternatives, making it more likely that a creative solution at least partly satisfying all participants could be devised. Thus the nature of the issue itself has a lot to do with the shape of outcomes.

The constitutional issue is also highly complex, and it is often impossible to predict the consequences of particular provisions. On the other hand, much more than the other issues it is a symbolic one. As a basic statement of the character of the federation it is likely to involve deeply held psychological positions on which the participants will find it difficult to trade. This is of course especially true for French Canadians who, as a minority, feel that constitutional guarantees are especially important. But a sub-issue like language rights may have equally important psychological effects for other actors, as the expressions of western premiers have shown.

The language rights issue, indeed, is one which on the face of it could have been defined in several different ways. That it in fact became defined in moral and symbolic terms, expressing English-Canadian fears of 'selling out to Quebec,' western fears of being the forgotten Canadians, and fears of other ethnic groups of losing out to the two dominant cultures, makes it both more conflictual and harder to resolve, especially if the negotiations are public.

But in other ways the constitution appears to share many of the characteristics of the pension issue which may well make trading possible. Indeed, a recent federal strategy appears to have been to tackle the various issues on a piecemeal one-by-one basis, thereby attempting to avoid the central symbolic and intractable issue of the basic confrontation between Quebec's desires for special status and federal resistance.

Finally some elements external to the particular issues under negotiation may impinge directly on the discussions. One of the side-issues is the existence of other subjects for debate simultaneously with debates on the major questions. Thus, during the pension issue we saw that finances, opting-out, student loans, and others were all on the federal-provincial agenda. In 1966 education and manpower training were also involved. More recently finances, medicare, and federal language policies in all their forms were involved in constitutional discussion. These intersecting issues can have several effects. They may make log-rolling more possible. This was clearly evident during the pension negotiations, when after the Quebec Conference it was possible for Quebec and Ottawa to develop a package solution to all issues. However, as we shall see, the amount of log-rolling is limited by a set of norms and constraints which make such tactics difficult. Another possible effect of intersecting issues is that good-will engendered by success on one issue may 'spill over' to make success on others more likely. Conversely, hostility on one issue makes conflict greater on others.[25] In this way 'traditions' of cooperation or conflict may develop. After the pension settlement with Quebec in 1964 tensions did appear to lessen considerably, and again, after the hostility of the 1966 October conference, provincial disgust at Ottawa's treatment of the Tax Structure Committee results appeared to lead to less willingness to cooperate in similar future endeavours and to the hardening of provincial actions.

When one party initiates the major issue, as Ottawa did with pensions and the constitution, other actors who may or may not be vitally concerned with it may introduce new side-issues. They hope that by doing so the other party will be willing to 'buy' support for its major proposal by making concessions on the side-issues. This, in addition to the simple coexistence in time of different issues seems to be a chief reason for the introduction of side-issues. The success of this tactic, of course, depends on how badly the initiator wants to achieve his goals on the main issue.

The second way events external to the immediate issue may affect the negotiations is that the political situation of the time may change. Since each actor is involved in his own political environment, as well as in the particular negotiations, it is obvious that such conditions as the electoral strength of the governments, their positions in their own legislatures, and events such as the growing outbreaks of separatist violence in Quebec in 1963 or the strength of the Parti québécois in 1970, will affect the goals, resources, and tactics of the actors. These matters will be examined at greater length in future chapters.

25 For a discussion of this concept, see Leon Lindberg, *The Political Dynamics of European Economic Integration* (Stanford, 1965), pp. 10–11.

Thus the issues themselves are important variables in the operation of the process. They have a lot to do with goals and conflict, resources, tactics, and outcomes. Issues arise in the federal-provincial arena for many reasons. Almost any issue conceivably could become a 'federal-provincial' one. But many issues do not arise for federal-provincial discussion, and on other issues federal-provincial negotiations are only a small part of the total decision process. The issues that do arise vary along several important dimensions, such as historical background, complexity, familiarity, relations to other issues, and degree of public and interest-group involvement. Each of these dimensions have important consequences both for the operation of the negotiating process and for its results. Closely related to these issues, of course, are the goals and objectives of the participants – indeed, it has been suggested at several points that the interests and values of the participants play a central role in defining many of the characteristics of the issues. In the next chapter we shall examine the actors' goals on pensions, finances, the constitution, and other issues in an attempt to better understand the nature of federal-provincial conflict and competition.

CHAPTER EIGHT

# Goals and objectives: the bases of conflict

Should the pension plan be funded or 'pay-as-you-go'? Should the federal government increase tax abatements to the provinces or let them raise their own money? Equal treatment for all provinces or a 'statut particulier' for Quebec? One equalization formula or another? A new constitution? If so, what will it be? On these and many other issues the federal government and the provinces have disagreed. This chapter investigates the goals and objectives each government brought to the negotiations and explores intergovernmental patterns of conflict.

Several questions underlie the chapter. First, what are the bases of conflict? Is it rooted in party differences, in ideology, in the economic interests of the regions the governments represent, or in political competition for voter loyalty and for status and prestige? Second, what sort of issues are most likely to involve the provinces, what matters do their governments most concern themselves with? Third, what are the cleavage lines? Is it Ottawa versus the provinces, the rich versus the poor, the large versus the small, the English-speaking versus the French-speaking, the east versus the west, or the Liberals versus the Conservatives? And indeed is it the case, as it is apparently in the United States, that intergovernmental disagreements are less important than intragovernmental ones? In part it is all of these, and it is possible to specify some of the conditions which determine the dominant lines of cleavage.

The first question to ask is what are the roots of agreement and disagreement? Why do governments conflict on some issues and not on others? Goals on any particular issue are to a large extent rooted in and derived from a set of on-going concerns. Therefore one should begin with an examination of some of the basic goals of the governments. These overall concerns may derive from many sources; some may provoke conflict, some not. Four sets of overall concerns seem to be most important in determining the goals of the Canadian governments in defining the nature of conflict and consensus among them. These are: basic economic conditions, ideology, status concerns for each government, and differences in reference groups and foci of attention.

## ECONOMIC INTERESTS

The most obvious potential source of conflict among the governments is differences in their economic positions, particularly in Canada where there is so much regional diversity. Table IV compares the overall economic positions of the provinces and demonstrates the regional disparities.

All provinces want money from Ottawa. But for some, the poorer

TABLE IV

Comparative economic positions of the provinces

| | Income per capita* (1965) | Index of fiscal capacity† (national average = 100; 1962–3) | Per cent revenue from federal sources‡ (1966–7) |
|---|---|---|---|
| Newfoundland | $1,173 | 48.0 | 40 |
| PEI | 1,370 | 64.4 | 37.3 |
| Nova Scotia | 1,483 | 72.0 | 34.3 |
| *New Brunswick* | 1,374 | 62.6 | 34.1 |
| *Quebec* | 1,754 | 86.9 | 15.0 |
| *Ontario* | 2,296 | 119.4 | 1.2 |
| *Manitoba* | 1,919 | 96.0 | 15.9 |
| Saskatchewan | 1,966 | 91.3 | 13.1 |
| Alberta | 1,974 | 104.9 | 2.3 |
| *British Columbia* | 2,280 | 113.7 | 0.4 |
| Canada | 1,988 | 100.0 | 9.5 |

SOURCES:

*Dominion Bureau of Statistics, *National Accounts, Income and Expenditure*, catalogue number 13-201.

†From James H. Lynn, *Federal-Provincial Fiscal Relations*, studies of the Royal Commission on Taxation no 23 (Ottawa, 1967). This index is based on a 'representative provincial tax structure,' using all provincial revenues except natural resource revenues.

‡From *Provincial Finances, 1967*, p. 26. A good discussion of the principle of 'fiscal need' is found in Eric J. Hanson, *Fiscal Needs of the Canadian Provinces* (Toronto, 1961).

provinces, the need is overwhelming. New Brunswick is a good example. Lacking a broad base for raising its own revenue the province is heavily dependent on federal sources. In 1966–7, 34.3 per cent of its budget came from Ottawa.[1] This economic dependence strongly conditions New Brunswick's goals. The province is led to defend a strong federal government, since if Ottawa gave up too much of its taxing power to the provinces it might be less able to assist the poorer members. The result is that New Brunswick sometimes advocates a stronger federal government than do federal officials themselves. Premier Robichaud said at one conference: 'The role of the federal government as the fiscal centre, the financial balance-wheel of Confederation, has always been recognized ... I affirm that nothing must be done to erode the strong central authority of the federal government in fiscal matters. Such national fiscal pre-eminence is essential to our federal system.'[2]

New Brunswick respondents echoed this concern: 'It is in our interests to have a strong federal government. Without it, what happens to any poor part of the country?' said one. This dependence also means that New Brunswick tries to avoid conflict with Ottawa: 'What's the point going out to buck Ottawa. You have everything to lose,' said one official. Not only does the province's poverty affect its overall goals but it also affects more specific ones. For example, because of its poverty more tax points would not assist the province much anyway. What is vital is equalization, which, in effect, gives New Brunswick more than if it controlled 100 per cent of the major taxes. 'For New Brunswick,' said Premier Robichaud in October 1966, 'equalization is the most important topic to be discussed at this conference.'[3] Thus New Brunswick is traditionally quiet on the question of tax-sharing, but is vocal and devotes much effort to equalization. Since Ottawa is strongly committed to reducing interregional disparities and does not want to give away more tax points, there is little conflict with New Brunswick in financial questions.

All the poorer provinces share these attitudes. A strong federal government, with power to redistribute funds through equalization and to engage in regional economic development programmes, is essential to

1 The figures are drawn from the Canadian Tax Foundation, *Provincial Finances, 1967* (Toronto, 1967), Chart 1, p. 26. This and its companion volume, *The National Finances*, are the best sources for current data on the revenue and expenditure positions of the Canadian governments.

2 In *Federal-Provincial Conference*, 24–28 Oct. 1966 (Ottawa, 1968), pp. 34–5. The premier went on to say: 'The federal government is responsible for the continued economic growth and social progress of the nation ... A strong federal government must have the powers, and use the powers to carry out this role' (p. 35).

3 *Ibid.*, p. 104.

their economic well-being. In both financial and constitutional discussions they have emphasized the necessity of maintaining federal primacy in fiscal matters. Premier Smallwood summed up this view in February 1968 in characteristic fashion.

... anything that tends in the direction at all of reducing Ottawa's importance, reducing Ottawa's authority, reducing Ottawa's strength, strikes a blow at us. We are weaker when Ottawa is weaker ... our protection ... is Ottawa.

*And we are absolutely opposed to anything that would weaken Ottawa!*[4]

For the poorer provinces, paradoxical as it may seem, a strong central government is a *condition* of strong provincial governments. Hence the maritime provinces insisted on the inclusion of the elimination of economic disparities as a topic at the Constitutional Conference and as a basic goal of Confederation. Hence too the fear of special status, increased federal tax-sharing, and limitations on the federal spending power. Economic inequality, they have argued, is every bit as much a threat to national unity as cultural or language problems.

At the other end of the scale of wealth are Ontario, British Columbia, and Alberta, the richest provinces. For them the crucial element in the financial package is tax-sharing, since they receive no equalization. Thus they have consistently advocated that Ottawa turn a larger share of tax resources over to the provinces. Ontario, in particular, has rejected Ottawa's argument that it can give up no more without the risk of losing its ability to manage the economy.[5] In 1966 Ontario argued that Ottawa would have sufficient leverage by controlling 40 per cent of personal income tax and 66 per cent of corporate tax.[6] British Columbia has demanded that Ottawa 'progressively vacate the fields of direct taxation.'[7]

4 Constitutional Conference, First Meeting, *Proceedings* (Ottawa, 1968), p. 189.

5 Thus an Ontario official circulated a paper at a continuing committee meeting during the summer of 1966 which argued that Ottawa could retain sufficient leverage over the economy with as little as 15 per cent control of the major taxes.
This view was not shared by an advisory group which reported to the government in April 1966. It felt that an upper limit of 50 per cent should be placed on the provincial share of personal income tax. Fortunately for Ontario's bargaining position, the report was not published until 1967. See Economic and Fiscal Subcommittee, 'Report on an Ontario Position in Federal-Provincial Financial Relations,' in Ontario Advisory Committee on Confederation, *Background Papers and Reports* (Toronto, 1967), pp. 229–321.

6 See 'Statement by the Hon. John Robarts, Prime Minister of the Province of Ontario, to the Federal-Provincial Tax Structure Committee, Ottawa, September 14, 1966,' in *Federal-Provincial Tax Structure Committee*, 14–15 Sept. 1966 (Ottawa, 1966), pp. 38–9. See also Ontario's statement to the Federal-Provincial Tax Structure Committee, in *Federal-Provincial Conference*, 24–28 Oct. 1966, pp. 65–7.

7 After arguing that the British North America Act granted exclusive authority

The rich provinces could be expected to oppose equalization, since it in effect represents a transfer from the rich to the poor. British Columbia 'remains highly critical of the principle of equalization payments ... Equalization has created a major problem for Canada, which at times has threatened Confederation, and yet has not eliminated the basic problem. Equalization payments unduly subsidize certain provinces and do not encourage fiscal responsibility.'[8] Instead the west coast province prefers direct assistance to poor persons, wherever they live. It interpreted a guaranteed annual income proposal as achieving this and thus rendering equalization unnecessary.

Ontario, on the other hand, favours equalization. An ideological concern for unity and fair treatment overrides the immediate economic self-interest, though it does want to limit the total amount paid out in equalization, to remove 'hidden equalization' in some shared-cost programmes, and to have the formula take into account the allegedly higher costs of providing government services to the richer provinces.[9] Said one respondent: 'With us, I think equity was the dominant consideration. We wanted the best possible formula for Canada. There is a strong feeling that it is in the interests of the province not to take a very selfish position.'

The richer provinces cannot argue that federal aid is essential to their survival. Rather they must base their arguments on the financial needs of all the provinces. They also argue that Ottawa must not risk weakening the richer provinces which are the source of most of Canada's wealth: 'There is the problem of assuring the continued financial and economic ability of the richer provinces. You've got to remember where the revenues are coming from right now. You can't screw the golden goose, and that's us.'

Manitoba is neither rich nor poor, sitting athwart the national average by most indicators. One result is that even small shifts in the equalization formula may entail a loss. This explains why, after having advocated a broader based formula in 1963, Manitoba opposed the federal proposal of 1966 as 'decidedly not in the interests of the Canadian people. Other provincial tax revenues are not normally good indicators of fiscal capacity

to the provinces in fields of direct taxation, Mr Bennett concluded: 'British Columbia requests the Government of Canada to vacate progressively the fields of direct taxation, so that the provinces may reassert their fiscal responsibility and rights of Confederation.' See British Columbia, 'Brief Presented to Plenary Session of the Federal-Provincial Conference, Ottawa, November 25, 1963,' Victoria, 1963. The province has returned to this position in the constitutional discussions.

8 In *Federal-Provincial Tax Structure Committee*, 14–15 Sept. 1966, p. 107.
9 *Ibid.*, p. 45.

and should not be used in computing equalization.'[10] It also explains why Manitoba has traditionally argued for a formula based on the top two provinces rather than the national average. Another result is that as equalization has come to mean less to the province, it has escalated its demands for more tax-sharing.'[11]

Another source of conflict based on economic differences arises from differences in the nature of provincial economies. For example, New Brunswick's weak economic base makes it particularly vulnerable to federal efforts to reduce inflation and the like. So New Brunswick urges federal economic policies which will be more sensitive to regional needs.[12] Another example is found in the west, where the economies are based mainly on primary industries which depend heavily on exports. Throughout Canadian history westerners have resented national trade, tariff, and freight-rate policies which were seen as protecting eastern manufacturing industries, forcing westerners to buy expensive equipment at unnecessarily high prices and to pay discriminatory rates to ship their products. This resentment is particularly strong in British Columbia and plays an important role in the latter's attitude to the federal government.

These examples show that basic economic interests are a major source of goals, and of conflict. This, of course, is most obvious in fiscal negotiations. In so far as all the provinces want a greater share of the fiscal pie, and Ottawa wants to retain a larger share, the cleavage is federal versus provincial. But on equalization, for example, the potential division is rich versus poor. On some economic policies it is centre versus west or east. Provincial goals are as much in conflict with each other's as they are with Ottawa's.

Economic self-interest may be tempered by ideology, as seen in Ontario's attitude to equalization. Conversely, economic – and other – needs can help shape the ideology, as in the case of New Brunswick. Finally, what economic interests are dominant for any government depends in part

10 'Manitoba's Statement to the Tax Structure Committee, 14th September, 1966,' p. 12. In 1963 Manitoba's brief said: 'We would like the conference to consider the extension of the equalization principle to the whole provincial revenue base, so that we may establish greater equity ...' 'Statement, November 25, 1963,' p. 7.

11 In 1963 Manitoba said: '... we make full equalization our first concern' ('Statement,' p. 7). The 1966 statements paid more attention to the need for a change in tax-sharing.

12 For example, at the September Tax Structure Committee meeting, New Brunswick Finance and Industry Minister L.G. Desbrisay observed: 'Because we lag, we are the first to feel the effects of national restraints. Because we are underdeveloped ... we are the last to benefit when national economic restraints are lifted ... [Monetary policy] is a weapon which punishes the economically weak more harshly than the economically strong.' See *Federal-Provincial Tax Structure Committee*, 14–15 Sept. 1966, p. 84.

on the government's perceptions of them and on the interest groups in the province it decides to respond to.

Different personalities may also vary in the stress laid on local economic factors. Liberal Premier Ross Thatcher of Saskatchewan has been far more aggressive in championing Saskatchewan's economic interests – to the extent of dismissing the constitutional negotiations as last on his priority list – than was his predecessor CCF government, committed to a more 'national' ideology. Similarly Ed Schreyer, also socialist, took a far more 'national' point of view than the preceding Conservative government of Manitoba when he joined the constitutional talks in mid-1969. So the emphasis placed on long-term economic interests can vary, but within fairly narrow limits. These interests are a fundamental basis of provincial goals – on constitutional as on more strictly financial issues.

## IDEOLOGY

If one conceives of ideology broadly, as providing a basic set of prescriptions about the nature and purpose of the system, then many elements of ideology should affect the nature of the bargaining process. Joseph LaPalombara has shown how ideological fragmentation in Italy affects the relations of interest groups and government.[13] A.H. Birch has indicated how conceptions of representation and responsibility have influenced the behaviour of British political leaders.[14] The purpose here is not to attempt a full analysis of the ideologies of the various political leaders in Canada; rather it is to show how some ideological factors affect the nature of federal-provincial adjustment.

Broadly, two basic elements of ideology are involved in federal-provincial negotiations: first are prescriptions about the nature of the political system, the proper balance of the governments within it, and the ways the decision process should operate; second are more substantive aspects relating to the kinds of policy goals the system should pursue. Both sets of elements may affect the specific goals of the actors: in a sense, goals in individual cases are deductions from a broader set of overall goals, though this operates within certain constraints. Ideological factors, primarily those which relate to the proper functioning of the system, will also affect the kinds of strategies and tactics the participants use. Finally, ideologies can be expected to affect the nature of the conflict. If conflict is rooted in ideological differences, it is likely to be sharper and more

13 *Interest Groups in Italian Politics* (Princeton, 1964), esp. chap. 3.
14 *Representative and Responsible Government: An Essay on the British Constitution* (Toronto, 1964), esp. chaps. 7 and 17.

intractable. But, on the other hand, if ideologies of the participants stress the need for compromise, accommodation, and peaceful solutions, then conflict will be muted.

Ideology in the sense of differences about the nature of the federal system and the rules of the political game have been more important than ideological differences over substantive policy goals. 'Left' versus 'right' has not been a salient characteristic of federal-provincial conflict, largely because at this level there has been substantial consensus among the governments. Virtually all Canadian governments have been committed to the notion of the welfare state,[15] though there are variations among them.

Substantive ideological differences have played a part in a few issues. The pension plan was defined by some, especially in Ontario, as a 'liberal' versus 'conservative' issue. Ontario's own Committee on Portable Pensions had rejected a government-operated pension plan for fear it would put too much money in the hands of the government, would be a 'welfare plan,' and would be a 'political football.'[16] Similarly, in the Canada Pension Plan negotiations, Ontario wanted to delay implementation of the plan to ensure that it would not threaten the 'over 5,000' private retirement plans then operating in the province, would not inhibit the flow of savings and investments, would not entail a redistribution of income, and so on.[17] Ontario's strong objections to universal government-financed medicare also involved elements of this conservatism.

The Ontario example also shows some of the constraints on the predominance of ideological views. It was felt the federal proposal was politically popular, so Ontario's criticisms should be circumspect: 'Robarts

15 For a good discussion of Liberal 'philosophy,' see J.W. Pickersgill, *The Liberal Party* (Toronto, 1962), esp. chaps. 5, 9, and 12. For an exposition of Liberal social thought by one of its more liberal but very influential thinkers, see Tom Kent, *Social Policy for Canada: Towards a Philosophy for Social Security* (Ottawa, 1962). Originally presented to a Liberal study conference in 1960, the paper was influential in setting Liberal policies for the 1962 and 1963 elections.

16 Ontario Committee on Portable Pensions, *Second Report* (Toronto, 1961), see esp. pp. 10–14. For a discussion of Ontario's pension viewpoint, see also Robert M. Clark, 'The Pension Benefits Act of Ontario and Its Relation to Federal Proposals,' in Laurence Coward, ed., *Pensions in Canada: A Compendium of Fact and Opinion* (Don Mills, Ont., 1964), pp. 27–44; and John P. Robarts, 'The Ontario Approach to Pensions,' in *ibid.*, pp. 1–5. The Committee on Portable Pensions was made up of two well-known Conservative academic experts on pensions, an executive of an association of life insurance officers, a professor at the University of Toronto School of Social Work, an officer of the Canadian Welfare Council, and a former chief economist and senior adviser to the Ontario government. The professor of social work and the Welfare Council official both were more favourable to a state-operated plan.

17 See Robarts, 'The Ontario Approach to Pensions,' and Ontario, 'Statement by the Prime Minister at the Federal-Provincial Conference on Pension Plans,' 9–10 Sept. 1963, Toronto, esp. pp. 4–5.

could not scuttle the plan and survive,' said one official. 'There was a limit politically to the kinds of criticisms we could make.' As a result many of Ontario's statements about the plan were of the 'yes, but' variety. Second, especially after the fund became available, the plan was very attractive to Ontario on other grounds. Third, Ontario's conservatism clashed with another ideological position, the goal of maintaining national unity. To have scuttled the agreement with Quebec would have been disastrous, and after May 1964 this viewpoint was far more salient than Ontario's views on the policy itself.

Saskatchewan, which was in 1965 the only CCF-NDP government in Canada, also took more ideological positions on the pension plan and medicare, in these cases acting as a pressure from the left. In the pension example it was an ally of Ottawa, urging that a national plan as generous as possible be implemented as soon as possible.[18]

Far more important than ideological 'left-right' differences are differences in viewpoint about the basic nature of the federal system, the appropriate roles and powers of the governments within it,[19] and the proper means of making joint decisions. And by far the most important conflict here, of course, lies in the clash between most of English Canada, both federal and provincial, on the one hand and Quebec on the other. The federal Liberals made a 'new deal' in federal-provincial relations a major part of their 1963 election programme.[20] Since gaining power the Liberals have been very concerned with minimizing conflict in federal-provincial relations, especially in dealings with French Canada.

Thus several elements in the federal ideology have made negotiations easier. First is an abiding concern with the need to maintain Canadian unity, and the concomitant fear that this unity is gravely threatened.

18 See, for example, comments by Premier Woodrow Lloyd at the July 1963 Federal-Provincial Conference: 'I want to emphasize the desirability and advantages inherent in this kind of federal programme.' He also urged extension of benefits as soon as possible. For a summary of his views, see E.N. Davis, 'Saskatchewan,' *Globe and Mail*, Toronto, 20 Nov. 1963.

19 Edwin R. Black has distinguished five strands of thinking about the nature of the federal state in Canadian thought and practice, ranging from the centralist, to the correlative (which is close to the notion in 'cooperative federalism'), to the dualist, which focuses on the bi-national character of Canada, to the compact, which stresses that Confederation was a result of independent colonies uniting to create a federal government with the implication that the central authority remains a creature of the provinces. 'Concepts of Canadian Federalism,' unpublished PHD dissertation, Duke University, 1962. See also J.R. Mallory, 'The Five Faces of Federalism,' in P.-A. Crépeau and C.B. Macpherson, eds., *The Future of Canadian Federalism/L'avenir du fédéralisme canadien* (Toronto, 1965), pp. 3–15.

20 See Pickersgill, *The Liberal Party*, chap. 14; also National Liberal Federation of Canada, *Canadians Together: Federal-Provincial Relations* (Ottawa, 1963).

'Above all we must work for national unity.' Prime Minister Pearson stated in 1966, 'Canadian unity must be more than our policy, it must be our passion.'[21] The theme has been restated time and again by Pearson, Trudeau, and others. Its centrality in Ottawa's belief system is difficult to exaggerate. It developed a new importance with the development of new demands from Quebec. A leading cabinet minister said: 'This was a new factor we had to deal with. I think we suddenly realized at the Quebec Conference [March 1964] that by God the country might break up ... It really was a dangerous situation, and the only way to deal with it was to make concessions to Quebec. We all realized the country could fall apart, and if it was not going to, then these sources of conflict had to be dealt with and quickly. We had to convince Quebec that we were prepared to deal with their legitimate grievances.' This quotation demonstrates clearly how the Liberals perceived the threat, and, more important, that they were prepared to make important concessions on many substantive goals in order to maintain unity. This was clearly reflected, for example, in the pension negotiations, and in Ottawa's attitude towards opting-out; federal negotiators desperately wanted a truly national pension plan and this meant making concessions to try to keep both Quebec and Ontario in. The commitment to unity is also seen in other federal policies such as the extension of bilingualism in the federal civil service and the appointment of a Royal Commission on Bilingualism and Biculturalism. Indeed it has often been suggested that this preoccupation has inhibited federal efforts for social reform.

This concern for unity may have eased the conflict with Quebec, but its vagueness leaves much room for dispute about how best to preserve Confederation. Federal thinking underwent some important changes between 1964 and 1970. In the earlier period, as the quotation indicates, Ottawa felt it must make concessions to Quebec, and these did go some way towards giving Quebec a *de facto* special status in Confederation. By 1966 several considerations, including the appointment of several forceful French Canadians[22] committed to a strong federal government,

21 Speech to the National Liberal Federation of Canada (Quebec), Montreal, 30 Oct. 1966, p. 4.

22 The three were Jean Marchand, head of the Quebec Labour Federation; Gérard Pelletier, former publisher of Quebec's largest newspaper, *La Presse*; and Pierre Elliott Trudeau, a noted writer and intellectual. All three had been in the forefront of Quebec's modernization. Trudeau had been a prominent member of the New Democratic Party, and Pelletier had been a supporter. Explaining their action, the three wrote:

'... the objective situation has changed: Quebec has become strong and the central power has become weak. The Quebecers are more and more turned towards the provincial sphere, and it is this sphere which attracts the most dynamic

had led to a change. Such concessions as opting-out, it was now felt, had resulted in a special situation for Quebec, and more concessions might lead in piecemeal steps down a 'slippery slope' towards eventual separation. The solution was for Ottawa to scrupulously respect the constitution – as seen in its 1966 proposals to turn over major shared-cost programmes to the provinces and in the form of the proposal to assist higher education. Ottawa would treat Quebec exactly as other provinces. At the same time, French Canadians must be assured of full participation in the national government and be permitted to feel culturally at home everywhere. This view, espoused particularly by the then Justice Minister Trudeau,[23] underlay much of the federal thinking in the 1966 negotiations. At the February 1968 Constitutional Conference the view was even more explicit, and constituted the cornerstone of federal policy. 'There can be no two interpretations of the constitution,' said one cabinet minister. This position, as we shall see, conflicts directly with the position of the Quebec government. But even it asserts the necessity of Ottawa's limiting its own substantive policy initiatives for the higher goal of national unity – a trade-off which many federal politicians object to.

A second aspect of overall federal ideology concerning the operation of the system is its emphasis on 'cooperative federalism.' The phrase has become a cliché, with, as one respondent put it, as many interpretations as there are Canadians. Basically, it reflects the view that Ottawa cannot dictate to the provinces; rather, it must rely on techniques of diplomacy, persuasion, and consultation if it is to maintain both national unity and an important voice in social policy. 'The talents required of federal leaders are no longer those of chieftaincy, but those of diplomacy,' a former justice minister, Guy Favreau, observed.[24] As outlined by Prime Minister Pearson in November 1963, cooperative federalism includes mutual respect for each other's jurisdictions, close consultation as a basis for coor-

politicians and the competent bureaucrats. The Quebecers continue to be governed by Ottawa, they still pay it half their taxes, but they are less and less present there, intellectually, psychologically and even physically ...

If men of competence and integrity do not go to reinforce the numbers of those who are already in Ottawa, the latter will be overwhelmed by insignificants and schemers and in the end Quebec will be represented by these last.

It is to try to prevent such an eventuality – to the best they can, that [we] seek to be elected to the Parliament in Ottawa.'

Quoted in John Saywell, ed., *Canadian Annual Review for 1965* (Toronto, 1966), p. 82 (my translation).

23 The best summary of Trudeau's ideas is found in his *Federalism and the French Canadians* (Toronto, 1968). He notes 'and so, to defend federalism, I entered politics in 1965' (p. xix).

24 'National Leadership in Canadian Federalism,' in Gordon Hawkins, ed., *Concepts of Federalism* (Toronto, 1965), p. 48.

dination, equitable tax-sharing, and equalization.[25] Cooperative federalism thus reflects the federal belief that some coordination can be achieved through cooperative discussion. It has been evident in federal sponsorship of the Tax Structure Committee, the yearly meetings of ministers of finance, and an expanded agenda of federal-provincial conferences at all levels. But, as with unity, the prescriptions are vague and open to many interpretations. 'Lack of prior consultation' remains a frequent provincial complaint. Cooperation is still an important goal, however, and in the absence of the ability to coerce it is, as former Finance Minister Mitchell Sharp has written, 'a practical necessity.'[26]

A third element of federal ideology which limits conflict is its emphasis on reducing inequalities among Canada's disparate regions. According to former Forestry Minister Maurice Sauvé: 'We must assure to all Canadians in all regions of the country a level of economic activity that will ensure full employment, and a living standard which is within the parameters of a well-defined national average.'[27] As a result, federal officials have spent much time developing methods of assisting the poorer provinces: the new equalization formula of 1966 was part of these efforts as were other efforts to promote regional expansion.

Coupled with the commitment to equalization is a belief that Ottawa must act as a protector for the smaller, poorer provinces. One official explained it: 'We must also bear in mind the interests of a number of provinces which only generally speak out on matters of their own direct interest ... These provinces rely on the federal government to speak for them, and I think we have to accept that function.' The desire to reduce regional disparities brings Ottawa into conflict with British Columbia, which opposes equalization on principle – it is seen as another example of Ottawa taxing British Columbia to benefit other parts of Canada. But this commitment does help to minimize conflict with the poorer provinces – including Quebec.

These three ideological concerns – unity, cooperation, and equalization – run through many federal policies. At the same time, federal officials are intent on maintaining the federal power, and many feel that the pendulum has already swung too far towards the provinces. Many federal respondents echoed this view: 'There definitely is one government superior to all the provinces – and that is the federal government,' said a French-Canadian minister. 'Otherwise there is going to be no country.'

25 'Statement by the Prime Minister to the Federal-Provincial Conference,' in *Federal-Provincial Conference*, Nov. 1963 (Ottawa, 1964), pp. 9–18.
26 'Learning to Be a Canadian,' *Queen's Quarterly* 72 (1965), p. 311.
27 'Canada's Need: A New Consensus,' in Hawkins, *Concepts of Federalism*, p. 20.

An English-Canadian official added: 'There is some resentment, some uneasiness that things have gone too far.' In particular, federal officials feel they must be free to take the initiative especially in promoting full employment and economic growth.[28] The fear that giving more tax shares to the provinces would eventually mean losing control of the fiscal tools necessary to economic management was a major element in the refusal of the federal government to give more tax points to the provinces in 1966. Federal officials also believe that only Ottawa has a national viewpoint; many consider provincial concerns narrow and parochial. They are reluctant to see the provinces as equals. These feelings may increase conflict.

Among the provinces ideology is clearly most important for Quebec. Its goals on the pension plan, education, finances, and of course the constitution can be traced to a strong and well-articulated ideology of nationalism. No attempt will be made to analyse the roots of this nationalism, but I shall try to show how it has shaped Quebec's goals and, to a great extent, the course of federal-provincial relations. While there is little consensus within Quebec on the exact nature of the demands implied by the nationalist ideology, and while there have been some changes in emphasis between the Liberal Lesage government which was in power during the negotiations, the Union Nationale government elected in 1966, and the Liberal Bourassa administration which came to power in 1970, some major elements do stand out. Prime Minister Bertrand observed in December 1969: 'It is perhaps in the constitutional field that we find in Quebec the greatest continuity from one government to another ... Regardless of which party is in power or who the Prime Minister has been, Quebec stands on this matter have preserved a truly remarkable historical coherence ... Of course, the styles may differ because times and people change. But the important thing is that the substance remains the same.'[29] It should be stressed here that we are describing some of the dominant attitudes of the Quebec government and its officials, not of all Quebecers,[30]

28 See statement by Finance Minister Mitchell Sharp, in *Federal-Provincial Tax Structure Committee*, 14–15 Sept. 1966, pp. 14, 25. 'There are also compelling reasons for the federal government to maintain a substantial position in the personal income tax field. This is the principal tax by which equity is achieved between rich and poor across the nation ... This tax, too, is one of the central instruments for regulating total demand in the economy, and Canadian governments must not allow total federal income taxes to be abated so much that they can be no longer used for this purpose. This means that the federal government must maintain a strong position in this field, despite the pressures it will continue to face for reducing its share in favour of the provinces' (p. 25).

29 'Notes for a Statement by the Prime Minister of Quebec during the discussion on income security and social services,' 8 Dec. 1969, p. 2.

30 A useful collection of statements by Quebec political figures is found in F.R. Scott and Michael Oliver, eds., *Quebec States Her Case* (Toronto, 1965). See

an increasing number of whom have adopted far more nationalistic positions.

The first element is the belief that Quebec is not a province 'like the others.' Rather, it is the homeland of a distinct national group. The provincial government is its political instrument and expression. 'Because the State of Quebec is alone responsible for the growth of a particular culture,' said Prime Minister Johnson in 1963, 'it needs greater freedom than the other provinces.'[31] These words have been echoed by almost every Quebec spokesman. They imply Quebec must have greater autonomy than other provinces, and that it, not Ottawa, should be responsible for most, if not all, those programmes affecting the social and cultural well-being of the populace. It also implies that policies will be examined from the point of view of Quebec first; Quebec, not Canada, is the reference point. Quebec should have 'special status,' and it should be recognized that Canada is not simply made up of ten equal provinces but also of two equal communities.

In the past French-Canadian nationalism had emphasized defence of Quebec's linguistic and cultural identity. As such, it imposed few demands on English Canada. More recently it has become what Léon Dion calls a 'nationalism of growth,' stressing Quebec's control of its own economic and social life.[32] Its thrust is summed up in the Liberal campaign slogan in 1962: 'maîtres chez nous.' Modernization and economic development by and for Quebecers became the prime goal. This has some important implications for federal-provincial relations: Quebec would need, for example, a much greater share of financial resources and a voice in federal economic, tariff, and monetary policies if it were to carry out successfully its own development. This need for greater financial resources was a major element in Quebec's financial and pension goals. Quebec insisted that any plan be funded, so as to build up a large pool of money which would be used for investment.[33] Said one official: 'The main advantage for us was the creation of a large fund. It would provide money for development

also Michael Oliver, 'Confederation and Quebec,' *Canadian Forum* 43 (1963), pp. 179–83.

For a collection of the views of Prime Minister Lesage, see Lesage, *Un Québec fort dans une nouvelle confédération* (Quebec, 1965). Prime Minister Johnson has developed his views in *Egalité ou indépendance* (Montreal, 1965); also, *The Government of Quebec and the Constitution* (Quebec, 1968).

31 In Scott and Oliver, *Quebec States Her Case*, p. 34.

32 'The Origin and the Character of the Nationalism of Growth,' *Canadian Forum* 43 (1963), pp. 229–33. Dion also makes the point that the dominant ideology fluctuates far more than does the underlying society. See his 'La polarité des idéologies : conservatisme et progressisme,' *Recherches sociographiques* 7 (1966), pp. 31–2.

33 See Jean Lesage, 'The Quebec Pension Plan,' in Coward, *Pensions in Canada*, p. 13.

here, and give us more liberty in the money markets. The fund was certainly the main reason for me; it was *the* reason.' In addition, the plan promised a means of channelling savings by Quebecers into development of their own province.

As the foregoing indicates, another element in the new nationalism is an emphasis on the role of an activist provincial government as the instrument of national development. French Canadians controlled neither Ottawa nor the English-dominated economy, but they did control the Quebec government. For Prime Minister Lesage the government of Quebec had become the lever which the Quebec citizens had resolved to use for their economic and cultural affirmation. It had the mission of safeguarding the culture of French Canadians.[34] Since the 1960 election there have been major reforms in the Quebec government. Several new departments, including the ministère des Affaires fédérales-provinciales[35] (later changed to Affaires intergouvernementales), have been created, and a group of highly educated young 'technocrats' have been recruited, largely from the universities and the federal government.[36] These changes have been associated on the one hand with a much more activist and dynamic government, willing to challenge Ottawa, and on the other with a much higher degree of expertise and sophistication in carrying out the policies.

A related element of the new nationalism is an emphasis on Quebec as *the* government of the province; Ottawa is the government of the English; French Canadians within it are ineffectual or worse. Satisfactory adjustment for Quebec will come not through working with French-Canadian representatives in Ottawa but by direct negotiations between Quebec and the federal government. Some comments illustrate this view:

It [Ottawa] can never be an instrument for us, for our development. It can never be ours. The federal government has never given us an opportunity to participate as a collectivity.

For the English Canadians, the Anglo-Saxons, the federal government is their government. Even the premiers, they feel the federal government is *the* government. But not here in Quebec. Here it is the opposite.

34 Jean Lesage, speeches to the Citizens' Foundation for the Fathers of Confederation Building, Charlottetown, PEI, 2 Feb. 1963, and to Le comité ukrainien de Montréal, 26 Jan. 1963, p. 2 (my translation).

35 For a description of its work, see Quebec, Ministère des Affaires fédérales-provinciales, *Rapport* (Quebec, 1965, 1966).

36 For a discussion of the recruitment and role of the new 'technocrats,' see Peter Desbarats, *The State of Quebec* (Toronto, 1965), chap. 8; Roch Bolduc, 'Le recrutement et la sélection dans la fonction publique du Québec,' *Canadian Public Administration* 2 (1964), pp. 205–14; Jean Lesage, 'L'administration et le bien commun,' *ibid.*, 4 (1966), pp. 345–51.

These views are often reflected in comments about French Canadians in Ottawa: they have no real power, they are apologists for federal power, or, simply, they are 'vendus,' the Quebec equivalent of Uncle Toms. These feelings are reflected in the negotiations. In a sense, part of the conflict between Quebec and Ottawa is about who does represent the people of Quebec. In 1963 and 1964 federal cabinet ministers appeared to accept the notion that the Quebec government spoke for Quebec; more recently the prime minister and other federal ministers have sharply challenged this view.

Another element in the ideology is resistance to federal incursions into areas of provincial jurisdiction. The Lesage government was firmly opposed to most federal shared-cost programmes and it negotiated the agreement by which Quebec could opt out of most existing programmes in return for an unconditional payment.[37] This view was restated by Prime Minister Johnson: 'Quebec will not enter any new shared-cost plans in fields of exclusive provincial jurisdiction.'[38] The opposition to federal incursions has taken other forms. Thus in 1963 and 1964 much of the Quebec-Ottawa conflict concerned new programmes which were part of the Liberal platform. All were considered trespassing on provincial jurisdiction.

Pensions were primarily a provincial responsibility. The mix of goals in the pension issue was well summarized by Resources Minister René Lévesque:

> Pension funds are one of a society's most powerful instruments, both social and financial. It would be unthinkable that Ottawa should run this system or that we should let her get away with it. Unthinkable not only because Quebec has such an acute need for this capital, but also because the individual social security of the citizen as well as the relations between employers and employees are matters of civil rights and thus of provincial jurisdiction ... It is Quebec that must establish its own comprehensive portable pension plan.[39]

Here lies a basic source of conflict, since so many of the areas within which federal policy-makers would like to operate are within provincial jurisdiction. Quebec officials are amenable to Ottawa's entering these fields in other provinces, but not in Quebec. The recent federal policy

37 The agreement is embodied in the Established Programmes (Interim Arrangements) Act, which was given royal assent 3 April 1965. For details, see A. Milton Moore, J. Harvey Perry, and Donald I. Beach, *The Financing of Canadian Federation: The First Hundred Years* (Toronto, 1966), pp. 88–90.

38 *Federal-Provincial Tax Structure Committee*, 14–15 Sept. 1966, p. 51.

39 In Scott and Oliver, *Quebec States Her Case*, p. 142.

of strictly adhering to constitutional provisions and minimizing use of shared-cost programmes was in part a response to Quebec.

This resistance to federal involvement is extended to a desire to take over programmes which at present are within federal jurisdiction. Mr Johnson stated this overall goal during the 1966 negotiations: '... the Quebec government would gradually become solely responsible within its territory for all public expenditures on every form of education, old age security, family allowances, health, employment and training of the labour force, regional development, and, in particular, municipal aid programmes, research, fine arts, culture, as well as any other social or cultural service within our jurisdiction under the present constitution. Existing federal programmes in these fields would be taken over by Quebec ...'[40] The proposal, with elaborate documentation and justification, has been repeated and extended in the constitutional discussions. Such proposals call into question the very existence of any direct link between the federal government and the Quebec citizen. They would involve the ending, at least in Quebec, of many of the federal government's most important programmes: family allowances, old age security, the Canadian Broadcasting Corporation, manpower training, and the like. Coupled with Quebec's financial demands, Quebec's proposals implied a massive weakening of the federal power, and sharply outlined the fundamental differences in outlook between Quebec and Ottawa.

A final characteristic of the new nationalism, and an area in which there is some difference between the Liberals and the Union Nationale, is a stress on the necessity of constitutional change. The Lesage government appears to have felt that suitable adjustments could be worked out within the framework of the existing constitution, and that to open the question of the constitution would have perhaps produced an unmanageable outpouring of demands. The Union Nationale on the other hand made reformulation of the British North America Act, to give expression to the 'legal and political equality of the two nations,' a major element of its programme. Prime Minister Johnson's book, *Egalité ou indépendance*, focuses primarily on the need for constitutional change, and this has remained a major objective.

If Quebec represents the most 'ideological' of governments, it also demonstrates some of the constraints on the extent to which ideology can dominate goals. One constraint is tactical. Thus in 1966 Quebec had a short-run goal: to get a substantial infusion of funds from Ottawa. It therefore had to frame its demands in a negotiable form, and in a way that would attract support from other premiers. As a result nationalism

40 *Federal-Provincial Tax Structure Committee*, 14–15 Sept. 1966, p. 52.

was almost totally absent from its briefs in October. Instead, Quebec argued in the same economic terms as other governments. Said one official: 'In October there was no need to repeat these [nationalist] arguments. He [Johnson] discussed the thing at the same level as the other premiers. We knew in September that the October meeting was going to follow. In October the premiers got together, and Mr Johnson spoke the same language as they.'

Another constraint is economic. After the heavy spending of the Lesage years Quebec was in a weak financial position. The province greatly needed increased funds from Ottawa and did not want to jeopardize the possibility. Quebec also still depended heavily on outside sources for investment in provincial development and for marketing its provincial securities. Too strong an emphasis on nationalistic goals, in particular on the possibility of separation, might lead to higher interest rates, difficulty in marketing bonds, and lower investment in the province.[41] There is some evidence that this happened. In particular there were reports that shortly after the September 1966 statement Quebec had trouble marketing $50 million in bonds. The financial constraint also helps to explain why Quebec accepted the federal manpower programme of 1966 on a 'temporary' basis. 'We needed the financial resources to meet our requirements,' said one official. 'To reject [the manpower proposals] would mean repercussions on all sorts of levels.'

This discussion of constraints suggests that we can think of the participants as acting in several 'games' at once. Here, for example, provincial governments take part in an electoral game where the main object is to maintain power at home; a federal-provincial bargaining game where the object is to gain the support of other premiers and win concessions from Ottawa; and an economic development game where one must woo invest-

41 For a brief summary of Quebec's borrowing requirements, see R.M. Burns and John Chant, *Provincial and Municipal Governments in the Capital Markets: The Implications for Monetary and Fiscal Policy* (Toronto, 1967). There were published reports that Quebec had great difficulty marketing a bond issue shortly after the September 1966 Tax Structure Committee meeting, and hints that this led to the more cautious approach in October. See article by Frank Howard in the *Globe and Mail*, 22 Oct. 1966.

In their attack on Quebec nationalism, French-Canadian federal cabinet ministers have made this point. Thus in a speech to the Richelieu Club of Cap de la Madeleine, 1 Nov. 1966, Minister without Portfolio Jean Chrétien argued that investment and economic growth in Quebec were slipping relative to Ontario, and he blamed '... the lack of confidence created by Quebec's hesitation and doubts about its own future.' In another speech to the Chicoutimi Lions Club, 6 Dec. 1966, he cited data showing Quebec had to pay a larger interest rate for its bonds than Ontario does, and he blamed nationalistic statements. 'A strike in Quebec is not news in New York, Chicago, London or Paris. But separatism is.'

ment. Occasionally the goals and the tactics in one game may conflict with those of others; and, to the extent that the games cannot be entirely separated, this puts an important constraint on the bargainer.

This discussion of Quebec has shown that for that province nationalism broadly defined has played a vital role in defining its position on specific issues, including the pension plan, finances, and the constitution. Prime Minister Lesage indicated the ideological significance of the pension plan for Quebec in a speech in 1963. It was, he said, not merely a jurisdictional quarrel. Rather, Quebec's goals were dictated by the French-Canadian desire 'to blossom out and accelerate their economic liberation.'[42] The discussion has also shown that conflict with Ottawa – and the other English-speaking provinces to some extent – has been based in large measure on fundamental differences about the proper nature of Canadian Confederation and the respective roles of its governments. This conflict became particularly clear in 1966, and again when Quebec made its propositions to the Constitutional Conference, when the federal outlook towards Quebec took a new direction and at the same time Quebec stated its overall demands much more clearly than in the past. Quebec officials were virtually unanimous that the new federal position was a dangerous one: 'I don't think special status would lead to separation,' said one official. 'On the contrary, it is a condition of unity.' Two others put it this way:

If the federal government does not move towards a special status, I do not know what will happen. There is a greater crisis now [1967] than there was [in 1963–4]. Quebec wants much more now, and can spell out very precisely what it wants. And I think public opinion has grown much more strongly to this point of view.

In 1964 the federal government did not understand us well. They thought that the policy worked out with Quebec would regulate the whole problem. But it was not like that. Then today they have this ideology of not giving Quebec any more. They feel that if they gave more, Quebec will continue to want more, and they are partly right. They do not want us to arrive at a certain point – and that is the point I want to arrive at.

This conflict, however, is not just with Ottawa. In addition to voicing many of their constituents' misgivings about developments in Quebec, the

42 Speech to le Conseil du travail du Québec et du district, Quebec, 2 Sept. 1963 (my translation).

provinces have more specific opposition. For example, western provinces have strongly opposed French Canadians on linguistic and cultural issues; the Maritimes are threatened by Quebec proposals which would weaken Ottawa.

For no other province is ideology so important. The English-speaking provinces share many goals with Quebec – especially the desire for more money – but they are not put forward with the same kinds of argument. An Ontario official summed up the difference well: 'We don't base our desire for more freedom on ideology or anything like that. Quebec is talking about a sociological problem of language, and culture and race, while we're talking about our ability to handle the problems and develop the policies better than the federal government can. It's not a matter of ideology. We feel we develop better policy. It's not emotional.'[43]

This difference shows up in provincial views about shared-cost programmes. Provincial officials voice numerous complaints about such programmes, but at the same time they have no basic opposition to them, and indeed often advocate establishment of new ones. Only Quebec took the option of opting-out. The provinces were unsympathetic to the federal proposal of 1966 to turn over to them the three major programmes.

Nevertheless, there are differences between Ottawa and the other provinces about their respective roles in the federation. All provinces wish to maintain a strong federal government – in particular, they grant its dominant role in fiscal and economic policy: 'Economic policy will always have to be more strongly centralized.' But at the same time it is believed that the provinces best understand the needs of the people in most areas. Said a Manitoba cabinet minister: 'We are the government that should deal with the people. These are our kinds of programmes. If a government did have to shrink in this country, then I think the federal government would have to start thinking of shrinking itself ... [Most of] running the country is a provincial problem.' 'The aspirations and needs of the farmer in Saskatchewan are best understood in Saskatchewan, not in Ottawa,' said an official. Related to this is the view that most of the important fields of government action at present lie at the provincial field. The solution, from the provincial perspective, is not to transfer responsibilities to Ottawa, but rather to transfer revenues to the provinces. An Ontario official: 'In most of the important areas of government – educa-

43 This approach is echoed by Prime Minister Robarts. Speaking of the constitutional division of powers, he said: 'I think powers must be allocated according to the functional criterion that the government most capable of doing the job efficiently should have the responsibility.' Ontario, Legislative Assembly, *Debates*, 1969, p. 7.

tion, highways, and so on – the provinces are responsible. These are the big areas and you are not going to get any constitutional change which transfers these to Ottawa. This implies the federal government has to consider our expenditure requirements on a par with its own.'

The provincial view was summed up by a New Brunswick official: 'Give us the money and let us decide.' Thus, though the differences are not great, provincial officials do have a slightly different emphasis – the provincial level is most important. Ottawa's role is not to legislate for the whole country, but to ensure that the provinces have the means to legislate for themselves.

The provinces are also strong believers in cooperative federalism. The federal government must be sensitive to regional needs. It must fully consult with the provinces before introducing policies which affect them. The difference, again, is one of emphasis, but an important one. Provincial participants frequently complain of federal 'faits accomplis,' 'blackmail,' and the like, alleging that Ottawa has not allowed adequate consultation. The complaint is less related to inadequacies in the mechanisms of negotiation than it is a recognition of greater federal political resources and differing foci of attention. Sometimes the allegation appears correct; at other times 'failure to consult adequately' is a handy charge to make against Ottawa when one's position has not been accepted despite long drawn-out discussions. Medicare is a good example.[44] For the provinces cooperative federalism implies they should be involved in policy formation at an early stage; for Ottawa it is less a question of joint decisions than a willingness to listen to provincial views after a policy has been developed. Clearly the latter strategy gives the initiator a partisan advantage.

Most provinces share the federal concern with minimizing conflict and maintaining national unity. They emphasize the need for moderation, compromise, and a 'national' point of view. Such views, again, are much more strongly expressed in the abstract than when it comes to specific policy differences. Many provincial officials are generally sympathetic to Quebec's demands, though the western provinces have been less willing to concede a special status to Quebec or to extend educational and other language rights to French Canadians in their own provinces. Sympathy with Quebec aspirations was particularly prominent in the New Brunswick, Manitoba, and Ontario interviews. The Ontario government has been especially concerned with the direction Canadian federalism is taking. It created an Advisory Committee on Confederation to examine

44 For a good discussion of this question, and a summary of several issues on which provincial complaints have been strong, see R.M. Burns, *Intergovernmental Liaison on Fiscal and Economic Matters* (Ottawa, 1969), pp. 126–33.

some of the broader questions and in 1967 sponsored the Confederation of Tomorrow Conference. These concerns directly affect Ontario's behaviour in the negotiations. Considerations of national unity were in part responsible for Ontario's concessions on the pension plan, and played an important role in its deliberations about whether to stay in the Canada Pension Plan or establish its own. These concerns also influence Ontario's tactics. The province usually eschews inflammatory tactics and tries to play a moderate role. 'Ontario always takes a national point of view,' said a federal official. 'Premier Robarts has done a lot for Confederation inside the conference room.' Ontario also sees itself as playing a mediating 'honest broker' role between Quebec and both Ottawa and the other English-speaking provinces. Said Mr Robarts: 'Ontario has a special role to play as an outstanding and understanding interpreter of the views of Quebec to some of the other parts of Canada.'[45]

The recent issues of language rights and the like have introduced a new ideological dimension to federal-provincial negotiations, one which is more symbolic and more emotional than other issues. Opening these areas to debate has revealed some deeply divided attitudes on some basic features of Canadian society. The differences in attitude are probably not new, but so long as they were not injected into the negotiating arena the conflict did not become clear. The most important dimension to this conflict is of course the role of French Canada in Canadian society. Three broad positions can be distinguished. First, the Quebec view that in order to survive and grow French Canadians must have control over their own 'state' with greater powers – hence the emphasis on increased jurisdiction

45 Ontario, Legislative Assembly, *Debates*, 1967, p. 3570. The statement occurred during debate on the motion to convene the Confederation of Tomorrow Conference. The whole debate gives an excellent view of the attitude of both the government and opposition in Ontario towards the federation.

Premier Robarts' statement to the Ontario legislature announcing his decision to participate in the CPP illustrates the point well. If Ontario had its own plan, he said:

'We would then have a plan which could be operated to our satisfaction, both efficiently and economically, for the benefit of the people of this province. We would preserve the constitutional rights which are ours under the British North America Act. We would have complete control over all the funds generated in this province. We would have complete control over any future amendments respecting contributions, benefits and other financial aspects ... In addition, although a provincial plan must be comparable to the federal plan, I am convinced that we could make improvements and simplifications ... if we were to devise and operate our own.

On the other hand, the province of Ontario and this government have traditionally worked for national unity and national standards of social services. We have participated in national social security programmes and in many other instances have provided support in the interest of national standards and stability.'

Ontario, Legislative Assembly, *Debates*, 1965, p. 24.

for the province and for recognition of the concept of 'two equal cultures.' Second is the view best expressed by Prime Minister Trudeau, namely that the best way for French Canadians to survive and prosper is not to give the Quebec government greater powers but rather to ensure that French Canadians can be at home anywhere in the country – hence the proposals to entrench language rights in the constitution, to make federal and provincial services available in French, and to promote bilingualism in the civil service. Ontario, too, has come close to this position on many occasions. Third is the view, most commonly expressed in the west, that Canada is not a bicultural but rather a multicultural nation, that French Canadians should neither have a stronger provincial government nor be favoured over other linguistic and cultural minorities by entrenchment of language rights and so on. These three positions and their variants obviously tap very deeply rooted sentiments, which have great emotional significance, as can be seen in the reaction to the strong position taken by Manitoba Premier Weir at the February 1969 Constitutional Conference. It is not easy to see how the three views can easily be reconciled. Indeed there is some evidence that the governmental leaders had in the past deliberately avoided raising them for fear of the consequences. Hence debate on them has taken a more emotional tone, very different from most previous negotiations. Whether these kinds of disagreements can be resolved in a forum like federal-provincial negotiation remains to be seen.

## STATUS GOALS: POLITICAL COMPETITION

In many respects, as we have seen, provincial governments act as spokesmen for the economic and political interests of their own regions. But they are more than just spokesmen. Rather, as complex organizations in their own right they have their own institutional goals as governments. We must therefore make a sharp distinction between the interests of a region and the interests of its provincial government. A government will presumably seldom pursue goals in conflict with those of the region, but it will have its own concerns and interests which are clearly distinct. It will ask not only how does this proposal affect my region but also how does it affect me as a government? These goals and interests, which I shall call *status* goals, are a crucial source of conflict in the system.[46] They include

46 This discussion depends heavily on Edward Weidner's discussion in 'Decision-making in a Federal System,' in Arthur W. Macmahon, ed., *Federalism Mature and Emergent* (New York, 1955), pp. 363–83. Weidner distinguished between programmatic or policy goals and expediency goals, which relate to the preservation and extension of the influence of individuals, agencies, or units of government. In his study of social work administrators in Minnesota, programmatic

three related types: the first electoral, the second psychological, and the third related to policy.

Let us look first at the electoral considerations. Here we come close to the heart of the nature of political competition in the federal system. The eleven governments jointly govern the same population, but they never actually campaign against each other. Why then compete? The reason can be stated simply: the federal and provincial governments compete *to gain credit, status, and importance,* and *to avoid discredit and blame.* They have in Anthony Downs' metaphor a 'territorial sensitivity.' If one views the politician as one who deals in policies in order to gain votes, it also becomes clear that the governments are competing for tax dollars, since revenues provide the wherewithal to produce policies.[47]

These considerations are most clearly seen in the financial negotiations. The tax abatement system, whereby Ottawa collected the major taxes and then turned over part of the proceeds to the provinces, had some clear advantages for them. Not only did they avoid the expense of collecting the taxes but also they could at least partly avoid the blame for doing so. On the other hand, the federal government had to bear the greatest part of the burden, in effect raising money for the provinces to spend. The decision in 1966 to end the abatement system and to make each province responsible for setting its own tax rates was based in part on the belief that the provinces should share the blame by raising the money themselves; equally, provincial resistance was based on a desire to avoid doing so. 'The federal government also wants to have enough funds to be able to offer some goodies in an election,' said one official. 'Why should we abate taxes to leave room for the provinces to have low taxes?' A federal minister added: 'Money is what they [the provinces] are interested in, always money. [They] wanted the federal government to take the blame by collecting the taxes, so it really is a political question.' The federal reply to the provinces' call for more money in October 1966 was: if you need it, raise it yourself. 'We are not going to take the political hell for raising your taxes so you can spend the money.'

Similarly, some of the recent federal reluctance about shared-cost programmes reflects these concerns. A cabinet minister: 'We pay for most of the programmes but we get no credit. We're not even invited to the opening of buildings we have helped pay for. Well, that's politically bad

values predominated over expediency values. He is here dealing at the level of officials rather than government leaders, and, more important, with a professional group, who, whether in Washington or the states, share many of the same professional values. Similar relationships between officials in federal and provincial operating departments have favoured shared-cost programmes.

47 *An Economic Theory of Democracy* (New York, 1957), p. 28.

for us. We pay all the money to the provinces and the public is inclined to think we do nothing for them in return for all the money we collect. It's a problem for every MP in his own constituency.' An official in the Manpower and Immigration Department gave as one reason for setting up the new manpower programme, and ending the old shared-cost programme, the fact that Ottawa was paying almost all the allowances to those undergoing training. 'Ninety per cent of the people receiving the cheques were completely unaware of the federal contributions,' he said; 'well, politically, that was a lousy deal for us.' 'The governments do compete for political credit,' agreed an Ontario official; 'they want to make sure their name is down.' When Ontario officials were examining the pros and cons of staying in the CPP or establishing their own pension plan like Quebec, one argument for having a separate plan was that then Ontario would get the credit for operating a popular programme. Quebec insisted that federal employees in that province join the Quebec pension plan, and that the joint registration card to be carried by members of both plans have no reference to Ottawa on it and use a maple leaf instead of the national coat-of-arms as its symbol. On the other hand, some provincial officials see federal initiatives, such as medicare, as attempts by Ottawa to reap political credit at the expense of the provinces' own priorities and programmes.

Political competition, while indirect, is thus a very important basis of conflict. It runs through many of the negotiations. 'At the political level,' said a British Columbia cabinet minister, 'we are really contending for the sanction of public approval.' 'The governments,' said an Ontario official, 'are competing for political credits, and, perhaps more important, for political prestige.' This conflict, which is generally unspoken in the negotiations, often makes coordination difficult. 'When governments compete for credit,' observed a BC minister, 'you are always going to have disorganized bickering.' Added a federal official: 'The basic barrier [to coordination] is simply the basic fact of the constitution and the fact that two levels of government are competing for the support and the taxation dollars of the same people. You cannot escape that. It is a fact of the federal system.' The competition, therefore, is not just about what policies will be made or what taxes collected; it is about who shall carry out these policies and who shall collect the money to pay for them.

A second aspect of these status goals is that provinces will react to proposals not simply on the basis of whether the proposed policy is good or bad but rather on how it affects them as institutions. A Manitoba official summed up the position well: 'On any deal, the first thing we want to know is how much we are going to get, and how this compares with what we got under the old arrangements.' This concern was well illustrated by the pension negotiations. On most questions concerning the plan, we have seen, only Ontario, Quebec, Saskatchewan, and Ottawa were deeply involved. For the others: 'We had no specific objectives. None of our fellows knew anything about it. It had always been a federal field before this ... We had no organization with which to evaluate them. It was a matter of reacting to the federal initiative.'

They *were* concerned only about those aspects of the plan which directly affected the provincial governments, in particular, the disposition of the fund, once it became clear there would be one. British Columbia was concerned about the fund. Like most provinces, the BC government operates a pension fund which serves all provincial, municipal, and school board employees in the province. In 1963 British Columbia demanded that they be exempted from the national plan. Why? First, British Columbia was reacting like an employer who operated a pension plan for his employees. 'We did not want to adjust our own pension plan,' said one negotiator; 'we feared a hassle over integration [of the two plans] more than anything else.' Second, the provincial pension plan itself created a fund which was used to invest in British Columbia's large development projects, and it did not want to threaten this source. When the CPP came to produce a fund, this objection vanished.

New Brunswick's reaction to the pension plan was similar: 'We just went neutral on the Canada Pension Plan,' said one official. 'We just eased right out of it. We just didn't have the capacity to tackle it.' What did interest New Brunswick was the financial aspect: 'My main interest as a Treasury Board-type was how much money would be available to New Brunswick. We didn't contribute many ideas. The two questions I was supposed to ask were the size of the fund and what were the strings going to be.'

These quotations suggest that governments will be selective about the issues in which they will participate actively. Leaders must decide if the issue raises questions of central importance for them, and if it is worth expending resources on them. In making this decision provincial leaders have considerable freedom.

To the extent both levels of government are activist and interventionist in their behaviour, the likelihood of conflict is increased. When one level is relatively quiescent few clashes are likely if the other is innovative. Thus a major reason for the heightening of Quebec-Ottawa tension in the sixties is that the new Quebec régime began to pursue much more aggressive policies at the same time as a relatively activist federal government took office.

Other examples of the way governments react on the basis of what implications a proposal has for them directly can be multiplied. The irate reaction by provincial governments, especially the departments of education, to the new federal manpower programme was largely based on the fact that the new programme posed a direct threat to the status of the bureaucracies which had been operating adult education and training programmes with federal assistance under the previous agreements.[48] Now Ottawa proposed to take over many of the functions of these bureaucracies. All the provinces were equally affected – and the case provides one of the few examples of all provinces being firmly united against Ottawa. Thus, it seems fair to say that provincial goals and provincial reactions to federal proposals are based very greatly on the ways these programmes directly affect the provincial governments themselves, quite apart from how they affect the provincial populations.

The second aspect of status goals is what I have called the psychological. It is much harder to document. It suggests that, in addition to, and complementary to, the status concerns based on the desire to maintain political support and to avoid threats to their programmes, each government's personnel are concerned with maintaining their own status, prestige, and power. They will try to enhance this prestige and influence and oppose developments which threaten it. 'The eternal struggle of politicians for recognition is one of the curses of the country,' Prime Minister Robarts observed to reporters at the December 1969 conference.[49] Thus, for example, no province proposes as a solution to the financial dilemma that Ottawa take over more functions.

In Quebec, several observers of the new nationalism have suggested that it is related to the status concerns of a developing middle class.[50] Applied to federal-provincial conflict, this suggests that for Quebec leaders, enhancing the role and importance of the provincial government enhances their own status; similarly for federal leaders from Quebec,

48 For a representative provincial view of the manpower programme, see paper delivered by N.A. Sisco of the Ontario Department of Education to the Canadian Education Association, Regina, Sept. 1967.

49 *Telegram*, Toronto, 10 Dec. 1969.

50 Albert Breton, for example, has argued that nationalism is a middle-class movement used as a device to gain access to positions of greater prestige and income; he sees it as imposing higher costs and thus running against the interests of the working class. 'The Economics of Nationalism,' *Journal of Political Economy* 72 (1964), pp. 376–86. See also Hubert Guindon, 'Social Unrest, Social Class and Quebec's Bureaucratic Revolution,' *Queen's Quarterly* 71 (1964), pp. 150–62; Charles Taylor, 'Nationalism and the Political Intelligentsia: A Case Study,' *Queen's Quarterly* 72 (1965), p. 162.

increasing provincial powers reduces theirs. That such a factor might be operating is suggested by the comments of several Quebec respondents who saw in federal resistance to Quebec's demands a fear by federal ministers that they were losing their importance. This concern helps to explain why Quebec says 'the solution to the problem of bilingualism lies in increasing the authority of the Quebec government' – and why federal politicians reply 'no, it lies in increasing the influence of French Canadians in Ottawa.' Observations by some federal respondents tend to confirm this view. Said a cabinet minister (English Canadian): 'The fact is, you have to have a guy at the top of the heap, and he has to hang on to as much power as he can. Otherwise he is not going to stay at the top very long.' 'The fact of the matter is the provincial governments are still in many respects the minor leagues,' said an Ottawa official; 'this is the big league here.' These comments indicate that some purely status concerns are operating, but it is very hard to separate them from other factors. Recent movements in Quebec sharply outline this status conflict, but in a less striking way the more general movement towards provincial autonomy Canada has witnessed in recent years points to an enhancement of provincial status over federal. The provinces have welcomed this change but it has led some federal officials to a heightened concern about their own position.

It is hard to overestimate the importance of status goals in the negotiations, and in the process of policy-formation generally. They are particularly important on those issues which do not arouse great public interest, since in such cases the participants are freer to indulge them. Herein lies a major part of the significance of the particular process of policy-formation we are studying. It ensures that the status concerns of the eleven governments will be central among the values considered in any policy. To this extent the governments can use the process to maintain and enhance their own status and prestige. And, to the extent a focus on these concerns leaves less time or attention for other possibly relevant values, the process conditions the overall activity of policy-making.

## DIFFERENT PERSPECTIVES

The final important basis of disagreement lies simply in the fact that the federal and provincial governments have different perspectives. Each government has a set of interests and priorities it is committed to, and each, not surprisingly, feels that its priorities are the most important ones. Each has a different electorate it must appeal to, and a different set of interest groups it must be responsive to. These differences in focus of attention take several forms. They are visible in all the negotiations under consideration.

First, the federal government tries to take a broad view. It tries to develop policies for the country as a whole. A federal official summed it up: 'There is a basic conflict in approach between the federal government and the provinces. The federal government must bear in mind the whole nature of the federal system and where it is leading to.' The provinces, on the other hand, are more concerned with their own regional needs and will judge policies in that light. Said a New Brunswick official: 'We talk to Ottawa in terms of specific projects for our specific regional needs. They talk of overall economic policy for the whole nation.' This sort of conflict is especially clear in fiscal relations. But it also shows up in reactions to other federal programmes. Said a Quebec official: 'They take general solutions and try to apply them across the country, so they don't apply to regional needs. That creates much waste and confusion. Many of the national programmes are tailored to a mythical Canadian who doesn't exist in any province.'

This difference in outlook often means provincial and federal governments will interpret the same programme in different ways. One example occurred in 1963, at the beginning of the pension negotiations, when Ottawa introduced a programme to provide low-cost loans to municipal governments. The purpose of this Municipal Loan Fund was to stimulate new capital projects and thus counter unemployment. The fund was to be administered by the federal government, and would be used mainly to finance previously unplanned projects to provide new jobs. The provinces reacted unanimously. They saw the fund as a device to finance municipal development rather than as an attempt to ease unemployment.

They worked to change the plan's emphasis so that a much wider variety of projects was eligible, and also demanded that the fund be allocated to each province on a per capita basis rather than by Ottawa on a basis of need. Finally, there was a status motive: the provinces have jealously guarded their authority over municipal governments and prevented large-scale direct relations between federal and local governments. Thus they demanded, successfully, that the funds be turned over to the provincial governments which would themselves grant and administer the loans. This status concern with regard to local governments explains, too, the reluctance of provincial governments to bring the former into formal participation in the constitutional conference and their refusal to consider direct federal aid to municipalities.

Another example of different perspectives is the new federal manpower programme. The federal emphasis was economic. It was interested in providing trained manpower for industry and in retraining adults in the work force who have been disadvantaged by lack of adequate skills. The federal programme therefore catered to those who had already been in the work force for three years or more. The provinces saw adult education as an extension of normal education: they wanted to use the funds to provide training to those, like apprentices or high school drop-outs, who had only recently left school. In part, the federal officials represented the views of the economists and the provinces those of the educators. Said a Manitoba official: 'They have the money, and they are interested in training adults, so that's what they pour it into. The provincial governments are more concerned with the younger people and they are being ignored.' Another federal goal was to assure a more equitable distribution of manpower training funds across the country. Previously, the richer provinces, with more resources of their own, had been in a much better position to make use of federal funds. The result was that in 1965–6 Quebec had received $25 per unemployed person while Ontario received $177. 'Least where the need was most.'[51] But of course what was rational from the federal point of view was not from Ontario's point of view, since its officials were most concerned with developing the best programme for Ontario.

The difference of focus shows up most clearly in financial negotiations. Each province is committed to its own set of priorities. These may not coincide with federal priorities; so when the latter involve the provinces in expenditures of their own, conflict results. An example is the federal medicare plan. The typical reaction of the provinces was that many other things were more important and should receive attention first. Provincial officials are unanimous in arguing that the chief priorities facing Canada lie in the provincial sphere. The implication is clear: Ottawa should turn over more finances to enable the provinces to meet these priorities. The federal rebuttal is that Ottawa has a prime responsibility for economic health, which requires that Ottawa control a major share of the main revenue fields, and that Ottawa has its own programmes which have high priority too. Said Finance Minister Mitchell Sharp at the September 1966 Tax Structure Committee meeting: 'The proposition that the federal government should reduce taxes to ease increases in provincial levies must ... be based on the assumption that Parliament is appropriating money for purposes less important. But we cannot accept as a general principle

51 Tom Kent, 'Intergovernmental Responsibility for Manpower Training,' paper presented to the Institute of Public Administration of Canada, Hamilton, 7 Sept. 1967, p. 16.

that federal expenditures are less important than provincial ones.'[52] Prime Minister Robarts of Ontario stated the opposite case: 'The provincial and municipal authorities can expect to be faced with an increasing need to undertake expensive types of expenditures, such as urban renewal, commuter transportation, regional development and school, university and hospital construction. This clearly demonstrates the need to secure a significant reallocation of tax resources between the federal and provincial governments.'[53]

Thus the line of conflict is clear: each level of government has programmes and policies; each is jealous – for the status reasons discussed earlier – to retain control over these policy areas; and, at the same time, each is faced with scarce resources. These different perspectives are perhaps the major source of conflict on broad policy matters like the ones discussed here; they are far less important on more technical issues where federal and provincial programme officials share common professional perspectives.

During the constitutional debate federal leaders often expressed frustration at the lack of provincial enthusiasm. Some provincial spokesmen on the other hand voiced the view that Ottawa was too concerned with abstract constitutional matters and not enough with immediate problems. This divergence manifested itself in disagreements about the agenda. Both sides, from their own viewpoints, were right.

Differences in the perspectives of each government have other effects. Each government operates in a different political environment, and must tailor its activities to that environment, even though the requirements imposed by it may mean conflict with other governments.

An important example is the federal handling of the pension plan. The Liberal government came into power on 8 April, during a time of concern about unemployment and other economic problems. The new administration also faced the problem of governing with a minority in Parliament. The Liberals had developed a wide-ranging set of social policies during the campaign, many of which, like the pension plan, had implications for the provinces. But in their concentration on economic problems, the need to get elected, and on Parliamentary difficulties, the policy-makers' calculations ignored the possible reaction in provincial capitals. A federal cabinet minister said:

> [We] had no consistent approach in 1963–4. We were concerned mainly with the problem of unemployment ... And then we were a minority government.

52 *Federal-Provincial Tax Structure Committee*, 14–15 Sept. 1966, p. 24.
53 *Ibid.*, p. 38.

We did have a hell of a time in the House. In the early days after the election we were thinking of the policy goals, the things we had been thinking about through two election campaigns. So we were less aware of the constitutional problems. We never thought we would be stopped on that. We had to pay a ridiculous price to get it through ... This [the need to negotiate with the provinces] was a new factor we had to deal with. Previous governments had not had to deal with it so much.

Therefore Ottawa dealt with the pension plan, observed one official, 'as if Canada were a unitary state, as if their only commitment was to the electorate and survival in the House.' It seems clear that if the federal focus of attention had included provincial reactions, its policies and means of promoting them would have been considerably different. As it was, the reaction of the provinces, especially Quebec, came as a rude shock.

In 1966 provincial officials were furious at the way Ottawa presented its complex new education and manpower programmes. They had been given little warning it was coming and were therefore unprepared to discuss it. Part of the reason for this method was undoubtedly tactical, but another important part was simply that the federal cabinet agreed on the package of proposals only a day or so before the October conference was to begin. Again the exigencies of the federal environment led to conflict and hostility in the federal-provincial environment; this is another example of how participation in several games at once affects the operation of the negotiating process and, in this case, the level of conflict.

Finally, Ottawa's preoccupation with the problems of Quebec and the Maritimes is an important element in conflict between the western provinces, especially British Columbia, and Ottawa. British Columbia respondents felt Ottawa systematically discriminated against the province in its economic policies, its refusal to help pay for provincial railroad and hydro-electric power projects, and so on. Instead 'the federal government is eastern-oriented,' said a senior minister; 'the heartland of federal policies is in Upper and Lower Canada [Ontario and Quebec] and that's who they listen to.' An official added: 'We feel that whenever Quebec sniffs, Ottawa has a cold.'[54] Such comments were general, and they contributed to the overall sense of grievance and tension between the two governments.

This became a constantly reiterated theme from the western premiers during the constitutional debate. They failed to see the need for constitutional revision; they denied that there was a crisis in French-English

54 By December 1969 that had escalated, in the words of one western premier, to 'Ottawa catches pneumonia.'

relations; and they insisted that the major topic of discussion should be economic matters. 'We want to get down to bread and butter issues,' said Premier Thatcher; 'we've had it up to here with the constitution.'[55] The expression was his, but the sentiment was shared.

The political world, then, simply looks different from different regional and governmental vantage points, and that leads to conflict. No one perspective is necessarily any more legitimate than another. The participants are simply led to consider different things as being most important. It is difficult if not impossible for any one set of decision-makers in the process to take into account fully the interests of all the others. The process means, in part, that they do not have to. It eases the problem of what Downs calls 'technical limitations,' which stems from a universally 'limited capacity for knowledge and information.' But even with perfect information the governments would continue to share often conflicting goals; federal-provincial conflict is not simply a matter of 'poor communications'; nor, therefore, could it be solved simply through establishing better coordinating machinery.[56]

## PARTY

Several writers on federalism focus on party differences as a major basis of conflict. William Riker and Ronald Schaps, for example, suggest that differences in party makeup between the federal and state governments in Canada, the United States, and Australia are responsible for most conflict.[57] Does this proposition hold true from the perspective of the Canadian decision-makers? Even a cursory glance at these cases indicates clearly that party differences have very little to do with federal-provincial conflicts. Party, in fact, seems to be almost the least important line of cleavage in the system.

The pattern of agreement and disagreement on the pension plan does not coincide with party lines. Ottawa's chief ally on pensions was Saskatchewan, a CCF government. Its chief antagonist was Quebec, its government bearing the same party label as the federal government. The same pattern emerges on financial questions. Here the three prairie provinces – one Liberal, one Conservative, and one Social Credit in 1966 – shared much the same goals. So did New Brunswick and Nova Scotia – one Liberal, the other Conservative. Both agreement and disagreement with Ottawa and with each other are no respecters of party lines. 'Party itself has absolutely no bearing on the negotiations,' said a Quebec official.

55 *Telegram*, 10 Dec. 1969.
56 Anthony Downs, *Inside Bureaucracy* (Boston, 1966), p. 50.
57 'Disharmony in Federal Government,' *Behavioral Science* 2 (1957), pp. 276–90.

This conclusion is supported by virtually all the respondents. They suggested that 'really, I don't think party makes such difference,' that it has 'no bearing' on the negotiations, and that the party label 'is not prominent at all.' A BC minister felt British Columbia has not had a 'poorer deal because its government is Social Credit,' and he pointed to the failure of previous governments as proof. 'They were even worse off.' Within the conferences, even at the ministerial level, 'There is an almost complete absence of any outward sign of partisan politics.' An observer could not discern to which party each premier belonged. Similarly, a federal cabinet member reported as much or more trust of Conservative premiers as fellow Liberal ones.

Thus partisan differences are not salient in the negotiations, much less a basis for deep disagreement. This is not to say party has no impact. It did get involved in the pension issue, when the Ontario Liberals made support for the Canada Pension Plan a major part of the election platform in a provincial election. Ontario's last-minute objections to the pension plan also appear to have been motivated at least in part by considerations of party advantage,[58] since the objections tied in neatly with those being made by the federal Conservatives. But this happened after the end of the federal-provincial negotiations and after Prime Minister Robarts had announced that Ontario would participate in the plan. These examples do indicate, however, that partisan differences are more likely to emerge in cases, such as the pension plan, when there is wide public interest and discussion and when the parties have made the issue important.

Partisan differences do have other marginal effects. One difference is in style. When dealing with a government of the same party there is often less aggressiveness. 'They might make the same demand, but in a very different fashion,' said a federal official. Party differences might also make communication a little less free. For example, there was more frank and open communication between Quebec and Ottawa during the Liberal Lesage years than there was during the Union Nationale régime. But again, both at the official and the political levels, Conservative Ontario communicates very freely with Liberal Ottawa and on an official level close Quebec-Ottawa contacts remained even during the Union Nationale's tenure.

Finally, partisan differences do appear to vary somewhat from province to province. In particular in the Maritimes, where federal and provincial parties are closely interconnected (and provincial parties depend on the national party for election finances), respondents felt New Bruns-

58 'Submission of the Government of Ontario to the Special Joint Committee of the Senate and House of Commons on the Canada Pension Plan,' Toronto, 21 Jan. 1965.

wick under a Liberal administration fared better at the hands of Ottawa because of the party connection. Said a New Brunswick official: 'Robichaud and Mike Pearson have a great deal in common, so [he] really gets his day in court with the federal government ... With this political thing, the federal people probably say to themselves the one thing we cannot do is screw Louis [Robichaud]. Of course, Diefenbaker thought he could screw Louis, and he did.' In other provinces, where there is less connection between federal and provincial parties, relations are much less close. Saskatchewan's Liberal Premier Thatcher and the federal Liberals regard each other with mutual distrust and dislike. The reason, as a British Columbian respondent put it, is 'The western Liberal is not the same fellow as the eastern Liberal and it's the same with the Conservatives.'

It seems clear, then, that party plays a marginal role. Cleavages do not follow party lines. Cooperation is not greater among Liberal governments; nor is conflict greater between Liberal and Conservative governments.[59] Other factors – regional needs and interests, ideology, and differences in the focus of attention of the various governments – override partisan differences. The tendency for federal and provincial parties to be separate entities and to be seeking support in different environments appears to be one reason for this phenomenon. Another reason for the lack of importance of party may be the lack of ideological coherence in Canadian parties.

## CONCLUSION

The basis of intergovernmental conflict is thus found in four main sources: varying basic economic interests of the various regions; ideological concerns, both in terms of substantive policies and in beliefs about the nature of the system; status concerns, in which the governments seek to protect and enhance their own importance and prestige; and, finally, differences in perspective occasioned by the different political, economic, and social environments. Partisan differences, we have shown, have only marginal effects on federal-provincial conflict. Agreement and disagreement among governments coincide with party lines only when other factors such as ideological agreement are at work; party is largely irrelevant to the major divisions among Canadian governments. The four factors which are important obviously interact with each other. For example, status concerns contribute to ideologies which emphasize either provincial or federal dominance, as the case may be. Differences in focus are at least partly

59 F.C. Engelmann and M.A. Schwartz agree with this conclusion; see their *Political Parties and the Canadian Social Structure* (Scarborough, Ont., 1967), p. 128.

related to differences in economic need. In addition, these factors help to account for agreement as well as disagreement. Thus most provinces do share an ideology that stresses the need for cooperation, unity, and compromise. This leads to moderation in the goals pursued and the kinds of tactics the participants use. All governments are also broadly agreed that each level has a right to exist; that the federal government does have some overriding responsibilities, notably in economic policy; and that all governments, being interdependent, must seek to coordinate their activities to some degree.

The patterns of cleavage among the governments will vary by issue. When all provinces are directly affected, in the same ways, then a straight federal-provincial division is likely. The disposition of the pension fund, some aspects of the manpower programme, and the Municipal Loan Fund are examples. But most issues are not that way. The provinces differ from each other as much as from the federal government in their relative wealth, economic needs, and political environment. Quebec's needs and interests differ greatly from those of the English-speaking provinces. On financial questions provinces are agreed on the desire for more federal financial help; they disagree, however, on the form it should take. The provinces can thus line up in many ways on different issues. For Ottawa, writes one observer, 'There was never need for a conscious policy of "divide and conquer," '[60]

Finally, not all governments wish to expend resources on each issue. They may all be expected to play an important part when their own direct interests and policies are at stake – notably on money questions. But on policy issues which concern them indirectly, like the pension plan, there is little incentive to get involved unless, as in the case of Saskatchewan, Quebec, and Ontario on pensions, important concerns of either the particular governments involved or their particular reference groups are at stake. Or where the immediate stakes and benefits are remote or unclear, as with much of the constitutional debate, governments will be inactive. In general, because of their central positions, Ontario and Quebec will be deeply involved in almost all major issues. Other provinces, with fewer resources, and a narrower range of interests will participate, but will not always play a major role.

Most conflicts are not fundamental. There is a broad consensus on the nature of the system among all but the Quebec government. At one level the conflict between Quebec and Ottawa is fundamental – their respective conceptions of the nature of the system are deeply opposed – but even

60 R.M. Burns, 'Intergovernmental Relations in Canada: Further Developments,' unpublished paper, 1965.

here the combination of a federal ideology which has in the past tended to stress accommodation and compromise and a Quebec position which also emphasizes discussion issue by issue and which is constrained by direct economic needs, means that much potential conflict is muted, though this appears to be changing. A major characteristic of the constitutional debate is that fundamental disagreements have been opened up and confronted with the attendant risk that resolution will be extremely difficult. Premiers Manning and Bennett warned of this in 1967. Opening the constitutional issue, they said, would only create unnecessary conflict and 'emotional strain.'

There are important differences in the goals and objectives of Canada's governments. But what of the personal relationships among the participants? There is conflict, but is there hostility? The limited nature of the dispute and the ideological desire for mutual accommodation suggest that there should be little. Such is the case.

## PERSONAL RELATIONSHIPS: 'IT'S LIKE A HOCKEY GAME'

In general, even when there are disagreements personal relationships among both officials and ministers are cooperative. Said a Quebec financial official: 'You know, it's rather like a hockey game. The players are fighting pretty hard on the ice – but have you seen them get together after the game? At the level of officials we are very close friends. There is great friendship, a very close relationship. The politicians have more differing interests, but even there, there is less disagreement than the press indicates.' Another official with experience in several governments used the analogy of a club: 'Despite all the differences and antagonisms and arguments, it's all very friendly. It's rather like belonging to a club.' A Quebec pension negotiator added: 'Throughout the discussions there was very little hostility. I heard a couple of times that such and such a minister was angry at the federal government, or that such and such a minister in the federal government was pretty angry at Quebec. But these were not the people who were taking part in the discussions. There was no hostility among them.' Comments like these come from most provinces.

But this does not mean tempers never get frayed. For example, the atmosphere at the Quebec Conference in March 1964 was very tense. Many of the officials who worked on the Tax Structure Committee projections were frustrated and annoyed when the results of so much labour were treated so cavalierly by the federal government. This, combined with federal refusal to concede and Ottawa's sudden introduction of a new manpower and education policy made the October 1966 Federal-Provincial Conference also tense and acrimonious. 'We were really mad as hell,' said an Ontario official. Thus at times the proceedings can get overtly hostile; but such occasions seem relatively few and short-lived. There is an element of ritual when angry words are said publicly.

Relationships can vary from department to department. Thus relations among financial officials of all governments appear to be good, despite the clear-cut disagreements. These officials meet often in the continuing committee, and consult frequently. Many have dealt with each other regularly for years. In addition, federal Finance Department officials have a very strong commitment to minimizing conflict, partly for ideological reasons and partly because of their belief in the need for cooperation in fiscal policies. The result is that the continuing committee in many ways resembles a club. The members share many of the same concerns and often the same type of professional training. This was not so much the case with the continuing committee on the constitution.

Similarly, the warmth of personal relations varies from province to province. Ontario and Quebec officials, for example, communicate very often with each other and with federal officials. 'I can pick up the phone and call Ed Gallant [then director of the Federal-Provincial Relations Division of the federal Finance Department] as easily as I can call someone downstairs,' says one Ontario official. Says a Quebec official: 'A marvellous thing has developed among the officials, with this great friendship and trust. Everybody has the greatest respect for Bob Bryce [then federal deputy minister of finance] and Al Johnson [then assistant deputy minister of finance], and I think this is reciprocated. You can tell them things and know they will never use it against us, and when they give it to us, we would not use it against them.' These personal friendships among key advisers from different governments undoubtedly lessen federal-provincial conflict and make agreement easier.

Not all governments – and not all individuals – have this type of relationship with federal officials. In British Columbia, especially, the pervasive sense of grievance against – and distance from – federal policies and officials shows up in the province's conduct and in personal relations. British Columbian officials and ministers are suspicious of the Ottawa 'centralizers'; Ottawa – and some other provincial – officials reciprocate these feelings. Thus at the personal level the worst relationship is probably that between British Columbia and Ottawa, but even here there is agreement on many things.

It might be expected that because they share many of the same professional interests, because they have more personal contact, and because they are less concerned with purely political matters, there might be a warmer relationship between officials than between politicians. Several respondents suggested this was in fact the case, but it appears that while officials do search more for positions of agreement rather than disagreement, there is little difference.

The foregoing suggests that, with some exceptions, the federal-provincial negotiations are conducted in a spirit of harmony. Seldom do policy differences become personal differences. Frustrations and annoyance are common, and individual personalities will often grate, but for most participants policy differences are not accompanied by deep-rooted personal antagonisms.

We have now described the nature and extent of federal-provincial conflict and competition, and examined the kinds of goals the governments pursue. What weapons do they have for attaining these objectives?

CHAPTER NINE

# Political resources

Given their goals and objectives the actors try to achieve them through the expenditure of political resources. But what kinds of resources do they have? What are they based on? What are their characteristics and limitations? Robert Dahl has stressed the rich variety of things which can provide the basis for political resources. He also noted that many participants do not fully exploit their potential resources; there is much slack in the system.[1] I shall concentrate on another vital aspect of political resources: their distribution is highly variable and relative to both the issues and the time. More important, resources are often not tangible, 'objective' facts; rather they are predominantly subjective. They depend on the beliefs and perceptions of the participants. This stress on the importance of subjective considerations may help to explain some difficult problems in assessing the influence of one actor over another. Often it is impossible to point to a specific legal sanction by which actor A influences actor B. In such situations the best answer is probably that B believes – or A has persuaded him – that A has power. Actor B acts on this belief, even though the reality, which no one can be sure of, may be quite different. A simple example might be: how does one explain a labour leader's influence. Presumably it is because the politician *believes* that somehow the labour leader exerts control over the votes of union

1 *Who Governs? Democracy and Power in an American City* (New Haven, 1961), pp. 226, 273.

members; in fact the leader might control very few votes. It is the perception that is important.

This chapter will explore some of these questions by examining some important bases of political resources and their limitations, and by assessing the distribution of resources among the governments on each set of issues. Finally, we shall draw some conclusions about the nature of political resources. Most observers of Canadian federalism have noted the apparently growing influence of the provincial governments vis-à-vis Ottawa. Here some of the dynamics – and limitations – of this alleged influence will be examined.

## LEGAL AUTHORITY

The most 'objective' type of political resource is embodied in legal authority to give or withhold consent. He who controls what Edward Banfield calls the 'requisite actions'[2] will have resources. The constitution, when it allocates responsibilities among the units, also allocates authority over requisite actions. A good example is found in the pension negotiations. The 1951 amendment to section 94 of the British North America Act[3] gave Ottawa authority only for simple old age pensions, and not for disability and survivors benefits. It also stated that no federal pension legislation 'shall affect the operation of any law present or future of a provincial legislature in relation to' old age pensions. Quebec was able to use the leverage this supplied at several points in the bargaining process; it was a valuable resource.[4] 'That put Quebec in a very strong position,' said a federal official, 'and any other province for that matter, if it had wanted to use the leverage.' Quebec had an advantage because, said a federal cabinet minister, 'the lawyers were on their side.' On pensions, Ottawa could not ignore the provinces.

Prime Minister Robarts frankly indicated this aspect of the constitution when he opposed, in 1969, a federal proposal to give Ottawa paramountcy in the pension field. Ontario, he said, would not like to give away its 'bargaining rights.' The province had been able to effectively bargain with Ottawa because of section 94A. 'With these rights we had

2 *Political Influence: A New Theory of Urban Politics* (New York, 1961), p. 309.
3 An Act to Amend the British North America Act, 1867, 14–15 Geo. VI, c. 32.
4 In November 1963 Quebec said it would not consent to the amendment of section 94A to allow federal survivors' benefits unless the federal plan had a 4 per cent contribution rate. This position was revealed by the Toronto *Globe and Mail*, 15 Dec. 1963. Mr Pearson denied it the next day. Both the respondents and the official summary of the meeting, however, indicate clearly that Lesage did make the statement.

some leverage to put our point of view and had it listened to ... I have some doubts if we would have achieved what we did [on the pension plan] had we given up the leverage that we had.'[5]

The constitution is, however, seldom so explicit as in the pension example. In raising taxes both levels of government have jurisdiction.[6] Equalization is simply a federal spending programme: 'they are Ottawa's dollars' and, though British Columbia has hinted it might test the constitutionality of the programme in the courts, there is little doubt about its legality. Tax-sharing is essentially a question of persuading Ottawa to abate more; equalization, for the beneficiaries, is similarly a matter of asking Ottawa to be more generous. In neither case do the provinces control requisite actions. The result is that the provinces have less leverage over Ottawa in these questions. 'You can argue a good case until you are blue in the face,' said an Ontario official, 'but if you are arguing against the guy who has the money, he has the power, and that's all there is to it.' Similarly, although constitutional authority over educational matters gives the provinces leverage over the *form* of federal assistance to education, the formula for aid to higher education put forward by Ottawa in 1966 was essentially a question of federal largesse to the provinces. They could demand more, but had no authoritative sanctions.

Other examples in which legal authority – which need not depend only on the constitution – confers resources can be multiplied. The undisputed provincial jurisdiction over local governments provided a good part of their leverage in getting the federal government to make changes in the Municipal Loan Fund proposed in 1963. Likewise, the provinces could ignore the federal proposal in 1966 to transfer three major shared-cost programmes to the provinces simply because the programmes themselves did not expire for two or three years. The provinces were able to force modifications in the new federal manpower programme because it depended on provincial institutions to provide the training courses. The provinces could – and one or two did – threaten not to sell any training places to Ottawa. Unless they signed the agreement there could be no federal programme. A Manitoba official said: 'The provinces can say well, if you are not going to come our way, if you are not going to improve the programme in light of our request, then we'll stop our cooperation, and you would be left holding the bag.'

Constitutional change had to be a joint exercise, since the provinces

5 Constitutional Conference, Third Meeting, 8–10 Dec. 1969, *Proceedings* (Ottawa, 1969), p. 110.

6 The most complete discussion of constitutional provisions concerning taxation is found in Gerard V. La Forest, *The Allocation of Taxing Power under the Canadian Constitution* (Toronto, 1967).

would have to agree to any results. Thus, when a federal proposal involves the constitutional rights of the other governments, or when it requires their cooperation, the provinces do control requisite actions, and hence resources. Where the action is more unilateral, the provinces have no legal authority, and fewer resources. This is one very important reason why the distribution of political resources varies from issue to issue.

Governments may try to protect or increase their resources in future negotiations by insisting on provisions which give them authority over future changes. One example is Ontario's insistence that future amendments to the Canada Pension Plan require consent of two-thirds of the provinces with two-thirds of the population. Similarly Quebec wanted to be included among the 'other provinces' for the purposes of amendment to the CPP. This would give Quebec a say over future changes without giving Ottawa a similar right over changes in the Quebec plan and would avoid giving Ontario a veto (which might prevent changes Ottawa and Quebec wanted). A 'national consensus' formula for approval of new shared-cost programmes would give a great deal more power to the provinces; arguments about the exact nature of the formula are really arguments about who should get what bargaining power.

Legal authority, whether conferred through the constitution, or through legislation, is also a constraint since it limits the freedom of each government to introduce policies where it has no authority. There are, of course, limitations on the extent to which the governments may use their legal authority. For example, withholding agreement to sell space for manpower training to the federal government would have been as costly to the provinces as to Ottawa. Thus, formal authority, expressed in laws or constitutions, provides fundamental parameters, which condition the behaviour and influence of all participants. But even here there can be room for dispute and argument, and authoritative allocations of resources are often non-existent or ambiguous.

## POLITICAL SUPPORT

Perhaps the most important political resource – or constraint – for negotiators competing in the same political environment is the degree of support they believe they have in the underlying population, or at least among attentive publics. Does the public support the federal or provincial government? If the participants believe support lies with the provincial governments, both generally and on individual issues, then it is likely the federal government will feel that to maintain its political following it must make concessions to the premiers. What is involved here is an assessment not only of the public mood but also of the influence the respective governments hold over their electorates. Conversely, if federal officials believe the public supports them, and is opposed to the views of the premiers, it is likely to be firm.

The underlying distribution of political loyalties is a question about which there are very few data. Politicians, like political scientists, operate in an environment of great uncertainty. This has two effects: first, because they must operate largely by guesswork, psychological factors play an important role in the assessments the politicians make; and, second, the participants will try to convince each other that they have support. Resources themselves become a matter for negotiation.

What is the reality? One unpublished study provides some data.[7] Asked which government is most important in affecting how one's family gets along, respondents in seven provinces were more likely to say the provincial government. There was great variation among provinces.[8] British Columbia voters were the most 'provincial' by this measure: almost 60 per cent said the provincial government was most important; 23 per cent said Ottawa was. Voters in the other western provinces also were more likely to say the provincial government. In Ontario, Ottawa had a slight edge. French-speaking voters in Quebec were more provincial.[9] The Maritimes varied: in Nova Scotia and Prince Edward Island almost identical proportions supported each government; Newfoundland and New Brunswick voters were more provincial. Another question, asking which government handled the most important questions, produced a much more 'federal' response.[10] Quebec respondents were the most provincial, followed by British Columbia, Ontario, and then the other provinces. The real distribution of loyalties is thus unclear; but it is certain that there is much variation among provinces. Quebec, as expected, is overall the most provincial, with British Columbia second; Ontario is the most 'national.'

Data on changes in the distribution of political support are even more sketchy. The Canadian Institute of Public Opinion (Gallup Poll) has asked its respondents several times if they felt 'Canada would be worse off if all provincial governments were abolished and the whole country

7 Jon Pammett, 'Canadian Politics and Party Support: Nationalization or Fragmentation?' unpublished paper prepared for Politics 820, at Queen's University, Kingston, under the direction of Professor John Meisel.

8 *Ibid.*, p. 7.

9 Interestingly, by this measure, British Columbians were more 'provincial' than French-speaking Quebecers, though in other questions the latter were always more 'provincial.' The figures reported here are for French-speaking voters in Quebec. English-speaking Quebec respondents were always more 'federal.'

10 *Ibid.*, p. 8.

governed from Ottawa?' In 1946 half the population felt so, and 25 per cent felt Canada would be better off. In 1960 the proportion feeling Canada would be 'worse off' had risen to 62 per cent, and in 1965 the figure was 66 per cent. Those feeling Canada would be better off declined to 18 per cent. On this and other questions the Gallup findings confirm regional differences mentioned above.[11]

It might be expected that questions about the 'appropriate' level of government will bring a different response from issue to issue. The Gallup Poll asked its respondents which government they thought should run a portable pension plan.[12] Nationally, 52 per cent said Ottawa, 31 per cent their provincial government, and 17 per cent were undecided. The differences between Ontario and Quebec were most striking: 58 per cent of Quebecers said the plan should be run by Quebec; 25 per cent said by Ottawa. The figures were exactly reversed in Ontario. In all other provinces large majorities favoured a federal plan.

Elections too provide little guidance. The problem of extracting a mandate from gross election returns is at best of times a tricky task. In a complex and esoteric area like federal-provincial relations, it is even more difficult. There is very little evidence that voters are motivated by federal-provincial concerns, though on occasion they are injected into the campaign by the candidates. Such concerns are only one set among many election stimuli, one which most voting studies would lead us to assume is of low salience. How can the decision-makers evaluate a Quebec electorate, to take one example, which in one provincial election returns a nationalist government and a short time later gives strong support to an emphatically federalist national Liberal party? Politicians at one level who try to influence an election at another in order to promote some policy goal seem to risk much while gaining at best very little. It seems to have been good strategy for the Union Nationale not to have risked its credibility by trying to defeat Trudeau's Liberals in the 1968 federal election.

Thus, whether through polls or elections, public opinion is a very uncertain factor in the negotiations. Nevertheless politicians, lacking certainty, grasp at what straws they can. The federal-provincial leaders do have beliefs and perceptions about political support, and they often act on the basis of them. It is in this subjective sense that political support is an important resource. Ontario provides a clear example. Ontario negotiators and their federal counterparts believe that Ontario citizens are

11 Mildred Schwartz, *Public Opinion and Canadian Identity* (Berkeley and Los Angeles, 1967), Table 32, p. 93, and pp. 93–5. Also Canadian Institute of Public Opinion, news release, 3 Feb. 1965.
12 Canadian Institute of Public Opinion, news release, 15 July 1964.

strongly identified with Ottawa. Two quotations illustrate the point:

It is almost bred in Ontarians to look at Canada first, not Ontario. It's very hard for these people to talk of Ontario as distinct from Canada. Ontarians tend to talk in terms of Canada, not in terms of a provincial government.

Ontario certainly could not have got these concessions [on the pension plan]. The Ontario people just wouldn't support it. They are for unity. They do not want measures that would weaken the federal government.

These considerations directly affect Ontario's conduct. On most issues the prime minister of Ontario cannot persuasively argue with federal ministers that if they displease him then they will displease Ontario voters; he cannot convincingly threaten Ottawa with loss of support in Ontario. Ontario officials believed it might be politically disastrous to kill the pension plan. Similarly, the province could never make a credible threat to pull out of Confederation. The result is to limit its bargaining power and to lead to moderation both in its goals and in the methods used to attain them. Seldom do Ontario officials publicly attack Ottawa. An Ontario adviser summed it up: 'There was not much attempt by Ottawa to persuade Quebec [on pensions] because they knew that Lesage had the support of the people. This fact gives Quebec great bargaining power, whereas Robarts knows that if there is conflict it will be difficult for him to get public support ...'

Even in Ontario, however, the immediate political situation may convey an impression of greater political support. Thus, when the Ontario Liberals campaigned on the issue of support for the pension plan the subsequent Conservative victory strengthened Ontario's hand and weakened Ottawa's. 'It did give us a breathing space,' said an Ontario official, 'The federal people tried to back us into a corner and they failed.' A federal official agreed: 'From that moment on, we were in the weakest possible position.' But even these feelings are subjective; there is no evidence that the pension plan was a significant determinant of votes in the election.

Manitoba operates under similar constraints. 'It is never very easy to put the blame on Ottawa,' said one official; 'the average person in the street, he just doesn't understand.' After the failure of Manitoba to achieve its objectives in 1966, the government did launch a public attack on Ottawa, 'but it just didn't work, and finally we had to drop it – you don't get far by damning the federal government here.' The response from both press and public was negative. Again, these factors limit Manitoba's resources and the tactics its representatives can use.

At the other end of the scale is Quebec, where all sides believe the provincial government to have a wide degree of political support. 'It's clear in Quebec that the provincial government is the most important,' said one official. A senior negotiator on the pension plan ably explained the feelings of many in the Quebec government – and in Ottawa – during the pension negotiations:

I think that at one point the Liberals in Quebec under Lesage really got almost total support from the population. There was a kind of identity of viewpoint between government and population. It was rather like Israel. The base of the government was very solid. The politicians and the wishes of the general public corresponded. There was a consensus. But with the federal government, there had been the year [1962] with the weak minority government of Diefenbaker, and then the Liberal minority which was very weak. So the Quebec government which was very strong faced a federal government which was very weak.

Quebec had wide support for its position on the pension plan from the Quebec press.[13] Provincial unity was clearly demonstrated to Ottawa when the government won unanimous support in the legislature for its resolution stating that Quebec would set up its own plan.[14]

This situation gives Quebec a set of political resources quite unlike those of any other province, and officials in all governments recognize it. A federal minister said: 'Certainly Quebec has more weapons than the other provinces. The biggest weapon in Quebec is that it is the only province that could wreck Confederation. This is their main weapon. They can make the threat and be taken seriously. It is not possible for the other provinces to do that.' A Quebec official agrees: 'At bottom the pressures we can exert are political – the threat of political retribution. This is particularly true in Quebec where most of the people look to the Quebec government. We can make that threat.' Quebec officials can, and do, argue credibly that if Ottawa does not accede to its positions, the federal government will lose support in Quebec. This argument is strengthened by the fact that the federal Liberals depend heavily on

13 This view was widely held by commentators in the press. Peter Newman wrote in 1963 that Lesage '... is probably in the strongest position a provincial Premier has ever held vis à vis Ottawa ... Not only is his cabinet and his party, but his opposition in the legislature, the province's press and most of the population are united behind him in the drive to extract concessions from the federal government.' See 'Backstage in Ottawa,' *Maclean's*, 10 Aug. 1963, p. 2.

14 23 Aug. 1963. The full text of the resolution is: 'That it is expedient for the Legislature of the Province of Quebec to pass as soon as possible an act to establish a public and universal retirement fund based on actuarial calculations, and maintained by compulsory contributions.'

Quebec's seventy-five seats in the federal Parliament for their power. It cannot afford to lose them. In 1965 the federal Liberals depended on Quebec for 30 per cent of their votes and fifty-six of their 131 parliamentary seats.[15] 'This gave Lesage tremendous leverage,' said a federal official, 'and they had to pacify him – thus there was a continual threat.'

The subjective nature of perceptions of political support means that assessments may change over time. The alteration in the federal viewpoint between the pension negotiations in 1963–4 and the financial discussions in 1966, and later, is a dramatic illustration. In the first period Ottawa leaders felt they were weak and the provinces strong and popular. The lesson, as the decision-makers saw it, was 'that the public is more likely to accept provincial policies than federal ones – the feeling was that we mustn't antagonize the provinces.' The real reason Ottawa was weak in the negotiations, said another official, was that 'on the whole the provinces have been strong in the sense that they have had firmly based majority governments. But for ten years now we have not had a federal government which is widely based on popular support. So this leads the federal people to feel it behooves us not to make enemies, especially among the premiers.' At the time it was felt extremely difficult to govern without a majority. While the Liberals had attained power with a very slim electoral margin, most provincial governments had recently been elected with large majorities. The new cabinet was weak and inexperienced, and the Quebec representation was considered especially mediocre, with little political base in the province.

Some developments early in the negotiations themselves reinforced the perceived lack of power. First was the débâcle following presentation of the first budget by Finance Minister Walter Gordon on 13 June 1963.[16] The budget, prepared with the help of outside advisers, contained many controversial provisions, and shortly after its introduction the government was forced into an undignified retreat. The impression of weakness was heightened only two weeks later when the provinces so easily won federal concessions on the Municipal Loan Fund. The whole atmosphere changed when the budget came out, said one federal official: 'Up to that time the federal government could have got away with all sorts of things without provincial protest. The moment the federal government proved itself vulnerable, the provinces were around its neck. The morale of the government was terribly hurt.' At the same time, federal leaders lost confidence in themselves while the provinces, correspondingly, felt more

15 John Saywell, ed., *Canadian Annual Review for 1965* (Toronto, 1966), p. 110.
16 For a discussion of the Gordon Budget, see Saywell, ed., *Canadian Annual Review for 1963* (Toronto, 1964), pp. 53–7, 195–204.

powerful. 'And naturally, when they saw the rug being pulled out [from under] the loan fund, they had no inclination to go easy on the pension plan,' said one official. Perceived political resources thus can change as the negotiations unfold, and events outside the federal-provincial arena can shape the positions of the governments in the negotiation process itself.

When it came to dealing with Quebec the subjective feelings of weakness had another dimension. At the time of the pension negotiations the Lesage government was well embarked on its ambitious programmes for provincial development. Moreover, the separatist movement was becoming vocal. It was the time of bombs in the mailboxes. The federal government realized that the country could break up. The Lesage government was difficult to deal with – but the prime minister was, after all, a fellow Liberal and a known quantity. Federal decision-makers feared that if he were defeated the replacement might be something far worse and harder to deal with. Therefore he should not be weakened.

The situation in Quebec had been strikingly brought home to federal and provincial officials at the Quebec Conference in 1964, when elaborate security precautions had to be taken, and when the chants of demonstrators on the Quebec Parliament lawn could be heard in the conference room. The Lesage government was embarrassed and apologetic. But this very embarrassment increased its resources. No one needed to say it, but the implication was clear: if we are defeated the alternative will be worse. A federal official described this attitude: 'In 1963–4 I think the ministers felt very weak. I think they probably realized a French-Canadian defection could bring them crashing down. They treated Quebec rather like a ticking time-bomb. They just couldn't judge to what extent Lesage was really speaking for the people of Quebec ... We were scared of him. We thought he was speaking for the people, and the bombs in the mailboxes only confirmed that.' This kind of feeling was echoed by provincial respondents. A Quebec official argued that: 'Most of the federal people felt that here was an understanding and flexible man [Lesage], but one who was also riding a tiger, so that they must not make things too difficult for him.' This last point illustrates another element of political resources, which again stems from their subjective nature. What may be a liability from one point of view (here nationalist opposition to Lesage) may be a resource from another, so long as it enables the actor to commit himself.[17] A similar combination of a federalist Quebec government, whose main opposition is a separatist party, should increase the bargaining power of the Bourassa government elected in 1970.

17 Thomas C. Schelling, *The Strategy of Conflict* (New York, 1963), p. 27.

All these factors contributed to federal officials' belief that they were weak, and that the provinces, especially Quebec, were strong. The provinces agreed. And this situation, which was largely subjective, seems to be a major reason for the federal concessions on pensions, finances, and other issues during the period. Political resources depended on beliefs about political resources.

By 1966 the federal assessment of the situation had changed considerably. It was still a minority government – but three years of experience had shown this was not an insurmountable barrier to effective government. The cabinet had gained in experience. Perhaps more important, the Quebec Liberals had been defeated, and their replacement, the Union Nationale, did not seem so fearsome after all. Separatism in Quebec had not declined, but the initial shock and fear had worn away. Most important, federal officials had changed their assessment of the way to maintain political support. Following the negotiations of 1963, 1964, and 1965 the government had been much criticized for weakness and vacillation in the face of provincial demands. Now federal officials felt that perhaps the best way to maintain support was not to concede to the provinces but to be firm with them. The result of this changed view of the nature of the environment was that Ottawa felt it could be much less conciliatory.

A federal adviser deeply involved in policy formation at both times summed up some of the dimensions of the change in federal attitude:

> There is much less a feeling of weakness now ... The government does not now fear a defeat or overthrow of Parliament ... But I suspect the most fundamental reason is the growing sense in the federal government that while there is no doubt the pendulum did swing very far and there is no doubt that there was a weakening in federal power, it [the experience in 1963–4] did reveal that public opinion was not so much in favour of the provinces when it came to a battle. The federal government was criticized for giving in. We realized that the people are not entirely provincially oriented. So this real sense that the provinces had this fundamental political power turned out to evaporate a bit.

Several advisers felt Ottawa had 'done itself a lot of good' by taking its firm stand in 1966. By 1969, of course, things had changed even more. There was a French-Canadian prime minister, who had led the national Liberals to a strong majority government on a strongly federalist platform, and strong French-Canadian representation at the highest policy-making levels. No longer did Ottawa feel on the defensive. It could and did pursue a much more aggressive strategy. It could directly challenge – in French – the Quebec government's claim to be the chief representative of French Canadians.

Thus between 1963 and 1966, and even more 1969, while it is unlikely the distribution of attitudes within the population had changed much – if, indeed, there is a consistent pattern to these attitudes at all – Ottawa's assessment of the pattern and of its consequences had changed, with important results. Ottawa perceived it had more resources and changed its behaviour accordingly, with successful (in the short run, at least) results. In effect, the distribution of resources changed, because perceptions changed.

This uncertainty also implies that the actors will try to change each other's assessments of reality. Quebec respondents frequently pointed out that in their view such federal Quebec ministers as Justice Minister Trudeau and Manpower Minister Marchand did not truly represent the views of Quebecers: 'I doubt if they have very much support at all. Trudeau was not elected in what you might call an ordinary constituency, Mount Royal, a largely English upper-class Montreal constituency and Marchand got in only by a hair's breadth.' More recently, Prime Minister Johnson, at the time of the September 1966 Tax Structure Committee meeting, asserted that in a referendum 80 per cent of Quebecers would support his 'two-nations' thesis.[18] And on the eve of the October Federal-Provincial Conference he reiterated that he, not the federal ministers from Quebec, spoke for the province.[19]

Federal leaders since 1966 challenged this Quebec position. In the fall of 1966 Mr Marchand, Forestry Minister Maurice Sauvé, Minister without Portfolio Jean Chrétien, and other Quebec MPs made strong speeches in the province defending the role of Ottawa and stressing the French-Canadian role in the federal government. Marchand said in a Montreal speech: 'Certainly, the position of a French Canadian is not easy. But when we are in Ottawa, and when we act within the mandates the population has given us, we act as much for Quebec as anyone does. No one alone can speak in the name of Quebec.'[20] Federal politicians, he argued, represent Quebec's views just as much as do Quebec politicians. Prime Minister Pearson echoed this view in a speech to the Liberal Federation of Canada (Quebec): 'The Prime Minister of Canada is as much Prime Minister for the people of Quebec as he is for the people of Ontario or

18 *Globe and Mail*, 16 Sept. 1966.
19 *Ibid.*, 21 Oct. 1966.
20 Reported in *Le Devoir*, Montreal, 31 Oct. 1966 (my translation). See also the commentary by Claude Ryan, 'L'ascension de M. Jean Marchand,' *ibid.*, 1, 2 Nov. 1966.

British Columbia or Newfoundland. The federal government is as much for the people of Quebec as it is for the people of any other province.'[21] Trudeau has expressed this view even more forcefully. Thus political support is a scarce resource; the participants compete for it; and this competition is part of the bargaining process.

Political support, despite its intangibility, provides one way in which federal-provincial negotiations are linked to underlying political attitudes. But the linkage is tenuous. Since there is so much uncertainty, it depends on the subjective assessments of the decision-makers themselves. These assessments may change quite independently of any real changes in public attitude. The politicians get few cues from the public itself. Support is also one of the most 'political' of political resources, since it depends on the politicians' calculations of what will win the most allegiance. The sanction ultimately is a political one: for Ontario, it is politically dangerous to fight too hard against Ottawa; for Ottawa, it alienates the Quebec government at its peril. Like most political resources, support is perceived to be unequally distributed. Quebec clearly is in a much stronger position vis-à-vis Ottawa than any other province: political support appears to be a major reason. For Ontario and Manitoba the distribution of political support acts as a constraint, both on their tactics and on their influence. British Columbia appears to have a more 'provincial' population than all provinces except Quebec. That this is not converted into greater political resources, however, can perhaps best be explained by the fact that, first, British Columbia's population is relatively small, but, second and much more important, it is clear that for Ottawa politicians Quebec is much more salient and important. Quebec occupies its focus of attention, again showing the importance of subjective factors.

## SKILLS AND EXPERTISE

Measuring the skill with which the governments pursue their objectives is well-nigh impossible, but at the same time differences in skills should be expected to play an important role in the negotiations. Two kinds of skills are most important – technical skills, especially among officials, and political skills, associated with the ability to persuade others, to exploit resources, and to devise winning strategies.

It is apparent that in recent years many provinces have greatly increased their technical expertise in federal-provincial relations. At the same time, the status of provincial civil servants has become much more equal to

21 The last sentence, following the time-worn practice of Canadian politicians to intersperse French and English, was in French.

that of federal civil servants. The provinces today are better equipped to react intelligently to federal initiatives.[22] Often they have thought out their own alternatives and are better prepared than their federal counterparts.[23] Following the Second World War the weight of technical expertise seems to have been overwhelmingly in Ottawa. The balance has shifted. A New Brunswick official with considerable experience in federal-provincial negotiations observed:

Especially on the continuing committee, around 1956 and 1957 the federal government had virtually all the strength. The provinces were extremely weak. The Atlantic provinces had a group of officials who had to be seen to be believed. Quebec was completely ineffectual and Ontario was no better. If any provinces did lead, it was the three western provinces. But the federal government had quite a battery. They would completely overpower the provinces ... But in recent years it's all changed ... The federal government is hard put to keep up with the provinces individually, let alone together. In the last round [1966] solid contributions were made by Nova Scotia, New Brunswick, Quebec, Ontario, even Saskatchewan, Alberta, PEI; and BC made a negative contribution because of ... Bennett who runs the show.

The reasons for this change are unclear. In part, with growing provincial responsibilities, provincial administrations have become more attractive and thus able to recruit better personnel. In addition, the governments have become more aware of the importance of federal-provincial negotiations and the need to be better prepared for them. Thus in Quebec the Lesage government recruited a group of brilliant advisers to work in this field. Ontario greatly increased its staff resources in federal-provincial relations.[24] The thrust in Ontario came partly as a result of dissatisfaction with the way the province had played its cards in the pension negotiations. Ontario also established the Advisory Committee on Confederation to advise and assist the government, especially in the constitutional debate. It also greatly expanded the federal-provincial relations section in the Office of the Chief Economist. When Premier Louis Robichaud's Liberal

22 See Edwin R. Black and Alan Cairns, 'A Different Perspective on Canadian Federalism,' *Canadian Public Administration* 9 (1966), p. 41.
23 Robert A. McLarty, 'Federal-Provincial Relations: Machinery and Policy,' unpublished paper, n.d., p. 12.
24 For a discussion of the role of the Office of the Chief Economist, see H. Ian Macdonald, 'The "New Economics" and the Province of Ontario,' *Ontario Economic Review* 4, no 4 (April 1966), pp. 4–9. For a good discussion of the operation of the Ontario executive, see Fred Schindeler, 'The Organization and Functions of the Executive Branch of Government in Ontario,' *Canadian Public Administration* 9 (1966), pp. 409–48.

government took power in New Brunswick, 'The first thing we had to face was the renegotiation of the tax agreements,' said a minister. 'We saw the immediate need for a strong staff to help us.' They recruited as deputy minister of finance D.D. Tansley, a highly respected official who had been a senior official in Saskatchewan, and added another former Saskatchewan official as economic adviser. Officials of all governments were agreed that New Brunswick was now far better equipped.

It is easy, however, to exaggerate this increased expertise in provincial capitals. Many governments continue to come to conferences with little preparation, so that, in Daniel Johnson's words, their premiers' contributions are little more than 'brilliant improvisations.'[25] Especially in the smaller provinces, where few persons are involved in federal-provincial relations, a shift of one or two men may have a great effect. Thus, under the CCF-NDP government, Saskatchewan had developed a group of extremely highly trained advisers. But shortly after the Liberal régime of Premier Ross Thatcher took office, several of the province's top personnel left, some to other provinces like New Brunswick, others to the federal government.[26] Saskatchewan's effectiveness was probably weakened as a result. British Columbia, largely because of the extremely personalized leadership of the premier, does not appear to have developed a strong group of advisers in federal-provincial relations. Both levels of government, moreover, face strong competition for trained personnel, particularly economists, from business and the universities, though several have used academic experts as consultants and included them in provincial delegations.

Nor should it be thought that Ottawa's talents have decreased. On many questions the federal government can still muster a wider array of experts than can the provinces. For example, in financial relations the Department of Finance has many professionals in the federal-provincial relations division, and can draw on others in the department and in the Privy Council Office. The provinces, said one federal official, 'do not have the depth we have. They are pretty thin.' 'The provinces have made terrific progress,' said another, 'but I still don't think they have gone much beyond the position where they can criticize ... intelligently.'

Skill and expertise also vary from issue to issue. This is partly because in some policy areas, which they are traditionally involved in, governments will have built up a background of knowledge and experience. On pensions, Ottawa could draw on its experts in the departments of national health and welfare, finance, and others; Quebec could draw on its own

25 Confederation of Tomorrow Conference, *Proceedings* (Toronto, 1967), p. 180.
26 Saywell, ed., *Canadian Annual Review for 1964* (Toronto, 1965), pp. 163–4.

interdepartmental task force; Ontario had a pool of its own from its earlier study of the question. Other provinces did not have this prior experience, so were much less well prepared. Pensions for them were remote, and they had little incentive to repair the gap.

Similarly, the resources available will depend greatly on the importance a government attaches to a question. The contribution made to the work of constitutional review in terms of study, preparation of position papers, submission of documented propositions, and the like appeared to vary directly with the significance the various governments attached to the review itself. Ottawa developed the most elaborate technical apparatus, followed by Quebec and Ontario. New Brunswick also devoted considerable effort to the review, supplementing weakness of staff resources in its own civil service by the use of outside advisers like Dean Maxwell Cohen of the McGill University Law School.

Political skills are harder to assess. To a great extent they lie in the eyes of the beholder, so it is impossible to spell out one set of qualities which add up to political skill. A politician skilled in one form of activity, such as winning elections, may not have the same abilities in negotiations with other governments. The most important kinds of political skill in federal-provincial negotiations include such elements as the ability to perceive or create new alternatives, to exploit and pyramid resources, and to devise arguments and tactics which best take advantage of the existing situation and which are most likely to win allies and persuade others. It is often easier to point to lack of skill than to its possession. Thus R.M. Burns, a long-time federal and provincial civil servant, has ascribed federal retreats in 1963 and 1964 to 'hamhanded,' hastily conceived proposals without adequate prior planning or consultation and to 'sheer political ineptitude.'[27] On the other hand, Quebec leaders effectively exploited their position after the Quebec Conference and many respondents commented on the skilful argument of Quebec delegates. One, said a federal official, 'is the best debater I ever saw – he will skate circles around you. You can never pull off a snow job when he is around.' Moreover, the political skills of individuals may provide resources for smaller governments with little other political weight. Premier Roblin of Manitoba, for example, was a dynamic participant in the negotiations, especially in 1966. 'I'm sure we had somewhat more influence than our economic or other role would justify,' said an official. The effectiveness of individuals is particularly strong in officials' meetings, where 'the influence of a person doesn't depend at all on the size and importance of his province.' Rather, 'it is the guy with the idea, the guy who is putting

27 *The Evolving Structure of Canadian Government* (Winnipeg, 1966), p. 39.

things forward, who is respected and listened to.' The abilities of New Brunswick officials thus gave New Brunswick considerable weight in the discussions, and especially in the development of the new equalization formula in 1966.

What are the consequences of the kinds of skill discussed so far? Do they have an effect on provincial influence? Quebec's success in the negotiations of 1963 to 1965 appear to be at least partly a result of its ability to formulate fully developed alternatives to federal initiatives, which were backed up with sophisticated arguments. On matters like opting-out, Ottawa reacted to a Quebec initiative. In addition, Quebec's expertise enabled it to develop a pension alternative which was in many ways more attractive than the federal plan. 'It is quite clear that Quebec got a very good deal on the Canada Pension Plan,' said a federal official, 'because they were able to convince everybody they had got a damn good plan.' 'The introduction of these new people has paid off – even in dollars and cents,' a Quebec financial adviser observed; 'they can bring more information to the discussions, the briefs are better, and there is better support.' This is true for all provinces – with better preparation and more skill they can develop sophisticated arguments in favour of their position. On matters which deeply concern them, the provinces will be as well prepared as Ottawa.

Thus it does appear that skills and expertise have been a factor in the growing influence of the provinces. Again, the respondents see it as unequally distributed. Quebec officials, many officials said, were often the best prepared and the most skilful bargainers. Ontario and New Brunswick representatives were also considered skilful. Several respondents felt that British Columbia, which invests little in federal-provincial relations, is generally less well prepared, and suffers for it.

## OBJECTIVE INFORMATION

A related resource is the possession of information which appears to back up the negotiator's position, especially when this information comes from a source which all agree is 'objective.' This kind of information is at least partly dependent on the expertise of the participants, since through their own research they can 'create' information. But as with many resources, there may not be agreement on the validity of the information or its import. Hence, again the resources themselves may be a subject for negotiation.

One example is the projection of revenues and expenditures for all governments prepared by the Tax Structure Committee between 1964 and 1966. All governments, with the partial exception of British Columbia, cooperated in the study. It showed what the federal officials had feared: provincial expenditures were rising far faster than revenues, and that while the provincial-municipal sector would be faced with a large deficit in future years, the federal government could expect a surplus. The study lent objective weight to the provincial arguments, and thus was an important resource for them.[28] Federal officials said the study did not take into account recent federal spending programmes, and therefore exaggerated the imbalance. The projection example also shows that possession of information is a limited resource. Despite the projections, the provinces were not able to get a major transfer of funds from Ottawa. Said a provincial official: 'I don't think we had ever been so well prepared as we were for last fall [1966], and yet we have seldom got so little. You can have the best case but you cannot get them to loosen those strings. It's a question of who has strength. Of course there is always another time, and I hope our preparation will pay off then.'

## SIZE AND WEALTH

It might be expected that the largest and richest provinces would also be the most influential in the negotiations, as R.J. May has recently argued.[29] In a sense this is obviously true: there are many more votes in the large provinces than in the small. But it is true only in a limited sense. Again the distinction between a region and its government is vital. While it may be true that Ottawa feels it must take into account the interests of Ontario *residents* in its policies, this does not necessarily mean the Ontario *government* will have resources. Rather, as we have seen, the participants do not believe the Ontario government could greatly influence a federal election. Quebec, though, because of its size, combined with its political support, does have more influence. Presumably if Quebec had a small population the government's political support would not be such an important resource. A BC respondent with many years of experience in the negotiations put it well: 'British Columbia's problem is that

28 Thus, in October 1966 Prime Minister Robarts argued: 'This work has provided unequivocal evidence that the present tax fields are maldistributed and that a major redistribution in favour of the provinces must now be carried out ... We believe that the projections of the Tax Structure Committee must be placed before the people of Canada ...' *Federal-Provincial Conference*, 24–28 Oct. 1966 (Ottawa, 1966), p. 65.

29 *Federalism and Fiscal Adjustment* (London, 1969), esp. chap. 1. May argues that in general 'central government policies will approximate the interests of big units rather than small units' (p. 7). He omits the crucial distinction between regional and governmental interests.

Bennett only represents 1.9 million people, while Johnson represents six million and that's a big difference.' Thus the smaller provinces do feel their influence is less because of their small size. 'Our influence has to be limited,' said a Manitoba minister. 'We are only 5 per cent of the country.' But it seems clear that size alone cannot make a province influential, nor does smallness make it weak.

Wealth in some circumstances may be a positive disadvantage in the negotiations; there is 'strength through weakness.'[30] One of the strongest arguments the provinces can make in financial discussions is their great need for funds. For the Maritimes the need is obvious, and, as we have seen, Ottawa is strongly committed to help alleviate the need. This gives the province a resource, as an Ontario official pointed out: 'Who has most influence? For hot political reasons Quebec must be number one. Then come the Maritimes. Their position is so dire they just cannot be ignored.' Ontario and British Columbia, on the other hand, cannot very persuasively argue they are in poor financial straits. Said one Ontario official: 'I think sometimes it is good in your relations with Ottawa if your province is in bad shape.' Said another: 'You have a big advantage by being small in Canada because the federal government is always going to take care of the smaller provinces and they think the big provinces can always look out for themselves.' Several federal officials echoed these sentiments. The result is that in federal-provincial relations provincial politicians will try to argue how poor they really are. In other situations the same premiers would argue the opposite. An Ontario minister told a story about Saskatchewan, which had recently joined the ranks of the 'have' provinces:

> I have to laugh at Premier Thatcher. You know it is really difficult to cry a lot about your position when it's really so much better than it was before. And that's what he has to do in a conference. I bet he says a different thing when he's down in New York talking to investors. I kidded him once at the Royal York [hotel in Toronto]. He was speaking at a Chamber of Commerce meeting and I told him you would never think you were the same person at the conference as you were at the Royal York.

Here again, the participants play in several games; what is appropriate in one is not in another. This is also another example that an embarrassment from one point of view – poverty – may be a resource from another.

This discussion of wealth and size shows that they do not necessarily

30 Edward A. Leonard, 'The Bases of Political Power: A Critical Re-examination,' paper presented to the American Political Science Association, Sept. 1969, p. 6.

lead to greater influence. They may even weaken it. In 1966 the rank order correlation (Kendall's Tau) between what each province gained (per capita) in the final result and per capita income was −.78; the correlation of gains with population was −.5. An argument like May's ignores the possibility that poverty can add to resources by giving the poor a kind of moral claim that is hard to resist. It also ignores the central fact of the focus of attention of federal decision-makers. They are more responsive to the interests of some governments than others and this makes some governments more influential than others.

## PROCEDURES AND RULES OF THE GAME

The structure of the negotiating process itself may give advantage to some participants and disadvantage to others. This explains why arguments over procedure can often play an important part in negotiations. In Canada, the rules of the federal-provincial game appear to favour Ottawa. The federal government has the dominant voice in preparing the agenda, and its representatives chair the meetings. Said one Ontario official: 'They provide the secretariat and the reports that come out afterwards, they supply the working papers, and they prepare the agenda. So they are able to structure the discussion pretty well. Very often it is little more than an information exercise as the federal government takes the delegates through their prepared positions ... If you're the chairman and control the agenda and you're in a position to call the coffee breaks and so on, you're going to have a tremendous advantage.'

Thus the structure of the meetings is determined primarily by Ottawa. The federal secretariat prepares a great deal of background material and statistics before the conferences, which helps to structure the discussion. In part, of course, this is a product of greater expertise and skill. The provinces could, and occasionally do, also provide working papers. Ottawa has more control over the timing of the discussion of issues. Thus Ontario in 1966 wanted to discuss what was for them the crucial question of tax-sharing before discussing equalization or shared-cost programmes. But Ottawa, which wanted to discuss equalization first, prevailed. As a result, by the time the ministerial meetings came in September and October, equalization had been virtually agreed on, but tax-sharing had been hardly discussed.

More important, the general pattern is for the provinces to react to federal proposals. Often they have little idea of what they will be before the meetings. Said a Manitoba official: 'Sometimes we don't get the agenda until the week before. That makes it very hard to do much preparatory work. We do try to anticipate what's coming and there is an unofficial grape vine by which we usually get the word, but occasionally – like last fall – we get caught. You get something new thrown at you and it's almost impossible to help out your politician.' There is little time to react, and a prepared provincial brief might even have to be scrapped.

This federal initiative was especially clear at the October 1966 Federal-Provincial Conference. The provinces had almost no advance warning of what was to come in the education and manpower fields. 'It looked from what we had heard that this would be very peripheral,' a senior Manitoba education official said, 'so we were entirely unprepared both in terms of our preparation and in terms of the personnel we sent. No one here had anticipated what was to come.'[31]

As well as putting the provinces as a disadvantage in the discussions, this method of presentation also enabled Ottawa to get a publicity jump on the provinces. 'So the federal government gets its programmes presented before the provinces can get theirs,' said a provincial official, 'and then it takes about one and a half days for the provincial responses to filter through.' A Manitoba minister suggested a related federal advantage: 'All the press material is handled through the Ottawa press gallery. They know their sources in the federal government and the federal press officers have a good relationship with them. They are provided with lots of press releases and background information. So how do you get your foot on the track when the federal government has this kind of advantage?' Ontario and Quebec do not appear to suffer from this weakness, since most major newspapers send their own correspondents to the meetings. It is also difficult to assess the importance of better access to the press. Like political support, its significance seems to lie mainly in the eyes of the negotiators themselves.

Nevertheless several elements in the procedures of federal-provincial conferences do provide the federal government with greater resources than the provinces, and provincial participants show much more concern with 'improving' the machinery than do federal actors.[32]

31 Thus, Quebec Justice Minister Jean-Jacques Bertrand told the press: 'We got a copy of the speech at ten last night and we worked until three this morning preparing our statement. A member of the Ontario delegation feels the same way we do. He just told me, "How can you expect people to come here and discuss such a problem when they throw this sort of thing at you on arrival."' *Globe and Mail*, 25 Oct. 1966.

32 This is supported by another study based on interviews with participants. See R.M. Burns, *Intergovernmental Liaison on Fiscal and Economic Matters* (Ottawa, 1969), pp. 121–2.

## FACTORS SPECIFIC TO THE NEGOTIATIONS

Finally, the distribution of resources in any set of negotiations will vary as the negotiations themselves proceed. Several examples may be cited.

First, an actor's commitment to one set of policy goals may affect his resources on other issues. For example, Ottawa's need to secure agreement on a pension plan gave Quebec a great deal of leverage on other issues of the day. It successfully exploited this advantage in the negotiations following the Quebec conference to achieve major concessions in fiscal and other fields. This is not to argue for a snowball effect in which every victory would increase the probability of victory on the next issue. Indeed, a string of victories may produce a reaction in which the opponent, as Ottawa did to Quebec in 1966, says 'no more.' More generally, Ottawa's commitment to avoiding conflict and maintaining unity can lead to weakness on more substantive issues. Said one respondent: 'As long as the federal government has this goal for keeping the country together it is vulnerable to being pushed into a corner by the provinces.'

Second, the action of one actor may give another resources. For example, Quebec's adamant refusal to participate in a federal pension plan gave Ontario more resources, since Ottawa could not have anything approaching a national plan if both the largest provinces were out. So during the fall of 1963 Ottawa sought ways to make the plan more palatable to Ontario; its revised plan of March 1964 embodied some of these concessions. Similarly, once a concession has been made to one participant, it can hardly be refused to others. Once it was clear Quebec would have full control of the funds produced in that province, Ottawa could not refuse the other provinces control of the fund too.

Third, if an actor can convince the others that he cannot concede to them because he is operating under a severe constraint, he will have a political resource.[33] Thus Prime Minister Lesage convinced Ottawa that it would be politically impossible for him to accept a federal pension plan. Again, Ontario and other provinces had little chance to make any major changes in the plan after Quebec and Ottawa had reached agreement with Quebec following the Quebec Conference, since Ottawa could argue that any major change would bring the tenuous agreement crashing down and lead to a reopening of the whole question. At a conference on the pension plan in July 1964 an Ontario delegate pointedly asked what was the purpose of the discussion since the conference was being presented with a fait accompli worked out between Quebec and Ottawa. The same

33 See Schelling, *The Strategy of Conflict*, p. 27.

question was raised later in parliamentary debate on the plan. As a final example, when Ontario was pushing for a provincial veto on future pension amendments, it was able to argue that it was under pressure from critics of the plan for 'selling out.' This gave Ontario resources, because, as a federal internal memorandum said, 'We cannot expect [Robarts] to be accommodating unless we provide safeguards which enable him convincingly to say [to his constituents] that he really has not sacrificed his future power.'

Fourth, internal relationships within governments may affect resources in the negotiations. Thus, Ontario's effectiveness in the pension negotiations appears to have been weakened by the fact that, especially in the early stages, its advisers were themselves divided, on occasion putting forward diverging points of view within the conference room. Similarly, one factor in the provincial success in delaying implementation of the federal medicare plan appears to have been a severe division within the federal cabinet.

Finally, completely idiosyncratic factors may be at work. For example, Prime Minister Lesage was particularly well equipped to debate pensions, since he had chaired the 1950 federal parliamentary committee which helped to draft the original Old Age Security programme. In addition, his experience in the federal cabinet equipped him well for dealing with Ottawa. Another example is the role of personal friendships. Thus, one reason for New Brunswick's success in financial questions has undoubtedly been the close relationship between A.W. Johnson, then assistant deputy minister of finance in Ottawa with major responsibility for federal-provincial relations, and D.D. Tansley and Robert McLarty, the two senior New Brunswick advisers, who had been colleagues in Saskatchewan.

## CONCLUSIONS

Political resources are subtle and complex. No fixed *a priori* classification of resources will suffice. Resources are rooted in the social context, the issue, and the time, and, even more important, in the minds of the participants. Not only does the balance of resources vary from issue to issue but also it is continually shifting as the negotiations on each issue progress. Therefore the participants must always be making calculations about their own and others' resources.

It is thus impossible to assess with certainty the resources of the participants in federal-provincial negotiations. To ask the respondents to assess their own and others' influence runs into the problem Joseph LaPalombara found in Italy; actors tend to see their own groups as weak and other groups as strong.[34] Nevertheless, some gross differences are clear.

First, overall provincial resources have increased in the last few years. 'Ten years ago the federal government could just overrun the provinces,' said a federal official.'Today it's much more difficult.' After describing the role he had played in one episode during the war, a federal minister said somewhat wistfully: 'The day for that sort of thing is past. Then we had the war and public support on our side. It's not like that any more.' A Manitoba official agreed: 'They used to think nothing of the provincial people at all. They'd just say, "Here, if you don't like it, you just get up and go home, and that will be it." But the provinces have much more influence now. I know when I was there [in Ottawa] the federal government was very strong. You just could not conceive then that the provinces would be as strong as they are now. They saw the provinces then as sort of overgrown municipalities. It was a tutelary kind of relationship.'

Among the reasons for this shift appear to be the relatively greater importance of matters under provincial jurisdiction, and a weakening of federal confidence and power, with the persistent minority governments as the chief symptom.[35] But neither of these factors account for the changes alone. For example the shift of the main tasks of government to provincial concerns could easily have resulted in Ottawa taking over these functions, as indeed it did with its postwar programmes of family allowances, unemployment insurance, old age security, and the like. What appears to be most important is a growth in the activism, competence, and, most important, self-confidence of provincial administrations, led by, but not restricted to, Quebec.[36] In recent years, they have exploited their resources to the full.

But this shift in resources can easily be exaggerated. In many areas Ottawa still retains the initiative and overwhelming administrative expertise. In particular, on those questions like finances, where the conflict takes the form of the provinces asking the federal government for something, the provinces have few resources. Where Ottawa depends on provincial actions, the balance is more equal. Most provincial officials still feel weak in the face of Ottawa. 'The provinces may propose,' said a British Columbia minister, 'but the federal government disposes.' 'They still hold most of the cards,' agreed an Ontario minister; 'you are sitting at their feet.' A Manitoba official put it this way: 'We are essentially at

34 'The Utility and Limitations of Interest Group Theory in Non-American Field Situations,' *Journal of Politics* 22 (1960), pp. 29–49.
35 Black and Cairns, 'A Different Perspective on Canadian Federalism,' pp. 35–6.
36 *Ibid.*, p. 39.

the mercy of the federal government.' These comments are clearly exaggerations, but they do indicate that Ottawa retains many political resources. They also indicate that these resources vary greatly according to the nature of the issue.

One reason for federal power is that the provinces are seldom united. Both provincial and federal respondents agreed that on most issues Ottawa would have great difficulty in resisting a solid front of the provinces. But, as we have seen, the provinces often differ among themselves. The federal government is often allied with some provinces against others. On those issues where the provinces have been agreed – medicare, the disposal of the pension fund, manpower – the provinces have been influential.

It is clear that the balance of resources between federal and provincial governments depends in great measure on federal and provincial beliefs about that balance. The shift in federal thinking between 1963–4 and 1966 represented a very real shift in resources, but it depended on shifting assessments of reality more than on changes in the allocation of authority.

The data also indicate that there are important differences among the provinces. Quebec clearly wields the greatest influence. Its political support, its activism, and its expertise – coupled with the others' realization of the need to avoid disastrous conflict – make it impossible to ignore. 'With Quebec,' said a Manitoba official, 'it is a moral and political suasion.' Ontario, too, is perceived as being very influential, bringing much expertise to the negotiations. But, as we have also seen, some of its strengths – such as wealth – act as a real constraint on its resources. British Columbia, most respondents agree, wields relatively little influence. Two factors appear to account for this. First, British Columbia devotes little effort to its role in federal-provincial relations; and, second, the federal government does not take it very seriously. Ottawa is more oriented to the Atlantic provinces, and this, plus its high level of expertise and its palpable need, gives New Brunswick more resources than might be expected for a small province. Manitoba appears to have few resources but, again, its expertise and the active role in the negotiations played by Premier Duff Roblin have made its voice heard.

The distribution of resources, then, varies from issue to issue and from time to time. The provinces had more resources on pensions than on finances, more resources in 1964 than in 1966, and more potential influence over the constitutional outcome than on tax-sharing. There are several reasons. The allocation of legal authority varies from issue to issue, as do the talents and expertise of the governments and the distribution of support and the attitudes of interested groups. Within each negotiation, particular events may give one or other participants great advantage.

The allocation of resources also varies greatly according to the subjective perceptions of the actors. A psychological dimension enters into their calculations about their own and others' resources. This stems from the ambiguity and uncertainty in the process. Assessments of the nature of political support and of the best way to maintain support must depend on fragmentary evidence. Nor is support the only resource about which there is uncertainty. In a real sense, therefore, an actor's resources depend on what resources he believes he has, and on what others believe he has.

It also means that the actors will attempt to shape others' perceptions about the distribution of resources. Competition for resources becomes an important part of the bargaining game. The participants may disagree about the distribution of political support, and will attempt to protect their resources for future negotiations.

An actor's resources depend greatly on his ability to commit himself credibly. As Thomas Schelling has shown, one important way to do this is to restrict one's own freedom to act.[37] Thus, what might appear to be a liability – such as Prime Minister Lesage's tenuous control over his own cabinet, or his fear of the separatists – may be an asset in the negotiations, just as a union leader's resources may be strengthened for contract negotiations by his inability to control his own men. Again, what may be an advantage in one game may be a disadvantage in another. Ontario's wealth is a boon in most ways; it is not in federal-provincial negotiations. The Atlantic province's poverty is a grave weakness – but not in the negotiations. This also suggests that in cases where the issue involves a relatively unilateral decision by one party, that party in effect decides who will have resources. Thus Ottawa's commitment to alleviating regional differences and its fear of divisive conflict gives the Maritimes and Quebec great resources; it is less concerned about, and less fearful of, British Columbia.

Many political resources are double-edged. As well as having political resources, the participants also act under political constraints. If resources represent factors which will help an actor to achieve his goals, then constraints operate to limit his action. This is not a matter of slack or unexploited resources. Constraints are the opposite side of the resource coin. Some of these constraints derive from the same elements as resources. Thus, the constitution grants authority, but also limits it. Percep-

37 *The Strategy of Conflict*, p. 22. 'Bargaining power,' he writes, 'is the power to bind oneself.'

tions of political support are a resource for Quebec, but a constraint for Ontario. The necessity of participating in several games at once is often another constraint on the actors.

This suggests there is an intimate link between political resources and constraints and the kinds of strategies and tactics used by actors. Tactics that are possible for Quebec, such as threats, are less available to Ontario or the other provinces. Ontario tactics are generally low-key; seldom do its disagreements with Ottawa spill over into public attacks on Ottawa. In general, we should expect that an actor's tactics will be dictated in part by his assessment of his own strengths and weaknesses. We shall pursue this question in the following chapter.

CHAPTER TEN

# Strategies and tactics

The mere possession of political resources does not ensure success, for they must be exploited in various strategies and tactics. This chapter examines some of the techniques used by the Canadian decision-makers. In the first section are suggested some of the factors which condition the kinds of tactics used. For while the potential range of actions may range the gamut from armed conflict to amicable discussion, in fact a series of constraints – some self-imposed by the decision-makers' own values, others stemming from the structure of the bargaining situation – places important limits on the kinds of behaviour that can be used, and encourages some tactics and discourages others. Among these are the participants' own widely shared norms and beliefs, the perceived attitudes of the wider publics about what is permissible and what is not, political resources, some dynamic characteristics of the process itself, and the individual personal qualities of the decision-makers. Rather than viewing the actors as perfect Machiavellians who judge various tactics simply on the basis of their effectiveness in maximizing goals, a more realistic view suggests that the means themselves may be as important as the ends. Nevertheless, the participants do have considerable freedom in choosing their own tactics and arguments, and in the second section of this chapter we shall look at some of the kinds of behaviour they engage in. Different actors at different times and on different issues may use different kinds of tactics.

## CONSTRAINTS ON TACTICS

### *Norms and beliefs: 'we don't bargain; we discuss'*

To listen to the participants, bargaining is hardly part of the Canadian political vocabulary. The respondents do not like to think of themselves as cynical negotiators; instead, they emphasize that the process is one of 'cooperative discussion.' Some frequently expressed norms demonstrate this feeling.

All suggestions of 'power politics' must be avoided. Asked whether log-rolling was a common tactic, an Ontario official answered: 'Ontario would not even contemplate this type of rough-neck approach. We were very disappointed when logic failed. But no one would even contemplate looking at threats or anything like that. You just don't look at discussions in that way.' A Manitoba official answered the same question: 'It's just not in keeping with the Canadian way, let alone that of Manitoba.' A New Brunswick official put it this way: 'It's not that sordid. You never get anybody saying, "if you do thus, I'll screw you in the next election." A person who did that would be as welcome as a skunk at a garden party. These people are pros; they know each other, they don't try and pull anything like that.' Throughout the interviews similar attitudes crop up: there are no 'back-room tactics,' there is 'little horse-trading,' 'you don't see much power politics at the meetings,' there are no 'quid pro quos,' and rarely is there 'brinkmanship.' The very use of such terms, with their heavy pejorative emphasis, indicates the reality and strength of the norms.

They can be summed up in a few rules. Most important is: 'don't gang up on Ottawa.' The provinces should not get together to work out joint positions or strategies with which to pressure Ottawa. 'There is one thing we really must avoid and that is ganging up on Ottawa,' said a Manitoba minister; 'that's just not the sort of thing that's done.' Said an Ontario official: 'We just wouldn't do that.' And a British Columbian minister, saying that 'making common cause against Ottawa would not be cricket,' added: 'This kind of thing would not be conducive to useful relations – we cannot have too much organized bitchery in federal-provincial relations.' Similar comments came from all provinces. While many respondents mentioned they would often exchange views and opinions with other governments before and during conferences, they usually added 'but we never work out of a joint position or anything like that.' A recent exception is the western provinces who have submitted joint positions to Ottawa. In December 1969 Premiers Bennett, Thatcher, and

Strom released a joint statement condemning the federal white paper on taxation which had recently appeared. Provinces like British Columbia and New Brunswick, which were relatively neutral on the pension plan, reported that there were no efforts by the main protagonists to enlist their support. 'There can be no suggestion of collusion,' said another BC minister; 'it would not be proper to influence other provinces.' Thus the norm 'don't gang up' – and again the term is pejorative – is an important one.

Another rule is: 'don't be a localist.' To be listened to, the participants are expected to frame their demands and positions in terms of the 'national interest,' not in terms of their own local or self-interest. 'It is essential for the provincial officials to take a national viewpoint and not be purely local,' said a federal official; 'if not ... they won't be too highly respected on the [continuing] committee.' The same official – and several others – strongly resented British Columbia's conduct in the negotiations, partly because the province allegedly violated this norm. An Ontario official said: 'There is a strong feeling in Ontario that it is in the best interest of the province not to take a selfish position ... Generally speaking in ... conferences there is a lot of cloaking of provincial self-interest in terms of the national interest. It's quite refreshing when you do hear someone say clearly that I need such and so for my province – but I guess that's because it's fairly rare.' Briefs to federal-provincial conferences usually emphasize national needs rather than provincial self-interest, though there are frequent exceptions.

A related norm is: 'don't attack other provinces.' 'We always have to be careful not to antagonize the other governments,' observed an Ontario cabinet minister. A New Brunswick official said: 'It's OK to take a crack at the federal government but it's bad form to take a crack at another provincial government. I can't figure out why. I've often said why not kick some of the other provinces in the shins, but it just isn't done ... There should be more of this. Bluntness would serve some purpose.' Federal officials often complain that even when they are defending the interests of the poorer provinces, the latter will not voice support for Ottawa. There are exceptions, of course. At the November 1963 conference, for example, Premier Bennett observed that the conference was just a big lottery – and Quebec was the winner. An important reason for this norm is that there is no point in provinces' attacking each other when the concessions they seek are usually from Ottawa. Why antagonize the other provinces when you may want their support on some other issue in the near future, and why waste resources?

Finally, the norms frown on threats, whether of non-cooperation or political retribution, on attempts to trade support on one issue for support on another, and on other similar tactics. Instead, one should be 'reasonable,' 'realistic,' and 'modest.' One should depend on logic and persuasion. Said a Manitoba official: 'In general, there's not very much horse-trading at these meetings. Threats have been made occasionally – Bennett sometimes has done that – but generally people try to convince with rational arguments. You don't see very much of power politics.' Similarly, there have been few overt attempts to use the constitutional issue as a lever on other issues. Said a federal official: 'Most premiers would see that as below them. Even a wheeler-dealer like Thatcher would not be that blunt – anyway, they couldn't get away with it.'

Thus an important set of informal rules helps to define what is and is not permissible in the negotiations. In general, they emphasize that explicit bargaining should be avoided – that it is a dirty business.

What is the explanation for these widely shared orientations? Several factors are working together. All act as direct constraints on the kinds of behaviour which the actors feel they can legitimately engage in. The first set of constraints are subjective and normative, rooted in the ideology of the participants. A comment by a senior Ontario official makes the point well: 'In the United States there is the feeling that you can have strong competition, but in Canada the question of survival is much more important. We're less inclined to draw swords. There's a tendency to think that if we cannot solve our problems by logic then we're in for real trouble. There is also the feeling that the facts will always emerge and there will always be a tomorrow. But if you do upset the apple cart, then maybe there won't be a tomorrow.' This quotation illustrates the pervasive feeling, especially among federal, Ontario, and New Brunswick representatives, that, largely because of Quebec's objectives, the very existence of the federation is in the balance, and that nothing must be done which might tip it irrevocably. Conflict should therefore be avoided. 'In a sense the provincial governments do have most of the cards,' said a Manitoba official, 'but they don't play them for fear of destroying the country.' Ontario officials, particularly, feel a sense of responsibility for minimizing conflict. 'We are the muscle in Confederation as the central richest province, and we cannot take advantage of our position,' said one. These normative feelings strictly limit the kinds of tactics the participants use. They partly explain Ottawa's flexible and conciliatory manner in the 1963 and 1964 negotiations, and they explain much of Ontario's activity. Several Ontario officials complained that perhaps Prime Minister Robarts was too responsible, and too reasonable. 'I sometimes wish he would throw his weight around a little more,' said one. This stress on the need for accommodation among élites to avoid threats to the system's survival suggests a pattern very close to the model of consociational democracy developed by Arend Lijphart.[1]

The strength of such internalized norms varies both among individuals and among governments. Quebec delegates are much more willing to use the vocabulary of bargaining and to use more explicitly tactical techniques. 'Most provinces have a very strong feeling against ganging up on the federal government,' said one senior official, 'but we don't feel any particular thing against it here.' Similarly, Quebec officials do not share the rule against localism. Rather they see their role as that of fighting for Quebec's interests. Interestingly, federal and other provincial officials appear to accept the fact of Quebec particularism. They do not condemn it – as they do condemn the alleged 'selfishness' of some other governments. The difference in beliefs about bargaining between Quebec and Ontario leaders is well illustrated by two contrasting quotations from Prime Ministers Robarts and Lesage. Said Robarts in 1963: 'We must at all costs ... avoid at all times any atmosphere of crisis because we will work out all our problems if we can just maintain our equilibrium and our balance.'[2] Premier Lesage summed up his approach another way: 'For my part I was never gentle but rather tough. That's the way you get results.'[3] These differences show up in the conference room. Quebec is much more likely to threaten, log-roll, and publicly attack Ottawa than is Ontario. British Columbian leaders too often appear to disagree with the norms against localism or publicly attacking Ottawa, as does Premier Thatcher of Saskatchewan.

What accounts for these differences? The Quebec example suggests that the kinds of tactics a participant is willing to use is in part a function of the degree of conflict. Within limits, the deeper the conflict, or the more strongly held the objectives, the more willing the actor is to risk potentially disruptive tactics. Thus Ontario's anger over medicare and federal tax-sharing policy led its leaders to be much 'tougher' and outspoken in its tactics during 1968 and early 1969. In addition, it is partly a function of their own reference groups and their own balance of loyalties. Quebec delegates, with Quebec itself as their object of loyalty, tend to judge their strategies simply by the criterion of whether they will enhance or impede their goals. Most English-speaking participants, on the other hand, have much more divided loyalties. They are more likely to ask

1 *The Politics of Accommodation* (Berkeley, 1968).
2 Ontario, Legislative Assembly, *Debates*, 1963–4, pp. 850–1.
3 Marcel Thivierge, 'M. Lesage commente l'attitude de Johnson à Ottawa,' *Le Devoir*, Montreal, 1 Nov. 1966 (my translation).

not only how the tactic enhances their own prospects but also how it affects the nation as a whole. The last point suggests that strictly personal factors, stemming from the participant's own role conception, personality, and ideology will play a large part in the kinds of negotiating behaviour he will consider legitimate or illegitimate to use.

Despite exceptions, these norms against 'rocking the boat,' 'throwing your weight around,' and the like are widely held. They are reinforced in the operation of the process itself. Thus, social pressures, especially within such groups as the continuing committee, act to discourage 'bargaining' in the pejorative sense and instead to emphasize 'cooperation.' There is a tendency for violators of the norm to be criticized by other members, and for their views to be taken less seriously. In part, too, these norms seem to stem from a wider élite political culture which attempts to deny the reality of conflict and disagreement. One respondent, for example, suggested the hierarchical norms implicit in strong party discipline, cabinet control, and in the civil service are associated with such rules.[4] Another, who had spent several years in the foreign service, contrasted the intensive negotiation between representatives of different agencies in American embassies with the situation in Canadian embassies. 'People in Canada don't like to talk about bargaining ... You had to take the overall generalist's approach.' Thus in their rhetoric at least some participants in the negotiations are far removed from single-minded partisans, who look out only for their own interests and use whatever means are at hand to attain them. Instead, the norms of the Canadian decision-makers emphasize 'discussion' over coercion and some 'national' interests over particular ones.

### *Political support and other resources*

But norms are not the only factors limiting the available tactics. Perceived political constraints – which are inevitably rather difficult to separate in practice from normative ones – also have an important effect. These stem primarily from calculations about political support discussed in the previous chapter. Not only do such calculations affect respondents' perceptions of their own and others' resources; they also affect what he feels he can safely do in the negotiations. Many provincial respondents believe that the public will not tolerate their indulging in what might be interpreted as rough-neck tactics. To publicly attack Ottawa risks criticism

4 See also Don Stevenson, 'Federalism and the Provision of Public Services: A Canadian Viewpoint,' unpublished paper presented to the seminar on federalism, University of Indiana, 1–7 June 1967, pp. 2, 11.

in the press and in provincial legislatures. 'From the political point of view, there is no mileage in attacking Ottawa,' said an Ontario official, 'and if the provinces got together to gang up on the federal government, well, they would tear you to pieces.' A Manitoba official agreed that 'no party locally which really damns the federal government can really do that well.' And, indeed, in 1966 the Manitoba government was severely criticized for its strong demands and for its public condemnation of Ottawa.[5] Ontario officials believe that if they assert the province's self-interest too greatly, 'people will say, "Oh, it's just those fat cats in Ontario again." ' These constraints extend to log-rolling and other such tactics. Asked why British Columbia could not have threatened to withhold agreement on the pension plan unless Ottawa met some of the province's other demands, an official said: 'Well, the pension plan was very popular – and anyone who tried to use it as a weapon would get very low marks.' Thus the participants feel constrained by attitudes which they believe to be widely shared in the external environment. What is important is not how much, if at all, the public actually is concerned that the negotiating tactics be decorous, but rather how much the élites themselves believe such attitudes exist.

Provinces operating under these constraints have their freedom of action severely limited. They have difficulty making threats, because they cannot make them credible. They cannot obviously log-roll because they feel that public reaction would be that this is a cynical misuse of power. They must be careful in carrying their disputes with Ottawa into the public arena. Instead, they must rely more on persuasion and logic, within the conference. They feel they have to expend much energy denying that they are 'raiding the federal treasury,' 'ganging up,' or using 'pressure tactics.'

Because perceived political support varies, so does the importance of political constraints. In British Columbia, several respondents reported, 'being anti the federal government is good election bait.' The same was true of Saskatchewan where 'it is politically popular to be against the federal government.' This belief means that leaders of the two provinces feel freer to carry their disputes with Ottawa into the public arena. In elections it may be profitable to campaign 'against Ottawa' – though such

5 Thus, Opposition Leader Gil Molgat said in the legislature: 'I think we have to get our facts and figures and we have to approach Ottawa in a sensible and straightforward manner, not the carping, complaining, blaming attitude the government is using ... The way to do it, Mr. Speaker, is to make a logical case, and not to be crying in the bushes.' Manitoba, Legislative Assembly, *Debates*, 1966, pp. 959–60.

tactics may have greater payoff at the polls than at the bargaining table with federal officials. Ontario and Manitoba leaders, on the other hand, feel it politically dangerous to engage in 'public' strategies.

For Quebec leaders the perceived desires of the electorate create strong incentives to attack Ottawa publicly. This leads to the phenomenon of Quebec participants being more vehement and forceful outside the conference room than inside it. In October 1966 Prime Minister Johnson created an entirely different impression outside the conference than inside. A leading Quebec journalist wrote:

> As is his custom, after each of the sittings he made all the usual declarations which it suits him to make in order to satisfy an electorate which he believes to be still thirsting for bloody tournaments ...
>
> However, at the gaming table of the conference, M. Johnson, once again, conducted himself in a quite different manner: reasonable to perfection, winning as only he is capable of being, a certain but delicate calculator, saying only what is necessary, and saying it well.[6]

Quebec, therefore, does not suffer the constraint of fear of alienating the public – if anything the normal constraint is reversed. Not only do Quebec leaders have beliefs which make explicit bargaining tactics *permissible* but also they have some resources which make them *possible*.

Political support and other political resources may be seen as providing the actors with incentives to undertake some kinds of action and not to undertake others. The actor will try to tailor his tactics to the kinds of resources he feels he has. If he feels he has political support, he will exploit that. If objective information is the chief resource, as it was for the provinces in the 1966 negotiations, then tactics will be built around its exploitation. New Brunswick, as a poor province, gains resources from Ottawa's concern with its plight, so it will adopt suitable tactics. 'Our strategy,' said an official, 'is not to offend the federal government.' New Brunswick respondents felt there was nothing to gain and everything to lose by adopting a belligerent stance. 'You catch more flies with honey than with acid,' observed a New Brunswick minister. Similarly, there is little point in Manitoba 'trying to throw its weight around.' 'It would look like Mighty Mouse trying to fight the devil,' said one official. 'We have to depend on sweet reason because there is nothing else to depend on.' Negotiating tactics, then, depend heavily on the amounts and kinds of resources available to the participants.

6 Jean-V. Dufresne in *Le Devoir*, 28 Oct. 1968 (my translation).

*Other constraints*

Other factors shape the kinds of tactics the participants use. One is that many tactics imply a cost to the user as well as to the person he is trying to influence. What makes a threat persuasive, says Thomas Schelling, is precisely the implication that the threatener commits himself to a mutually harmful course.[7] If the bluff is called, and the threatener is not willing to make good, then the credibility of his future commitments will be questioned.[8] The Canadian decision-makers are well aware of this. A Quebec adviser noted that threats cannot be used very often: 'If you make a threat, you have to be prepared to carry it out – and that's a very dangerous thing to do.' Similarly a province could threaten to hold a referendum on an issue, or participate actively in a federal election campaign to defeat the incumbents in Ottawa. 'But that's very tricky,' said a Quebec official. 'If you are not successful you lose face, and even if you do succeed, it is not clear what it means.' Many other tactics involve potential risks. For example, the provinces could refuse to participate in a joint programme unless it were suitably modified – but that risks the programme's failing completely, with possible condemnation from affected groups and loss of needed funds. Another possible move in financial relations is for a government to attempt to preempt more tax points by unilaterally raising its own taxes, and then trying to blame Ottawa. Ontario came close to this in 1966 when the budget speech announced a 4 per cent rise in personal income taxes, but it was not implemented. In this case Ottawa may not reduce its own taxes, or the province may be unable to put the blame on Ottawa. Thus many possible moves require taking risks. When the payoffs are uncertain – as is often the case – politicians may be unwilling to take the chance, especially when the norms discourage this behaviour anyway. An Ontario official summed up the dilemma well:

You cannot get any bargaining at the table without backing it up with political action. The premier would have to say, 'Now look you bastards, if you do this, then I am going to go out and make things hot for you.' That's crisis-type diplomacy and you really don't know what would happen if you did have to go out and make a fuss – and of course the federal government can always retaliate. Bargaining strength is always dependent on political strength and

7 *The Strategy of Conflict* (New York, 1963), p. 35 ff.
8 This is related to Fred Iklé's concept of the 'bargaining reputation.' *How Nations Negotiate* (New York, 1964), chap. 6, esp. pp. 77–8.

that means you have to go out and test it. And that people really don't want to do. Horsetrading in the sense that if you do this, I'll do that, really doesn't take place.

Another constraint on available tactics is the fact that the participants are operating in several different environments at once. What is appropriate in one situation may not be in another. Even though much of the discussion takes place behind closed doors, it still remains difficult to keep action in one arena separated from that in others. This helps to explain the difference in Quebec's actions inside and outside the conference room. In addition a nationalistic statement by Quebec leaders designed to influence Ottawa or the electorate – like the September 1966 brief to the Tax Structure Committee – may cause repercussions with bond buyers and potential investors in New York or Toronto.[9] It may well be that Quebec's less aggressive stance in 1969 was related to the general problem of provincial financial difficulties – reduced level of private investment and growing unemployment.

Similarly, many actions taken in the federal-provincial arena are designed to further the actors' goals in other arenas. Thus, all briefs to conferences are as much directed at the voters back home as to the influencing of federal policy-makers. Quebec's nationalist brief in September 1966, for example, represented a translation into concrete form of the Union Nationale's recent election platform and was directed as much at the government's standing with Quebec voters as at Ottawa. Since the different roles leaders play and the different arenas they participate in can never be completely separated, some element of trying to reconcile the perceived imperatives of different arenas or to forward goals in more than one arena simultaneously will be a feature of most tactics.

This is of course directly related to the argument over 'open' or 'closed' conferences. A prime reason for the failure of the televised constitutional conferences to make much progress is that the cameras forced the participants to play two games simultaneously: to mobilize and seek support among the voters back home and to negotiate with the other governments. This tension was clearly felt by the participants themselves. Among several governments the former purpose became more important. This will

9 See Frank Howard in the Toronto *Globe and Mail*, 26 Oct. 1966. Quebec, he said, needs dollars and the confidence of the financial world more than a nationalist victory. Similarly, Peter Newman, in the *Toronto Star*, 29 Oct. 1966, wrote that 'The imperatives of the province's financial situation have, for the time being, triumphed over his [Johnson's] dream of splitting Canada into associate states.'

be a problem, of course, only so long as the participants believe that there is a conflict between the positions demanded by their electorates and the positions necessary to get federal-provincial agreement.

The dynamics of the process itself also help to condition tactics. For example, the high degree of communication among participants means they know and understand each other's positions well, which makes dissembling or bluffing more difficult. 'The limits of bluff are easily seen,' said a British Columbian minister; 'if we had done that [bluffed], the federal government would have known it was a bluff and it wouldn't have been useful at all.' Finally, it must be remembered that the negotiating process itself is subtle and complicated. As it unfolds, and as other actors engage in their own tactics, the situation itself changes for each actor, ruling out some courses of action and making others more attractive. Thus Quebec's irrevocable commitment in the summer of 1963 that it would not participate in a federally operated pension plan meant that federal bargainers had to adapt their strategy to trying to reach an agreement with Ontario.

Finally, internal relationships within governments may make planning well-developed and coordinated strategies extremely difficult. Any one negotiation is only a small part of a complex network of relationships and concerns for all participants. Many different interests within governments must be balanced. This is especially true of the federal government which is larger and more diverse than others. A senior official described how hard it was for Ottawa to develop a coordinated strategy on the pension plan: 'We were not only playing poker with Quebec, but also trying to see what we could get our cabinet to agree to, who in turn were thinking about electoral considerations. It is very difficult, too, when you get into a group of twenty-five cabinet ministers of differing interests in a very technical discussion.' In response to this problem, the federal government has greatly strengthened its internal coordinating machinery for dealing with the provinces both in the Prime Minister's Office and the Privy Council Office.[10]

Similarly, Ontario never developed a coherent strategy in the pension negotiations. Said one adviser: 'I am quite sure we could have played our

10 This machinery included a much more active cabinet committee on federal-provincial relations. A set of controversial 'regional desks,' primarily concerned with political intelligence, was established in the Prime Minister's Office, and several advisers to the cabinet on constitutional and other matters were appointed. Within the Privy Council Office a federal-provincial relations secretariat was established. It too was divided into a set of 'regional desks,' each with a dual responsibility – to oversee and coordinate the activities of federal departments in various functional areas as they relate to federal-provincial relations, and to communicate with particular provincial governments.

cards better, but the problem is it's rather like a ball game. You have to react instantly. Suddenly you have the ball and you have to run with it ... And then we tended to be divided within ourselves. We didn't resolve our differences on funding, for example. And so we tended to adopt a wait and see attitude. It was a big mistake.' Many provinces resented the method Ottawa chose to present its proposals in October 1966. But the method was only partly a result of strategic calculations. Equally important was the failure of the federal cabinet itself to agree on the proposals until just before the conference began. In circumstances like this, as governments ponder complex issues in a diverse environment, complete with uncertainties about the effects of various actions – all under pressure of little time – it is easy to understand why cold tactical calculations are often impossible.

Thus the range of action open to most negotiators is a relatively narrow one because of the character of resources, prevailing norms, and the nature of the negotiation process.[11]

*Personal style*

Another basic factor conditioning the behaviour of the participants is their own personal style or character. Many of the constraints previously discussed are quite loose. Neither prevailing norms nor political constraints provide fixed rules for action in all cases, and, anyway, some participants might not agree with the norms or might feel it is worth risking political support by violating them. As a result the way the participants behave is in part determined by more idiosyncratic factors like personality. The variable is an elusive one, but it is particularly crucial in a case like the Canadian one, when the number of participants is relatively small. This effect is reinforced by the fact that most provincial government establishments are small and centralized, making it easy for the premier to place his own personal stamp on the whole administration. Considerations of personal style thus have important consequences for the operation of the process.

On the federal side, for example, respondents reported a great difference in style between former Prime Minister John Diefenbaker and Lester Pearson. Diefenbaker 'would harangue the premiers,' said one: 'It was a whole new world when Pearson came in,' said another. Pearson's own style was low-keyed and flexible, dedicated above all to reaching agreement and avoiding conflict and dissension. This appears to be one cause

11 For a discussion of such constraints in another context, see Aaron Wildavsky, *The Politics of the Budgetary Process* (Boston, 1964), pp. 6, 63 ff.

of the frequent criticisms that he was weak and vacillating. Pearson gave a revealing description of himself in a 1966 television address: 'Indeed, my whole career, my deepest instincts, have been dedicated to the resolution of disputes, to the search for agreement, to the avoidance of controversy and to find solutions to difficult problems. I don't like conflict and controversy unless it is over high principles.'[12]

This approach is clearly reflected in the way the government handled itself in the negotiations, and in the way Pearson chaired federal-provincial conferences. Respondents unanimously praised his considerate, flexible chairmanship. Another leading federal participant in the pension negotiations, Health and Welfare Minister Judy LaMarsh, was well known for her combativeness and partisanship, and this was seen in some of the ways she defended the pension plan. She frequently antagonized negotiators from other governments. In 1966 a major factor in Ottawa's ability to hold the line against strong provincial pressures to increase tax-sharing appears to be due to the determination of Finance Minister Mitchell Sharp himself. Many respondents felt that were it not for him concessions would have been made. Premier Bennett seemed to be expressing this view when on the last day of the October 1966 conference he suggested that perhaps everything could be settled satisfactorily if only Prime Minister Pearson and the premiers could have lunch together alone.

Prime Minister Trudeau's style appears different again. He is also praised as a good chairman but is more analytical and abstract in approach. He seems less willing than Pearson to accept *ad hoc* muddling through solutions to problems – a difference readily apparent in the different ways each prime minister approached constitutional negotiation.

On the provincial side the 'responsibility' and moderation of Ontario respondents seems to stem in large measure from the example set by Prime Minister Robarts. His commitment to national unity and the avoidance of conflict are reflected not only outside the conference room but inside it as well, where he speaks relatively infrequently and is known for his calm, phlegmatic style. Other premiers have their own well-known characteristics. Premier E.C. Manning of Alberta was known not only for his very conservative ideology but also for his willingness to act as a compromiser and moderator. Premier Bennett's flamboyant style together with his suspicion of federal officials seems to lead him to stress an external approach, making public demands on Ottawa, but not trying to work through 'quiet diplomacy' either in officials' meetings or in the plenary conference. Bennett's highly personalized leadership ('There's

12 Address on 'The Nation's Business,' CBC-TV, 8 June 1966.

an amazing Treasury Board here,' said a former official; 'it's just Bennett.'), his secretiveness, and his distrust of civil servants all combine to affect British Columbia's strategies. Bennett's reluctance to participate in the Tax Structure Committee projection exercise, for example, was partly because 'he has always had a deep skepticism as far as civil servants are concerned,' and because he 'did not want to give away all his marbles' before formal discussions began. Similarly, Bennett gives very little freedom to his officials who participate in the continuing committee. 'The clamp came down,' said one former senior official, 'and they were scared to talk – it certainly does harm British Columbia's effectiveness.' Often no BC representative is sent to officials' meetings, and occasionally only an official will be sent to a ministerial meeting. Such behaviour does not appear to stem from explicit tactical calculation, but rather from Bennett's own personal predilections.

The importance of individual characteristics is well illustrated by the contrast between Prime Minister Lesage's tactics and those of Prime Minister Johnson. Lesage was described by the other participants as 'a real tension builder,' who would 'wave his arms and beat the table and shout down the phone.' One premier is reported to have said of Lesage: 'Every time I see Lesage, I marvel at the humility of General de Gaulle.' Such a characterization is obviously an exaggeration, but it does illustrate something of the Lesage style. By contrast Johnson, even though in some ways more nationalistic than Lesage, was a surprise to those who met him at the conference. He was described as 'smooth,' 'charming,' 'courtly,' 'a real gentleman.' Said an Ontario minister: 'Lesage would like to pound the table a lot – Johnson would never do that.' These comments by the English-speaking respondents indicate that they felt Johnson was more attuned to the norms than Lesage. While Johnson's charm in October 1966 and at the later constitutional conferences was certainly partly a calculated bid to enlist the support of other premiers for Quebec's goals, it is also clear this style suited him personally. The same may be said of Johnson's successor, Jean-Jacques Bertrand.

It is difficult to judge the effectiveness of the two approaches. Most generally, the Lesage strategy seems to be most effective if the object is to coerce Ottawa; but by the end of his tenure it risked losing the goodwill of the English-speaking provinces. Johnson's strategy ran less risk of doing so. Interestingly, a Quebec Liberal spokesman commenting on the compliments Johnson had received from English-Canadian leaders suggested that they really implied he had not fought hard enough for Quebec.

Thus the personal styles of the participants is an important factor conditioning the kinds of tactics they use. Even here, however, there is a relationship between personal style and more general social factors. The environment may provide greater or lesser constraints on the degree of freedom the individual leader has for exercising his own personal predilections. More important, different environments may encourage the recruitment of different kinds of leaders. Thus, we have seen that Premier Bennett has adopted a flamboyant style, but one reason for his election may be that the British Columbian electorate welcomes such behaviour and elects politicians who will 'bait the federal government.' Similarly, Prime Minister Robarts' style seems to have been shared by his immediate predecessors, suggesting that Ontario is less likely to elect someone like Bennett or a Joey Smallwood. Nevertheless, the interaction of situational factors, like the electorate, and specific personality factors remains unclear. Certainly there can be few more striking differences in style than that between Premiers Lloyd and Thatcher, both products of Saskatchewan.

Thus some general elements combine to help shape the kinds of behaviour that the actors in the federal-provincial negotiations can engage in, and so shape the character of the debate as it proceeds. Some of these factors, like norms and personalities, depend on the personal qualities of the negotiators themselves. Others, like political support, depend on the participant's perceptions about a wider set of political attitudes. Still others stem from the complex nature of the environment within which the policy-makers operate and from the dynamics of the process itself.

## MOVES AND COUNTER MOVES: HOW THE ACTORS EMPLOY TACTICS

Within these constraints, however, there remains a wide variety of possible actions which the actors can and do engage in.[13] One large group of activities is designed to change the *perceptions* of other participants about the probable advantages and costs of different courses of action, both for themselves and for others. Here the actors exchange 'information and appeal' in what Lindblom calls 'partisan discussion.'[14] A second group of

13 Charles E. Lindblom, *The Intelligence of Democracy: Decision-making through Mutual Adjustment* (New York, 1965), pp. 32–4, and chaps. 3 and 4. See also Jack Sawyer and Harold Guetzkow, 'Bargaining and Negotiation in International Relations,' in Herbert Kelman, ed., *International Behavior* (New York, 1965), pp. 489–96.

14 *The Intelligence of Democracy*, pp. 69–73. Lindblom defines partisan discussion as 'A form of partisan mutual adjustment in which X, as a recognized condition of making his own decision effective, induces a response from Y by effecting through communication a reappraisal by Y of his partisan interests and the means to satisfy them without X's actually altering the objective consequences for Y of any of his possible responses, where Y may or may not, in a symmetrical relation, do the same with respect to X' (p. 71).

activities includes tactics which *actually* change the situation and the real costs and advantages of different moves, either by the proposing of new alternatives, through taking unilateral actions or through the exchange of threats and promises. Both categories have played an important role in the negotiations. Some tactics, in addition, involve direct exchanges between the actors, while others are more public, designed to bring pressure to bear indirectly. Throughout this discussion a vital element is the calculations of the individual participants. Developing appropriate tactics is a creative art. Tactics must continually be reassessed and modified as the negotiations unfold.

*Partisan discussion*

By far the most common form of adjustment in the Canadian case falls under the rubric of partisan discussion. This is largely because the norms which govern the process legitimize it while frowning on many other techniques and because the kinds of resources available to many of the actors make it difficult for them to invoke other sanctions. The manipulation and communication of information in partisan discussion is therefore the dominant means used by the actors as they seek success. It takes many forms.

First, and perhaps most important, the actors will try to structure the discussion in terms favourable to themselves. It is generally true in policy-making that the act of defining an issue – what are the general principles involved, how high are the stakes, is it soluble or not, and so on? – is crucial to the final outcome. The act of definition suggests that the problem will be viewed from a certain perspective. A particular set of precedents, prior experiences, arguments, and general rules will be called into play and will structure future action. Equally, others will be ruled out. So when the terms of an argument are defined, the range of possible outcomes is drastically reduced. At the extreme, to state the problem in a certain way is, in effect, to state the final result. Hence, in federal-provincial negotiations, defining the issue itself becomes a partisan process. The actors try to persuade each other that issues should be defined in their way. In practice a large amount of time in the negotiations is taken up in just this debate. What is at issue in financial questions – the ability of all governments to meet their constitutional responsibilities (the provinces win) or the need for central control to enable overall direction of the economy (Ottawa wins)? Is the general principle to be invoked 'he who spends the money should raise it' (Ottawa wins) or 'transfer resources to those governments which need them' (provinces win)? Is manpower training really an economic matter (Ottawa wins) or an educational one (provinces win)? And so on, for virtually every issue. This kind of argument was perhaps even more important in the constitutional case since it was so wide and diffuse. But few issues arise from the environment in such unequivocal terms that there is no argument about what they mean or involve.

The debate at the September and October 1966 federal-provincial conferences is a good example of the form many such arguments take. The provinces exploited the information provided by the results of the Tax Structure Committee projections, saying that they proved the need for a redistribution of resources to the provinces. Ottawa responded first by minimizing the significance of the findings: 'projection is still an art not a science,' 'it doesn't include several new large federal expenditure programmes and is therefore out-dated,' and 'the provinces exaggerated some of their figures.' Second, Ottawa altered the terms of the argument. Turning more funds over to the provinces was not the real issue, said its spokesmen. Rather the issue was that all governments were going to have to raise taxes, and why should Ottawa continue to be the 'fiscal crutch' for the provinces. Ottawa had to maintain control of taxes for fiscal management purposes. Most important, in response to provincial arguments stressing their undeniable financial difficulties and the priority of provincial functions, Ottawa raised quite another basic principle: fiscal responsibility. Each government should be fully responsible to its own taxpayers for the money it decides to raise. Yes, said the provinces, but independent taxing raises the danger of destructive intergovernmental taxing competition and the creation of a 'tax jungle' like that of the 1930s. And, in addition, if there is to be independent taxing, there should at least be an initial transfer, so that each government starts off on roughly equal terms.[15] Both governments here were invoking general rules. They were not disagreeing over their validity, in the abstract, but over their applicability to the issue in question. Such debate was the stuff of the conferences, as each side sought to persuade each other of the consequences of different courses of action. In doing so, each will stress the arguments most favourable to his position, and try to deny, minimize, or outflank those of others.

Another tactic is to try to show that the weight of expertise or of 'objective' information is on your side. This may be done through making use of 'evidence' developed by others, through joint efforts, as with the Tax

15 See briefs by various governments to the September 1966 Tax Structure Committee meeting, collected in *Federal-Provincial Tax Structure Committee*, 14–15 Sept. 1966 (Ottawa, 1966), and the briefs to the October federal-provincial conference, in *Federal-Provincial Conference*, 24–28 Oct. 1966 (Ottawa, 1968).

Structure Committee projections, or through the participants creating their own information through research and related activities. The last, especially, is costly; it requires considerable staff resources, and, as we have seen, this disadvantages some governments. In the pension debate Ontario and Ottawa traded rival assessments of some important features of the plan. Ontario, for example, pointed to analyses which seemed to show that costs would rise very rapidly; Ottawa pointed to a study by the International Labour Organization which supported the idea of a 'pay-as-you-go' plan. At one point at the November 1963 meeting the discussion was, as one participant put it, 'your actuaries versus my actuaries.' Governments will also produce their own analyses to back up their positions, like the paper an Ontario economist presented to the continuing committee in 1966 attempting to demonstrate in deliberately 'academic' terms that Ottawa did not need to control half the major direct taxes in order to be able to control the economy. Again in 1968, perhaps showing an uncharacteristic concern for lower income taxpayers, Ontario produced an analysis showing that the Social Development Tax Ottawa had imposed but not shared was 'highly regressive.'[16] Similarly, British Columbian delegates used figures purporting to show that there was a huge imbalance between the amount British Columbians paid to Ottawa in taxes and the amount that Ottawa returned to the province.[17] Information is seldom neutral.

At the same time, the governments will manipulate information in order to defend their positions. Thus Ottawa, outlining possible alternative equalization formulae in February 1966, deliberately did not include figures which showed what each province would get (to the provinces' chagrin) because it wanted to ensure 'objective discussion.' The desire to have the Tax Structure Committee figures come out 'right' helps to explain the ways some provinces supplied information for the calculations. Similarly, at the end of the 1966 negotiations, the figures Ottawa prepared showing what each province was going to get diverged greatly from provincial estimates. There was much uncertainty about the real amounts so Ottawa used assumptions which showed how generous it was, and the provinces did the opposite. Ottawa, for example, compared what the provinces were to get in 1967–8 under the new arrangements with what they got in 1966–7 under the old ones. But the proper comparison, said the provinces, was between what the provinces were to

16 Taxation and Fiscal Policy Branch, Department of Treasury and Economics, 'Explanatory Notes on the New Federal Social Development Tax,' Toronto, Oct. 1968.

17 Vancouver *Province*, 23 Nov. 1963.

get in 1967–8 and what they would have received if the old arrangements had been continued. Similarly, of course, participants will try to withhold or downplay information unfavourable to their positions, as Ontario withheld a paper on tax-sharing prepared by the Advisory Committee on Confederation, since its approach clashed with government policy.

Another device is to suggest that a certain possible solution constitutes a 'prominent solution,'[18] so that if it were broken there would be no logical stopping place. Thus in 1966 Ottawa made much of the '50 per cent line' beyond which the provincial share of personal income taxes could not go because if it did there would be no compelling reason not to let the provincial share slide to, say, 75 per cent. This 'limit' had the added advantage of apparent equity. 'It was obviously the decent thing.' Interestingly, at the time, only Quebec's share of the income tax (because of its opting-out) approached 50 per cent, and several respondents felt one reason for the offer of seventeen more points in return for shared-cost programmes was to raise the provincial share so it would approach the 50 per cent limit, making it difficult to ask for more. 'They really sucked us in,' said an Ontario official. Ottawa's stand on 'equal treatment for all provinces' in recent years is a similar argument – if we let Quebec have special status with regard to A, what is to stop us giving it on B, C, and D.

Another form of partisan discussion is to turn the opponents' arguments against them. Thus during one exchange with Prime Minister Robarts, in early 1964, Prime Minister Pearson noted in a letter that one Ontario suggestion 'would clearly be incompatible with your principles of a closer relationship between contributions and benefits.'[19] Similarly in defending its proposal to turn three of the major shared-cost programmes over to the provinces, Ottawa used many of the provinces' own arguments about the influence of shared-cost programmes on provincial priorities and the like.[20] Justifying the end of shared-cost programmes in the manpower training field, Manpower and Immigration Minister Jean Marchand told the delegates: 'Perhaps I might point out to Premiers ... that the contrary view was not taken by us; it was taken by the [provincial] Ministers of Education ...'[21] More recently Ontario and others pointed out that federal insistence on medicare and other spending

18 See Schelling, *The Strategy of Conflict*, pp. 111–12.
19 Pearson to Robarts, 25 Feb. 1964, in House of Commons, Sessional Paper 202H.
20 See, for example, *Federal-Provincial Tax Structure Committee*, 14–15 Sept. 1966, pp. 18–19, and statement by the prime minister in *Federal-Provincial Conference*, 24–28 Oct. 1966, pp. 6–21.
21 *Ibid.*, p. 49.

programmes violated its own insistence on controlling inflation and holding down spending. Prime Minister Trudeau's debating style leans heavily on this sort of argument.

Finally, the actors can try to change others' assessments of the consequences of certain actions. Thus, the Lesage government could and did argue that if Ottawa did not make concessions to it, that would be the best guarantee that the extremists would arise, or that a new government, even harder for Ottawa to deal with, might be elected. In 1968 Daniel Johnson pointed to the challenge of separatist groups. Similarly Premier Bennett at the September 1966 Tax Structure Committee meeting said that he was 'reporting to this conference ... widespread resentment' in British Columbia to federal treatment of the provinces.[22] In the same category as these examples are predictions, like those made by Ontario and others in 1966, that 'independent' taxing would lead to a 'tax jungle.'

Thus partisan discussion is a prevalent form of negotiating tactics. This is so because the norms favour it, especially if it is 'objective' and because often few other resources are available. Through it the participants hope to be able to convince and persuade others of the validity of their positions, and to point out consequences of different courses of action which the opponents might not have thought of. These devices do not change reality itself, but only perceptions of reality. It is one important way in which new information is brought to bear on the decision-process since each actor is motivated to provide as much information as possible to back up his position. The dominance of partisan discussion in the negotiations was summed up by a Quebec respondent, asked to summarize Quebec's strategies: '[They] are to make a very good presentation of its case and then to utilize this preparation in the best possible way to prove our point ... It is not a battlefield, you know, you base your demands on facts.'

### *Changing reality*

The second category of tactics involves those which actually change the situation which confronts the other actors, forcing them to react. One important way to do this is to take the initiative, to pose new alternatives which might not otherwise have been thought of. Ottawa has consistently used this approach. Thus, instead of simply telling the provinces it would like to discuss pensions, equalization, or manpower training, Ottawa

22 *Federal-Provincial Tax Structure Committee,* 14–15 Sept. 1966, p. 107.

initiated concrete detailed proposals, thereby largely setting the ground rules for future debate. Mr Pearson expressed this point shortly after the compromise with Quebec: '... to put forward a piece of federal legislation in detail, submit that to the provinces and then if necessary accept changes to that legislation after provincial discussion. That, I think, is the most effective way of negotiating ... We are not playing a defensive game in this government. If you play a defensive game, and I am thinking of hockey now, you are not likely to get so many penalties, but you are certainly not going to score any goals. I think we are scoring some goals.'[23]

Quebec also has used this technique with great success. Its pension alternative, which 'added a whole new dimension to the argument,' was a notable example. Because it was broader and more generous, and especially because it showed the other provinces the potential value of a fund, it won the support of most governments, and drastically altered the terms of the debate. Quebec followed this strategy on many other issues, including opting-out and the Municipal Loan Fund, when, said Prime Minister Lesage, 'We did not content ourselves with opposing this intrusion, we submitted concrete and acceptable counter-proposals.'[24] 'It seems to us that a critique of the federal régime is sterile if not accompanied by suggestions presented in a constructive way.'[25] Similarly Quebec has taken the initiative in the constitutional discussions, with elaborate, well-documented, position papers. Other governments have occasionally also taken the initiative in this way, but much less often than Quebec or Ottawa. Many lack the skill, expertise, and interest necessary to formulate well-developed alternatives. They prefer to react to federal initiatives.

A closely related tactic is to try to structure the timing of issues. This was one important reason why Ottawa submitted its education and manpower proposals to the provinces with little warning at the full Plenary Conference in October 1966:

> This was a way of preventing the provinces from moving into a position and preparing a response to the programme before it had been officially announced. If we had done that, there would have been leaks from the various governments and all the initial press would have been unfavourable to our plan. The provinces would have been able to manœuvre and prepare all sorts of objections, and we might never have got off the ground. As it was, we were able to take the initiative ... So it was a tactical thing.

23 Quoted in John Saywell, ed., *Canadian Annual Review for 1964* (Toronto, 1965), p. 63.
24 Speech to l'Union des municipalités de la province de Québec, Montreal, 18 Sept. 1963 (my translation).
25 Speech to the Université de Moncton, 17 May 1964 (my translation).

The provinces, as we saw in chapter 4, were caught unprepared and off-guard and their subsequent disarray testifies to the effectiveness of the tactic. Numerous other examples of this 'pre-emption tactic' can be cited. The federal Social Development Tax was announced just before the finance ministers met to discuss new tax collection agreements in the autumn of 1968. At the meeting, Ontario Treasurer Charles MacNaughton complained that for the third year in a row the federal budget had been brought down just before the federal-provincial meetings, thus pre-empting provincial positions. The federal spending power, as the medicare example shows, gives Ottawa many opportunities to use this tactic. However, the resentment and hostility created by such moves shows that they may well increase the overall level of conflict and make agreement harder.

Associated with initiation and timing, of course, is the desire to structure the agenda for debate. Quebec, we have seen, has done much to set the agenda by introducing new issues. But again, Ottawa has the advantage. Governments commonly try to inject side-issues of particular concern to them into the agenda of conferences. They also argue about the order of discussion of items. Similarly, in the constitutional debate Quebec argued for a discussion of transfer of legislative powers, which most concerned it, before discussing entrenchment of a bill of rights, and other provinces insisted that various economic questions had at least as much priority as linguistic and cultural ones. They were successful.

Another way of changing the objective situation faced by others is for an actor to bind his own hands by making a firm commitment.[26] The force of this strategy depends on the ability to persuade the other side that one could not make the concessions even if one wanted to, or that any concession would imply such a high cost to the participant that the opponent could not decently ask for it. The most difficult task for the tactician, then, is to make the commitment a credible one. The clearest example of this tactic is provided again by Quebec. In August 1963, at a special session of the Quebec legislature, the Lesage government's resolution stating that Quebec would have its own pension plan passed unanimously. The main purpose of the resolution was to convince Ottawa there was no possibility of getting Quebec to join a national plan. It was successful – Ottawa admitted soon after that there would have to be two pension plans. When, later in the negotiations, federal officials sounded out their Quebec counterparts on the possibility of Quebec's joining a modified federal plan, the Quebec delegates replied: 'We are bound by our resolution.' Their hands were tied. The resolution had the added ad-

26 Schelling, *The Strategy of Conflict*, pp. 227–8.

vantage of demonstrating to Ottawa the Quebec government's wide political support, since all opposition members voted for it.

Ottawa used a similar tactic several times. When approached by Quebec officials about the possibility of making the original federal plan compulsory for the self-employed (as Quebec's was) Ottawa officials replied that they saw the sense of Quebec's point, 'but the federal cabinet had decided on many points and did not want to reconsider.' At another point, Quebec was thinking of pressing Ottawa to turn the whole social security field over to the province. 'We told them we could not face our Parliament or cabinet ministers with anything like that,' said a federal official, 'And they respected it.' In these examples the commitments were made credible by saying 'my hands are bound' because higher authority (the cabinet) had decided or because the concession would never be tolerated by some third party. This is another way that a liability from one point of view can be an asset from others.

The commitment may also be made credible by taking a position publicly and then saying to the opponent that I will lose too much prestige if I give in to you. Or it can be made by saying 'we would like to help you, but we just don't have the money now.' Thus shortly before the September 1966 conference, when formal negotiations on finances began, federal Finance Minister Sharp declared in a major budgetary speech that 'Our present economic situation and our foreseeable federal financial position do not permit [a tax abatement] on our part now.'[27] He backed up the statement by announcing that Ottawa anticipated a large budgetary deficit. 'We would like to help you, but ...' was a frequent refrain in the subsequent negotiations. These prior commitments limit the users' own freedom, but at the same time make it harder for others to demand concessions. They are unilateral actions in the sense that they do not constitute any direct claim on the other participants – they simply change the objective situation they are confronted with, and thus force them to adapt to the new circumstances.

This sort of commitment, as we have said, is risky. It is only successful if it really binds the one who makes it. That creates expectations on the part of audience groups and greatly reduces future flexibility, especially if it is public. Resolution when both parties have deeply committed themselves to opposing views is much more difficult. For example, it is

27 *Globe and Mail*, 9 Sept. 1966. The tactic was seen as a violation of the rules of the game by several premiers. 'I thought this was a matter that was to be discussed at the Conference,' said Prime Minister Robarts. 'Apparently the decision has been made before we get there.' *Ibid*. Ottawa, said Prime Minister Johnson, has 'started playing the game before the other team is on the ice.' *Ibid*., 10 Sept.

difficult at present to see any way out of the Quebec-Ottawa impasse on social security.

A fourth tactic in most negotiations is the exchange of conditional threats and promises. 'If you do (or don't) do this, then I will ...' They run all through the pension and financial negotiations, and they take many forms. But in order to make a threat credible, or to make a promise, one must have something to withhold or to offer. Therefore, threats and promises, more than most tactics, require the possession of certain kinds of resources. In the financial negotiations, for example, the provinces were simply making demands on Ottawa; there was little they could give in return. The pension and constitutional cases were quite different because each side possessed sanctions over the other. Quebec as we have seen, can make the most credible threats. For example, at the Quebec Conference in March 1964 Lesage warned federal officials that his budget speech, soon to be delivered, would be a very severe attack on Ottawa unless something was done. A year earlier Lesage had delivered his 'ultimatum' to Ottawa demanding '25-25-100.' 'This then is the last time I am putting the case in these terms,' he said. If by the next budget the federal government had not taken Quebec's demands into account, then 'We in Quebec shall on our side ... have seen to it that the necessary decisions are taken.'[28] Prime Minister Johnson, too, occasionally threatened Ottawa. 'If Ottawa wants to drive us out of Confederation,' he said in a television speech before the October 1966 conference, 'that's their business. This [the refusal to give tax shares] is the best way of doing it.'[29] In 1971 Quebec made it clear that its agreement on a new amending formula and on entrenchment of civil rights was conditional on Ottawa's conceding Quebec broader powers in the field of social security. But even for Quebec, threats must be used sparingly. Made too often, they lose their force and become like cries of 'Wolf!' More important they might have to be carried out – which explains why the threats are very seldom bluntly stated. Rather the consequences are left unspecified and vague.

Other provinces are much less able to make threats, though occasionally they do. British Columbia has hinted it might test the constitutionality of equalization in the courts. In 1966 Premier Thatcher of Saskatchewan said that if Ottawa persisted with its new equalization formula, he would pull his Liberal government out of the National Liberal Federation. In 1964 Prime Minister Robarts strongly hinted that Ontario would not par-

28 Budget speech, 5 April 1963, reprinted in F.R. Scott and Michael Oliver, eds., *Quebec States Her Case* (Toronto, 1964), p. 30.
29 *Globe and Mail*, 21 Oct. 1966.

ticipate in a pension plan without Quebec, and in 1966 he told the Tax Structure Committee Ontario would be 'unwilling' to agree to a new equalization formula before 'our position in tax-sharing has been satisfactorily determined.'[30] But such cases are rare. It is difficult for the provinces to make threats, or even to try to trade support on one issue for concessions on another. The lack of sanctions or inducements, fear of political condemnation, and the norms of the game all make it difficult.

### *Public and private strategies*

As the examples have shown, some tactics involve direct communication between the actors themselves. Others appear more designed to win public support, and so bring pressure to bear indirectly. Thus at all conferences the delegations are anxious to get their views to the press. Briefs are as much designed for the voter back home as for persuading Ottawa. 'The public' then is a very important consideration for the participants as they participate in their negotiations, even though the reference is often a vague one, and it is unclear what interest the public does have. What is important is that the participants generally feel that they should justify their positions to the public. Some participants, like Quebec and British Columbia, rely much more on strategies which involve appeals to the public than do others. Again, this seems due partly to the personal styles of the particular leaders and partly to assessments of the nature of perceived public support. When an actor believes that in general his government has support, or that his position on a particular issue is more popular than others, he is more likely to include tactics which exploit these advantages.

This is true even with the normally constrained Ontario. Fairly confident of his position on constitutional matters, Prime Minister Robarts, against some advice, opened the Confederation of Tomorrow Conference to television and press, thereby setting a precedent. At the February 1969 conference, again, Robarts made a direct public appeal on the medicare issue: 'I hope all the people in Ontario are watching and listening to me on television this morning, because I am speaking to them.' This change in Ontario tactics, which I mentioned earlier, stems at least in part from a changed perception of the political environment.

## CONCLUSIONS

These tactics cover a wide range of behaviour, but the most common ones can best be described as 'partisan discussion' – the participants try to

30 *Federal-Provincial Tax Structure Committee*, 14–15 Sept. 1966, p. 46.

persuade, cajole, convince, and appeal to others. Other tactics play a much less important role, though for some governments, notably Quebec, they are more common.

Tactics vary from issue to issue not only because resources vary, but also because issues which like the pension plan involve wide public interest lend themselves to strategies designed to involve the public, while others encourage more private activities. In addition, the federal government's strategy will differ greatly from an issue like the pension plan where the object is to persuade the provinces to go along with a federal initiative to one like finances where the chief federal aim is defensive, to give away as little as possible. Similarly if a province's goals coincide with those of other governments its tactics will be different from cases when others are opposed or neutral. Quebec has been very skilful at phrasing its goals in terms that will gain the support of other provinces. This cannot easily be done for its more nationalistic aims or its claims for special status, but where possible the Quebec leaders take care not to phrase positions in ways that would antagonize the others. Thus Quebec made clear the advantages to all governments of its proposed large pension fund. In 1966 and in other financial negotiations the fiscal demands made the case for all provinces. 'Here all the provinces were in the same boat – our tactic was to align them against the federal government.' It succeeded – '[Johnson] put the provincial case very well,' said a Manitoba official.

Procedures, too, help to condition tactics. Private sessions, and continual interaction in forums like the continuing committee, encourage private strategies and partisan discussion rather than more 'outside strategies.' Televized conferences both encourage public strategies and make it more difficult to keep strategies in different areas separate.

Similarly, an actor will tailor his behaviour to his own goals. When goals are strongly held or when conflict is great it is likely the participants will be less bound by the norms (or hold different ones) and that they will be more willing to indulge in potentially risky tactics. As Ontario's frustration at federal intransigence on tax-sharing has grown, so has its willingness to 'gang up' and to attack Ottawa more bitterly and openly. In addition, of course, strategic calculations will enter into the formulation of goals and objectives. Thus when preparing their positions governments must decide how much to push for, balancing what they hope to get with what they realistically expect to get, developing arguments which they hope will persuade Ottawa and win the support of other provinces, and so on. Again individual participants may make different judgments. For example, equalization was the central issue for both Nova Scotia and New Brunswick, but the former advocated a different and more generous formula than Ottawa proposed while New Brunswick backed the federal formula. 'We made more or less a bargaining position out of it,' said a New Brunswick official. 'We asked for what we thought we could decently get. We didn't ask for the moon – if everyone insisted on the income approach we might have ended up simply with a revision of the old formula.' Another New Brunswick negotiator put it this way: 'If it won't wash, I won't waste my time on it.' He would disagree with Manitoba tacticians, who obviously believed it best to aim high and hope for something less when they demanded twenty-six more personal income tax points in 1966.

Another example of the way goals and tactics are related is provided by Ottawa. 'We knew we would have to raise our bid during the conference,' said one senior official of the federal education and manpower proposals in 1966, 'and we didn't want to make it look too much like a retreat – so why not start out a little bit vague.' This was one reason for the difficulty all sides had in figuring out what the federal brief in October 1966 really meant.

More generally, all Quebec goals in the Lesage years were formulated with a basic overall strategy in mind. 'There are two theories in the matter of autonomy,' said Municipal Affairs Minister Pierre Laporte. 'There is that of the global refusal; there is that of the lucid and realistic claim.'[31] Quebec opted for the latter, pushing hard on a few issues at a time and working only for what was thought possible. 'We always had a certain limited position that we wanted to achieve,' said a cabinet minister, 'and we drove very hard on that. We would work on specific issues, and specific limited positions.'

Finally, Ottawa's whole approach to the 1966 financial negotiations was the product of an extensive rethinking of the federal position, in an attempt to develop an overall strategy which would permit Ottawa to regain the initiative and to resist further provincial demands. What emerged was strategy in which policy goals and tactical considerations were deeply intertwined. 'This was really the first time we had a basic position we could defend in front of the provinces,' said one official. The federal brief to the September 1966 Tax Structure Committee was both an important statement of Ottawa's philosophy of federalism and a tactical document.

Resources are also intimately related to tactics, as we have seen. Indeed, one particularly important political resource is the skill to devise appropriate strategies and tactics in a complex and ever-changing en-

31 Québec, Assemblée législative, *Débats*, 1964, p. 101.

vironment. Differences in political resources go a long way towards explaining why different actors use different tactics.

Thus many factors operate to help shape the kinds of tactics used in the negotiations. The range of possible actions is therefore limited. But there is nevertheless a great deal of room within which the participants can plan their own tactics and arguments. And, while it is hard to assess the effect of specific tactics on the final outcomes, it is clear that the kinds of tactics the participants do use are a crucial element in the final result. Unless exploited creatively, political resources are lifeless. Without the new strategy in 1966, with its outflanking of the Tax Structure Committee results, it is much more likely Ottawa would have done less well in the negotiations. If Quebec had not made the unequivocal commitment to its own plan in the August resolution, Ottawa would probably have behaved much differently; if Ontario had not been able to persuade Ottawa of the validity of its claim that the end of conditional grants for vocational school construction would threaten a series of planned community colleges for which the money was already committed, then Ottawa might not have made the concession it did, and so on. It might be thought that partisan discussion would seldom affect outcomes because it has no tangible sanction behind it. This view, however, assumes a zero-sum form of conflict. Perceptions can be changed, and governments can be persuaded. In many cases the new information fed into the process can and does suggest new possibilities, and changes the participants' perceptions and goals. In addition to affecting outcomes, tactics affect other elements in the process – as, for example, when conflict and hostility increase because the tactics of one participant are considered illegitimate by the others.

We have now examined some of the major elements in federal-provincial negotiations – issues, procedures, goals, resources, and tactics. Let us turn to the results of this process, and examine its outcomes and consequences.

CHAPTER ELEVEN

# The outcomes

What is the result of the negotiating process? How can different cases be explained? Does the federal-provincial bargaining process we have described really make a difference for the kinds of policies that get made? The answers are of great significance for understanding the effects of a particular form of policy-making on actual policy results. The outcomes described in this chapter differ in some important ways. These differences arise from variations in the patterns of the central variables – issues, procedures, goals, resources, and tactics – which have been previously considered.

## THE PENSION OUTCOME

The pension plan which emerged after two years of negotiations was very different from that first proposed by Ottawa. Most obvious, there were now two pension plans, the Canada Pension Plan serving nine provinces, and the Quebec pension plan for Quebec. Both had identical provisions, though the wording in the legislation differed somewhat. The two schemes were completely integrated and coordinated. A series of agreements were signed for the exchange of information and for arrangements to permit an individual who had contributed to both plans during his lifetime to receive just one pension cheque.

The major provisions of the scheme were also greatly changed. Both plans were now partially funded. Contributions would exceed benefits in the first years of operation, and the resulting fund would amount to about $8 billion by 1985 before beginning to decline. The full amount would be turned over to the provinces for them to invest in their own projects. The contribution rate was higher than that originally proposed, benefits were more generous, and the coverage was wider. A wide range of supplementary benefits for widows, orphans, and the disabled was included. The plan now involved some income redistribution since the $600 exemption for contributions meant that lower income employees would in effect pay a lower rate. All provinces had the right to opt-out of the national plan and establish their own at any time, and the consent of two-thirds of the provinces with two-thirds of the population was to be required for any substantive changes. Both benefits and contributions would automatically increase as wages and prices rose, and the plan would come into effect gradually over ten years.[1]

The first question to ask of the outcome is who won and who lost? Did all actors manage to reach their goals? First, how did Ottawa fare? It did achieve its basic pension goal: a national contributory pension plan ensuring the same provisions for all Canadians. Several features of the revised plan – like broader coverage and supplementary benefits – were elements Ottawa would have liked to include in the original proposal but omitted because of constitutional and administrative problems. Ottawa prevailed on matters like automatic escalation which it had been most deeply committed to. But Ottawa also made some important concessions, such as the higher contribution rate, funding, turning the funds over to the provinces, and restricting future freedom of action through provincial veto on amendments. Many federal respondents, however, felt that the plan as finally enacted was better than their original plan.

The pension settlement also contributed to some of Ottawa's other goals. The solution averted what could have been a very serious clash between Quebec and Ottawa, and contributed, in the short run at least, to the goal of national unity. There was a price: a large financial concession. Ottawa also conceded that henceforth Quebec citizens would look to their provincial government, not Ottawa, for their pension benefits and that future changes in federal legislation would depend on provincial approval. These concessions seemed to weaken the status of the federal government, and enhance that of the provinces. Thus Ottawa achieved some of its goals, but failed on others.

Quebec was the clearest victor. It had its own pension plan. The final

1 For a summary of the provisions, see William Mercer, *Canadian Handbook of Pension and Welfare Plans*, revised by Laurence Coward (3rd ed., Don Mills, Ont., 1967), pp. 209–20.

scheme came closer to its proposal than to Ottawa's. Quebec's major concession was the length of the transition period; Quebec had wanted it longer, to permit building up a larger fund. Another Quebec gain was Ottawa's agreement to negotiate arrangements for opting-out and to give Quebec fiscal compensation for the student loan and family allowance programmes.[2] More generally, the settlement contributed to Quebec's broader goals. It was a recognition of Quebec's special status. 'It was a turning point in the history of Quebec,' said one respondent. Said another: 'It showed that Quebec can have a *statut particulier* and yet the rest of Canada can satisfy its goals too.'

If Quebec gained most Ontario gained least. Ontario had throughout the negotiations presented a shifting and sometimes divided position. One group of advisers, especially those most active in the early stages of the discussion, appeared to be opposed to any pension plan, and throughout Ontario had voiced criticism about its cost, generosity, effect on private plans, and the like. From these points of view the final settlement was worse than the original proposal. At the same time, Ontario shared Ottawa's concern with national unity and thus welcomed the settlement with Quebec. It also benefited greatly from the pension fund and the tax concessions that all provinces won. Ontario's success in gaining the right to opt-out and the virtual veto of future amendments of the pension plan, enabled it to preserve its influence on future developments, and to reply to criticism that it had 'sold out' the conservative interests it represented by saying it could guard against any future expansion of the plan.

The other provinces also gained, though many respondents remained critical of certain provisions. They won unequivocally on the issue that most interested them – the fund. In 1966 it produced $500 million, well above initial estimates.[3] Ontario alone received $298.4 million. Quebec's fund yielded $176.6 million.[4] Such amounts would obviously increase the fiscal weight and independence of the provinces, and would ease their dependence on the private bond market at a time of rising needs and high interest rates. Most provinces also welcomed the broader coverage and benefits. In particular the maritime provinces, with a large proportion of the labour force in self-employed occupations like farming and fishing, had wanted compulsory inclusion of the self-employed. Saskatchewan, which throughout had been a pressure on the left, was much more pleased with the final outcome than with the original proposal.

2 For an analysis of the opting-out procedure, see J. Stefan Dupré, 'Contracting-Out: A Funny Thing Happened on the Way to the Centennial,' Eighteenth Tax Conference, *Proceedings* (Toronto, 1965), pp. 209–18.
3 Canadian Tax Foundation, *Provincial Finances, 1967* (Toronto, 1967), p. 47.
4 La régie des rentes du Québec, *Rapport annuel, 1966* (Quebec, 1967), p. 47.

Thus the pension outcome had important benefits for all participants, though some gained more than others. The negotiations ended with a definite decision on a policy, rather than agreement to disagree. Most important, the settlement was not based simply on splitting-the-difference or finding a lowest common denominator. Rather, the negotiations produced alternatives which had not been thought of before. The final settlement was a plan which was, for many participants, preferable to both the original federal proposal and Quebec's alternative. In addition, the pension model, in which there would be two separate but completely coordinated pieces of legislation, seemed to point to a creative way of satisfying some of Quebec's basic goals while not preventing the English-Canadian majority from achieving its objectives. Finally, a broad range of values were satisfied by the pension settlement: Ottawa's concern for unity, Quebec's for special status, and the other provinces' desire for funds.

## THE FINANCIAL SETTLEMENT

No such agreement emerged in the financial negotiations. At the final conference in October 1966 tempers ran high. The conference was, said Prime Minister Robarts, 'an exercise in futility.'[5] Premier Roblin said it had been bad for both Manitoba and the country.[6] Prime Minister Pearson summed it up as 'equalized unhappiness.'[7]

In tax-sharing, Ottawa held firm to its intention to abandon the abatement system and not turn over a greater share of the major taxes to the provinces. The provinces would receive only four points of personal and one of corporate income tax as a federal contribution to higher education.

The most important result was probably the new equalization formula, which brought total equalization payments to the seven recipient provinces to $546.8 million in 1967–8,[8] almost $200 million more than the previous year. The formula was based on a much more comprehensive measure of fiscal capacity than previously, and, because the measure was based on the combined taxing decisions of the provincial governments, the total amount of equalization would rise automatically in the future.[9]

5 *Globe and Mail*, Toronto, 29 Oct. 1966.
6 *Le Devoir*, Montreal, 29 Oct. 1966.
7 Maurice Western in the *Winnipeg Free Press*, 31 Oct. 1966.
8 *H. of C. Debates*, 1966, p. 9291. The figure was later revised downward to $535.3 million. *Ibid.*, 1967, p. 13789.
9 For details on the theory and method of calculation of the formula, see *ibid.*, 1967, pp. 13687–9 and 13787.

No decision was made on Ottawa's plan to turn over three of the largest shared-cost programmes to the provinces in return for seventeen points of income tax (plus a complicated adjustment formula). The federal government would now pay half the operating costs (or $15 per capita) of higher education, in the form of an unconditional abatement. An extra payment would be made to cover any difference between the yield of the abated taxes and actual operating costs.

The largest federal concession at the October conference was the increase in the capital grants to the provinces for technical and vocational school capital costs. For the provinces, the most important question was the total amount of money the new arrangements would provide. Because of many unanswered questions about the exact financial effect of the educational grants and about how fast the added funds for technical and vocational schools would be used, there was considerable debate at and after the October conference about what the outcome means in dollars and cents. Each side used figures for partisan advantage. Estimates provided by the federal government indicated that the provinces would receive just under $400 million more in total payments than the previous year. The provinces' estimates were considerably lower. Table v summarizes the results.

TABLE V

Results of 1966 negotiations: comparison of provincial receipts in 1966–7 with those of 1967–8 (estimated)

| | Equalization increase (million) | Total increase: equalization + education transfer + vocational grant (million) | Per capita increase |
|---|---|---|---|
| Newfoundland | $29.2 | $34.4 | $65.20 |
| PEI | 3.5 | 5.2 | 44.90 |
| Nova Scotia | 23.2 | 33.7 | 43.10 |
| New Brunswick | 20.1 | 24.2 | 37.20 |
| Quebec | 109.8 | 163.6 | 27.00 |
| Ontario | | 55.6 | 7.60 |
| Manitoba | 1.8 | 14.7 | 13.70 |
| Saskatchewan | −6.6 | 7.0 | 6.80 |
| Alberta | | 23.0 | 15.10 |
| British Columbia | | 16.8 | 8.60 |
| Total: | 181.0 | 378.2 | 18.1 |

The table shows how unevenly the 'winnings' were distributed: from only $6.80 per capita for Saskatchewan to $65.20 per capita for Newfoundland – both, incidentally, Liberal governments. The distribution was also determined primarily by Ottawa; it differed little as a result of the negotiations.

Finally, Ottawa bowed to provincial arguments that the financial question should be reopened before the usual five-year agreement was up. The arrangements would be renegotiated after two years, raising the possibility that the provinces would do better then. In fact, of course, they did not; in 1968 Ottawa held firm.

The federal government won a substantial victory, successfully resisting pressure for more tax-sharing, holding to its principle of 'independent taxing,' and winning provincial approval for its new equalization formula. Its only concessions on equalization had been an extra $3.5 million for Prince Edward Island and a transitional payment to Saskatchewan, which under the new formula would have lost its equalization payment entirely. It had not increased its offer for higher education, and its concession on grants for vocational school construction was relatively cheap.

But there were costs. One reason for the apparent victory was that many potential concessions had been made prior to the meetings. In addition, Ottawa took measures to assert the equal treatment of all provinces and thus resist special status for Quebec. This, however, meant that Ottawa had admitted that the central government would not play any role in determining the overall structure of higher education in Canada. More broadly, in moving away from shared-cost programmes, and stressing it would no longer get involved in areas of provincial jurisdiction, Ottawa seemed to be narrowing its own role. Much of the debate within the government had been around these questions. In addition, Ottawa's stress on 'fiscal responsibility' raised the danger of increasing tax competition among the governments now that Ottawa had abandoned its central coordination. Ottawa's ignoring the Tax Structure Committee projections also raised the danger that provincial resentment might inhibit this kind of cooperation in the future and again make coordination of taxation and fiscal policies more difficult. However, it is clear that Ottawa had regained the initiative in financial relations. It had come to the negotiations with a cohesive, coherent programme and had prevailed over strong pressures to change. By 1968 it had reversed what had become an accepted pattern of provincial expectations: that each time the financial agreements were negotiated a further fiscal transfer would be made.

Ontario gained very little in the negotiations. Tax-sharing, the most important issue for Ontario, yielded nothing. Nor did equalization. The concession on capital grants for vocational schools meant only that the province would be able to meet existing commitments. With one-third of Canada's population, it got only one-seventh of the $378 million increase in total funds. Ontario officials were also disturbed that consideration of long-term requirements – which had been implicit in the Tax Structure Committee projections – was sacrificed to short-term needs, and that successive fiscal arrangements were profoundly affecting the nature of the federal system without the basic assumptions being questioned. Ontario's only gain – but an important one – was the decision to base the higher education payments on *actual* costs in each province rather than on the national average, thus raising the Ontario grant and avoiding the implicit equalization factor which Ontario strongly opposed. Its frustration was summed up by one official, 'We have never been so well prepared for that round, and we have seldom got so little.' Manitoba representatives shared this sentiment. The new arrangements had little for the province or for British Columbia, and for Saskatchewan, which gained less than any other province.

The maritime provinces had every reason to cheer because the equalization formula benefited all (except Prince Edward Island, which got a special grant). Even Nova Scotia, which to the end had advocated an alternative formula, had little reason to protest. The $15 per capita option for higher education especially benefited Newfoundland and Prince Edward Island, since $15 per capita was almost twice as much as half the operating costs of their educational institutions. In addition, the poorer provinces were pleased that Ottawa did not increase abatements, since they wanted Ottawa to maintain its fiscal predominance, which makes equalization possible. 'We're happy,' said Premier Robichaud at the end of the conference. Newfoundland gained $65 per capita; Prince Edward Island, $45; Nova Scotia, $43; and New Brunswick, $37.

Quebec benefited greatly from the new equalization formula and from the education grants. But it too failed to get the major transfer of resources that it had wanted. In addition, Quebec representatives fundamentally disagreed with Ottawa's view that all provinces should be in the same relationship to Ottawa, and that Quebec should not have a special status. 'It's not so much a question of money,' said an official; 'it is this refusal to consider a reorientation of the system, this feeling of the federal government that we are strong and we can and will resist the provinces.' One beneficial effect for Quebec was that now it was firmly aligned with Ontario, Manitoba, and British Columbia on the tax-sharing question.

## THE CONSTITUTIONAL NEGOTIATIONS CONTINUE

No final outcome has been reached in the constitutional debate. With the depth of disagreement on the main issues, and the failure of the Victoria Charter, it is dangerous to speculate on what the final outcome will be.

In mid-1971 the outlook for a far-reaching consensus was not bright. All governments had made concessions to arrive at the tentative agreement in Victoria, but Quebec possessed an effective veto and used it. It remained to be seen whether any governments retained either the will or the ability to try once again to resolve the disagreements or to salvage some tangible results.

Even if it had been accepted the charter would have represented a lowest common denominator compromise, especially in the provisions concerning civil rights, language rights, and the Supreme Court. Ottawa gained agreement on entrenching language and civil rights, but those governments with major reservations assured that the statement of rights would be greatly limited. The revised section 94A, dealing with social policy, did split the difference between Quebec and Ottawa. But it represented a defeat for those poorer provinces especially concerned with maintaining a strong federal presence, and, ultimately, was not enough for Quebec. During much of the discussion Ottawa had appeared to be dominating the debate, but the provinces were able to alter the agenda and in the end Ottawa's views did not prevail, despite support from several provinces. Nor, of course, did Quebec's. The costs of the failure to achieve a creative consensus out of the complex divisions are yet to be counted, though there remained the possibility of agreement in the future.

## THE RESULTS

Outcomes can be evaluated along several dimensions. One is simply how well each participant did in terms of his own goals. Who prevailed? On this dimension, there are important differences between negotiations. Ottawa made major concessions on both pensions and related issues in 1963 and 1964. It substantially prevailed in 1966. Quebec prevailed in the pension case, but did not in 1966. Ontario got little out of the pension issue; and virtually nothing out of the financial settlement. British Columbia achieved its very limited goals on pensions, but gained very little in 1966; the same is true for Manitoba. New Brunswick was successful in both cases. Thus overall the provinces were much more influential on one issue than on the other.

Another dimension is how explicit and definitive the outcome is. Is the issue 'resolved,' and thus removed as a bone of contention, or is it simply postponed for future negotiations? The pension result was much more 'final' than the financial one. In finances, no resolution was reached. The conflict was as great or greater after the negotiations as before. Federal legislation giving effect to the equalization formula and the abatement for education was passed; but the issue remained, and would be reopened soon. After years of discussion, it is hard to conceive of the constitutional debate ending with an agreement satisfying all parties and laying the issue to rest.

A third dimension of outcomes is suggested by Ernst Haas.[10] There are three types of accommodation, each indicating a certain measure of integration. First is accommodation on the basis of the lowest common denominator, in which the participants exchange concessions, but the solution never goes beyond what the least cooperative bargainer is willing to concede. Second is 'splitting the difference,' in which some mid-point between the final bargaining positions of all actors is chosen. The third, which suggests the greatest level of integration, is the finding of a creative solution, in which all parties are satisfied and their common interests upgraded. The pension outcome approached this 'highest' level. The result was a plan different from that proposed by any of the participants, and one which went further towards meeting the goals of all than any of the alternatives. The financial settlement, on the other hand, more nearly approximated the first level. The participants did not discover any broad overall interest. There was no creative solution to the difficult question of sharing of revenue fields. Nor was there any searching for a new approach to shared-cost programmes which might have satisfied both Quebec's concerns for autonomy and other governments' desires for maintaining shared-cost programmes. Nor was there a productive discussion of how best to finance higher education within the federal framework. Instead, there was no decision at all on shared-cost programmes and a 'lowest common denominator' solution to the problem of higher education. A difficulty of the constitution is that several of the issues involved in it – such as Quebec's status – do not easily lend themselves to lowest common denominator or splitting-the-difference solutions, because of the basic matters of principle concerned and because a requirement for a successful constitution is widespread consensus about its legitimacy. Thus the outcomes appear to differ considerably in some important ways. Why? How can these differences be explained?

## EXPLANATIONS

The first reason for different outcomes lies in the nature of the issues themselves. Finances were much more nearly a zero-sum conflict. Every

10 'International Integration: The European and Universal Process,' *International Organization* 15 (1961), pp. 367–8.

dollar gained by the provinces was a dollar lost to Ottawa. This sharpened the conflict and made it much harder to find a creative solution satisfying the interests of all. Gains and losses were more visible and easy to assign, again sharpening the conflict. By contrast, the very complexity of the pension issue encouraged much trading back and forth on specific provisions. The same complexity also meant there was much room for the participants to frame new alternatives; finances were much more cut and dried. In its complexity, the constitution more nearly approaches the pension example. But its emotional significance, together with the fundamental if unclear consequences, make agreement more difficult.

Similarly, the participants' goals and the degree of conflict between them helps to account for differences in the outcome. In the pension case there were substantial areas of consensus. There were far fewer areas of common interest between the actors in finances. In addition the financial issue and the constitution involved the direct self-interest and status concerns of the governments much more deeply. They directly affected each as institutions. Pensions, except for the fund, were much more peripheral to these direct concerns. This is not simply to repeat the truism that agreement is harder to reach when conflict is greater. Indeed, the very existence of severe conflict may be a powerful incentive to find agreement, as the rapid settlement following the débâcle of the Quebec Conference in 1964 clearly demonstrated. The very feeling that mutually destructive conflict could result meant Quebec and Ottawa officials were highly motivated to find a solution – and provinces like Ontario were motivated to go along with it. Thus conflict itself does not make agreement difficult; what is important is that the participants are able to find some common ground. Finally, when one or more participants place a very high value on getting agreement, and are thus willing to make large sacrifices in their policy goals to do so, agreement will be easier to reach. This was the case with Ottawa in 1964, when the goals of unity overrode many policy commitments. In 1966 Ottawa placed much less value on reaching agreement, and much more on winning its substantive point. Again, the result was to make agreement less likely.

In addition, several characteristics of goals help to explain why some actors have more influence in the outcome than others, and why an actor's success may differ from one negotiation to another. If a government's goals are firm, well formulated, and internally consistent, they will likely be more successful. Ottawa had not developed a well thought-out approach in 1963 and 1964. This left much of the initiative to the provinces. Ottawa was stronger in 1966 and 1968–9 partly because it had a much more viable position to defend. Similarly Quebec gained from putting forward detailed proposals like the pension alternative in 1964. Moreover, if a government can convince others that its goals represent a set of very strongly held basic values, as Quebec was able to do in 1964, then it will probably have more influence. This is true partly because the other actors will feel that it is in some sense unfair to expect the other to sacrifice his most fundamental values, and partly because they realize that he is likely to escalate the conflict if those values are threatened. When fundamental values for *both* sides are at stake, as in the constitutional debate, common ground is hard to find.

The most important determinant of the outcome, and of the relative influence of different actors, is the distribution of political resources. The distribution was quite different in different years and on different issues. In some ways the provinces had more resources in 1966. The results of the Tax Structure Committee supported their contentions. Most had much more technical expertise to draw on than in the pension case. But in most ways they had fewer resources. Authority over pensions and the constitution was shared among the governments. The provinces therefore controlled some 'requisite actions' which they could use to gain leverage. There were no such sanctions available in 1966. The provinces were in the position of asking Ottawa to turn funds over to them, which meant there was little they could give or threaten in return. Most important, perceptions of political resources had changed. Ottawa felt in a stronger position: it no longer feared the provinces so much and had decided that perhaps the best way to maintain public support was not to give in to the provinces but to be firm with them. It felt better able to stand up to Quebec because of the recent recruitment of a much stronger Quebec delegation in the federal cabinet, and because the defeat of the Lesage Liberal government took much of the power out of the implicit threat that 'if you don't please us, something worse will take place.' These factors were of course even stronger after the 1968 federal election. As in the pension case, however, Ottawa's focus of attention gave resources to some provinces and not to others. Thus the greatest resource for the Atlantic provinces, which gained so much from the 1966 outcome, was Ottawa's own commitment to improving their lot through equalization.

Differences in resources not only help to explain who won and who lost, but also cast some light on the nature of the outcome. When one actor possesses many more resources than the others, he is able to dictate the outcome. It approaches a hierarchical situation, and the resources of the other actors depend mostly on how well the central actor takes their views into account. Under such circumstances he does not really have to trade, offer compromises, and the like. This makes it less likely that the outcome will meet the goals of all or most participants. It also means that it is less likely the solution will upgrade the common interests of all participants, since the actor who controls most resources is less motivated to search for such an agreement. The outcome seems most likely to approach a creative solution when resources are distributed relatively equally, since each participant is then forced to undertake a search for areas of mutual agreement and for new mutually acceptable alternatives. Thus it seems likely that in 1966 there would have been more extensive joint decision-making and consideration of alternatives on such matters as tax-sharing and university financing had resources been more equally distributed. The distribution of resources on both pensions and the constitution required joint decision-making.

The actors' tactics, too, vary from case to case, and these differences may have an effect on the different outcomes. But since tactics are so closely related to resources, it is very difficult to isolate their effects. Nevertheless, it seems clear that Ottawa's tactics were much more skilful in 1966 and in the constitutional discussions than in 1964, and this helps to account for the different results. With more resources in 1964 and 1965 the provinces were able to use a much wider variety of tactics. In 1966 they were restricted to the various forms of partisan discussion. The effectiveness of partisan discussion, however, depends greatly on the willingness of the opponent to be persuaded and to listen to appeals. Ottawa's firmer goals and changed assessment of its political resources made it less likely to be swayed by provincial arguments.

Finally, the different tactics used by different governments help to account for the relative success of different governments in the negotiations. Quebec's success clearly depended heavily on both the availability of a wide range of tactics and the willingness of Quebec decision-makers to utilize them. On the other hand, one reason for British Columbia's lack of influence appears to lie in the kinds of tactics its leaders use.

This discussion suggests, then, that a great deal of the difference in results can be explained by looking at variations in the central variables. Because the nature of the issue, the participants' own goals, the resources they possessed, and the tactics they used varied, the outcomes differed. Had they been different, the results would likely have been different too. Moreover, by looking at some of the central characteristics of each of these variables it should be possible to predict who will win and who will lose, which governments will be influential, and what kind of solution will be attained in other cases. Since the central factors interact so strongly with each other, it is difficult if not impossible to separate the influence of one from another. In most cases they operate together.

The issues that arise are directly related to the sites used for the negotiations, to the goals and objectives of the participants, to the kinds of resources they possess, and to the tactics they will use. The sites and procedures, we have seen, have implications for the resources of the participants and encourage some tactics and discourage others. The decision-makers' own goals and perspectives have much to do with their resources, with the sites and procedures, and with the tactics they will utilize. The kinds and amounts of political resources the participants possess will play a large role in shaping the range of possible tactics. Some of these relationships have been described in more detail in previous chapters.

All this implies that the federal-provincial negotiations did make a difference in the development of the pension legislation and in the 1966 financial settlement. They will profoundly shape the outcome of the constitutional issue.

## DOES THE PROCESS MAKE A DIFFERENCE?

A general question must be answered before the significance of federal-provincial negotiations can be fully assessed: are policy outcomes significantly different because the policies are negotiated between federal and provincial governments? If so, how do they differ?

One way to help answer this question is to ask what might have happened on each of these issues had the policy been decided in some other framework. Four alternatives may be considered:

| | |
|---|---|
| Central government dominant | no provincial role |
| Provinces dominant | no federal role |
| Federal system | interaction at other sites |
| Federal system | each government acts independently |

Let us first consider the fate of the pension plan if the federal government had been in a position to legislate on the matter with no provincial interference. Under these circumstances, and with a cabinet form of government, it is reasonable to assume that the final legislation would have looked much like that originally outlined by Ottawa in July 1963. Contributions would have been much lower, and benefits less. It might well, however, have included supplementary benefits, since they were not included in the 1963 proposal partly because of the constitutional difficulty, which would not apply with this model. In addition, it is probable that the Old Age Security increase would have been separated from the CPP, as it was under provincial pressure, because this change had been strongly urged by all opposition parties. There would, of course, have been only one pension plan. It would have been a pay-as-you-go plan with little money for investment. It would, in the early years of operation at least, have been less generous and have less broad coverage. The plan would probably have been enacted more rapidly than it was with federal-provincial negotiation. Some major features of the present plan would most likely have been missing.

Development of the legislation would have varied in some other important ways. A different set of participants would have been involved, and with them a different set of interests and concerns. Thus Parliament and the opposition parties would probably have had a greater role to play. As it was, the parliamentary role was extremely limited despite extensive debate on the plan. The joint committee which examined the legislation in detail operated under the severe constraint that if it proposed any major changes the agreement with Quebec would be broken. It is not certain, of course, that the committee would have had much more freedom if the government had not had to deal with the provinces, since the cabinet system gives relatively little policy-making role to committees. But what does seem clear is that parliamentary considerations would have bulked much larger in federal thinking than they did. As it was, a minority federal government had to have one eye on Parliament and the other on the provinces.

Similarly, interest groups would probably have played a greater role. Federal respondents reported that the difficulties of modifying the plan to meet provincial objections left little room for consideration of the objections raised by interest groups. It is reasonable to expect that if it were not for the provinces such considerations would have played a larger role in federal thinking; and that private interests would have been more extensively consulted in the development stage. Again, it is a matter of the reference groups and focus of attention adopted by the policy-makers. In so far as opposition parties in Parliament and interest groups would have raised different concerns the outcome would likely have been different.

Finally, the side-benefits produced by the pension plan – especially the financial gain for the provinces in the fund and tax-sharing concessions – would not have arisen. The possibility of log-rolling which developed in 1964 between Quebec and Ottawa would not have occurred, raising the possibility that conflict between Ottawa and Quebec on the financial question during that period would have been much more severe.

The second model assumes a system where pensions were entirely a provincial responsibility, with Ottawa playing no role at all. Under such circumstances it is most unlikely that a plan comparable to the CPP would have been enacted. There would have been pension legislation, perhaps like that Ontario passed providing for regulation of private pension plans, and specifying that all employers with a certain number of employees must provide them a pension plan meeting certain standards. Since this alternative was inexpensive, it is likely that other provinces would have followed with similar plans. Indeed, in 1965 and 1966 Ontario led a successful effort to get provincial agreement on such regulatory legislation passed in most provinces to supplement the CPP. But it is unlikely much broader pension legislation would have been developed. Most provinces had neither the expertise nor the resources needed to establish a contributory pension plan. In most, the small population would have made a pension plan difficult to operate. If some provinces had set up such plans and others had not, barriers to interprovincial mobility would be set up and coordination of the schemes would have been very difficult. Most provinces simply had not worried about pensions. Thus, if the provinces had acted independently, it is likely that no plan would have been generally available, and that, if plans had been adopted, the standards would have varied greatly among the provinces.

The third model suggests that regional interests would be heard, but they would be expressed through central political institutions like Parliament rather than in the process of direct government-to-government negotiations I have described. It is more difficult to speculate on this model because there are so many possible variants. How much, for example, should the party discipline assumption be relaxed? What degree of provincial government influence on members of Parliament and cabinet ministers should be assumed? If the MPs were merely delegates of the provinces, the situation would approximate the direct negotiation model, with the important exception that the federal government would be even more oriented to provincial interests that it is now. Let us instead assume that MPs and cabinet ministers represent *regional* interests, but not directly those of provincial governments, and that this regional representation is only part of their role. In this case, it is unlikely the results would have been very much different from those obtained with the central government dominant, since regional interests themselves were not a central feature of the pension dispute. What were important were the status concerns of the provincial governments, in particular the value of the fund and the maintenance of provincial control over future amendments. It is unlikely Quebec members in the federal Parliament would have recommended that Quebec have a separate plan, because that would be a threat to their own status. Thus even if central and regional interests were adjusted in a different form the results probably would have differed in some important ways from those that finally emerged.

The outcome of the pension negotiations, then, took the shape it did largely because of a certain pattern of federal-provincial interaction. It ensured that a particular set of interests – those of the provincial governments – was injected into the policy-making process. Coordination might have been achieved without federal-provincial negotiation, but the shape of the final result was in large measure a product of this form of negotiation.

What about finances under another model of policy-making? If one or other government were completely dominant in all revenue fields, almost by definition the problem of sharing would not exist. The most interesting model to speculate about here is that in which each level of government would make its own taxing decisions independently, without any explicit discussion with other governments, though, as with Lindblom's adaptive adjustment,[11] the governments might take some account of the effects of their actions on others. Unless each government were assigned specific revenue fields finally and unequivocally, such independent taxing decisions would still affect other governments; they would still be interdependent. Broadly, the United States follows this model. It also applies to a large part of the Canadian system of governmental finance. The governments typically do not consult each other when they impose new taxes or raise old ones. The financial negotiations are about narrower questions, notably the sharing of personal and corporate income taxes and the form and amount of federal assistance to the poorer provinces, though broader questions of overall fiscal policy coordination are discussed.

It would of course be possible for the governments to achieve coordination under independent taxation without formal negotiations. Governments would have to adjust their actions automatically to the actions of others. But the important point is that the outcome, or result of such coordination, could vary very widely, with great consequences for the status and financial power of the various governments. It might, for example, lead to intergovernmental tax competition, administrative duplication and overlapping, 'double taxation,' or great disparities between

11 *The Intelligence of Democracy: Decision-making through Mutual Adjustment* (New York, 1965).

revenue needs and actual revenues, as happened in Canada during the depression, when 'the uncoordinated efforts of all governments to maintain solvency reduced the tax system to chaos.'[12] Even with the direct negotiation process, it is possible such developments could occur, but they would appear less likely. If both levels of government controlled large shares of the major revenue sources, adjustment through independent taxing could also make coordination of fiscal management policies more difficult, with the possibility that the various governments would pursue contradictory policies. Thus two Canadian economists suggest that the combined spending, taxing, and borrowing decisions of Canadian provinces and municipalities have been slightly 'procyclical.'[13] Again, it is by no means certain that negotiation will produce harmonized federal and provincial policies, but it is likely to increase the probability of complementary measures, if only by making all governments aware of the problems.[14] Another consequence of such a system might be that the financially weaker units would be ignored, as the central government felt less incentive to provide special assistance. All these factors played a part in the development of formal federal-provincial financial negotiations since the war. Coordination through completely independent action failed to meet the goals of many participants.

A perhaps more important consequence of independent taxing is that the equilibrium reached in the sharing of tax fields would likely adhere closely to the status quo. In Canada, we have noted, the postwar years have seen a progressive shift in the major revenue sources to the provinces, so that the provincial share of personal income taxes in 1966 was an estimated 33.5 per cent of the total collected.[15] By contrast, starting from a similar wartime centralization, the American states in 1964 collected only 7 per cent of all personal income taxes.[16] In 1970, provincial

12 A. Milton Moore, J. Harvey Perry, and Donald I. Beach, *The Financing of Canadian Federation: The First One Hundred Years* (Toronto, 1966), p. 10.

13 A.W. Johnson and J.M. Andrews, 'The Basis and Effects of Provincial-Municipal Fiscal Decisions,' in John F. Graham, A.W. Johnson, and J.M. Andrews, *Inter-Government Fiscal Relationships* (Toronto, 1964), p. 66. See also Jacques Parizeau, 'Prospects for Economic Policy in a Federal Canada,' in P.-A. Crépeau and C.B. Macpherson, eds., *The Future of Canadian Federalism/L'avenir du fédéralisme canadien* (Toronto, 1965), pp. 45–57.

14 Thus, Johnson and Andrews found in discussions with provincial financial officials that they were 'on the whole, prepared to co-operate with the federal government in any effort to counteract business cycles. But they feel unable to do so by themselves, and can do so only within the context of a federal-provincial plan.' 'The Basis and Effects of Provincial-Municipal Fiscal Decisions,' p. 66.

15 Marion Bryden, *Occupancy of Tax Fields in Canada* (Toronto, 1965), p. 20.

16 Advisory Commission on Intergovernmental Relations, *Federal-State Coordination of Personal Income Taxes* (Washington, 1965), p. 1.

income taxes claimed 3.7 per cent of GNP, state income taxes represented 1.4 per cent.[17] It is possible that through independent decisions the contemporary Canadian division of resources would have arisen, through the provinces unilaterally imposing and increasing income taxes of their own and by Ottawa unilaterally deciding to assist the poorer provinces through equalization. But it probably would have been politically dangerous and costly for provincial governments to raise their own income taxes above those of other provinces, and would have been even more difficult for all provinces to raise taxes high enough to force Ottawa to reduce its own by the amount that it has. Thus, it is likely that a system of independent taxing would find equilibrium close the pre-existing status quo. So might negotiations. But the negotiations have permitted the provinces to bring direct pressure to bear on the federal government and to exploit their resources to the full. In Australia direct financial negotiations, much like the Canadian in form, have taken place without the federal government's giving up its full control of income taxes – though the states have been able to win larger unconditional grants.[18] The difference between the Australian and Canadian cases can be explained largely by the fact that for several reasons the Canadian provinces have greater political resources than the Australian states. The negotiations provide the framework within which to utilize those resources. Thus, it is difficult to imagine that the division of financial resources would be the same as it is without the process we have examined, even though the 1966 round did not produce much gain for the provinces.

Finally, what results might interaction from other arenas yield in financial relations? Again, because regional interests would be represented instead of governments, we would expect different outcomes. Thus while there would be debate within Parliament and the cabinet about how the impact of federal spending and federal fiscal policies was distributed across the country, the form of federal assistance to regions would probably change. It would be in the form of federal programmes and projects, not provincial ones. Hence there might still be special payments to the poorer regions, but it is less likely they would be in the form of unconditional grants like equalization. In the United States, for example, about one-third of recent grant-in-aid programmes have involved an equalization component, but unconditional equalizational payments have never

17 Advisory Commission on Intergovernmental Relations, *Intergovernmental Fiscal Issues in the United States Evaluated against Recent Canadian Experience* (Washington, 1971), p. 14.

18 See Geoffrey Sawer, *Australian Government Today* (rev. ed., Melbourne, 1961), pp. 13–16.

been a major issue.[19] Similarly, there is no reason to expect a federal government in which regional interests were strong to give up its central control of the major tax fields to other governments or that it would choose an abatement as a way of aiding universities.

Thus in finances, too, the negotiations do make a difference to the policy outcomes. The results are shaped in large measure by the kind of decision-process that operates. There is no legal requirement that federal and provincial governments negotiate directly. That they continue to do so, and that this negotiation appears to take place on a wide range of issues, indicates that most of the participants believe that the process has important advantages in terms of policy outcomes.

Although there is as yet no final outcome on the constitutional issue, it does seem clear that because the matter was discussed in the federal-provincial rather than some other forum, the nature of the debate itself took a certain form. Indeed, it is significant that the first substantive agreements to come out of the constitutional debate were one allowing the provinces into some indirect tax fields and a federal commitment to limit its spending power by giving provincial *governments* a veto over some federal spending projects. Both agreements show a response to the institutional interests of governments, and both, presumably, are matters of more interest to governments than to other groups.

Thus, to debate the constitution among these people – the political executives of the eleven federal and provincial governments – and in this forum – the federal-provincial conference – seems to have had some crucial consequences for the values which were considered, for the points of view to be examined, and for the language and rhetoric of debate. Ultimately we may expect the shape of a revised constitution itself will be profoundly affected by the decision-making mechanism used. An examination of the constitutional debate suggests that the premiers and prime ministers who are the main participants injected first those matters which concern their immediate status interests most. Hence, for example, the widespread desire to talk about taxing and spending powers. Hence the frequent raising of non-constitutional issues. Matters like entrenching constitutional rights were remote; few wanted to talk about them. The discussion took off from the problems facing governments rather than from the problems facing individual citizens. Many potential issues were simply not discussed. The participants tended to concentrate on relatively short-term matters rather than long-term possibilities. They stressed structural over substantive problems. One participant, who ob-

19 Advisory Commission on Intergovernmental Relations, *The Role of Equalization in Federal Grants*, Commission Report A-19 (Washington, 1964), p. 5.

jected to this characteristic of the debate said: 'It is a cock-eyed way of going about looking at a constitution; it is extremely short-sighted. It predetermines the discussion in favour of retaining, by and large, the existing fabric; it closes the door on a whole range of alternatives.' Said another, 'We are still thinking in terms of existing forms and structures.' To mention this point is not to agree with the criticism: one may well argue that this is the most appropriate way to conduct the exercise, that any alternative method would be doomed to failure and would not produce useful results. The point is that this form and content of discussion are to a large extent implicit in the unspoken – and undiscussed – choice of the forum and the participants.

Similarly the rhetoric of debate seems to have been shaped by the characteristics of the participants. The debate was conducted in pragmatic unemotional tones. The first ministers, said one observer, went about negotiating the constitution just as if they were negotiating another tax-sharing agreement. 'I just cannot get dewy-eyed over the constitution,' said an Ontario official. 'I take a purely pragmatic view.' There was no sense that the participants were the latter-day fathers of a new confederation; 'There was no spirit of Philadelphia here.' The exception was Quebec, but even its spokesmen pitched their arguments pragmatically to suit their audience.

These characteristics of the debate seem to stem not only from the fact that governments were the main participants but also that within governments it was the first ministers and their immediate advisers in premiers' offices, finance ministries, and attorneys general's departments who were most involved. Few officials or ministers from substantive programme departments were widely consulted.

Thus, as with the other issues, the debate would have been very different in other settings, and with other points of view brought to bear. For example, if municipal governments had been involved – as they had requested – we would expect wide discussion of the constitutional position of municipalities and of the establishment of direct relations between central and municipal governments. If the parliamentary committee had been involved before 1970 surely there would have been more discussion of the constitutional role of Parliament and cabinet in a modern state. If party leaders had been involved we might expect there to have been more consideration of the constitutional role of parties and of constitutional provisions strengthening their position. Thus the German Basic Law to a large extent reflects the interests of those most involved in its drafting – the major parties on one hand and Land politicians on the other. The issues considered – and they were only a few of a very large set of possible questions touching on the constitution – reflect to a large extent the interests and concerns of those who participate in the decision-process. The three cases studied here demonstrate this. In choosing the forum they did for constitutional revision it was clear that a series of other choices were implicitly made. Clearly there would be no weakening of the constitutional powers of the provinces. In the current Canadian context it was almost unthinkable that any other forum be used for constitutional revision – especially when the original demand came from several provinces themselves. The participants wished to restrict the degree of involvement of other actors: the constitutional debate began and remained an intergovernmental affair. The outcome will reflect that.

All this is not to suggest that all policy outcomes are the result of federal-provincial negotiation, or that the results depended entirely on the discussions. Demands for an expansion of pension legislation had been made frequently by interest groups and parties like the New Democratic party before 1963. The federal government had formulated its original plan well before it was introduced to the provinces, so the issue was well defined by the time it got into the federal-provincial arena. The discussion was not so much whether there would be a plan, but what its provisions would be and who would run it. The basic decision, to have a national pension plan, was made outside the federal-provincial arena, though it was possible that events in the negotiations could have defeated the plan.

Similarly, the whole question of finances is not discussed in any one round of financial negotiations, and actions the participants have taken outside the negotiations also profoundly affect the financial division. In 1966 the question was not should Ottawa make abatements or have an equalization programme, but rather should it abate more and how should it modify equalization? The participants were not remaking the financial system but making incremental adjustments. The starting point for the negotiations was the existing arrangements. This is true despite the fact that several provinces did want to make the 1966 negotiations a synoptic consideration for the basic problem with a view to a fundamental realignment of fiscal resources and despite the Tax Structure Committee's work which was designed to make just such a study. Thus the alternatives are circumscribed in the negotiations and events in the wider political system have a major effect on the outcomes. But even here the process itself plays a major role, because the influence of the wider system is to a large extent channelled through the negotiation process. It is reflected in the nature of the issue, in the goals and objectives of the participants who react to the exigencies of their own political environment and to the interests and concerns of their reference groups, in the participants' political resources and constraints, and in their strategies and tactics. In being channelled through these elements the effect of the wider environment is altered and adapted to the federal-provincial bargaining game.

Because of the way federal-provincial negotiations brings in to the decision-making process certain interests and concerns which would not otherwise be involved, and because it gives provincial governments, as institutions, a major voice in national policy-making, the kinds of decisions made in the system and the interests brought to bear in policy-making are distinctive. Furthermore, differences in some central characteristics of this adjustment process help to explain why the results in one case differ from that in others.

CHAPTER TWELVE

# Consequences

The process of federal-provincial negotiation depends broadly on some of the basic social and institutional characteristics of Canadian federalism. The process, in turn, shapes policy outcomes in some important ways. Finally the process and its outcomes have consequences for the system and for particular groups within it. There is a feed-back process, and through it some of the broader implications of federal-provincial negotiations for Canadian federalism may be examined. It is difficult to measure such effects, since they mingle inextricably with other complex factors, and since one or two incidents may make little discernible impact in themselves. Furthermore, the impact may not become apparent until long after the event. It is impossible yet to tell, for example, if a mutually harmful taxing conflict between governments will result from Ottawa's abandoning the abatement system, or whether it will make coordination of fiscal policies more difficult. Nevertheless, some suggestions can be made.

## EFFECT ON OTHER NEGOTIATIONS

First, the operation of the process in one case will affect its operation in others. Financial questions interacted strongly with both the pension and constitutional issues. The pension and other negotiations in 1963 and 1964, said a federal official, were 'far too large an experience not to have had a very large permanent influence on federal policy-making and on federal-provincial relations. More than any other single event it ... burned on everybody's consciousness how much there had been a shift in power.' One result was to stimulate federal decision-makers to modify their goals in a response to this new situation. Another result was to force Ottawa in future policy planning to pay much more attention to provincial attitudes: 'Now we ask,' said a federal official, 'how can we manœuvre so we can get things done with the necessary degree of acceptance from the provinces – we take that into account now.' Two sets of regional desks, in the Prime Minister's Office and the Privy Council Office, represent an institutional response to this development. Thus the pension experience led to a change in Ottawa's goals, tactics, and focus of attention. It also altered some resources for later negotiations. The amending procedures and wording of the British North America Act amendment ensured that in future pension discussions the provinces would possess authority. One set of negotiations may modify or add to the procedures used for others. The Tax Structure Committee's projection exercise may be a model for future negotiations. For another example, the 1966 Interprovincial Conference, for the first time, devoted itself to federal-provincial matters, and this has continued in later conferences. Finally, the outcome on one issue may directly affect that on others, by setting precedents or by suggesting new models which could be used in future cases. Thus one negotiation is intimately related to others, past, contemporary, and future.

## CONSEQUENCES FOR PARLIAMENTARY DEMOCRACY

'This Parliament cannot be allowed to become a rubber-stamp for ten provincial Premiers,' said Liberal MP Ron Basford during the pension debate. 'I can assure them that the people of this country look to us in this Parliament to solve some of the problems besetting Canada.'[1] 'Only the Parliament of Canada ... the one institution which is responsible to all of Canada seems to have ignored the on-going discussion of constitutional evolution in Canada,' complained Opposition Leader Robert Stanfield in 1968. 'Only the Parliament of Canada seems to have stood aloof and above the controversy.'[2] This complaint underlines the frustration felt by many federal legislators who feel their status – and Parliament's – is threat-

1 *H. of C. Debates*, 1964, pp. 23–4. Robert Prittie, a New Democratic Party MP, agreed: '... many people ... are fed up with the posturing of the provincial premiers ... They think they have a mandate from their people to make life miserable for the federal government, and I suggest this is not the case at all. They act like heads of sovereign states.' *Globe and Mail*, Toronto, 3 March 1964. In 1955 a Conservative leader, Gordon Churchill, worried about the long-term effect of federal-provincial conferences on the 'prestige, authority and development of the Parliament of Canada.' *H. of C. Debates*, 1955, pp. 3643–4.

2 *H. of C. Debates*, 1968, p. 1485.

ened by the increasing policy-making role of federal-provincial negotiation. The failure of Parliament to act as an arena for federal-provincial adjustment is an important reason for the negotiation process itself. But at the same time, the more important the negotiations become, the more Parliament gets bypassed, and the less central it is in the adjustment process. This is not to say Parliament was irrelevant to the pension outcome – the difficult time the government had piloting the legislation through attests to that. But in the last analysis it could do little more than ratify legislation worked out in another arena. The case demonstrated some of the incompatibilities between parliamentary government and federalism. 'You have to recognize and try to compromise with them,' said one MP. Similarly Parliament has had virtually no role to play on the constitution, despite opposition demands for establishment of a special committee. It was finally established after two years of negotiation.

At the same time, writers in many countries have discussed the so-called 'decline of Parliaments.' In a cabinet system the role of Parliament in policy-making is limited anyway, as the British experience shows. Thus Canada is not unique; the requirements of federal-provincial bargaining simply add one more dimension to the wider process. It has also become commonplace to note that the real political opposition in Canada comes not from opposition parties in Parliament but from the provinces.[3] This is only a partial view. Minority governments in Ottawa between 1962 and 1968 made the legislature a vocal site for opposition, to which governments have had to pay great attention. It is more accurate to suggest that in Canada there are two main sites for opposition – Parliament *and* the provinces. The need to respond to both at the same time helps to account for some of the difficulties faced by Canadian governments. In many cases the interests voiced by the provinces are different from, and sometimes opposed to, the interests voiced by the parliamentary opposition, making it very hard for a government to satisfy both at once.

## CONSEQUENCES FOR INTEREST GROUPS

Interest groups were extremely active and vocal in the pension discussions, since the immediate outcome would have a direct impact on many of them. They were less active in the financial or constitutional issue because they did not perceive their direct policy interests to be at stake. In no case did interest groups have a significant effect on the outcome, once the issue had

3 R.B. Bryce, 'Discussion of "Coordination in Administration,"' Institute of Public Administration of Canada, Ninth Annual Conference, *Proceedings* (Toronto, 1957), pp. 162–3.

entered the federal-provincial arena. John Porter[4] and others have argued that the federal system, by providing veto points and complicating decision-making, is inherently conservative. They also suggest that, because they lack resources and because they are more vulnerable to group pressure, the provinces are generally conservative, so business and other such groups will favour provincial autonomy. This hypothesis is plausible, but it is clear that the relationship of interest groups to the process of federal-provincial negotiations needs further study. Certainly, the pension industry had a great deal of influence on Ontario's pension goals. But against this must be placed Saskatchewan, which took the opposite position, and Quebec, which consulted few interests – and certainly not business – in the formulation of its plan.

Some characteristics of the negotiations do give interest groups access. There are eleven possible points of contact rather than one. Delays in getting provincial agreement may give interest groups time to mobilize and thus be more effective. The experience of the 'Fulton-Favreau formula' for amending the constitution is a case in point. After much negotiation the formula was approved by all governments, including Quebec, but in the meantime nationalist groups in Quebec mobilized to mount a major attack on the proposed formula, and it was eventually rejected.[5] Finally, the lack of financial resources in many provinces makes it difficult for them alone to introduce major social policies which might offend conservative interests. Yet, Saskatchewan's CCF government was able to introduce medicare, government automobile insurance, and other such programmes by itself; British Columbia could nationalize the electric power industry and ferry fleet; Quebec could nationalize power, to name but a few examples.

Moreover, some other central characteristics of the process seem to weaken the impact of interest groups. First, the focus of attention for governments as they plan their policies may leave out interest groups. Ottawa, worrying about the provinces and Parliament in the pension case, had little attention to spare for the concerns of interest groups. 'It was difficult to deal with them [pension industry critics] because we were engaged on so many fronts,' said a federal pension planner. Similarly, faced with extensive demands for assistance to higher education, Ottawa had to worry about the provinces more than the universities. The universities would have preferred direct federal aid to the institutions, but Ottawa chose to make an abatement to the provincial governments, with no con-

4 *The Vertical Mosaic: An Analysis of Social Class and Power in Canada* (Toronto, 1965), pp. 380–1, 384–5.

5 John Saywell, ed., *Canadian Annual Review for 1965* (Toronto, 1966), pp. 47–53.

ditions whatever on its use. In doing so Ottawa helped to strengthen the control of provincial governments over the universities, and made federal support for such 'national' universities as McGill in Montreal impossible. The provinces, not universities, were taken into account in Ottawa's planning.

Second, the operation of the process itself tends to freeze out interest groups. There is no provision in the procedures of federal-provincial conferences to consult interested groups, unless, as with Ontario in some of the pension discussions, group representatives are part of the provincial delegation itself. The Canadian Federation of Mayors and Municipalities has been unsuccessful in its demand for attendance in constitutional negotiations which clearly affect them directly. 'It's very hard to assess federal-provincial relations,' said a representative of one large interest group concerned with the pension plan; 'we have so little access.'

Another reason for the lack of interest-group effectiveness in the process is that the kinds of preoccupations of provincial policy-makers are seldom the same as those espoused by the interest groups. Thus a prime issue for both employers and pension companies was how the CPP could be integrated with existing private plans. The federal government took the position that it would not be difficult, and that it was simply a matter for employers and unions to settle. In fact, it was a complex job.[6] But no province voiced this concern. 'The interests that got heard,' said one official, 'especially the provincial interests, just didn't give a darn about integration.'

This is related to a further factor: the dynamics of the process itself. Even if a government does act as a spokesman for a particular interest in the negotiations, these interests may be sacrificed. At best interest-group concerns will form only a part of a government's goals and, to the extent that they are less central than status or ideological goals, they will be the first to be jettisoned in the conference room. This will be especially true when there is great pressure to reach agreement, as there was after the Quebec Conference. Ontario until then appears to have represented the insurance companies, but when it came to the crunch the province's desire for the fund and for such normative values as national unity became controlling, and Ontario welcomed the Quebec-Ottawa agreement.

This is not to say that interest-group concerns would not be sacrificed in other forms of decision-making, but it does appear to be characteristic of federal-provincial relations. Canada, which shares so many of the

6 See Judy LaMarsh, speech delivered to the British Columbia Federation of Labour, 28 June 1965, p. 14. For reactions of pension industry leaders to the problem, see Canadian Pension Conference, *Proceedings*, vol. IV, no 3 (Toronto, 1965).

characteristics of British government, does not appear to have developed to the same degree the institutionalized pattern of policy-making by negotiations between government and groups which Samuel Beer[7] and others have described. Perhaps the predominance of federal-provincial negotiations helps to account for this. This does not mean that such negotiation favours no interest groups. Rather, by giving a strong voice to provincial interests in policy formation, it is likely that regionally based groups have their voice increased while national ones have relatively less influence.

## CONSEQUENCES FOR THE CONSTITUTION

The pension negotiations added a new wrinkle to Canada's operating constitution: that the sovereignty of future Parliaments could be bound by an external agency – the provincial governments. The 'national consensus' doctrine announced in June 1969 would make a similar limitation on Parliament's spending power even more binding. These particular changes may not be profound, but they do illustrate how the policy decisions that emerge from federal-provincial discussions modify the operation of the constitution.[8] More generally, the structure of federal-provincial conferences 'is the most significant unwritten development in the constitutional life of the country,'[9] and may well become legitimized in a new constitution. This does not arise from just one or two series of negotiations, but slowly over time. The two cases merely reflected and reinforced these developments. Thus even those cases not explicitly involving constitutional matters can have constitutional consequences.

## CONSEQUENCES FOR STATUS OF GOVERNMENTS

One of the most important stakes in the negotiations is the status of the various governments, and the results have immediate consequences for their positions. The pension outcome, for example, increased the financial independence and fiscal weight of the provinces. Their status was also increased by the CPP amending provisions and by the provincial freedom to opt-out. Perhaps more important, the whole experience contributed to provincial status and prestige by demonstrating how much influence the

7 'Group Representation in Britain and the United States,' *Annals of the American Academy of Political and Social Science* 309 (1958), pp. 130–40.

8 Edward McWhinney writes: '... Canada's present dominion-provincial conference system seems responsible, much more now than the Supreme Court, for the many and far-reaching informal constitutional changes that have occurred since World War II.' 'The Nature of Bicultural Constitutionalism,' in Ontario Advisory Committee on Confederation, *Background Papers and Reports*, II (Toronto, 1970), pp. 54–5.

9 R.I. Cheffins, *The Constitutional Process in Canada* (Toronto, 1969), p. 15.

provinces could have and how much Ottawa's freedom of action was limited. For Quebec the settlement meant even more. It demonstrated that Quebec could have a special status and implied that Quebec citizens would have less contact with the central government, looking instead to Quebec to provide pensions, student loans, and other services. On the other hand, Ottawa had proved vulnerable, weak, and occasionally inept. There is little doubt that these factors contributed to a decline in the status and prestige of the federal government and a corresponding increase in that of the provinces.

Federal planners recognized this in preparing their 1966 position, and tried to reassert their status. Ottawa's firmness in resisting provincial demands and its assertion of responsibility for manpower training as a federal economic programme illustrate this change. At the same time, Ottawa asserted that Quebec should not have a special position and that Ottawa had primary responsibility for management of the economy. But in some ways this new policy simply recognized existing reality, and it may have the effect of further decreasing Ottawa's status. The new policy on shared-cost programmes meant largely abandoning what since the war had been the main device for federal involvement in areas of social policy. Ottawa was caught in a painful dilemma – to allow Quebec to continue its special relationship (which risked, in federal eyes, a threat to national unity), or to assert that all provinces should have the same degree of autonomy as Quebec (which risked 'a possible paralysis of the federal initiative in dealing with important national problems'[10]). There was thus 'a basic, if not fully voiced, concern that loss of the federal presence in the way proposed carried the principle of decentralization and the narrowing of federal power too far for the long-run cause of national unity and national growth.'[11] Ottawa's admission of its lack of influence over higher education in its proposal for post-secondary education financing and the actual experience of the first years of the programme demonstrate the reality of this fear.[12] A similar dilemma for Ottawa was posed in tax-

10 T.K. Shoyama, 'The New Federal-Provincial Fiscal Arrangements,' paper presented to the Ottawa Chapter, Canadian Political Science Association, 22 Nov. 1966, p. 18.

11 *Ibid.*

12 Lamenting Ottawa's lack of control over its own budget engendered by provincial spending, Mr Trudeau said at a press conference in August 1969:

'... because of the agreements that we have with the provinces, we are not in a position to determine what we spend for post-secondary education ... This we can't control at all.

You see, much of the difficulty of the federal budgeting is that we're locked into so many of these open-ended programmes.'

Quoted in *University Affairs* 10, no 8 (Oct. 1969), p. 1.

sharing. By stressing that each government should bear 'fiscal responsibility' for its own taxing decisions, Ottawa has come almost full circle from the fiscal centralization of the wartime years, again raising potential difficulties for effective economic policy unless voluntary mechanisms of coordination can be developed. Thus, paradoxically, the 1966 results demonstrated both a reassertion of federal status and a recognition of federal weakness. In the short run, Ottawa helped to erase its image of weakness and vacillation, but the long-run price may be further increases in provincial status, since so many of the politically attractive areas of policy – including such questions as urban development – lie within provincial jurisdiction.

More generally, the negotiation process both reflects and contributes to a greater provincial role. Provincial governments are major participants in national policy formation. They come to conferences as Ottawa's equals and benefit from national publicity and recognition. Provincial premiers play a major role on the national stage. Again, this is a cumulative process. The more they do so the more likely the press, interest groups, and the like are to pay attention to provincial reaction in future issues. And the more likely provincial governments are to insist that they be consulted.

These shifts in relative status have not, however, made Ottawa powerless. Rather, the pension case demonstrated that even when faced with major provincial opposition Ottawa could still achieve its basic goals. 'Cooperative federalism' has not meant federal paralysis. As we have seen, Ottawa has many resources in the negotiations. Few provinces can match its expertise and personnel in many areas. By 1966 federal leaders could say that they had enacted most of the major planks in their 1963 election programme, in the face of challenges not only from the provinces but also from a vocal parliamentary opposition. Thus the federal government remains not merely one among eleven governments; it plays a more central role at the heart of the system. This is recognized not only by federal officials but also by those in the provinces. The lines of communication run between each province and Ottawa, as the hub of the system, rather than between capitals.

The question of status and prestige is, of course, a relative one. Status with regard to what? And in whose eyes? In this study we have looked primarily at governmental élites. But to measure fully the effect of these negotiations, and their results, on the status of governments we would also want to examine changes in the attitudes of mass publics and particular élite groups. Are they becoming more oriented to one level of government for the voicing of demands, the provision of public services, and, most important, in terms of emotional or affective loyalty? If so, then the behaviour of these groups in trying to influence policy should change, and this in turn might be expected to affect policy outcomes.

In this study we have focused primarily on some of the centrifugal forces. There are, of course, pressures acting in the opposite direction. The recent creation of national symbols like a Canadian flag, recent efforts by the federal government to better integrate French Canadians into national political life through measures like encouraging bilingualism in the civil service, and the outpouring of national sentiment associated with the 1967 Canadian Centennial and with Expo 67 in Montreal may all help to 'nationalize' Canadian political attitudes at least among English Canadians, and thus weaken the status of the provincial governments in the long run. This remains a subject for future research. Other factors, like election of a majority government and a dynamic prime minister, seem to have enhanced federal stature, at least in the short run. It seems probable, however, that the outcomes in the negotiations studied did, on balance, help to weaken federal and enhance provincial status, contributing to the further decentralization of Canadian federalism, and to the increase of the role of *federal-provincial* decision-making on national issues.

## THE PROCESS AND THE MANAGEMENT OF CONFLICT

The process has a direct effect on the kinds of conflict in the system, and on ways of resolving it. The basic causes of conflict appear to be rooted in the social system and in the demands and ideologies of leaders. But the methods and procedures developed in federal-provincial negotiations add their own dimension to conflict in the Canadian system. The process fosters certain kinds of conflict and channels disagreement in certain ways. Because federal-provincial negotiation is so important, major issues tend to become defined as federal-provincial ones. In doing so, the status and prestige concerns of governments, which may be harder to resolve, are superimposed over simple policy differences. This is encouraged by the relative centralization of the governments. Although many minor issues do get settled in horizontal relationships among officials, there is a tendency for a high proportion of issues to get moved up the political ladder. And, while the politicians may have the advantage of being able to authoritatively solve disputes, this means again that the concerns of status, prestige, electoral advantage, and the like will become more dominant. Added to this is a great visibility of the process at the political level. A few times each year the premiers and prime ministers come together in what are widely described as 'confrontations.' In addition, each issue involves the same relatively small group, meaning that disagreement on one issue is more likely to spill over onto other issues. Thus A.H. Birch suggests that the tradition of conflict in Canada over financial arrangements has spilled over to make cooperation on matters like social policy more difficult.[13]

This pattern of conflict focused narrowly at the political level contrasts strongly with the American pattern. In the United States state and federal political systems are tightly interlocked through the party system, simultaneous elections, mobility of office-holders from one level to another, and so on;[14] in Canada the whole process is much more narrowly focused. The very complexity of the relationships in the United States, suggests M.J.C. Vile, mutes and diffuses conflict and promotes compromise. If there were an artificial separation between state and federal politics, he suggests, conflict would be greater and harder to resolve.[15] This appears to be broadly the case in Canada. With fewer units, more centralized governments, and less broad-scale interaction between federal and provincial political systems, the pattern of conflict in Canada is more visible and more simple. It tends to put *governments* in conflict with *governments* and thus adds an important dimension to the conflict.

Another feature of the Canadian pattern which makes conflict resolution more difficult is the absence of third parties who might play a mediating or arbitrating role, and to whom individual governments could appeal. We have seen the weakness of the Canadian Supreme Court in this regard; its role is far different from that of the United States court. Nor is there a relatively independent body like the Common Market's Commission which could initiate new policies or suggest compromises. It could be argued that the adversary relationship encouraged by the process was particularly harmful in the constitutional debate – and that wider participation by other elements might have made consensus easier to achieve by introducing other issues.

Yet, given certain kinds of disagreement, the process does appear to provide some relatively effective ways of managing it. This study has focused primarily on issues which provoked conflict – as indeed do the participants. Nevertheless, the federal-provincial arena is also a forum for building consensus. It produced wide agreement on the pension plan, and, while it will probably never do so on finances because of the nature of the issue, even here it is likely that the continuing exchange made possible by

13 *Federalism, Finance and Social Legislation* (Oxford, 1955), p. 239.
14 Herbert Kaufman, *Politics and Policies in State and Local Governments* (Englewood Cliffs, 1963), chap. 1. Herbert Wechsler, 'The Political Safeguards of Federalism,' in Arthur W. Mcmahon, ed., *Federalism Mature and Emergent* (New York, 1955), pp. 97–114.
15 *The Structure of American Federalism* (London, 1961), p. 93.

frequent conferences played an important role in building support for the value of equalization, for better coordination of fiscal policies, and so on. In addition, the frequent meetings, combined with norms of trust and honesty, do facilitate communication, and thus lessen the chance of conflict on extraneous issues. They may also permit the settling of disagreements without their breaking out into public view. They enable participants from various governments to learn about the problems and perspective of others, and to develop common values. In addition, by ensuring that regional values do get taken into account, the process helps to ensure that federal and provincial actions will not ignore others' interests to the extent that widespread resentment results. Again, however, the process is not perfect in this respect. Important regional grievances, especially in the west, remain. Misunderstandings are still common.

Ultimately, however, the effectiveness of the process in managing conflict depends on the attitudes and perspectives of those who operate in the system. The structures and institutions of federal-provincial negotiations are extremely flexible and fragile. There are few formal rules and little formal structure. The sites and procedures have little independent life of their own, which might itself influence behaviour. Few government officials and no interest groups have their status bound up in the process itself, again in contrast to the Common Market with its Eurocrats.[16] Yet, in most governments, senior officials and politicians value the process, and wish to maintain it. Part of the reason is that, given the structure of the Canadian political system, it does help to manage moderate levels of conflict. In severe conflicts, it is unclear what role it would play.

## CONSEQUENCES FOR ETHNIC CONFLICT

A particularly vital source of conflict in Canada is ethnic conflict between French and English Canadians. Managing it has been a central task of the system from 1867 right up to the present. In recent years the conflict has taken the form of a series of demands by Quebec on the rest of Canada, especially on the federal government. Such demands, we saw, were intimately involved in all issues. Robert Dahl suggests that such 'subcultural' conflict is especially bitter and intractable;[17] few nations, developed or undeveloped, have managed it successfully. One Canadian solution to the problem has been federalism itself. The logic of this solution is that by, in effect, disengaging the parties, each is free to pursue its own interests with-

16 See Jan Schokking and Nils Anderson, 'Some Observations on the European Integration Process,' *Journal of Conflict Resolution* 3 (1960), pp. 406–7.
17 *Political Oppositions in Western Democracies* (New Haven, 1966), p. 357.

out requiring the assent or cooperation of the other. Such a solution works only so long as the actions of one party do not spill over to affect the other, and so long as the goals of one side do not imply demands on the other. The interdependence of modern states, and the nature of the recent claims by Quebec, however, ensures that for large areas of crucial importance to both Quebec and English Canada, these conditions are not met.

How does the process handle the ethnic conflict? French-Canadian nationalists have often criticized the process of cooperative federalism. René Lévesque suggests that the process – 'the ancient hobble of a federalism suited to the last century' – can only lead to unproductive confrontations which will only produce mutual frustration.[18] Jean-Marc Léger has called it 'one of the most monumental trickeries of the century,' since it is nothing but a mask for the true centralizing interests of the federal government: 'Very certainly two out of three times Ottawa will have to revise its initial project, consent to modifications, optional formulae, particular schemes for this or that province: little of importance, the essential will be achieved, the principle of intervention will have been admitted, the mechanism of centralization will have been put in place.'[19] Others criticize federal-provincial conferences because they give Quebec only one voice out of ten, giving the homeland of a nation no more weight than Prince Edward Island.[20] This is true in the narrow sense that formally Quebec has no more authoritative sanctions than any other province. But there is no doubt that in fact Quebec's political resources far outweigh those of other governments. What the process does not give – and what many nationalist critics wish it would – is formal authority for Quebec as a nation dealing on equal terms with the English-Canadian nation.

It nevertheless seems clear that the negotiating process has played a role in mitigating the ethnic conflict. The pension outcome in particular demonstrated that on some kinds of issues at least it is possible to devise solutions which go a long way to meeting both Quebec's demands for a special role and English-Canadian goals of national leadership. It is unlikely such a creative solution could have emerged without the process of negotiation. Opting-out, the solution on student loans and family allowances, and even, though in a less creative way, the aid to higher education outcome in 1966, are other examples of such solutions. In addition, the negotiating process has given Quebec leaders the chance to explain their goals and

18 René Lévesque, *An Option for Quebec* (Toronto, 1968), p. 26.
19 'Cooperative Federalism or the New Face of Centralization?' *Canadian Forum* 43 (Oct. 1963), p. 155.
20 Daniel Johnson, *Egalité ou indépendance* (Montreal, 1965), pp. 68–70; also 'Les phrases et les faits,' *L'Action nationale* 53 (Jan. 1964), p. 416.

intentions to English-Canadian politicians and officials. The result is perhaps a wider sympathy for Quebec's aspirations. Many suggested this was the chief result of the 1967 Confederation of Tomorrow Conference. It is unlikely that premiers like Robarts of Ontario would have taken such a sympathetic view were it not for the communications encouraged by the process. Quebec and the other provinces also agree on many issues, such as tax-sharing. This helps to prevent the conflict polarizing into a French versus English one, and ensures Quebec allies. Furthermore, working through the process, Quebec between 1960 and 1966 did achieve some of its more important goals.

The system of negotiation also makes the ethnic conflict relatively institutionalized. So long as the conflicting forces are diffuse, incoherent aggregates, Ralf Dahrendorf suggests, the regulation of conflict is almost impossible.[21] The federal-provincial conferences provide a framework for discussion and decision. They help to channel the conflict through leaders who, although they may disagree, can be made aware of each other's problems, of the possibilities for compromise, and of the dangers involved in an irrevocable split.

The personal contact which takes place in the negotiations may help to reduce barriers to effective compromise such as personal hostility, lack of trust, and inadequate communications.[22] Quebec officials active in these cases felt the process was effective in reducing these barriers. Finally, while it is true that in many ways the conflict between French and English Canada is a fundamental clash of values about the nature of the federal system and the place of different groups within it, that is not the way issues have typically arisen in the federal-provincial arena, at least until recently. Rather issues have arisen one by one as concrete, limited disputes. Agreement on these is much easier than on matters which involve the whole range of basic value conflict. Finally, the process gives Quebec much greater weight in national policy-making than if it were simply represented in the federal Parliament, and this may reduce the overall level of conflict.

On the other hand, it could be argued – as some present federal policymakers do – that the special status Quebec has achieved will in the long run weaken national unity and exacerbate ethnic conflict by reinforcing Quebecers' loyalty to the provincial government and reducing their sense of involvement with Ottawa. In addition, the character of Quebec's demands is continually shifting, meaning that concessions on one issue or

21 *Class and Class Conflict in Industrial Society* (Stanford, 1959), p. 226.
22 K.J. Holsti, 'Resolving International Conflict: A Taxonomy of Behavior and Some Figures on Procedures,' *Journal of Conflict Resolution* 10 (1966), pp. 279–80.

group of issues may have the effect of increasing demands for further changes, rather than bringing agreement.

Thus the process has had some important effects on the nature of ethnic conflict in Canada. It has helped to shape the nature of the conflict by making it largely a contest between governments. The Quebec provincial government has given concrete form to Quebecers' demands, and has pushed for these demands within federal-provincial conferences. In doing so it has given a particular shape to these demands, calling for an increase in provincial autonomy rather than, say, urging a greater role for French Canadians in the national government. Indeed an increased French-Canadian role in and identification with the federal government – as many federal policies are now trying to encourage – is not in the interests of Quebec government leaders. In this sense the process and the role it gives to the institutional interests of governments does perhaps serve to exacerbate ethnic conflict and reinforce the French-Canadian cleavage. At the same time, the process has provided a means for the French-Canadian minority to satisfy some of its aspirations, though many would argue only by winning concessions at Ottawa's expense. Whether it will continue to do so depends partly on the willingness of English Canadians, both in the electorate and at the political level, to make the kinds of changes Quebec spokesmen demand. In the short run the contact encouraged by the process would appear to provide an incentive for French Canadians to moderate their demands by framing them in terms that will win support of other governments. The process thus facilitates piecemeal adjustments of the ethnic conflict rather than development of grand solutions, and is more capable of dealing with moderate levels of conflict than with severe conflict.

More generally, the pattern of English Canadian-French Canadian bargaining through federal-provincial meetings closely approximates what Arend Lijphart has called consociational democracy.[23] Given hostile or widely differing subcultures with widespread potential disagreement, he suggests, conflict may be best regulated through a process of relative isolation of subcultural members from each other, coupled with overarching élite cooperation. This solution rests on several conditions, two of which are crucial in the Canadian context: first, there must be considerable deference of non-élites to élites, to leave them relatively free to engage in the bargaining process. Second, the élites themselves must agree on at least some overall goals, the most important being a common commitment to maintaining the system itself; without that agreement, the incentive to

23 *The Politics of Accommodation* (Berkeley, 1968), and 'Typologies of Democratic Systems,' in Lijphart, ed., *Politics in Europe: Comparisons and Interpretations* (Englewood Cliffs, NJ, 1969), pp. 46–84.

reach agreement on specific issues is limited. Neither of these conditions are fully met in Canada and it may well be argued they are met less completely in the early seventies than they were in the early 1960s. Thus, federal negotiators, as we saw, have a very strong commitment to national unity. Quebec leaders have been less committed to this goal, and it seems fairly clear that the Lesage government had a stronger determination to maintain the federation than did subsequent governments. Moreover, all indications were that in the early sixties Quebec citizens were to a large extent united behind the federal-provincial policies of the government. That consensus seems to have broken down more recently, with a wide variety of competing currents not only on the issue of nationalism but on a wide range of other issues as well. With modernization appears to have come also a breaking down of traditional mass deference to relatively authoritarian leaders. This puts Quebec negotiators under greater constraints from their citizens and diverts their attention to other issues. It also means that the Quebec government has less authority among their own citizens, and less ability to make binding commitments. If these two trends do exist, then it suggests that, especially when combined with rising nationalist demands, the efficacy of federal-provincial negotiation as a forum for the management of ethnic conflict is weakening.

## THE PROCESS AND POLITICAL CHANGE

In the period covered by the cases, Canada has been undergoing some major political changes. They are in large part a continuation of trends begun in the 1950s and their roots lie primarily in the wider environment.[24] But to a great extent they have been expressed through and mediated by the federal-provincial bargaining process. The immediate instruments of many of the changes have been the federal and provincial executives who participate in the process. Their goals and behaviour reflect measures of the wider environment, but, at the same time, their perspectives and attitudes give concrete form to these pressures; often the pressures for change come from the decision-makers themselves.

Political change may be thus viewed as the product of the interplay between the underlying social environment, the constitutional and institutional structures, the kinds of problems and demands facing the system, and the attitudes and behaviour of the decision-makers. The negotiations are an important nexus for this interplay.

Out of it come many kinds of changes. They may not be a deliberate

24 Donald V. Smiley, *The Canadian Political Nationality* (Toronto, 1967), chaps. 2 and 3.

goal of the participants, nor do they typically come in large steps. Rather many of the changes may be unanticipated consequences, and take the form of piecemeal adjustments. Thus in 1966, according to one major participant, 'important new directions were established *implicitly* for Canadian federalism, without joint federal-provincial discussion about the direction or the philosophy of Canadian federalism.'[25] The contracting-out legislation for Quebec in 1965 was a response to immediate Quebec demands; few federal decision-makers at the time perceived the consequences this *de facto* special status would have for the future. The fact that a synoptic total consideration of the whole question of the relation of governments and of public finance was implicit in the Tax Structure Committee's mandate – and that so little was achieved in this direction – indicates one of the difficulties of synoptic, overall consideration of alternatives.[26] Despite many officials' wishes to the contrary, the decision-makers commonly react to immediate interests and immediate problems, so change is slower and more piecemeal.

We have already discussed some of the changes in the system that the process has helped to shape. Most obviously, the process is an instrument for changes in policy. The Canada Pension Plan is one of the most significant pieces of legislation in recent years, with a direct impact on every Canadian. Change may also come in the structures and procedures of government. Thus, the Tax Structure Committee and the secretariat of the constitutional conference were building blocks in the institutional structure of federal-provincial relations. Combined with the earlier establishment of the continuing committee of economic and financial advisers in 1955, the annual meetings of ministers of finance and provincial treasurers in 1964, and the re-establishment of the interprovincial conferences in 1960, it suggests that the process itself, largely as a result of its own operation, is changing in the direction of greater formality and institutionalization, even though the evolution is slow. This change in turn has implications for other political institutions, including the national Parliament.

Perhaps the most significant political change in recent Canadian history has been the relatively greater influence of the provincial governments vis-à-vis the federal government. Many reasons can be advanced: Quebec's demands, the growing self-confidence of provincial governments, failure of many federal policies to adequately take into account regional

25 H. Ian Macdonald, 'Commentary on "The Dynamics of Federation in Canada,"' paper presented to the Canadian Political Science Association, 1967, pp. 4–5.

26 Another reason was that the governments were still awaiting the report of the Royal Commission on Taxation.

differences, a weakened federal government with less than a majority in the national Parliament (until June 1968), and so on. All these forces have come to bear in the negotiation process itself, being reflected in the goals, resources, and actions of the participants. The outcomes of the process itself – on the pension plan, the Municipal Loan Fund, finances, and other matters – have contributed to this change, and reinforced the growing provincial influence. Success in one round of negotiations is likely, all other things being equal, to lead to greater success in the next; it is a cumulative process.

This is not to say that the federal-provincial negotiations are the only reason for the change, or that the relative balance of power will not shift again. Indeed Canadian history has seen several fluctuations in relative influence. Crises like war or depression, or greater orientations to the federal government by interest groups or mass publics, could produce centripetal tendencies. But again this change will be reflected in the resources the federal-government brings to the negotiations. Moreover, the strong position the process puts the provinces in provides them with many resources with which to resist centralizing forces.

## THE PROCESS AND THE PUBLIC

'The dispute between levels of government in Canada,' Marc Lalonde has written, 'is essentially connected with the power politics of the various groups involved, and has very little to do with the welfare of the individual citizens of the country.'[27] Several respondents made similar remarks. A former Manitoba civil servant remarked that 'sometimes the officials get so wrapped up in their little game which they play by their own little rules that very often the public interest and the interests of the people they are serving get ignored.' 'There's a great distinction between what is nice for the prestige of a government,' said a federal New Democrat MP, 'and what is nice from the point of view of the people.' These comments suggest that the process is undemocratic, first, because it tends to freeze out the public, and, second, because the values at stake are simply governmental status concerns, irrelevant both to good policy and to the views of individuals. It further suggests that the norms and procedures of the federal-provincial negotiations impel the participants to become so wrapped up in playing the federal-provincial game that the 'public interest' somehow gets slighted. The critics would agree with Anthony Downs' observation about

27 'Commentaries,' in P.-A. Crépeau and C.B. Macpherson, eds., *The Future of Canadian Federalism/L'avenir du fédéralisme canadien* (Toronto, 1965), pp. 82–3.

interorganizational conflict generally: 'A second effect of territorial sensitivity is that bureaus consume a great deal of time and energy in territorial struggles that create no socially useful products.'[28]

There is some truth to such assertions. Certainly considerations of status and prestige figure prominently in the goals of all participants. It is true that press and public have been excluded from federal-provincial conferences, just as they are, for example, from cabinet meetings. It is also evident that the difficulties of operating the process do tend to channel the energies of the decision-makers towards a concentration on the problem of federal-provincial relations *per se* and away from evaluation of substantive policies. James D. Barber's suggestion that 'In cybernetic terms feedback from within the system itself tends to overload the communications network, reducing its capacity to handle feedback from outside the system,'[29] seems to apply to the Canadian case.

On the other hand, the process ensures that regional interests, which might not be effectively represented in a single cabinet or legislature under strict party discipline, do get brought to the fore. In a sense, each voter is represented twice in national policy-making – by Ottawa and by a provincial government. Participants from both levels, concerned with maintaining their own power, are responsive to their electorates, as they perceive them. In addition, the feedback problem suggested by Barber, and the predominance of status goals, are common to all decentralized systems.

Another criticism – really more a comment on the federal system itself than on the particular negotiation process – is that the system frustrates widespread demands for policy changes. Thus, A.H. Birch suggests that 'greater progress [in social legislation] would have been made but for the complications of federalism.'[30] But given these complications – divided jurisdiction, lack of provincial resources, and the like – the process has facilitated the output of new policies. A wide variety of programmes, including the pension plan, have been enacted after discussion in the federal-provincial arena. Many could not have been developed by the federal government without negotiation, since they lay within provincial jurisdiction; nor could they have been developed by the provinces alone, since they lacked the resources. The process provides one way in which the 'complications of federalism' can be overcome. In addition, while the process may slow down enactment of new policies, it provides fewer veto

28 *Inside Bureaucracy* (Boston, 1966), p. 216.
29 'Some Consequences of Pluralization in Government,' unpublished paper, 1968, p. 6.
30 *Federalism, Finance and Social Legislation*, p. 204.

points than some other systems, such as the American, with its high degree of decentralization within governments. Compared with a centralized unitary system, the process is a 'complication' for policy-making; but given a decentralized federal system with strong provincial governments, it is a valuable device for policy development. There is little evidence that it has frustrated widespread public demands in recent years.

Ultimately judgments about how democratic the process is depend on the observer's own conceptions of democratic representation. If he prefers a system in which a majority will be elected and then govern with relatively few restrictions, the system is undemocratic, since 'federal' majorities are constantly checked by 'provincial' majorities. If, however, he believes that a multiplicity of checkpoints enhances the changes for rational decision-making and for maximizing consent, and that provincial – especially ethnic – majorities should be accorded a special weight in decision-making, the process is more democratic.

The question of whether 'good policy' emerges also depends greatly on the observer's point of view. To most respondents the pension outcome was better than most alternatives. One writer suggested that the issue 'will likely become a case study in the beneficence of the diversity of viewpoints that federalism makes possible.'[31] Others, however, felt that many of the changes – such as the fund – were irrelevant to the goodness or badness of a pension plan itself, and were instead introduced for extraneous reasons, related to other provincial goals. However, the ability of a decision to satisfy a wide variety of divergent values can be one test of its effectiveness. To insurance companies and others opposed to the whole idea of a government-run pension plan, the final outcome was worse than earlier alternatives, but polls showed wide public support for the plan. Similarly, assessment of the financial outcome depends on one's point of view. To those interested in maintaining federal leadership, or concerned with the need for one government to unequivocally control the economy through dominating the major revenue fields, the progressive increase in the provincial share of major taxes is lamentable. To those, however, who stress the virtues of provincial control of such matters as education and recognize the need for the provinces to have access to the funds necessary to perform such tasks efficiently, decentralization of revenue sources is good, and federal-provincial negotiations can help to reconcile this with the need for a national federal policy.

31 J. Stefan Dupré, 'Contracting-Out: A Funny Thing Happened on the Way to the Centennial,' Eighteenth Tax Conference, *Proceedings* (Toronto, 1965), p. 215.

It is clear, then, that the process of federal-provincial negotiation has some important consequences for Canadian federalism – for the policies generated, for the participants themselves, for the way the process operates in other cases, for the constitutional and institutional arrangements of Canadian government, for different groups within the system, for responsiveness of the system to democratic values, for individual interest groups, and for political change itself. On one hand the process is dependent on the wider environment; on the other it is an instrument through which the participants alter that environment.

CHAPTER THIRTEEN

# Conclusion: federal-provincial diplomacy

This study has shown that negotiation between federal and provincial governments is a central feature of the Canadian federal system. I have tried to suggest some of the reasons why this process is so important, how it works, and what some of its consequences are. What can we conclude about the nature of this process? What implications does the study have for some basic questions about relations between central and state governments in federal countries? How does the Canadian case help in understanding the relationship between broad structural characteristics of political systems and the process of policy-making? What does it tell us about the general problem of coordination among units which are at the same time interdependent and relatively autonomous?

What could be emerging in Canada, writes A.R.M. Lower, is 'a new governmental form, a government of governments.'[1] All federations, of course, are governments of governments in one sense; but Lower's comment suggests further that legislative power is coming to rest with a group of senior federal and provincial executives, meeting as governments in formal conferences. Power over many important policy decisions is distributed not to one government or the other, but rather to governments acting jointly. Through the mechanism of federal-provincial negotiation, the Canadian system has undergone some important changes in recent years, the most important being an alteration in the *de facto* distribution of power

1 *Evolving Canadian Federalism* (Durham, NC, 1958), p. 47.

among the governments. There has been an extension of provincial authority which, in the words of one veteran participant, at both levels 'may perhaps be incompatible with the effective conduct of our national affairs.'[2]

The federal-provincial negotiation process is facilitated by some important features of the Canadian social and institutional system. It deals with a wide range of issues and operates largely through a distinctive set of institutions, the federal-provincial conferences. The participants – the political heads of the eleven governments and their senior civil servants – conflict on a wide variety of issues. The conflict stems from differences in regional economic conditions, ideological interests, perspectives of different governments, and the competition for status and prestige. At the same time, the participants substantially agree on some basic overall goals for the system, on certain procedures for resolving disputes, and on the need for compromise and cooperation. In seeking their objectives the governments possess a wide variety of political resources, which are unequally distributed and which vary from issue to issue and time to time. They engage in a wide range of behaviour to gain their ends, though possible tactics are limited by procedural norms, by the limitations of political resources, and by the actions of others in the operation of the process itself. All these factors combine to produce different outcomes, which vary – in their finality, in the success and failure of various actors, and in the degree to which the participants are able to find creative solutions.

This description suggests that the negotiations are in many ways similar to international negotiations, especially in international organizations. It is probably not a coincidence that the former director of the federal-provincial relations division of the federal Finance Department had previously been on Canada's delegation to the General Agreement on Tariffs and Trade (GATT) negotiations, or that the secretary of the constitutional conference is a former diplomat. What distinguishes the Canadian case from international negotiations? First, in Canada the extent of interaction and the degree of interdependence are much wider than in most international organizations. Politically, socially, and economically the Canadian governments are much more closely tied together than, for example, are United Nations or NATO members. At the same time some international organizations, especially the European Common Market, do foster a very high degree of interdependence and interaction, more closely approaching the Canadian model. A second difference between the Canadian and international patterns is that in Canada one government, the federal, is in a unique position, depending on an electorate drawn from all

2 R.M. Burns, *The Evolving Structure of Canadian Government* (Winnipeg, 1966), p. 50.

the other units, with distinct legal and constitutional powers, and acting in large measure as the hub of the process. While, as with France in the European Economic Community, one member may play an especially crucial role in international organizations, it is not a separate level of government. A third and related difference is that the eleven governments in the Canadian system jointly govern the same population; each voter participates in both the federal and provincial electorates. This in turn is related to the fact that in the federal system sovereignty is shared among the governments, whereas in most international organizations, except the EEC, each unit retains full sovereignty, at least in law. Finally, despite the similarity of federal-provincial to international negotiation, Canada remains a single political system, where citizens hold dual loyalties and share a much wider range of common history, experience, problems, and political culture than do citizens of members of most international organizations. All these differences have important implications for the number and kinds of issues that arise for negotiation in the two types of systems, and for the procedures that will be followed. Yet the striking parallel between intergovernmental negotiation in Canada and international negotiation does suggest that the same variables that have been used to study the Canadian case would be a useful way of examining interaction in other settings.

The Common Market perhaps comes closest to the Canadian pattern. Ironically, most students of the market examine it from the point of view of the integrating of previously separate systems, while the Canadian example is more nearly a case of disintegration or at least decentralization. Indeed, the processes and procedures of Common Market decision-making do suggest in some ways a higher level of integration than the Canadian model. Sites and procedures are much more elaborate, complex, and institutionalized. Supra-national bodies like the Commission have developed much authority and influence and there is more continuous communication among the members through the Committee of Permanent Representatives and the Council of Ministers than in Canada. However the market's operations are primarily in the economic sphere, and at the level of mass publics it seems evident that citizens of member nations are not nearly as integrated into the EEC system as Canadians are into the Canadian political system.

The operation of the federal-provincial negotiation process also raises the question of how the Canadian pattern of relations among governments differs from that in other federations. Such relations may vary along several dimensions. Three especially important ones are (1) the degree or frequency of interaction; (2) the forms this interaction takes; and (3) the relative influence of the different governments. In Canada, many issues become involved in the federal-provincial negotiations; there is a high frequency of interaction, which often takes the form of direct relations between executives of different governments. The provinces appear to have a high degree of influence. What about some other federations?

In the United States, while there is much federal-state interaction at all levels, relatively few major political issues appear to become defined primarily as 'federal-state' issues. The development of the Social Security Act, part of which is directly analogous to the Canada Pension Plan, illustrates the difference. While many of those debating the scheme were conscious of maintaining a state role, the states did not participate directly in the programme's development.[3] Similarly it has been possible to write studies of policy-making in such areas as education and public housing, both involving many 'federal-state' issues, with virtually no reference to state government involvement in the policy-making process.[4] That would be unthinkable in Canada. The form of federal-state relations is also very different in the United States. State interests are mediated primarily through the Congress, the parties, and the federal bureaucracy, rather than through direct negotiations between the president and state executives as on the Canadian model.[5] Finally, there appears to be a general consensus that while state functions have indeed increased along with all governmental functions, the federal government is predominant, and that the states have less influence in national policy-making than do the Canadian provinces.[6]

3 See Edwin W. Witte, *The Development of the Social Security Act* (Madison, Wis., 1962), passim, and A.J. Altmeyer, *The Formative Years of Social Security* (Madison, 1966), passim.

4 Eugene Eidenberg and Roy Morey, *An Act of Congress: The Legislative Process and the Making of Education Policy* (New York, 1969), and Leonard Freeman, *Public Housing: The Politics of Poverty* (New York, 1969).

5 See, for example, Herbert Kaufman, *Politics and Policies in State and Local Governments* (Englewood Cliffs, NJ, 1963), pp. 2–15. After discussing the large number of bodies like the Governors' Conference and the Joint Federal-State Action Committee, set up in 1957, M.J.C. Vile concludes that there are no federal-state bodies comparable to the Australian [or Canadian] premiers' conferences. The United States, he suggests, 'is almost entirely lacking in centres for real decision-making, or bodies which can effect genuine agreements between federal and state governments.' *The Structure of American Federalism* (Oxford, 1961), pp. 171–2.

6 Thus William Riker describes American federalism as 'centralized,' while Canada is relatively 'peripheralized.' *Federalism: Origin, Operation, Significance* (Boston, 1964), pp. 81–4, 116–19. 'National supremacy' is a basic element of American federalism, suggests Daniel Elazar. See 'The Shaping of Intergovernmental Relations in the Twentieth Century,' *Annals* 359 (May 1965), p. 11. See also William Anderson, *Intergovernmental Relations in Review* (Minneapolis, 1960), pp. 137–40.

In Australia there is also a high level of interaction.[7] It takes place largely through the Conference of Commonwealth and State Ministers and other Commonwealth-state bodies, in a form strikingly like the Canadian pattern.[8] Financial sharing (through unconditional Commonwealth grants) is 'determined by a process of bargaining and compromise between governments,'[9] much as in Canada. However, most observers agree that in these negotiations the federal government has the upper hand, and state influence appears to be less than in Canada.[10]

Finally, in West Germany only the relatively few issues which directly affect the integrity of Land governments become federal-Land disputes.[11] The chief site for adjustment of the Land interests is the Bundesrat, which also acts as a representative of bureaucratic interests, and which on most 'national' issues is dominated by the national parties.[12] In Germany the influence of the Länder in national policy-making – though not in administration – appears to be small. Paradoxically, the more influential the Länder became in policy-making, through the Bundesrat, the more national parties exerted control over the Land parties.[13]

Thus there is considerable variation between federations in the patterns of federal-state relations. How might such differences be explained? Does the framework used in this study offer any possibilities for fruitfully comparing federal systems? Patterns of decision-making, I suggested at the outset, may result from the interaction or interplay of three levels of

7 See J.D.B. Miller, *Australian Government and Politics* (London, 1954), chap. 6; Geoffrey Sawer, *Australian Government Today* (Melbourne, 1961), pp. 19–23. For an example of one joint effort, see 'The Introduction of the Commonwealth-State Tuberculosis Scheme,' in B.B. Schaffer and D.C. Corbett, eds., *Decisions: Case Studies in Australian Federalism* (Melbourne, 1966), pp. 104–23.
8 For a description of Commonwealth-state bodies, see A.J.A. Gardner, 'Commonwealth-State Administrative Relations,' in R.N. Spann, ed., *Public Administration in Australia* (2nd rev. ed., Sydney, 1962), pp. 234–57.
9 R.J. May, 'Politics and Gamesmanship in Australian Federal Finance,' in Henry Mayer, ed., *Australian Politics: A Reader* (Melbourne, 1966), pp. 123–4.
10 See, for example, Sir Robert Menzies, *Central Power in the Australian Commonwealth* (Charlotteville, Va., 1967), passim; Alexander Brady, *Democracy in the Dominions: A Comparative Study in Institutions* (3rd ed., Toronto, 1958), pp. 178–9.
11 Edward Pinney, *Federalism, Bureaucracy and Party Politics in Western Germany: The Role of the Bundesrat* (Chapel Hill, NC, 1963), chap. 5. For a general study, see Roger H. Wells, *The States in West German Federalism* (New York, 1961), passim. See also Gerald Braunthal, 'Federalism in Germany: The Broadcasting Controversy,' *Journal of Politics* 24 (1962), pp. 545–61.
12 Riker, *Federalism*, pp. 123–4.
13 Pinney, *Federalism, Bureaucracy and Party Politics*, p. 240. See also Arnold Heidenheimer, 'Federalism and the Party System: The Case of West Germany,' *American Political Science Review* 52 (1958), pp. 826–8.

factors: the social and cultural setting, the institutional and constitutional framework, and the particular goals, attitudes, and behaviour of incumbent leaders and the demands and problems facing the system. This perspective suggests that the first dimension of variation – the frequency and extent of federal-state conflict or interaction – will depend on several related factors. First, at the sociological level interaction will be more frequent the more politically relevant cleavages and interests are regionally distributed. This is particularly true when highly distinctive subcultures, like French Canada, are concentrated in one area. In such cases the state government is likely to become the advocate of the minority interests in national policy-making. When demands and cleavages are not regionally based, regional governments are less likely to play a part in articulating and debating them.

Next is the institutional and constitutional level. One immediate determinant of the frequency of interaction is the formal constitutional division of powers. When the constitution allocates functions jointly to both levels, or is silent or ambiguous on important powers, or the financial resources assigned to governments do not permit them to carry out their assigned functions, then interaction will be more frequent. In addition, *intergovernmental* interaction is likely to be more frequent the less the institutional arrangements at the national level accommodate regional interests.

Finally, the extent and frequency of interaction will depend on the attitudes and perspectives of leaders at each level and on the demands and problems facing the system. Thus, when the major problems or demands cut across formal divisions of powers, adjustment will be more necessary. When important interest groups define some problems, such as education, as 'national,' but the constitution allocates them to states or provinces, states and federal governments will need to coordinate their efforts either through interstate or federal-state arrangements. When leaders at both levels perceive that they can best achieve mutually held goals through collaborative effort, formal procedures for interaction are more likely to develop. Finally, when government leaders at both levels are activist and jealous of their powers, interaction will be more frequent than when leaders at one level are relatively quiescent and prepared to leave the initiative to the other level.[14] This activism in turn will depend on such factors as how much important problems facing the system fall within state

14 Thus, D.V. Smiley suggests that one reason for the centralized Canadian federalism immediately after the Second World War was the general acquiescence of provincial leaders to an expanded federal role and their relative ineffectiveness compared with federal leaders. *The Canadian Political Nationality* (Toronto, 1967), pp. 51–2.

or federal jurisdiction, and the effect of the recruitment process on the goals, skills, and leadership styles of leaders at each level. A final determinant of the frequency of interaction, and particularly of its salience in policy-making, is the importance of local or municipal institutions. Thus in Canada local government is both legally and in fact subordinate to provincial governments, and the latter have insisted that direct city-federal relations, bypassing the provinces, not develop. In the United States on the other hand, where local governments carry much political weight, an extraordinarily wide range of direct federal-local relations has grown up, frequently leaving out the state government. This is in part a consequence of the weakness of state governments, especially of their failure to respond to urban problems and needs; but its growth also contributes to weakening of state governments and reduces the salience of state-federal relations in formation of major policies.

What about the specific form of intergovernmental relations? It too depends largely on three levels of factors. Most important however, are the institutional variables. Thus, in Canada and Australia parliamentary government with strict party discipline, together with centralization within both levels of government, appears to have been a sufficient condition to inhibit the effectiveness of national legislative bodies as arenas for adjustment and so to facilitate the development of a new set of institutional arrangements, the federal-provincial conferences. This contrasts with the United States, where lack of party discipline and decentralization within governments has meant that the Congress has served as an important arena for adjustment. Moreover, the larger number of units and the fact that senior executives cannot easily authoritatively commit each other in the United States would make federal-state conferences on the Canadian model difficult if not impossible. In addition, the form interaction takes also depends on the attitudes and expectations of leaders, especially when the procedures are relatively fragile, as in Canada. Moreover, the social environment also helps to condition the form negotiations take, since ultimately the machinery of policy-making depends on beliefs by citizens that it serves their interests. Thus, the form interaction takes, like its frequency, also depends on the interplay of the three levels of factors.

Finally, what about the relative influence of the governments? Like frequency of interaction, relative influence is extremely difficult to measure. The degree of influence varies from government to government, from issue to issue, and from time to time. Nevertheless, a few suggestions can be made.

First, at the social and cultural level the more citizen loyalties are directed to state governments, and the more voters and interest groups look to state governments for the solution of their problems, the more influential the regional units are likely to be. They will have greater political support. Great regional diversity is likely to be associated with such a 'provincial' focus. The existence of regionally based subcultures may also give the provincial government greater legitimacy in the eyes of many minority group members and increase provincial orientations. One source of tension in a federal system, as the Canadian case shows, arises when some groups favour a relatively stronger federal government and others powerful provincial governments. In addition, the more citizens look to municipal governments, and the more politics at city and national levels are aligned, the weaker the states are likely to be. If the national government can bypass the states to deal directly with local governments, the states bargaining power is reduced.

At the institutional level the distribution of powers in the constitution is directly related to the influence of the governments. The constitution allocates both responsibility and authority which can be exploited as a political resource. The constitution and the social environment are obviously related to each other. But the relationship may be far from perfect, so that in the short run constitutional provisions are an independent determinant of each government's influence, and governments may exploit its provisions to slow down, or block, the pressures of broader social influences towards centralization or decentralization. The role of national political institutions, especially parties and the national legislature, also affect the distribution of influence. If interregional adjustment takes place largely in the national legislature, then the goals of state government (though not regional) interests are less likely to have an impact on national policies than when the state governments themselves participate continuously in the adjustment process. The more decentralized national parties are, not simply in terms of recruitment but also in terms of actual party policy-making, the more influential the states are likely to be, especially if it is state (rather than local) politicians who play the crucial role. Finally, the institutions developed for the federal-provincial interaction affect the influence of the various governments, since the procedures typically give advantage to one or other government.

At the third level the demands and problems facing the system and the characteristics of the leaders of different levels affect the relative influence of governments. Faced with the severe national crises of depression and war all western federations underwent a period of centralization. When the system does not face such overwhelming national problems and when instead the major problems facing the system fall into provincial jurisdiction, the states are likely to have more influence, since they will possess authority, and citizens are more likely to direct their interest and attention towards them. This in turn would likely encourage the recruitment of activist, skilled politicians and administrators to the state level, as appears to have happened in Canada, and thus increase state influence through their increased skill and expertise.

These suggestions indicate that differences among federal systems – and changes within individual countries – can best be explained by variations in three kinds or levels of factors. The three are closely interrelated but they are nevertheless distinct from each other. None of these factors alone can explain differences in the relationship of federal and state governments. It seems evident that even the laudable aims of parsimony in political science do not justify sweeping generalizations based on one factor, like William Riker's assertion that one institutional element – the party system – controls the nature of the federal bargain.

This discussion has hinted at some of the ways broad background factors like the social and institutional framework shape the decision process in particular cases. Let us confront the question more directly.

First, how are some of the basic social and economic underpinnings of the federal system related to the major elements in the decision-making process? To begin, they shape the issues that get raised for discussion. Regional economic disparities lead to debate on such questions as aid to the poorer units in Australia and Canada. Subcultural differences provide the basis for another set of issues. The same elements help to determine many of the goals of the participants in the negotiation, since leaders of each government will respond to the interests of their own regions. To the extent that regional or subcultural interests diverge, and that the issues for negotiation stem from these differences, then they will be a basic determinant of the level of conflict. The sites and procedures also depend in part upon the attitudes of the broader public, in particular its views about whether the process facilitates translation of public demands into policy output. The social environment plays a central role in the distribution of political resources. The balance of loyalties, we have seen, is a crucial determinant of political support. Differences in political culture also condition the skill of each government's leaders by influencing the attractiveness of careers in one or other level of government. Thus Quebec participants were generally considered particularly able; one reason is that the cultural differences made service in the provincial government more attractive than in the federal government, so the province has been able to recruit leaders who otherwise would have gone to Ottawa. Finally, the social environment helps to condition the kinds of tactics the participants use by setting up constraints about what is and is not permissible behaviour, though the force of such constraints is perhaps more dependent on the participants' perceptions than on public attitudes themselves. Thus the social environment affects the decision-making process directly through such things as the generation of issues for debate and indirectly through its influence on institutions and through the constraints and opportunities it provides the decision-makers.

Similarly many elements in the institutional framework affect the process. The constitutional division of powers shapes not only what issues will arise, but how they will be defined. This framework may itself become an issue when there is lack of consensus. The constitution defines the channels through which the decision-makers must work, or which they must modify and adapt to their own purposes. It also allocates authoritative resources – 'legality' – and through this affects the tactics the participants use, and their success on particular issues. In Canada we have seen the major consequence of the traditional institutional structure has been not to serve as a channel for federal-provincial interaction but rather as a block to such interaction and an incentive to the creation of new institutions. This example indicates that the formal institutions – like the constitution – may serve as barriers to be side-stepped as well as more positive determinants of decision-making behaviour. The participants may themselves develop new institutions to suit their needs.

The underlying social and institutional factors are far from completely determining the operation of the decision process and its results in particular cases. Rather, their effects are often indirect. They are filtered through and mediated by those who operate the process itself. The governmental élites at both federal and provincial levels play a crucial independent role. The dynamics of the process itself, expressed in the nature of the issue, the goals and resources the participants bring to bear, the procedures and rules of the game they have developed, and so on are vital to an understanding of the operation of the decision process, and even more to the specific decisions made. The social environment conditions the nature of the issues that will be raised, but the participants also raise some of their own, and, more important, they define the stakes and shape the terms of the discussion. The sites and procedures are to a large extent determined by institutional factors, but the specific procedural norms which govern the process are developed by the participants. Similarly, the actors' goals are greatly affected by the social and cultural environment within which they work. But at the same time they have their own goals, stemming from their own personal styles, their own role-conceptions, their own ideologies, and their own positions in governmental institutions with status and maintenance needs. Moreover, the way goals are framed depends on the participants, as does definition of the degree of agreement or disagreement. Similarly, not only do many political resources depend on the skills and expertise of the decision-makers, but also on the ways they perceive and interpret the effects of the environment. Finally, the participants have their own norms and rules about what kinds of tactics are legitimate or not. The decision-makers themselves decide what arguments to make, what tactics to use, when to offer alternatives, concessions, or compromises, and so on. Thus, to understand the decision-making process it is crucial to study the decision-makers.

The participants operate in a complex environment. They are active on many fronts at once: in the federal-provincial negotiations, in trying to woo investors, in dealing with their own legislatures, and in efforts to maintain themselves in power. Goals in one arena may conflict with those in another; a resource in one game may be a liability in another; and tactics appropriate to one set of concerns may be inappropriate to another. This means the actors must continually balance the perceived requirements of one arena with those of others.

Combined with the complexities and uncertainties of the process itself, the need to participate on many simultaneous fronts means that the decision-makers must constantly be making difficult calculations about their own and other actors' goals, resources, and strategies, and about the positions and reactions of important audience groups. These calculations often involve extensive negotiations and balancing of interests within the various governments.

The need for calculation also means that the actors will try to simplify and reduce its costs. This is one function of norms and rules of the game. The participants also have relatively fixed goals and stable attitudes about such matters as political support and permissible tactics, and this too lessens the need for calculation in every case. Finally, the actors can simplify their calculations by concentrating on making changes at the margins, rather than in continually having to consider whole policies anew. This possibility, however, is greater on some kinds of issues than others, and the Canadian case shows that the range of issues coming up for negotiation is too broad to permit application of a few simple decision rules, such as is possible in areas like budget politics in the United States, where essentially the same operations are performed repeatedly.[15]

Many characteristics of the decision-making itself play an important independent role in shaping the operation of federal – and other – systems. Moreover, it seems clear that a useful way to approach the question of how broader social and institutional factors affect the process of decision-

15 See Aaron Wildavsky, *The Politics of the Budgetary Process* (Boston, 1964).

making is to focus on the participants and ask how they perceive and react to these forces.

A final question underlying the study has been how autonomous but interdependent governmental units can coordinate their activities and jointly make overall policy for the nation. This is a problem of all decentralized systems. In Canada coordination on many matters cannot be achieved by central direction in which one government dictates decisions to the other. Rather coordination must come largely through a process which Charles Lindblom calls 'partisan mutual adjustment,'[16] in which the actors bring to the decision process different goals, perspectives, attitudes, resources, and strategies. We have seen that through this process the Canadian decision-makers have been able to coordinate their activities not only in the minimal sense that their respective decisions are adapted to each other but also in the broader sense that they have been able to develop jointly some broad basic policies for the country.

At the same time, however, many Canadians, observers and participants, have stressed that more efficient machinery must be developed to improve the coordination of federal and provincial policies. Thus, R.M. Burns suggests that 'if we wish to conduct our affairs like interchanges between sovereign states in international alliances, we must develop a more sophisticated machinery of internal diplomacy.'[17] In part such comments appear to be based on the belief that central coordination, at least on some issues like economic policy, is somehow better and more efficient than the 'messier' process of negotiation. Whether the results of hierarchical coordination are considered to be better than those of coordination through mutual adjustment would appear to depend greatly on the value judgments and policy preferences of the individual observer. It seems impossible to weigh the alleged benefits of central coordination against those of more decentralized processes, though Lindblom has argued persuasively for the superiority of partisan mutual adjustment, both as a process for rational calculation and as a means of ensuring consideration of the widest possible set of values in decision-making.[18]

Nevertheless, the Burns comment does suggest that coordination of interdependent units will be facilitated when regularized machinery and procedures have been developed in which to carry it out. This is particularly true when the parties interact on a very wide range of issues, when they are as highly involved with each other as the units of a federal state,

16 *The Intelligence of Democracy: Decision-making through Mutual Adjustment* (New York, 1965).

17 'Choices for Canadian Federalism,' *Canadian Tax Journal* 13 (1965), p. 516.

18 *The Intelligence of Democracy*. For a strong, though largely implicit, attack on this notion, see Theodore Lowi, *The End of Liberalism* (New York, 1969).

and when the policies to be decided are complex. Coordination can be achieved without such a framework, but the costs and delays of reaching decisions might be greater and there is less likelihood of the system's responding adequately to the demands placed on it by the electorate.

Regularized, agreed-on procedures and institutions can have several effects on the ease of achieving joint policy-making. First, they can simplify the actors' calculations since the procedures will be familiar and the rules of the game clear. Second, they can reduce the level of conflict. If the 'machinery of internal diplomacy' facilitates communication, 'artificial' conflicts based on misunderstanding of others' goals are less likely to arise. This communication may also permit the actors to re-evaluate their goals, and perhaps to develop new common values. The participants can make each other aware of their own needs and aspirations, and thus encourage respect for each other's positions and strengthen norms of reciprocity and compensation. It is possible, however, that the communication process may have the opposite effect, actually sharpening the conflict by making it clearer and more open, and it is an interesting empirical question how often this happens.

Another piece of machinery that appears to play a vital role in facilitating coordination is the existence of third parties or joint bodies independent of the participants themselves which act as mediators, developers of new common interests, initiators of compromise, and so on. Members of such groups, more than the other participants, are likely to have their own goals and status tied to the maintenance of the organization, and thus to place a very high value on getting agreement. Such groups may become a new focus of loyalty for important élite groups, again strengthening the machinery. One barrier to coordination in Canada is the absence of such a group in the federal-provincial arena.

Another aspect of the machinery is the kind of decision rules that obtain. When procedures for terminating debate are clear, and when there is consensus on them, then again calculations are simplified, and it is likely coordination will be easier. In Canada the machinery of federal-provincial relations does not provide formal voting procedures (and the difficulties of devising a voting formula would be formidable) nor does it make formal decisions itself. This appears to complicate the decision-process and make it less likely that firm decisions, recognized as legitimate by all parties, can be found. It is a particular problem in the constitutional debate.

The relative secrecy of the procedures may also affect the ease of reaching coordination. The more open the negotiations the more pressures there are on the decision-makers and the more actors are brought into the negotiations.[19] This may make it more difficult for the actors to communicate freely and make it harder to reach agreement. On the other hand, more actors might enhance the changes for agreement by bringing in more values which could be traded and would build public support for the process by reducing the frequent criticism that the premiers divide up the tax pie behind closed doors with little thought for the taxpayer. The emphasis on *in camera* discussion, so evident among the Canadian decision-makers, seems to imply a belief that the decision-makers themselves share many more common interests than do their constituents, since it is believed that if the conferences were public the participants would be given to public posturings rather than constructive discussion.

Thus it does appear that several aspects of formal machinery for negotiations can have some important effects on possibilities for achieving coordination. The machinery itself, of course, is dependent on the participants' belief that it is useful both for achieving coordination and for furthering their own goals. This is particularly true in Canada where the machinery is relatively fragile, without its own independent existence based on tradition, precedent, and the loyalty of particular groups with an interest solely in maintaining it.

Several more general factors affecting the success of joint decision-making in decentralized systems can be suggested. If, as in most international negotiation, there are few connecting links between the parties themselves, coordination may be more difficult. For example I suggested in chapter 2 that, compared with the United States, federal and provincial political subsystems in Canada were relatively isolated or separated from each other. American state leaders are much more likely than Canadian ones to have national aspirations and to move between the two levels. When the levels are separated as in Canada, it seems more likely that status conflicts will arise, and that there will be fewer areas of common interest and understanding between representatives of each government. The participants will be less likely actually to have experienced the problems and interests of others and would not imagine themselves as occupying in the future the positions now occupied by their opponents.

Another institutional factor affecting the ease of coordination is the degree to which the participants can speak authoritatively for their governments. Coordination should be easier if they can make binding commitments, as in Canada.

Despite the importance of institutional mechanisms, however, the chief

19 Jack Sawyer and Harold Guetzkow, 'Bargaining and Negotiation in International Relations,' in Herbert Kelman, ed., *International Behavior* (New York, 1965), p. 492.

factors facilitating or impeding coordination lie with the decision-makers themselves. Coordination will be more difficult the more fundamentally their goals diverge. In particular, if the conflict involves the divergence of basic value systems, it will be less amenable to compromise than disagreements over substantive policy. Conflict based on status or prestige concerns is likely to make coordination more difficult. More generally, consensus on some broad values for the system, such as unity, and on specific procedures for managing the conflict should make coordination simpler, by providing incentives to agree on more immediate issues. Consensus on basic values, as Herbert Kaufman showed in his study of forest rangers, can greatly reduce the costs of achieving coordination.[20] When the norms and rules of the game stress compromise, cooperation, and reciprocity, the participants are likely to be able to find agreement and to be willing to trade support on one issue for support on others. Reciprocity and willingness to compromise also imply that even when they strongly disagree the participants recognize the legitimacy of the others' points of view and recognize their right to promote these goals. The kinds of tactics the participants use may also condition the ease of attaining coordination. In particular, it should be more difficult when the participants use tactics which violate the rules of the game. Thus a wide range of the actors' own attitudes play a crucial role in achieving coordination. Most important is their belief that coordination is necessary or desirable. Given this basic decision, the particular machinery can assist the process by facilitating communication, increasing awareness of others' problems, producing new information, and so on. Without that consensus, no machinery is likely to be useful. Any particular form of coordination, like the direct negotiation between government executives we have examined, depends ultimately on the belief by the participants that in the long run such procedures provide benefits for them. The participants can often agree on procedures even when their substantive interests differ considerably.

The Canadian case thus suggests both some of the conditions facilitating effective joint policy-making, and some of those which make it more difficult. These conditions apply to other systems in which the units are autonomous, yet interdependent, and in which the members feel the need to develop mutual policies applying to all.

Federal-provincial negotiation – diplomacy is perhaps a better word – is a central process in Canadian policy-making. The pattern, indeed, is one of the most distinctive characteristics of Canadian federalism. The system is not an easy one to operate: conflict and tension are inherent in the process; governments often seem far more concerned with their own status

20 *The Forest Ranger* (Baltimore, 1960), chap. 6.

needs and goals than with concrete programmes and policies; much of the debate is far removed from public scrutiny and involves obscure questions which only those who do the negotiating seem to understand. These are some of the costs of federal-provincial diplomacy. But this analysis has attempted to show that the pattern evolved as a response to some basic characteristics of Canadian society and institutions. It has permitted accommodation of central and regional interests, though with results that both centralists and regionalists on occasion deplore. Federal-provincial diplomacy has also firmly placed its stamp on the character of a large number of public policies developed in recent years: they have taken the form they have because they were worked out in the federal-provincial arena. We have attempted to answer basic questions about the relationships in Canada between political structure on the one hand and policy-making on the other. The description is only a partial one; many other lines of research suggest themselves. The system itself is constantly changing. But it seems safe to say that many of these changes will take concrete form in the discussions of the premiers and prime ministers sitting at their horseshoe-shaped table in the great waiting room of what was until recently the Ottawa Union railway station.

# Index